HIKING SOUTHWEST CANYON COUNTRY

HIKING SOUTHWEST CANYON COUNTRY

SANDRA HINCHMAN

4TH EDITION

MOUNTAINEERS BOOKS

MOUNTAINEERS BOOKS is dedicated to the exploration, preservation, and enjoyment of outdoor and wilderness areas. www.mountaineersbooks.org

1001 SW Klickitat Way, Suite 201, Seattle, WA 98134
800.553.4453, www.mountaineersbooks.org

First edition 1990. Second edition 1997. Third edition 2004. Fourth edition 2019: Second printing 2025.

Distributed in the United Kingdom by Cordee, www.cordee.co.uk

Manufactured in China

Copyeditor: Diane Durrett
Cover, book design, and layout: Heidi Smets
Cartographer and illustrator: Hannah Hinchman
All photos by author unless otherwise noted

Cover photographs, front: *Jacob Hamblin Arch in Coyote Gulch, Grand Staircase-Escalante National Monument (photo © Omer Salom, @osalom)*; back, left to right: *Ladders to ruins at Mesa Verde National Park, striking pictographs in the Great Gallery in Horseshoe Canyon, Canyonlands National Park*
Frontispiece: *Hoodoos wearing hard rock caps abound near Lake Powell.*

Library of Congress Cataloging-in-Publication Data
Names: Hinchman, Sandra, 1950- author. | Mountaineers Books (Firm)
Title: Hiking Southwest canyon country / Sandra Hinchman.
Other titles: Hiking the Southwest's canyon country
Description: Fourth Edition. | Seattle, Washington : MOUNTAINEERS BOOKS, [2019] | "Third edition 2004"—T.p. verso.
Identifiers: LCCN 2019006867 (print) | LCCN 2019009661 (ebook) | ISBN 9781680511475 (ebook) | ISBN 9781680511468 (paperback)
Subjects: LCSH: Hiking—Southwest, New—Guidebooks. | Day hiking—Southwest, New—Guidebooks. | Walking—Southwest, New—Guidebooks. | Backpacking—Southwest, New—Guidebooks. | Mountaineering—Southwest, New—Guidebooks. | Rock climbing—Southwest, New—Guidebooks. | Trails—Southwest, New—Guidebooks. | Southwest, New—Guidebooks.
Classification: LCC GV199.42.S68 (ebook) | LCC GV199.42.S68 H56 2019 (print) | DDC 796.510979—dc23
LC record available at https://lccn.loc.gov/2019006867

ISBN (paper): 978-1-68051-146-8
ISBN (ebook): 978-1-68051-147-5

MIX
Paper | Supporting responsible forestry
FSC www.fsc.org FSC® C188448

An independent nonprofit publisher since 1960

CONTENTS

7. Canyons 291

Tafoni and desert varnish adorn a golden cliff face in Crack Canyon.

INTRODUCTION

Most of the places featured in this book lie within a day's drive of one another. With some notable exceptions, they occupy the Four Corners region of the Colorado Plateau, where Utah, Arizona, Colorado, and New Mexico converge at a single point. Colloquially, this region is sometimes known as "canyon country," a landscape with scenic endowments second to none. Artifacts of prehistoric tribes that once inhabited the area remain amply in evidence. Rivers that helped shape the high desert's topography provide access to remote locales and offer the most scenic and thrill-packed rafting in the United States. The towering, geologically unusual mountains that frame this arid land contribute yet another dimension to its allure. Even a rudimentary grasp of the Southwest's natural and human history will enhance the visitor's experience.

Geologic Forces at Work

The Colorado Plateau represents an exciting yet accessible geologic classroom. Natural features stand forth starkly, without cover of topsoil and dense vegetation. The neophyte geologist need not search for road cuts to study underlying layers, for the distant past is everywhere on display.

The dominance of sedimentary rocks simplifies the task of understanding regional geology. Because wind and water deposited their components in layer-cake fashion, deeper-lying strata are almost always older than their higher counterparts. Rank amateurs can easily learn to distinguish different types of sedimentary rock, recognizing the colorful badlands of the Morrison Formation, the weirdly eroded Entrada Sandstone goblins and arches, the massive domes of Navajo Sandstone, and the severe, vertically fractured Wingate Sandstone cliffs. Each stratum delivers clues about the kind of environment that prevailed when its materials were set down.

For instance, Coconino Sandstone in the Grand Canyon is composed of rounded sand grains of roughly equal size, arranged in layers that often meet at odd angles (a phenomenon known as cross-bedding). This formation suggests that the present-day Grand Canyon must have been covered by vast dunes when the Coconino was deposited, since shifting winds arrange desert sands in exactly such patterns today.

But high-desert geology is hardly as simple as rock-layer diagrams make it appear; close inspection reveals unimagined complexities. First, sedimentary rocks are never laid down in strata of uniform thickness. Ancient ecosystems of relatively limited extent—estuaries, beaches, dune fields—determined the depth and size of each layer. Consequently, formations characteristic of some sections of the Colorado Plateau may thin out or even vanish elsewhere. For example, the Elephant Canyon Formation so prominent in the Needles District of Canyonlands National Park is entirely absent, whether above or below the surface, in neighboring Arches National Park.

Second, because sediments can be deposited only in basins, whenever sections were uplifted, they began eroding away. Sometimes the result is an "unconformity":

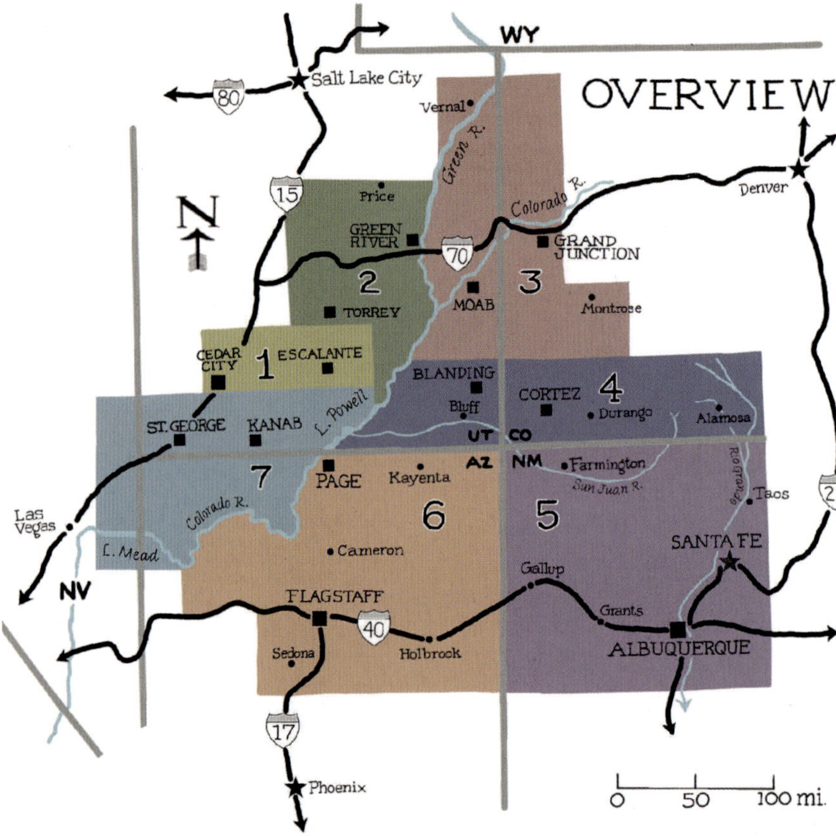

two layers of rock with no trace of the strata that once lay between them. Thus, sedimentary rocks in the Southwest offer a fragmentary and incomplete guide to its geologic history. Whole pages, even chapters, of that history are missing (though a "grand tour" of the region enables visitors to reconstruct much of it).

Third, faulting and uplifting have disturbed many strata that elsewhere form unbroken beds, pushing one part of the bed above, or dropping it below, another. The Moab Fault, near Arches National Park, provides a vivid illustration. Wingate Sandstone cliffs, capped by Navajo Sandstone, tower above the west side of the valley. On the east side, by contrast, the Wingate layer is buried beneath the surface, while the Navajo and Entrada layers form the backdrop for the visitor center. In places, the offset of strata along this fault reaches 1500 feet.

Finally, ancient vulcanism and mountain building have played dramatic roles. Areas on the periphery of the Colorado Plateau, such as Bandelier National Monument, owe their peculiar geology to vast amounts of ash and lava from ancient volcanoes. Elsewhere, the region is crossed by long "folds" or "reefs," such as Utah's Waterpocket Fold and San Rafael Reef, which arose when subterranean forces lifted up overlying rock strata and tilted them at crazy angles—sometimes to a nearly vertical plane. Often the uplift occurred so slowly that preexisting streams cut into the rocks as fast as those rocks were elevated, creating slot canyons that run perpendicular to the Reef.

In addition, canyon country boasts several mountain ranges that rise 10,000 feet or more above sea level. Many ranges—including the La Sals, Abajos, and Henrys, as well as isolated, turtle-shaped humps such as Sleeping Ute Mountain and Navajo Mountain—are laccoliths: roughly, failed volcanoes that created large bulges in the earth but never actually erupted. The rocks in and around them are mostly igneous types, such as granite. Deep canyons, similar to the slots that cut through folds and reefs, formed on the flanks of these peaks as meltwater rushed through soft sedimentary rock. Navajo Mountain's Bridge Canyon, the locus of Rainbow Bridge, provides a choice example.

Rock Strata

Clear and simple on a grand scale, the geology of the high desert remains complex and unique for each specific area.

Some of the region's deepest strata, Precambrian rocks over two billion years old, appear in the Grand Canyon. Even the youngest layer there, the Kaibab Limestone Formation, dates back 250 million years to the Late Permian age. Look especially for the buffy bands of Coconino Sandstone near the canyon rim and the brick-colored Redwall Limestone farther below, both of which form sheer cliffs for miles.

Utah contains some extremely ancient Paleozoic rocks. The Needles of Canyonlands National Park are composed of pale Cedar Mesa Sandstone, like the nearby cliffs of Natural Bridges National Monument. Cedar Mesa Sandstone is actually a "member" of the Cutler Formation, which includes other, quite different strata. The Cutler weathers into crimson spires, gargoyles, and standing rocks, visible in Canyonlands' Maze District and at Fisher Towers north of Moab. In Capitol Reef National Park, although Chimney Rock and similar monoliths near the western boundary resemble the Cutler, the layers are actually composed of the newer, Triassic-era Moenkopi Formation. A harder cap of Shinarump Conglomerate retards the erosion of the chocolate-colored mudstone and sandstone Moenkopi layer beneath.

The most spectacular formations in the region belong to the Glen Canyon Group of the Triassic and Early Jurassic periods, the heyday of the great dinosaurs. Notable among these is Navajo Sandstone, the classic white-to-tan slickrock of the high desert, which mineral oxides often stain. This stratum, more than 1500 feet thick in places, composes the muscular domes of Capitol Reef and forms features like Zion's Great White Throne. Because of its relative hardness, the Navajo layer can also produce nearly vertical cliffs in places like the Escalante River and the slot canyons of the San Rafael Reef.

Below Navajo Sandstone, you usually see the reddish, easily weathered rocks of the Kayenta stratum, which forms ledges, Swiss cheese walls, and magnificent arches such as those found in Capitol Reef's Upper Muley Twist Canyon. Some remarkable

Common Rock Strata of the Colorado Plateau

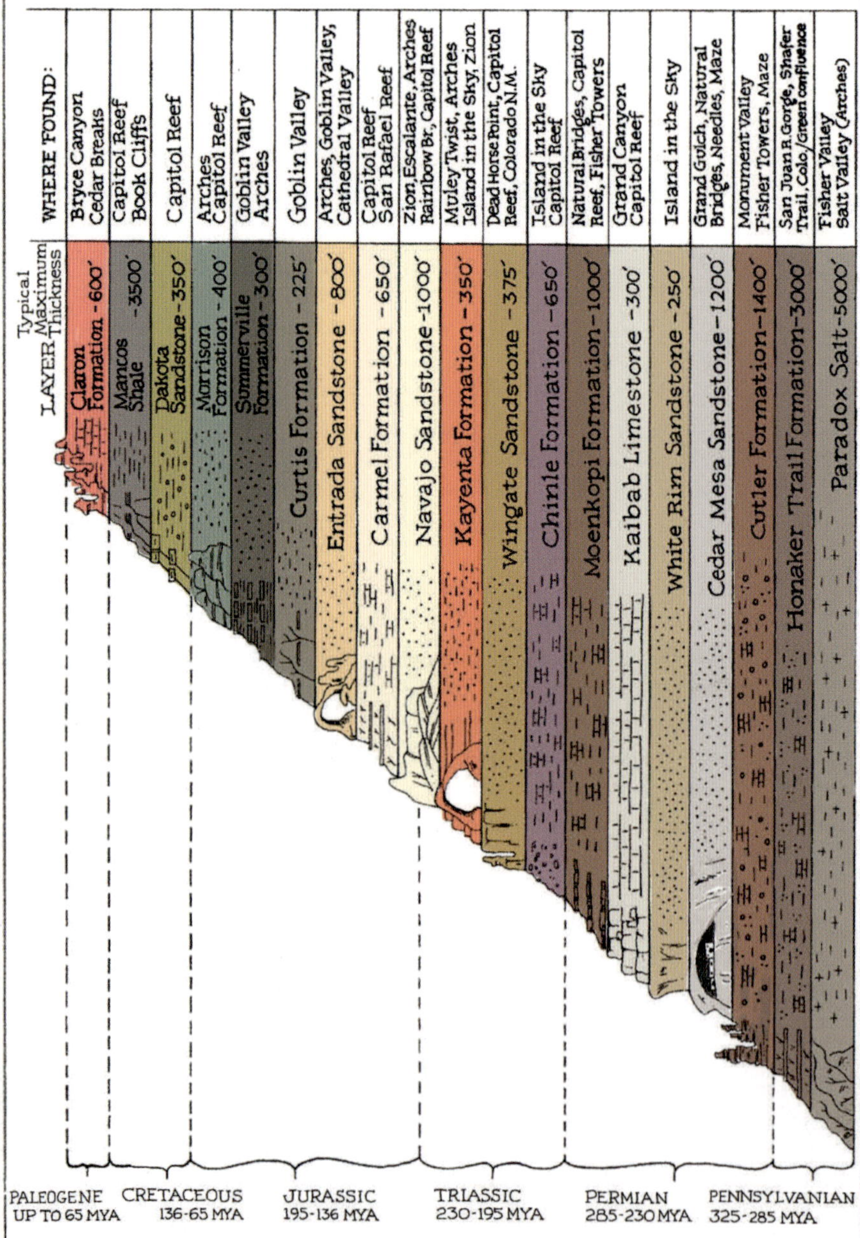

A unique plaid wall stained with mineral oxides in Buckskin Gulch

narrows cut through the Kayenta Formation, too, like those of Crack Canyon in central Utah.

Wingate Sandstone, a fairly hard rock prone to long, vertical fractures, is the final member of the Glen Canyon Group. Sometimes it erodes into towering, golden cliffs such as those of The Castle in Capitol Reef or along the Colorado River north of Moab. Elsewhere, it weathers into isolated buttes and spires; the Six-shooter Peaks of Canyonlands' Needles District offer a prime example. Usually at the base of the Wingate is the sloping, rubble-strewn Chinle Formation, a uranium-bearing layer that often produces colorful badlands.

Two other formations deserve mention because of the manner in which they erode. Above the Navajo Sandstone in some places lies Entrada Sandstone. In Arches National Park, this is a relatively hard, gold or reddish layer out of which most of the natural spans and fins were carved. But at Goblin Valley State Park, where Entrada Sandstone presents as much softer, more crumbly, and mudlike, it produces grotesque and comical knobs, hoodoos, and pillars.

Farther west, at Bryce Canyon National Park, Navajo Sandstone constitutes the oldest rock that has been found, and that only by drilling. The other formations present date as far back as the Cenozoic era (starting about 65 million years ago), capped by the brilliant pastel and white Claron Formation, a combination of limestone, shale, and sandstone. The Claron has weathered into the ethereal, dreamlike world of Bryce's Pink Cliffs.

In sum, if you were to travel from the Grand Canyon through Capitol Reef and Zion and then on to Bryce, you would encounter the "grand staircase," a series of rock strata displaying geologic history from Precambrian times to the demise of the dinosaurs and the emergence of early mammals.

Topographic Features Glossary

The following glossary should help you to recognize and interpret certain topographic features of the Southwest.

Alcoves (overhangs, amphitheaters) are shallow caves in cliffs or fins that result from flaking or falling rock.

Anticlines are domes or ridges formed when rock layers are pushed upward and bowed by subterranean forces. They often erode in the center, leaving valleys bounded on either side by upward-tilting strata.

Arches are natural openings formed when water percolates into porous rock, such as sandstone, and gradually breaks it down either by freezing and thawing or by dissolving its chemical "cement." *Potty (pothole) arches* result when those rock openings occur at the tops of alcoves.

Badlands are dry, barren, often multihued clay hills fluted by mechanical and chemical weathering.

Balanced rocks develop as the pedestal on which a caprock sits erodes rapidly, becoming thinner over time.

Benches are the flat areas above the banks of rivers or streams.

Buttes form when the action of water, frost, or wind causes mesas to weather drastically and unevenly, until only tall remnants are left. These are capped with hard, resistant rock that protects softer layers underneath. Unlike mesas, buttes typically are higher than they are wide.

Canyons (gorges, gulches) are carved into plateaus by streams, sometimes aided by simultaneous uplifting caused by underground forces. Soft rocks erode into canyons that are wide and shallow, whereas hard rocks create deep, narrow ones. In contrast, *arroyos* form when streams gouge out deep channels in the floor of a canyon; such ditches can result from flash flooding, especially when the landscape is denuded of vegetation by overgrazing.

By definition, balanced rocks have attained an angle of repose.

Chockstones are boulders wedged tightly between canyon walls, complicating or even blocking a hiker's forward passage.

Desert varnish is a dark oxide stain produced when minerals like iron and manganese are dissolved by water.

Escarpments are long, steep cliffs formed either by faulting or erosion that separate areas with significantly different elevations. Arizona's Mogollon Rim, which delineates the southern boundary of the Colorado Plateau, provides a classic example.

Fins and domes develop when parallel vertical joints in solid rock are widened by erosional agents, eventually yielding freestanding formations. In contrast, *needles* are standing rocks that result when such joints run perpendicular to one another.

Grabens are sunken fault blocks that show on the surface as narrow valleys or trenches bounded by steep walls. Examples include Cyclone Canyon and Red Lake Canyon in Canyonlands National Park, which formed when underlying salt beds leached away.

Hanging canyons occur when a tributary does not cut into its bed at the same rate as the main stream but instead becomes suspended above it.

Hoodoos (goblins) are standing rocks, sometimes found along the bases of cliffs, that have eroded into improbable shapes.

Laccoliths are isolated mountains formed when subterranean molten materials force their way up without breaking through the earth's crust. The magma travels horizontally between thick beds of sedimentary rock, warping those layers.

Meanders are sinuous bends or curves in a river or stream.

Mesas are high, flat plateaus with sloping or cliff-bounded sides.

Moki (or Indian) marbles are roundish stones that were freed by erosion from the conglomerate rock by which they had been engulfed.

Monoclines (hogbacks) are sudden tilts or jogs in the plane of sedimentary rock strata. The term may designate the structure of one side of an anticline; Arizona's Cockscomb Formation represents a case in point.

Narrows are canyon walls pinched very close together, creating a tunnel-like effect.

Natural bridges are spans created by the surge of water against a rock wall, such as when a stream cuts off a meander by breaking through a fin.

Oxbows (goosenecks) occur when a canyon stream has meandered enough to form a loop, turning back on itself. An *entrenched stream* forms when a meandering watercourse cuts into its bed as the land around it is uplifted.

Pour-offs (dry-falls) are found when canyon floors take sudden, steep plunges, posing obstacles for hikers.

Reef is a colloquial term applied by early settlers to any barrier to travel. In the Southwest, it refers to drastically tilted ridges, such as the Waterpocket Fold monocline.

Rincons are abandoned meanders that occur as a stream cuts through a narrow neck between loops to create a new channel. Where this happens, *natural bridges* can develop.

Saddles are low points or depressions along a ridgeline.

Slickrock is an informal term referring to expanses of bare, undulating sandstone. It is generally not slick at all, except after a rain.

Spires (pillars, towers) originate when relatively soft rock strata are thinned out by weathering or when erosion breaks off vertical slabs of harder rock from isolated buttes, reducing them to slender pinnacles.

Synclines are slumps in the earth's surface; the opposite of anticlines.

Tafoni is a term referring to rocks that have weathered to produce a honeycomb or "Swiss cheese" effect.

Tanks are permanent or semi-permanent water sources found in potholes.

Tent rocks are cone-shaped remnants of volcanic tuff, usually formed when boulders shield softer underlying rocks from erosion.

Unconformities are gaps in the geologic record that develop when the rocks that once separated two strata gradually erode away.

As this fossil track reveals, a three-toed dinosaur once crossed this area when it was an ancient sand flat.

Paleontology

Dinosaurs roamed the Southwest during the Triassic, Jurassic, and Cretaceous periods of planetary history. During times of drought, individuals would congregate near water sources, where many perished. Eventually, their petrified tracks and bones were preserved in muddy sediments. The Morrison Formation, in particular, houses a paleontological treasure trove. The best-known working sites are Dinosaur National Monument and Cleveland-Lloyd Dinosaur Quarry. Museums in Fruita, Colorado, and Moab and Price, Utah, will enhance your appreciation for prehistory's "terrible lizards."

Climate

What makes the Four Corners region a desert is not simply the small amount of precipitation it receives (averaging under 10 inches annually) but the fact that much of this precipitation occurs in brief but sometimes torrential thunderstorms during July and August, instead of falling evenly throughout the year. Because the parched, sparsely vegetated ground cannot absorb the moisture from such deluges, much of it runs off, contributing to rapid erosion. Storms can cause flash floods and quicksand in previously dry washes or gullies. They also replenish drinking water and kill off much of the insect population. Summer visitors to the region thus can expect hot, buggy, dry conditions during its first half and wetter, cooler, relatively bugless conditions during its second. Temperature-wise, the ideal months for most high-desert travel are April, May, September, and October, though in order to avoid crowds, it's smart to plan your visit for the off-season.

Generalizations aside, what matters most is the altitude at which you hike. Huge temperature variations distinguish places such as Cedar Breaks National Monument at 10,000 feet and the Grand Canyon's Tonto Rim at 3500 feet. In the former, you might need a sweater even in summer, while the latter might be delightful on a mild winter day.

Flora and Fauna

The distribution of plant and animal species in the Southwest can be explained by the "life zone" concept formulated by 19th-century botanist Clinton Hart Merriam. Merriam observed that the climate and latitude of an area help determine what flora and fauna flourish there. "Communities" of plants and animals develop as the species residing in an area grow interdependent over millennia of evolutionary changes.

However, climate and latitude don't tell the entire story; here again, altitude also must be considered. Air temperature decreases and precipitation increases with altitude, producing an environment that supports different life-forms. Every 1000 feet of elevation gain is equivalent to about 300 miles of latitudinal movement toward the pole.

Merriam posited the existence of seven life zones, from the Tropical to the Arctic-Alpine, of which three prevail in the high desert: the Lower Sonoran, Upper Sonoran, and Transition zones. They and their residents overlap considerably, and the vegetation and wildlife found where water is relatively ample (lakeshores, riverbanks, intermittent streams, springs, potholes) may be anomalous.

Claret cup cacti steal the show in spring.

Top: Globe mallow superbloom along the upper Escalante River; *bottom:* Indian paintbrush, a parasitic plant, takes root near a fallen juniper in Arches National Park.

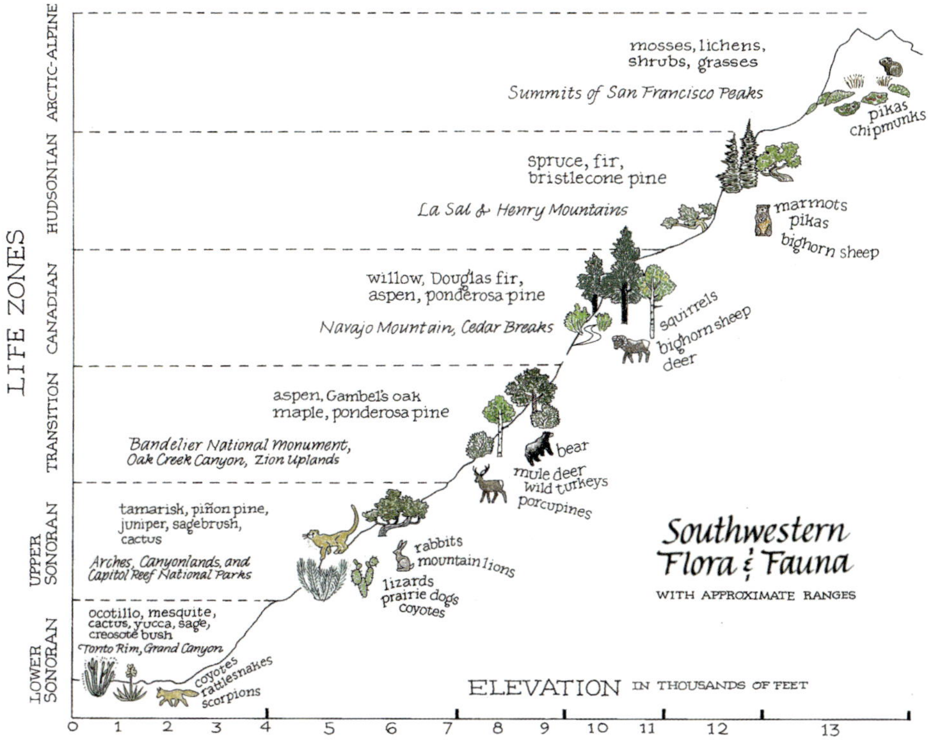

Lower Sonoran Zone

Reaching to about the 3750-foot line, this zone includes the bottom of the Grand Canyon, the banks of the Rio Grande, and the Virgin River lowlands of western Utah and Arizona. Cactus, mesquite, yucca, Joshua trees, agave, creosote bush, blackbrush, rabbitbrush, and snakeweed are among the dominant flora. The zone's wildlife includes rattlesnakes, deer, coyotes, scorpions, lizards, kangaroo rats, bats, skunks, desert tortoises, cactus and rock wrens, and hummingbirds.

Upper Sonoran Zone

From about 3750 to 7000 feet in altitude, this zone occupies by far the largest portion of the Four Corners region. Most typical of the Upper Sonoran is the so-called pygmy forest of pinyon pines and Utah junipers—"pygmy" because these trees are dwarfed as a result of scant rainfall. Oaks, box elders, and cottonwoods grow where the water table is high. But the zone's bushes and shrubs are even more diverse: sagebrush, blackbrush, bottlebrush, Mormon (or Brigham's) tea, rabbitbrush, tamarisk (an exotic riparian species), willow, canyon grape, mock orange, cliffrose, buffaloberry, snakeweed, and greasewood. Late spring floral displays can be extravagant, especially in years with high precipitation. Flowering plants include prince's plume, mule ears, bee plant, datura, sego lily, penstemon, prickle poppy, geranium, globe mallow, phlox, four o'clock, evening primrose, scarlet gilia, Indian paintbrush, sunflower, and monkeyflower.

Pronghorn antelope, a New World species, have been clocked at speeds of 60 miles per hour.

The prevalent animal species are coyotes, bats, rattlesnakes, scorpions, lizards, prairie dogs, kangaroo rats, mice, rabbits, squirrels, skunks, gray foxes, pronghorn antelope, bighorn sheep, and mule deer. Among bird species, look for wrens, swallows, kinglets, vultures, jays, ravens, magpies, nighthawks, larks, hummingbirds, towhees, and eagles.

Transition Zone

A buffer between deserts and mountains (from about 7000 to 9500 feet), this zone contains two distinct associations of plants and animals. At lower altitudes, you find Gambel's oak, maple, ponderosa pine, Rocky Mountain juniper, serviceberry, chokecherry, mountain mahogany, and manzanita. Higher up, Douglas and white fir, aspen, common juniper, and mountain ash predominate. You may see wild turkeys, deer, porcupines, bears, squirrels, chipmunks, foxes, marmots, skunks, bobcats, and mountain lions. Common birds include swallows, swifts, nuthatches, robins, flickers, jays, ravens, and chickadees.

Ancient Cultures

Centuries before Europeans arrived in the New World, several Native American cultures flourished in the desert Southwest. All descended from Central Asian nomads who crossed the land bridge connecting Siberia with Alaska during the last ice age. Of the three main groups, the Anasazi, believed to be ancestors of the modern Hopi and Pueblo tribes, inhabited the Four Corners area, with the Fremonts concentrated north of Utah's Abajo Mountains and the Sinaguas residing in Arizona.

Desert Archaics

Beginning around 5000 BCE, the Colorado Plateau and environs were inhabited by nomadic hunter-gatherer peoples, today called the Desert Archaic culture. Although little is definitively known about them, it is easy to admire their skill in painting enigmatic figures on the walls of cliffs partially protected by overhangs from weathering. Many of these pictograph panels depict mysterious shaman figures, often life-size or larger, sometimes with trapezoidal bodies lacking limbs but displaying huge hollow eyes. Excellent specimens abound in the Maze District of Canyonlands National Park and Buckhorn Wash, in Utah's San Rafael Swell. Over time the Desert Archaic world changed, as new techniques and food sources came into more general use: the cultivation of corn, beans, and squash; the bow and arrow, a borrowing from the Plains Indians, which made hunting more efficient; and the development of so-called pit houses, partially dug into the earth and framed in with wooden poles.

The Fremonts

In later centuries, the northern reaches of canyon country were home to the Fremont culture, a name given to a variety of semi-nomadic tribes and clans that gradually formed small communities in much of present-day Utah. They too left vast galleries of outdoor art, mainly petroglyphs incised into the rock. Representative samples appear in the vicinity of Dinosaur National Monument, Capitol Reef National Park, and Nine Mile Canyon. Although the Fremonts erected the first masonry and adobe structures, they used them as granaries rather than dwellings.

The Sinaguas

The southern zones of canyon country were inhabited by yet another Neolithic group, the Sinaguas (Spanish for "without water"), who ranged from around modern-day Flagstaff south to the Verde Valley between around 500 and 1400 CE. Most likely they were an offshoot of the Mogollon culture that had settled in the mountainous regions of eastern Arizona and western New Mexico. The Sinaguas benefited greatly from contacts with neighboring peoples, particularly the Hohokams (ancestors of today's Tohono O'odham or Papago tribe), who may have taught them both the art of irrigation and the joy of competing in masonry ball courts reminiscent of those found farther south in Mexico. Eventually they learned how to construct aboveground dwellings, both in the open and in cliff recesses at sites such as Arizona's Tuzigoot, Wupatki, and Montezuma Castle National Monuments. They also left intriguing rock art, of which the most renowned is at the V-Bar-V Ranch site near Sedona.

The Anasazi

As impressive as the accomplishments of these other peoples may have been, they were overshadowed by the sociocultural and economic system created by the Anasazi (from the Navajo for "ancient ones" or "ancient enemies"), as they are familiarly called, or Ancestral Puebloans, as they are more formally known. The Anasazi inhabited a vast area covering most of northwestern New Mexico, northern Arizona, and southeastern Utah. Anthropologists typically divide their history into two broad phases: Basketmaker and Pueblo. During the late Basketmaker era, lasting until about 700 CE, the Anasazi lived in underground pit houses in settled communities, where they began to rely on farming as well as hunting and gathering for their sustenance. A technological breakthrough came with the transfer of pottery-making techniques from the Mogollon area farther south. Clay pots proved to be far superior vessels for preparing food than the fine woven baskets that they previously had employed.

In their subsequent Pueblo phase, the Anasazi embarked on a remarkable period of change and expansion. They moved to masonry surface sites and/or cliff dwellings, often grouped into small villages or even great cities accommodating hundreds of people. The pit house of yore evolved into a kiva, or subterranean ceremonial chamber, which was used for religious, social, and educational functions. The usual entrance to the kiva was from the top, by ladder. Each kiva also had a hole in the floor called a sipapu, or symbolic entrance to the spirit world.

Cliff dwellings, erected in the 12th and 13th centuries, often were accessible only by toeholds and handholds laboriously pecked into solid rock. These stairways were coded, such that a person had to know whether to begin climbing with the right or left foot or else risk dangerous mid-cliff corrective maneuvering. Rural Mormons, anglicizing the Spanish word for Hopi, referred to these primitive ladders as Moki steps; they assumed that because the doors of Anasazi houses have extremely low clearance, a munchkin-sized race had built them. In fact, the Anasazi, like the Fremont and Sinagua peoples, were comparable in stature to the Europeans of their day. The typical life span was comparable as well, at 30 to 35 years, with very high infant mortality (a 50 percent death rate for children under age five).

Below the cliff dwellings were the middens, a sort of dump where items such as broken pottery and old sandals were discarded. The dead were sometimes buried in these middens, not out of disrespect but because digging proved easiest there. Mysteriously, few corpses have been found in or near cliff dwellings. Some Hopis maintain that the Anasazi, having perfected themselves through harmonious dealings with nature and one another, ascended to the fifth level of creation, leaving behind our fourth level's suffering and strife.

Many of the Southwest's most breathtaking Ancestral Puebloan sites were found and publicized by the Wetherill brothers in the late 19th and early 20th centuries. Ranchers from Mancos, Colorado, the Wetherills became amateur archaeologists after stumbling upon abandoned dwellings on nearby Mesa Verde. Excited by these finds, they spent years exploring the Southwest, scouring ruins for artifacts to sell to museums and private collectors. Although by today's standards this practice would be considered looting, in their time it was neither illegal nor even seen as unethical. During his travels, Richard Wetherill formulated the distinction between Basketmakers and Puebloans, referred to above.

The de facto capital of the Anasazi world was broad, dusty Chaco Canyon, in what is now western New Mexico. In its heyday during the 10th and 11th centuries, Chaco boasted nine so-called great houses: multistoried structures that combined residences, storage rooms, and kivas (still utilized today in the pueblos of New

Mexico). Chaco also held many small farmsteads that presumably supplied food to elites inhabiting the great houses. But why were the great houses built? It appears that they were both religious and political centers and entrepôts responsible for shifting foodstuffs to areas of deficit, with high-quality pottery as a universally accepted medium of exchange. To facilitate trade, the Chacoans built 400 miles of wide, poker-straight roads to outlying settlements. One of these, the Great North Road, lines up almost exactly with the north star, Polaris. The roads also enabled them to transport large ponderosa pine logs that could be used in construction.

Chaco fell into decline and partial abandonment as rains either became more erratic or failed entirely in the late 11th and early 12th centuries. By the end of the 1100s, most farmsteads and great houses had been abandoned. There seems to have been a general drift of population northward toward higher, cooler, and wetter terrain as people reverted to the ancestral semi-nomadic, semi-agricultural way of life that they never had entirely relinquished. Yet by 1200, the Ancestral Puebloans again began erecting impressively large structures, this time cliff dwellings such as the ones seen today in Mesa Verde National Park. The shift to homes that often were notoriously hard to access may have reflected a rise in intra- or intercultural tensions. It should be noted that other Anasazi groups had been building smaller and usually less defensively minded versions of such dwellings for centuries, especially around today's Cedar Mesa in Utah and Navajo National Monument in northern Arizona. But those settlements too were abandoned, typically after just 50 to 75 years of occupation.

Controversy remains not only about why the Anasazi left their towns but also about exactly what became of them after they did. The developing consensus is that they sought refuge with neighboring peoples with whom they had previous ties, perhaps by clan lineage, language, or religion. The highland populations of southern Colorado and northwestern New Mexico probably joined existing pueblos along the Rio Grande, while the indigenes of northern Arizona may have migrated to the Hopi Mesas, as many contemporary Hopis believe.

The Ancestral Puebloans' most serious problem always had been the impermanence of their settlements. In combination with certain technological innovations, making the move to the Hopi Mesas, the Rio Grande, and outlying pueblos such as Acoma and Zuñi enabled them to solve that problem. The settlements they founded near the Rio Grande typically extended from the riparian lowlands to far cooler and wetter uplands. Hence, if crops failed at lower elevations, their counterparts higher up most likely could fill the gap, while also providing edible wild plants and meat from game. Crucially, the lowland Anasazi learned to irrigate their crops by digging ditches that utilized the water supplied by the Great River's more tractable tributaries. As a result, they began to flourish in the 15th century, entering into a sort of golden age that endured until the Spanish conquistadors arrived, bringing diseases to which the natives lacked resistance. But the story of modern pueblos over the past five centuries would take us too far afield. Suffice it to say that most eventually recovered from the population crash that they suffered during the conquest.

Ladders provide access to the floors of Anasazi cliff dwellings.

Native Cultures Today

The region's present-day Native Americans include the Ute, Navajo, Hopi, and Pueblo peoples. Tribal members live suspended between the traditional, animistic world of ceremony, in which everything on Earth is seen as alive, and the larger society, with its high technology and metaphysical religions.

The Utes

Some anthropologists believe that the Ute tribe (whose self-designation is Nuchu, meaning "the people") descended from the ancient Fremonts. Others think their forebears were the Shoshones, who entered the region in the 12th and 13th centuries. Before they were vanquished by the US Army, the Utes lived as semi-nomadic hunters and warriors. Once pushed onto reservations, they were compelled to live in a more sedentary manner, dependent on agriculture and on rations from the Bureau of Indian Affairs. The largest of these reservations are in northern Utah and southwestern Colorado, adjacent to Mesa Verde National Park. Livestock raising and agriculture, their economic mainstays, are handicapped by the absence of reliable, good-quality water supplies.

The Navajos

Calling themselves Dineh ("the people"), the Navajos are ethnically unrelated to the region's pre-Columbian inhabitants. Like the Apaches, they descended from nomadic hunters on the plains. Their common name comes from the Spanish corruption of another tribe's word for them, Apache de Nebahu, or "enemies with cultivated fields." More than 175,000 strong, the Navajo Nation exceeds all other US tribes in both population and territory, occupying a reservation that encompasses half of northern Arizona and spills across the borders of Utah and New Mexico. Previously, the

Navajos were believed to have migrated into the region during the 17th century, but recent findings suggest they were present in New Mexico as early as the 1200s. Some anthropologists have postulated a link between the coming of the Navajos and the exodus of the area's aboriginal peoples.

In many ways, the Navajos fared better than other tribes in their dealings with the federal government. Although they endured terrible woes, including the destruction of their homes, livestock, and orchards, and the death of many of their kin on a forced march to eastern New Mexico in 1864, they ultimately succeeded in keeping their land. And that land, which at first appeared worthless to Anglos, turned out to contain uranium and fossil fuels, especially coal. The discovery of coal was a mixed blessing, since with it came the construction of slurry lines that depleted local water supplies and of lucrative but polluting power plants intended to supply energy to distant cities. Currently such plants are being phased out. While the environmental impacts of that change for the greater Southwest are welcome, its economic consequences for the already-underprivileged tribe will prove decidedly negative.

Some citizens of the Navajo Nation are employed as energy workers. Others earn their living by selling high-quality wool rugs and turquoise and silver jewelry, while more traditional Navajos raise sheep and goats. Unemployment rates here, as on some other reservations, hover around 50 percent, and many families still lack electricity and running water. Although prefabricated dwellings are common on the reservation, Navajo lands are also dotted with more traditional structures such as sweat lodges, ramadas, and hogans (one-room homes composed of earth, logs, and modern materials, oriented by custom toward the rising sun).

Most of the land on the Navajo Reservation has been severely degraded from overgrazing. Already-sparse desert vegetation, eaten to the quick by livestock, gives way to dune fields that generate sandstorms so ferocious that they can strip the paint off cars.

The Hopis

A small tribe of fewer than ten thousand members, the Hopis have been relatively successful in preserving their cultural traditions ever since the days of Spanish conquistadors and missionaries. Their northern Arizona reservation is completely encircled by Navajo land, a long-standing source of friction. In recent decades, it occasioned a bitter lawsuit over disputed joint-use territory that resulted in the displacement of many families.

Unlike the Navajos, the Hopis are primarily farmers. They live on arms of Black Mesa in villages such as Oraibi, the oldest continuously occupied town in the United States. Although the tribe has its outspoken faction of modernizers, many members continue to observe their old customs, evidently derived in part from Anasazi practices. Like the Navajos, the Hopis regard certain mountains in the area to be sacred, particularly the San Francisco Peaks north of Flagstaff, where their nature gods—deified spirits of ancestors (or *kachinas*)—supposedly reside. Assuming the form of clouds, these beings send welcome rains. Another sacred place is the Sipapu, a travertine dome on the Little Colorado River. The dome has an opening through which traditionalists believe humans and animals emerged into our world.

Outdoor ovens called "hornos" are still in use by New Mexican cooks.

The Pueblos

This population is scattered among nineteen independent villages, located primarily in New Mexico's Rio Grande Valley. Conquest by the Spanish in the 17th century led to pillaging, enslavement, and attempts at forced religious conversion. Bloody revolts and reprisals ensued. Somehow, the Pueblo peoples managed to retain much of their cultural integrity in the face of both long-term dominion by the Spanish and subsequent waves of Mexican and Anglo immigration.

Today some villages seem relatively prosperous, with economies based on agriculture and on crafts like pottery and jewelry making. As on the Hopi Reservation, kivas remain in use, though many are now aboveground structures. Sacred dances are held in the villages several times a year, in keeping with ancient rituals. Visitors are generally welcome to tour the pueblos for a small fee.

This brief survey of the natural and human history of canyon country should help enrich your experience as you travel through the region.

PLANNING AND PREPARING FOR YOUR TRIP

To maximize the chances of an enjoyable trip, do your homework. Step up your exercise program well in advance. Determine how much time is at your disposal and how best to allocate it. Boil down hiking options based on your available time, the fitness and experience of your party, and the limitations of your vehicle. Calculate how long your chosen routes will take, provisioning accordingly. Obtain maps or literature and secure reservations or permits months ahead for popular campsites and backcountry trails (see Contact Information at the end of this book). Above all, remain flexible, recognizing that circumstances on the ground may necessitate changing your plans.

Where and When

I strongly urge you to concentrate on relatively compact geographic areas so as to maximize your time in the great outdoors and minimize the time you are cooped up in a car. Nothing could be less satisfying than to whiz across vast distances in an effort to check off items on a standardized bucket list. Travelers determined to race from Zion to Bryce after a three-hour tour have not "seen" the park, except in the most superficial sense. For that matter, try to spend time in places that are off the beaten track. Oftentimes, these are just as enchanting as the more well-known locations and even more enjoyable, since they are not jam-packed with visitors struggling to elbow their way to a photo-op.

By the same logic, consider an off-season trip. Although most people, especially families with schoolkids, are locked into summer visits, high seasonal temperatures can make hash of even the best-laid plans. Come in spring and fall if at all possible, though ideally not on big holiday weekends like Memorial Day and Labor Day. Winter visits to canyon country, especially at lower elevations, promise comfortable hiking, fewer crowds, and bargain-basement motel prices. As a bonus, nothing is more breathtaking than red rocks dusted with a fresh coat of powder.

Camping

Most national and state parks have campgrounds with modern facilities. Some remain open year-round, though services may be curtailed during the colder months. The days when you could expect to swoop in and bag a campsite in season are over. Although some venues still adhere to a first-come, first-served policy, increasingly the trend is toward requiring reservations. To avoid disappointment, apply online as early as possible.

Hikers use safety ropes to ascend through an arch.

Except in archaeological parks, backcountry primitive camping remains an option. Even here, however, designated sites have become the norm. Where not expressly forbidden, freelance camping is possible in areas administered by the Bureau of Land Management (BLM). Don't be intimidated by fences and gates, which on BLM lands are intended not to keep you out but to keep livestock in. Leave gates open or closed, as you find them.

An underappreciated perk of canyon country camping is that because of both low humidity and minimal light pollution, the night sky dazzles with stars. As of 2019, several national parks and monuments had been designated as International Dark Sky Parks, among them Arches and Canyonlands in Utah. City-dwellers in particular may be astonished by the sheer number and brilliance of the constellations that illuminate moonless evenings.

Negotiating One-Way Hikes

Many of the Southwest's best trails are one-way affairs that begin and end at different, possibly far-flung, points. For these, you have several options.

- **Double back to the trailhead,** especially if the hike is short.
- **Establish a vehicle shuttle system.** With two vehicles, drop one off at the end point before setting forth. Mountain bikes sometimes suffice for this purpose.
- **Hire a driver** to take you to the trailhead.
- **Swap keys** with people doing your hike in reverse.
- **Hike separately in opposite directions.** Your party can split up, starting at either end of a trail. When the hike concludes, those with access to the car then pick up the others.

- **Hitch a ride** back to your starting point, if that is within your comfort zone. Bear in mind that because many of the region's roads are lightly traveled, you could be in for a long wait.

Equipment

Outfitting yourself for desert treks need not involve extraordinary effort or expense. If you are an experienced mountain hiker, most of the gear you already own will suffice. Make sure your equipment is in good repair, and always carry the Ten Essentials, which were developed by The Mountaineers:

1. **Navigation**—map and compass and/or GPS unit
2. **Headlamp or flashlight**—make sure the batteries are fresh and strong
3. **Sun protection**—sunglasses, sunscreen, and hat
4. **First-aid supplies**—bring the basics, including bug repellent and glue for cactus spines
5. **Knife**—ideally included as part of a repair kit (duct tape, safety pins, shoelaces, multitool)
6. **Fire**—waterproof matches, firestarter, and a portable stove
7. **Emergency shelter**—options include a small tarp, waterproof backpack cover, large garbage bag, bivy sack, or space blanket
8. **Extra food**—pack enough to keep you sustained for a few additional days
9. **Extra water**—bring more than you'll need for the entire hike, plus spare bottles and a water filter
10. **Extra clothes**—options include a fleece or down jacket, as well as a waterproof rain jacket

For hikes in watery canyons, plan to pack river shoes: either amphibious footwear designed expressly for that purpose or old boots or sneakers that you are willing to sacrifice to the elements. Flip-flops and other open-toed shoes are generally unsuitable for trails described in this book.

Hiking Safety

Backcountry travel entails unavoidable hazards and risks. Trips vary greatly in difficulty and in the amount and type of preparation required to enjoy them safely. Routes can change or deteriorate rapidly. Excursions that are safe for seasoned, well-equipped travelers may be unsafe for ill-equipped novices; a hike that is safe in good weather may prove unsafe in weather that is adverse. If situations arise that you are unprepared to handle, alter your plans.

Always inquire locally about weather, water, road, and insect conditions before beginning a major hike. Consider the fitness and experience of the members of your party. Be cognizant of your limitations and alert to your surroundings. Beginners should stick to short, well-established trails through terrain that is not too rugged or challenging. Even veterans may need time to adjust to the temperature and altitude. For everyone, training in first aid is a must.

Logs wedged between cliffs mark the crests of past flash floods.

To minimize danger, inform yourself about potential hazards and how to avoid them or remedy their effects. The problems identified below are exacerbated by remote locations and difficult topography.

Water

During summer, plan on at least a gallon of water per person each day for drinking, washing, and cooking. This amount may seem excessive, but it is not, so don't be tempted to skimp. Wherever you can't count on finding groundwater, you must carry all that you need. Because water weighs nearly 8.5 pounds per gallon, this can be a heavy proposition.

Sometimes water is available from springs, pools, or perennial streams. Conditions change seasonally, even weekly. Because map and guidebook information regarding water sources may be outdated, always confirm such information locally.

Poor water quality presents an increasingly serious problem for hikers throughout the US, and the desert is no exception. Many water sources—even those that look pristine—have been contaminated by cattle, horses, or wild animals, not to mention careless campers. The main contaminant is *Giardia lamblia*, a protozoan released as feces decompose. When ingested, the bacterial cysts can cause severe diarrhea and dehydration. Although symptoms may not appear for several weeks, they usually persist until treated with antibiotics. To avoid contracting waterborne diseases, use a high-quality portable purifier. You can attach a drip coffee filter to the intake valve with rubber bands to prevent clogging. Never drink from any source that supports no life, since it may contain arsenic or another toxic compound.

Flash Floods

In the Southwest, mid-July through late August is a time of frequent afternoon thunderstorms. These brief but heavy downpours (called "male rains" by Navajos) can cause flooding even in faraway streams. Sometimes it takes 12 to 24 hours for waters to recede, though minor floods will not delay you for so long. The debris piles and quicksand that often appear in the aftermath of flash flooding may make it difficult to complete a hike. You can hear a flash flood coming—it sounds like a locomotive—but you may be inconvenienced, injured, or even killed unless you observe certain guidelines.

- Never camp in or near the bed of a wash or in any narrow section of canyon lacking an easy and obvious escape route.
- Listen to weather reports and pay attention to phenomena that signal impending storms, such as sudden shifts in air temperature or wind direction, or deterioration in stream clarity.
- Check with local rangers for the weather forecast before your hike.
- Avoid travel in remote areas when storms seem imminent.
- Never try to cross a wash during a flash flood, or to race a flood down a canyon.
- Should you be trapped in a canyon during a flood, move to high ground and wait for the water to subside. If high ground is unavailable, try to position yourself behind a boulder large enough to break the force of the water.

A NOTE ABOUT SAFETY

Safety is an important concern in all outdoor activities. No guidebook can alert you to every hazard or anticipate the limitations of every reader. Therefore, the descriptions of roads, trails, routes, and natural features in this book are not representations that a particular place or excursion will be safe for your party. When you follow any of the routes described in this book, you assume responsibility for your own safety. Under normal conditions, such excursions require the usual attention to traffic, road and trail conditions, weather, terrain, the capabilities of your party, and other factors. Keeping informed on current conditions and exercising common sense are the keys to a safe, enjoyable outing.

–Mountaineers Books

Quicksand

Sometimes encountered in or along streambeds, especially on the inside of bends, this supersaturated "jelly mud" rarely presents a genuine hazard. People tend to sink gradually and no farther than knee- or (at most) waist-deep. Remove your pack, extend your arms, fall on your back, and concentrate on pulling your legs free. Stay calm and avoid unnecessary movement.

Heat

Foot travel on hot desert days can result in dehydration, muscle cramps, heat exhaustion, or even sunstroke. To avert such ailments, drink small amounts of water frequently, accompanied by salty snacks to maintain the body's electrolyte balance. Give yourself time to acclimatize before tackling strenuous trails, rest sodium-depleted muscles at the first sign of cramping, and plan on an extended midday siesta. If temperatures are extreme, alter your plans.

Usually the onset of heat-related illness is gradual. Initial symptoms include dizziness, weakness, nausea, headache, and/or disorientation. The best treatment is to find shade, remain quiet, consume cool water (adding a pinch of salt or electrolyte drink powder), and wet down your clothing. Ignoring these early warning signs can result in heatstroke, a life-threatening condition characterized by rapid pulse rate, high temperature, loss of consciousness, delirium, dry skin, and/or profuse sweating. Cool the victim's body immediately, and seek emergency attention.

Hazardous Terrain

To hikers in the Southwest, sheer drop-offs pose a significant danger, since many appealing trails either descend into or wind along the rims of steep-walled canyons. Certain varieties of rock are notoriously crumbly, and sand and rounded pebbles can create slippery conditions. The use of trekking poles and/or safety ropes is sometimes

Sandstone and sky define a slickrock hiker's world.

recommended. Since medical help may be far away, prudence dictates caution on exposed trails.

Getting Lost

Desert trails can be difficult to follow, particularly when they traverse slickrock, talus, or lava fields. To avoid getting lost, never proceed far until you have located the next trail marker. As insurance, inform someone in advance about your hiking plans. If you do get lost, stay where you are, signal your position in some obvious way (such as laying out colorful gear in an open area), and wait for help to arrive. Bear in mind that cell phone coverage tends to be spotty in remote locations and deep canyons. Backcountry rescues, especially those involving helicopters, can break the bank.

Poisonous Creatures

Although the Southwestern deserts are home to rattlesnakes, scorpions, and black widow spiders, you rarely see such creatures, which are largely nocturnal, preferring to take shelter under rocks or in woodpiles or brush during the heat of day. Rattlesnakes usually give fair warning of their presence. Their bites are seldom fatal, and about one in three does not inject when it bites, having already spent its reserves on prey; but if you should be among the unlucky, wash the wound, splint the affected limb, and slowly make your way to civilization. The bites of black widows are likewise rarely fatal, for although their venom is even more toxic, they inject a much smaller amount. Among scorpions, only a short and slender yellow species is potentially deadly (mainly to young children or unhealthy adults); of the areas covered in this book, only the depths of the Grand Canyon normally host this species.

Old mining and livestock routes attract modern bike and jeep traffic.

Common sense suggests taking precautions. Be careful when climbing rocks or turning them over, and try not to place your hands anywhere that you can't first examine visually. Shake out your shoes, and inspect the underside of your tent before rolling it up. And note that poisonous creatures often frequent wet environments, such as perennial streams.

Dangerous Plants

One of the most common desert hiking injuries is getting pricked by cactus spines, which are mildly poisonous and easily become embedded under the skin. Avoid contact with cacti by watching where you step. If you do pick up some spines, squirt the affected area with plain white glue (like Elmer's), then let the glue dry and peel it off. In a pinch, you can use duct tape. The sharp tips of *yucca* and *agave* leaves can also irritate skin, though to a lesser degree. Beware, too, of poison ivy and poison oak, unwelcome occupants of some canyon floors. Wear long pants in such environments.

Insect Pests

Prime bug season on the Colorado Plateau is late spring and early summer, prior to the onset of storm season. Aside from mosquitoes, which breed in stagnant pools, there are three especially annoying species. Red ants inflict a painful sting, best treated with cold-water immersion. Biting gnats, which favor pinyon and juniper vegetation, go after the tender eye and ear areas, producing itchy welts and even swollen glands. Like mosquitoes, gnats are most bothersome around dusk. Deerflies, concentrated in moist, reedy places where livestock have grazed, are attracted to motion and usually aim for the back of the knees.

Repellents containing DEET (diethyltoluamide) or Picaridin are effective against many pests. You also can take measures to foil them: Use only unscented beauty and hygiene products. Wear light-colored clothing, hats with "no-see-um" netting, long-sleeved shirts, and long pants. Choose breezy, exposed campsites and build a smoky fire where regulations allow. As a last resort, try another trail or even another geographic area, since bug populations vary with altitude, water supply, and other local conditions.

Driving Safety

Desert driving is usually delightful and unchallenging: Vistas are grand, skies are clear, and traffic is light. Yet remote locations, extreme temperatures, and rough roads may pose unaccustomed hazards.

Scanty Services

Because towns in the Four Corners region are few and far between, and because service stations often close early, keep plenty of gas in the tank and check fluid levels frequently. Always have extra food and drinking water on hand in case you break down miles from nowhere. Remember that service stations may have to order any parts needed to repair your vehicle. Towing fees can be prohibitive, especially if you lack the relevant insurance.

Unpaved Roads

Reaching some trailheads featured in this book requires the use of a high-clearance or four-wheel-drive vehicle. The absence of guardrails on secondary roads poses a danger, as does the presence of livestock on the open (unfenced) range. Avoid driving on unpaved tracks at night if at all possible.

On gravel surfaces, slow down when approaching other vehicles to avoid sustaining a broken windshield should a rock get thrown by spinning tires. Also, sharp rocks on the road surface may cause flat tires or blowouts.

Dirt roads can be rough when dry and impassable when wet, either because they cross wash bottoms or because their beds have clay-based soil. On washboards—the closely spaced, parallel ridges that typically bedevil dirt roads—slow down to maintain control. Reduced speeds are also advisable when a road is bumpy or twisty and when it descends into gullies or traverses exposed rock. By contrast, when driving through soft, deep sand, gun your accelerator to avoid bogging down. Twist the steering wheel back and forth and don't stop moving, no matter what! Carry a shovel in the trunk, and consider deflating your tires in advance to 18 pounds per square inch of pressure.

Carefully study road maps, especially when planning to travel off main highways. Remember that maps rarely show all unpaved roads, and that GPS devices sometimes lead unsuspecting motorists astray. Seek precise directions and current road-quality information locally before starting out.

If you will be driving on poor or remote roads, it is best to travel in the company of another vehicle, and to inform a responsible party of your intentions. Cell phones may not suffice in emergencies, because the rural Southwest is short on transmission towers, and canyon walls may block reception.

Trailhead Theft

Car clouting poses problems in certain locations. Play it safe to avoid break-ins. When dropping off your vehicle at a trailhead, lock up, pack an extra set of keys, and try to leave nothing of value inside, especially not within plain sight.

Wilderness Ethics

The desert is a fragile environment, easily harmed by thoughtless practices. Decomposition is slow, erosion is rapid, and unsightly scars made by vehicles, fires, and even lug-soled boots may take decades to heal. Therefore, it is even more vital here than elsewhere to camp in a low-impact manner, as epitomized in the familiar mantra, "Take nothing but pictures, leave nothing but footprints." In particular, visitors should abide by the following guidelines.

- Never drive off established roads.
- Stay on trails and designated routes. Avoid cutting switchbacks, which hastens erosion.
- Resist the temptation to make souvenirs of cacti, exotic plants, rocks, pottery fragments, arrowheads, or petrified wood from protected areas.
- Avoid trampling the black "cryptogamic" (a.k.a. cryptobiotic) soil that retards erosion throughout the Southwest. Composed of lichens, mosses, algae, and fungi, this living substance stabilizes the sand and locks in moisture, permitting larger plants to take root. Be mindful of its presence both when hiking and when choosing a place to camp. Don't bust the crust!
- Camp in previously used sites, if possible.
- Use a backpacking stove instead of building a campfire. Fires are prohibited in many places. Where they are permitted, gather only dead wood lying on the ground; use a fire pan or established fire ring; set up far away from vegetation;

pack out all trash; and afterward douse the ashes with water, stirring to make sure no live coals remain.

- Animal-proof your camp by hanging food in bags in sturdy trees (4 feet from the trunk and 10 feet off the ground), storing it in your car, or employing a canister designed to foil break-ins.

Hygiene

Camp and wash dishes at least 300 feet away from groundwater. Never pollute pools or streams with soap, even the biodegradable kind.

Use established toilets when available. Bury human waste in cat holes 6 inches deep and 300 feet from water sources. Pack out your toilet paper and feminine products. In certain fragile environments, such as river corridors, hikers are required to carry portable toilets, or “wag bags.”

Antiquities

Appreciation for the Southwest’s archaeological heritage has led federal and state governments to make laws protecting ancient ruins, drawings, and artifacts from vandalism, damage, and theft. It is illegal to remove, deface, or destroy antiquities found on public land. Violation of these laws carries stiff penalties, including fines and jail terms. Please respect any antiquities that you find. Avoid touching rock art; standing, sitting, or leaning on ruin walls; walking on middens; and “arranging” found objects such as potshards and corncobs. Disturb nothing, take nothing, and make sure that others follow suit.

Don’t put ancient potsherds on display; leave specimens exactly as you found them.

Evanescent agave flowers beautify a desert spring.

Sustainability

The fact that guidebooks such as this might have a bad effect on canyon country is an irony not lost on me. Authors run the risk of attracting people who will love an area to death, transforming it from the pristine landscape that they knew into the crowded, littered, trampled-down kind of place they had hoped to escape. Partly offsetting this risk is the need to forge a strong progressive constituency. I am gambling that people who hike in the Southwest will come to care about it and work on its behalf, whether by writing letters to the editor, lobbying their elected representatives, joining environmental organizations, or simply encouraging others to treasure pristine nature. For too long, canyon country has been besieged by proposals to construct nuclear power plants or waste dumps, highways designed to subsidize extractive industries, massive water diversions to serve profligate cities, and other assorted horrors, any one of which would cause more damage than thousands of hikers.

Movements to privatize public lands or turn federal property over to the tender mercy of states, counties, and localities have gained traction, particularly in my home state of Utah, where powerful interests champion untrammeled development at nature's expense. Recent years have witnessed unprecedented attempts to gut the Antiquities Act and the Clean Air Act, outlaw future wilderness designation, and roll back restrictions on grazing and mining. Ecotourism potentially can create the political will and muscle needed to oppose such measures. People are unlikely to champion what they have not come to know and appreciate. Needless to say, visitation must be managed prudently so that it does not become part of the problem.

As a gesture of support for the health and integrity of canyon country, I pledge to donate a substantial portion of any royalties generated by this book to organizations such as the Sierra Club, Southern Utah Wilderness Alliance, and Grand Canyon Trust. These groups have struggled tirelessly, sometimes heroically, to preserve, protect, and enlarge wild places. Our world would be a far poorer place without their efforts.

HOW TO USE THIS BOOK

This book was written by an average hiker for the average hiker. It addresses people seeking beauty, wonder, and spiritual renewal in the outdoors rather than opportunities for gonzo adventure. While the featured trails vary in length and difficulty, most are gentle on the nerves, demanding neither technical expertise nor superhuman endurance. If you are a daredevil who hungers to test your mettle by swimming frigid pools, braving hair-raising rappels, or negotiating boulder-choked defiles, you should look elsewhere for enlightenment.

The book contains seven chapters, each covering a different region of the Southwest. Every chapter designates two municipalities as its central hubs, with spokes radiating from them in various directions. The featured hikes are numbered consecutively. A few scenic drives and cultural or historical attractions are also included.

By design, consecutive chapters deal with geographically contiguous areas, and overall the chapters are arranged in a clockwise direction. For example, Chapter 2 concentrates on south-central Utah, which is adjacent to the southeastern Utah venues of Chapter 3. At the extremes, Chapters 1 and 7 also link up geographically.

Some itineraries may hold appeal for special audiences. Readers intrigued by archaeology should select hikes in Chapter 4 or 5, while serious backpackers may be most attracted to the hikes in Chapters 6 and 7. Shorter hikes predominate in Chapters 1 through 3. Those who prefer to seek creature comforts at the end of the day should consider hikes in Chapters 3, 5, and 7.

In describing individual trails, I've tried to steer a "Goldilocks" course, aiming to hit the sweet spot between being unhelpfully sketchy and bombarding readers with superfluous detail. When a hike is straightforward, I give a bare-bones write-up, but when executing a hike is complicated, I offer considerably more guidance. Many, but not all, hikes are shown on hand-drawn maps. Each route description begins by specifying its degree of difficulty, distance (rounded to the nearest quarter mile, unless greater precision seems desirable), average hiking time (rounded to the nearest quarter hour), and corresponding topographic map (either a USGS 7.5-minute or 15-minute map or a commercial Trails Illustrated map). If a permit is not listed in the hike summary, then one is not required.

Very easy trails have good walking surfaces and may even be paved. They are usually short, more or less level, unproblematic to follow, and suitable for almost everyone.

Easy trails demand minimal physical exertion. Although they may involve some elevation loss or gain, it is of the slow, steady variety. They are usually well-maintained and clearly marked with signposts or cairns (rock piles), and although they tend to be longer than trails rated very easy, they remain good family hikes.

Moderate trails require more skill and endurance. Some, by virtue of their length, are practical only for backpackers. Most presuppose at least minimal routefinding ability, as well as tolerance for ups and downs. Climbs can be short and steep or

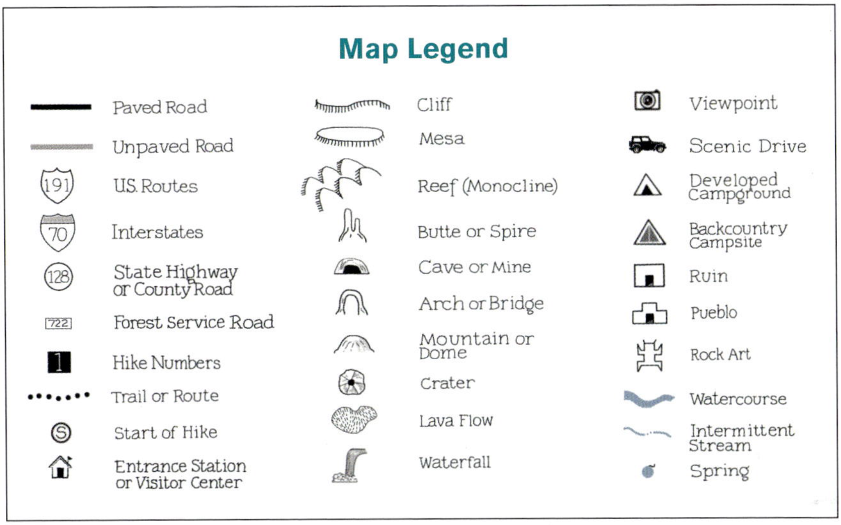

longer, with gentler gradients. Routes may require slogging through sand or hopping boulders.

Difficult hikes put significant demands on the traveler. Often located in remote areas, they involve more serious planning. Many are backcountry trails not suitable for day trips. Complications can include long, tiring routes; dramatic elevation gains on steep, exposed slopes; deep wading; rock scrambling; long waterless sections; unmarked or poorly marked routes; or precipitous drop-offs.

Very difficult routes are recommended only for experienced hikers in tip-top condition. The same hardship factors evident in difficult hikes apply, but to a higher degree or in greater concentration.

Prefacing each hike, the section entitled **Getting there** covers driving directions, usually from a notable landmark within a park, such as a visitor center or entrance station, or from the nearest town. Sometimes directions to the general area are in the park or area overview. **On the trail** describes the hike itself, including trail junctions and, where useful, distances of certain sections, what to look out for along the way, and so forth. Some hikes end with a **Nearby** section that highlights other hiking opportunities in the area, options for extending the featured hike, and more.

Finally, a brief word about two things that this book does not provide. I include GPS data (WGS 84, with decimal degrees) only in cases where special attractions may prove difficult to locate without them. My working assumption is that people are more in touch with the landscape when relying on a map or compass rather than a distracting electronic device. Likewise, I refrain from specifying my favorite hikes or supplying a must-do list. In part, this decision rests on my desire to spread people out rather than to concentrate them in a few places. But it also reflects my view that all hikes included in a guidebook should be "star-worthy"—ones that the author would recommend warmly to friends. Accordingly, any hike that failed to meet that criterion did not make the cut for this book. I consider all of these hikes to be the best of the best. Happy trails!

A hiker braves lower Coyote Gulch (Hike 28) on a rainy afternoon.

CHAPTER 1
DESERT RIVERS

With hubs in Cedar City and Escalante, Utah, this chapter explores the Paria and Escalante drainages. Bryce Canyon and Capitol Reef National Parks, Cedar Breaks and Grand Staircase-Escalante National Monuments, and three state parks receive top billing. Also featured is the Kolob Canyons section of Zion National Park. Because many of the hikes involve either splashing through deep, watery canyons or wandering high plateaus, they tend to be suitable for hot-weather travel.

Hubs: Cedar City and Escalante, Utah

Occupying the cool uplands of the Markagunt Plateau, **Cedar City** (population 31,300) is a university town that hosts the annual Utah Shakespeare Festival. Its name derives from the plateau's abundant juniper trees, locally called cedars.

Escalante (population 800) was named for a Spanish padre commissioned in 1776 to establish an overland route from New Mexico to California. The town received a shot in the economic arm during the late 1990s, with the creation of **Grand Staircase-Escalante National Monument**. Aside from the tourist industry, which has brought a wider mix of people into the community, ranching and mining are its mainstays. Just northwest of town is **Escalante Petrified Forest State Park**, where short trails wind through deposits of petrified wood, fossilized dinosaur bones, and prehistoric Fremont artifacts.

ZION NATIONAL PARK: KOLOB CANYONS SECTION AND VICINITY

Although Zion's dazzling Kolob Canyons unit rivals the main section of the park for beauty, it attracts far fewer visitors. From Cedar City, drive south on Interstate 15 for 17 miles to exit 42. Turn east onto the scenic road, pass through the park visitor center, and then continue on the scenic road, following the canyon carved by Taylor Creek before terminating at a glorious overlook.

1. Double Arch Alcove

Easy 5-mile out-and-back; allow 2.5 hours
Map: Trails Illustrated 214: Zion National Park

GETTING THERE: From the park visitor center off I-15, drive 2 miles up the scenic road and park in the designated lot.

ON THE TRAIL: This hike leads up the Middle Fork of **Taylor Creek** to a dramatic alcove containing two blind arches, "blind" because they do not completely cut through the surrounding rock. Begin by traversing a wooded area.

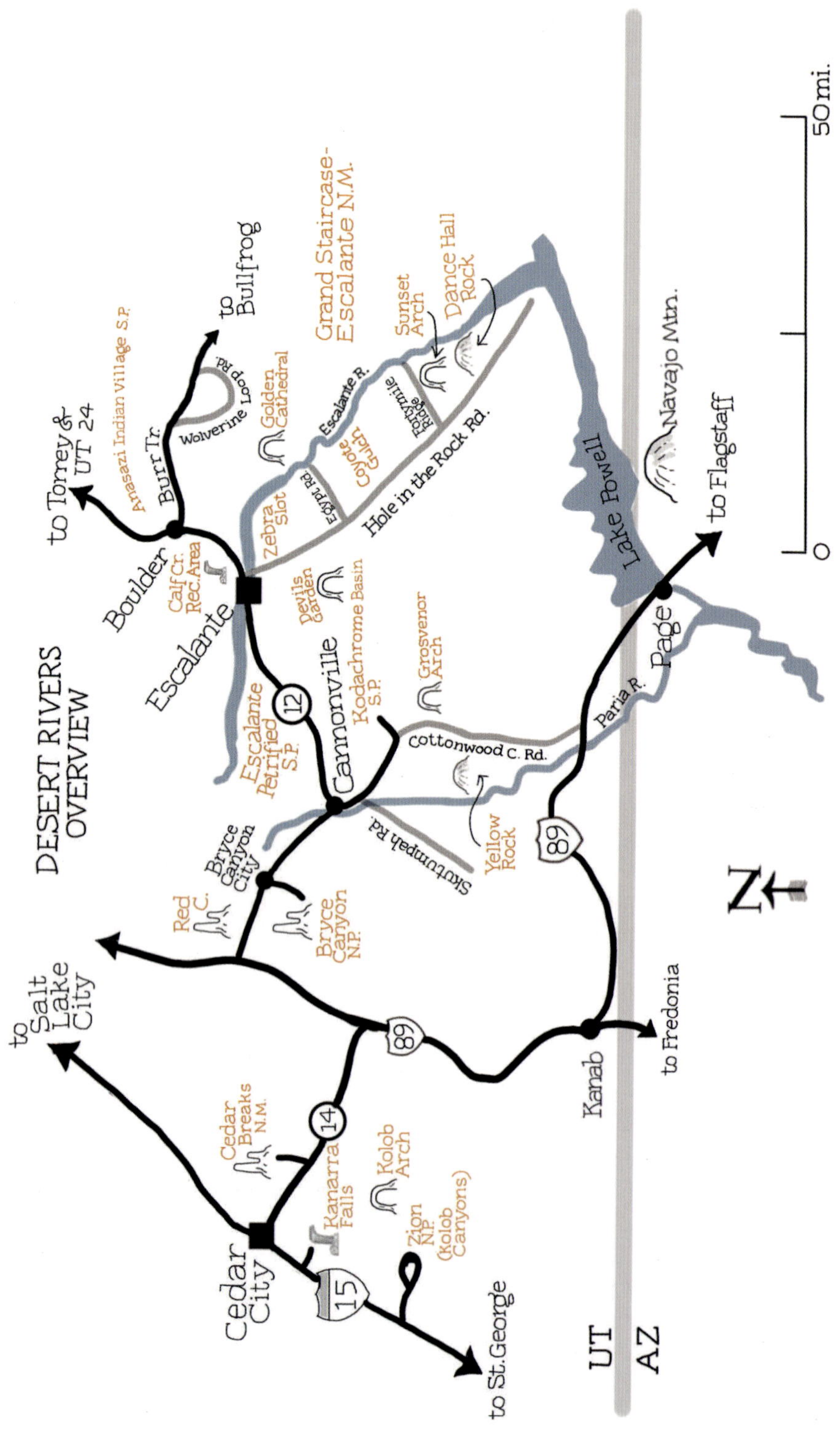
DESERT RIVERS OVERVIEW
to Salt Lake City
to Torrey & UT 24
to Bullfrog
Anasazi Indian Village S.P.
Burr Tr.
Wolverine Loop Rd.
Boulder
Calf Cr. Rec. Area
Escalante
Golden Cathedral
Grand Staircase-Escalante N.M.
Zebra Slot
Egypt Rd
Coyote Gulch
Escalante R.
Fortymile Ridge
Sunset Arch
Dance Hall Rock
Hole in the Rock Rd.
Devils Garden
Kodachrome Basin S.P.
Grosvenor Arch
Escalante Petrified S.P.
12
Cannonville
Cottonwood C. Rd.
Skutumpah Rd.
Yellow Rock
Paria R.
Page
Lake Powell
Navajo Mtn.
to Flagstaff
89
Bryce Canyon City
Red C.
Bryce Canyon N.P.
Cedar Breaks N.M.
14
Kolob Arch
Kanarra Falls
Zion N.P. (Kolob Canyons)
Cedar City
15
to St. George
Kanab
to Fredonia
UT
AZ
N
0
50 mi.

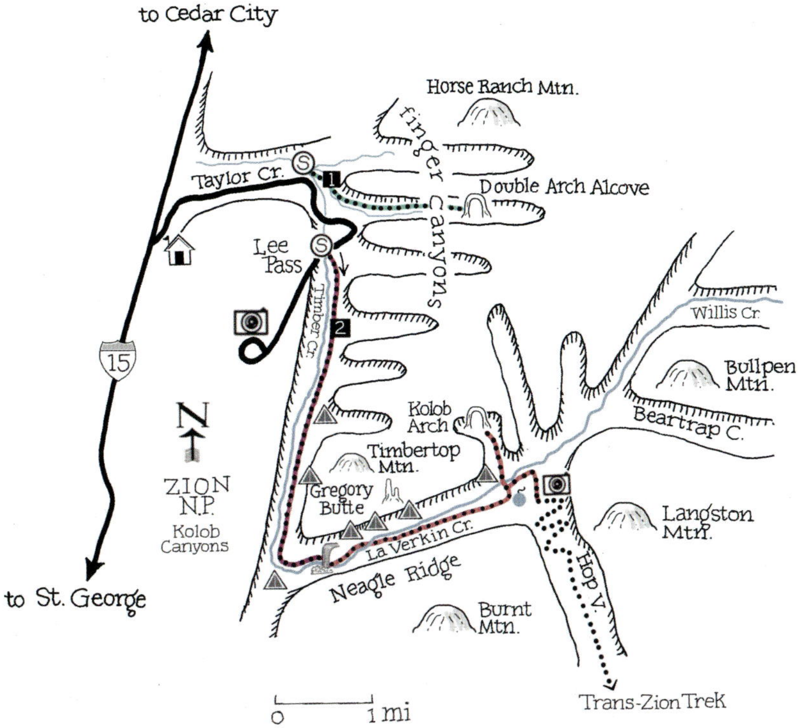

At about mile 1, bear right upon reaching a pioneer cabin at the confluence of the Middle and North Forks. Past this point, the canyon closes in, framed by craggy red peaks of Navajo Sandstone. The trail ascends slowly, alternating between benches and the creekbed. Just before a dry-fall, Double Arch Alcove occupies a sharp bend. Desert varnish and hanging gardens contribute to its allure.

2. Kolob Backpack

Moderate 15-mile out-and-back; allow 2 days
Permit required; water filter recommended
Map: Trails Illustrated 214: Zion National Park

GETTING THERE: From the park visitor center off I-15, drive 4 miles up the scenic road to the Lee Pass parking lot.

ON THE TRAIL: Your trip begins with a rapid 1.25-mile, 500-foot descent to cottonwood-lined **Timber Creek**. Enjoy views of wild and narrow finger canyons along the way. After following the creek for a while, the trail climbs to a low saddle. The rushing stream of **La Verkin Creek**, hundreds of feet below, sports a small waterfall and shallow pools. The trail meets the creek at mile 4.75. The prominent cliffs of Gregory Butte and Neagle Ridge loom on either side; composed of Navajo Sandstone, they sit atop the Kayenta Formation, through which the stream cuts its channel.

The trail gradually ascends, crossing the creek several times. At about mile 6.5, drop your pack and enter the first side-canyon on the left, following an obscure, brushy

This crude ladder offers a thrilling, chilling finale to the hike up Kanarra Creek.

trail to gigantic **Kolob Arch**. The arch, perched high in a cliff, is in an arm of the side-canyon. At nearly 300 feet across, this is one of the world's largest spans.

Designated campsites line La Verkin Creek. The recommended turnaround point is an overlook of tranquil **Hop Valley**. More ambitious hikers might want to consider the **Trans-Zion Trek**, extending 47 miles from Lee Pass to the east entrance station.

3. Kanarra Creek

Moderate 4-mile out-and-back; allow 2.5 to 3 hours

Permit from Town of Kanarraville required (available online or at trailhead); trekking poles, river shoes, and dry bag recommended

Map: USGS: Cedar City

GETTING THERE: From Cedar City, take I-15 south to exit 42, New Harmony/Kanarraville. Turn left (east) and proceed for 4.5 miles to the street named 100 North. Go right and continue to the official town-sponsored parking lots.

ON THE TRAIL: Families love this hike in Dixie National Forest, which follows a wooded gorge to an enchanting waterfall. Because the trip necessitates some twenty stream crossings, it represents an ideal summer option. Avoid the area during the spring runoff, when the water will be cold, deep, and swift, and on weekends, when it surely will be mobbed.

On foot, follow a dirt road as it climbs about 500 feet. Where the road ends at mile 1, pick up a trail to the left of a fenced-off facility. Soon the fords begin in earnest. Normally, the water level is ankle-to mid-calf-deep. Trekking poles help you maintain your balance while crossing the rocky stream. At about mile 1.5, skirt a small cascade on the right. Near the end, the canyon narrows to a rose-colored slot that requires constant wading. To the right of a short but scenic waterfall, climb a metal ladder to a second cascade. Although most people turn around here, under suitable conditions you can continue 0.5 mile to a highly photogenic double waterfall.

CEDAR BREAKS NATIONAL MONUMENT

Less than 20 miles east of Cedar City is Cedar Breaks National Monument. To reach it, take UT 14, a scenic road through Dixie National Forest, to UT 148 and continue to the visitor center.

Cedar Breaks sits high in the evergreens of the **Markagunt Plateau** at 10,000 feet. The road through the monument stays close to the lip of a 2500-foot-deep amphitheater, providing extravagant views of the pastel badlands ("breaks") below. Like lower-lying Bryce Canyon, Cedar Breaks features rows of Claron Formation spires marching down a limestone cliff. Overlooks and short trails enable you to inspect at close range the monument's pillars, alpine glades blanketed with wildflowers, and gnarled bristlecone pines, the earth's oldest living trees.

4. Ramparts Trail

Moderate 4-mile out-and-back; allow 2 hours
Map: USGS: Cedar Breaks

GETTING THERE: Start at the Cedar Breaks visitor center.

ON THE TRAIL: This picturesque trail follows the amphitheater west to Spectra Point and other overlooks. Total elevation change is 600 feet.

NEARBY: The **Alpine Pond Trail**, an easy 2-mile lollipop loop from Chessman Ridge Overlook, wanders through forested uplands to a bucolic pond on Rattle Creek.

RED CANYON

Carved out of the Dixie National Forest, Red Canyon resembles Bryce Canyon, minus the crowds and fees. Anywhere else, it would be a national park. The well-appointed visitor center is 3 miles east of US Route 89 on UT 12. Obtain a map at the visitor

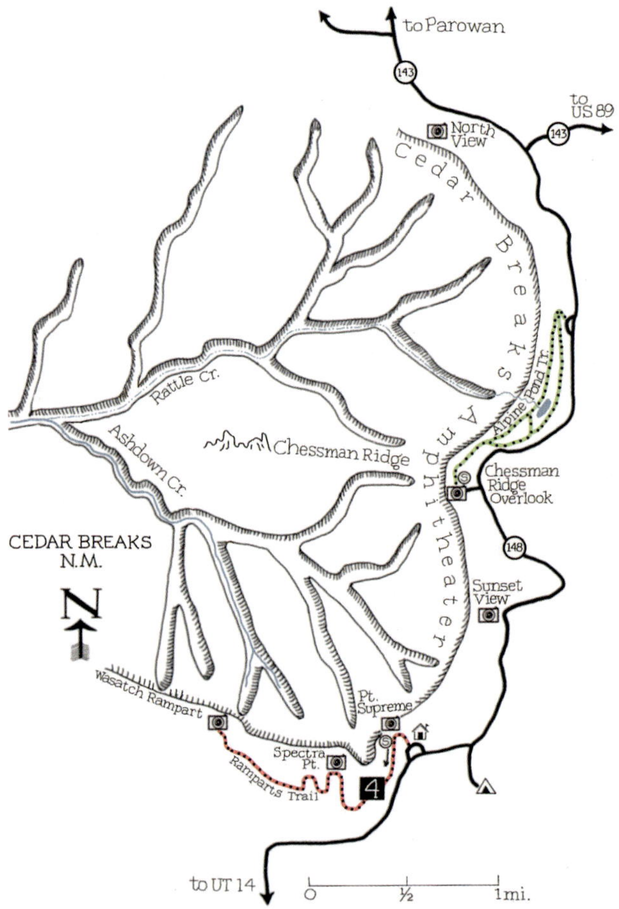

center and stroll the delightful **Pink Ledges Nature Trail**, an easy 0.75-mile loop that begins to the left of the building. Longer alternatives are described in Hikes 5, 6, and 7.

5. Arches Trail

Moderate 1-mile lollipop loop; allow 30 minutes
Trekking poles recommended
Map: USGS: Wilson Peak

GETTING THERE: From the Red Canyon visitor center, drive 1 mile west on UT 12. Turn right onto unpaved Casto Canyon Road and proceed 2 miles to the parking lot.

ON THE TRAIL: Starting at the north end of the parking lot, the trail crosses Losee Creek, usually dry. Intersecting the loop, turn right to walk in a counterclockwise direction. Soon the trail makes a hairpin turn to the right. An unofficial path on the left climbs a scree slope to the first, and largest, arch.

Back on the trail, ascend the mesa on a flight of stairs. Numerous rock windows come into view. Just before arriving at another set of stairs, detour right to an overlook.

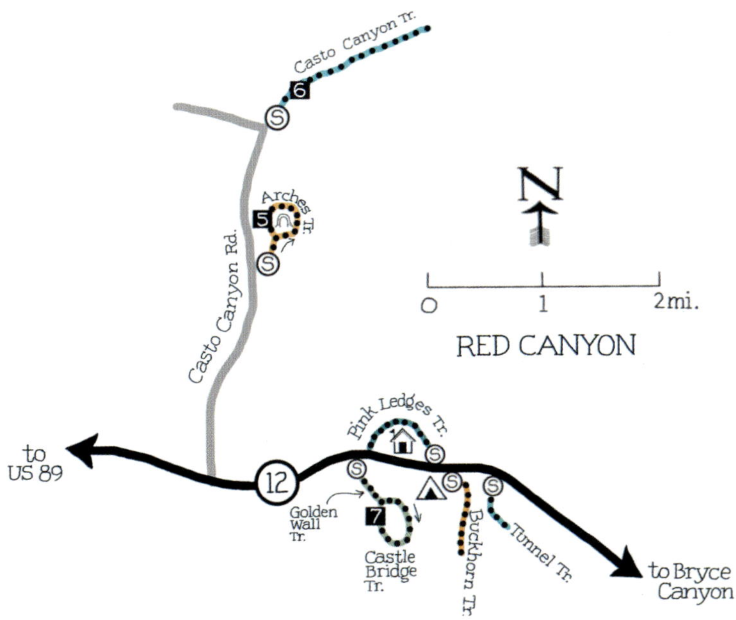

Despite some exposure, the wide spur poses no danger. Returning to the main trail, descend to close the loop.

6. Casto Canyon

Very easy 2-mile out-and-back; allow 1 hour
Map: USGS: Wilson Peak

GETTING THERE: From the Red Canyon visitor center, drive 1 mile west on UT 12. Turn right onto unpaved Casto Canyon Road and continue 3 miles to the trailhead.
ON THE TRAIL: Shared by hikers, bikers, equestrians, and small ATVs, this trail passes through a gate and follows a jeep road up a major wash. The limestone spires and hoodoos are as fanciful as, and even more colorful than, their Bryce Canyon counterparts. Walk in at least 1 mile for maximum enjoyment.

7. Castle Bridge Trail

Moderate 2-mile lollipop loop; allow 1.25 hours
Trekking poles recommended
Map: USGS: Wilson Peak

GETTING THERE: Pick up the trail on the south side of UT 12, 100 yards west of the Red Canyon visitor center.
ON THE TRAIL: Begin by walking 0.5 mile up the **Golden Wall Trail**, which ascends gently alongside a rocky wash. Turn left at the first junction onto the **Castle Bridge Trail**. Switchbacks make the subsequent climb to a ridgetop less punishing than it otherwise would be. Enjoy expansive vistas at the top. Descend on another set of switchbacks to rejoin the Golden Wall Trail at mile 1.5. Return to your vehicle, wondering why the promised bridge never materialized.

NEARBY: Two short, moderate out-and-backs start east of the visitor center. Drive 0.5 mile up UT 12 to the campground; the 2-mile round-trip **Buckhorn Trail** (which takes off from site 23) zigzags 500 feet to an exposed, knife-edged ridge. Farther east on UT 12, between mileposts 3 and 4, hike the **Tunnel Trail**, 1.5 miles round trip, which crosses a wash before ascending to a low bluff amid bristlecone pines.

BRYCE CANYON NATIONAL PARK

Bryce Canyon always has stirred the imagination and inspired metaphor. The Paiute Indians, whose myths depicted its tall hoodoos as individuals petrified and painted by a vengeful deity, called it "red rocks standing like men in a bowl-shaped canyon." But to Mormon rancher Ebenezer Bryce, it was simply "a hell of a place to lose a cow."

Technically, Bryce comprises not a single canyon but a series of amphitheaters biting into the **Paunsaugunt Plateau,** where the headwaters of the Paria drainage are found. The park's high altitude—up to 9100 feet—makes it a comfortable venue during summer. Indeed, freezing temperatures and even snowstorms can persist into May.

More than 60 miles of trails wind through Bryce's pastel needles, which were formed by mechanical and chemical weathering. An easy **Rim Trail** connects Fairyland View with Sunrise, Sunset, Inspiration, and Bryce Points. All trails from the rim to the floor of the amphitheater are at least moderately difficult, requiring climbs of several hundred feet, but other trails are suitable for people of any ability level. From April through October, free shuttle buses run between Bryce Canyon City and Bryce Point, with several intermediate destinations.

To reach the park, from the junction with US Route 89, follow UT 12 for 14 miles to Bryce Canyon City (formerly Rubys Inn). Turn right onto UT 63 and head south to the entrance station.

8. Fairyland Loop

Moderate 8-mile loop; allow 4 hours
Trekking poles recommended
Map: Trails Illustrated 219: Bryce Canyon National Park

GETTING THERE: Access the trail from Fairyland View overlook, just north of the park entrance station. Be advised that the shuttle does not stop here.

ON THE TRAIL: Start by descending a ridgeline 850 feet to cross the upper reaches of Fairyland Canyon. After rounding Boat Mesa and passing exotic formations such as the Palace of the Fairy Queen and the Ruins of Athens, you enter Campbell Canyon. Here the trail intersects a short spur on the left to **Tower Bridge**, one of two substantial spans in the park. Beyond this point, the trail starts its ascent, affording views of the **Chinese Wall.**

At the top it forks; the path on the left leads to Sunrise Point, while the Rim Trail on the right climbs to North Campground, hugging the lip of the bowl back to Fairyland View.

9. Queens Garden Trail

Moderate 1.5-mile out-and-back; allow 1 hour
Map: Trails Illustrated 219: Bryce Canyon National Park

GETTING THERE: Drive south on the park road to the parking area for Sunrise Point, near the park visitor center. Park in the large lot and strike out for the rim.

ON THE TRAIL: Queens Garden, the easiest of the trails to the amphitheater floor, descends 325 feet, past Gullivers and Queens Castles, before ending at a viewpoint of **Queen Victoria's Profile**. From here either retrace your steps or take the connecting trail to the Navajo Loop. If you ascend to Sunset Point on the Navajo Loop (see Hike 10), a very easy 0.5-mile stroll along the Rim Trail returns you to the parking lot.

10. Navajo Loop

Moderate 1.5-mile loop; allow 1 hour
Map: Trails Illustrated 219: Bryce Canyon National Park

GETTING THERE: Drive south on the park road, following signs to Sunset Point. Locate the trailhead on the canyon rim.

Bryce Canyon's vibrant pastels intensify when the sun shines low.

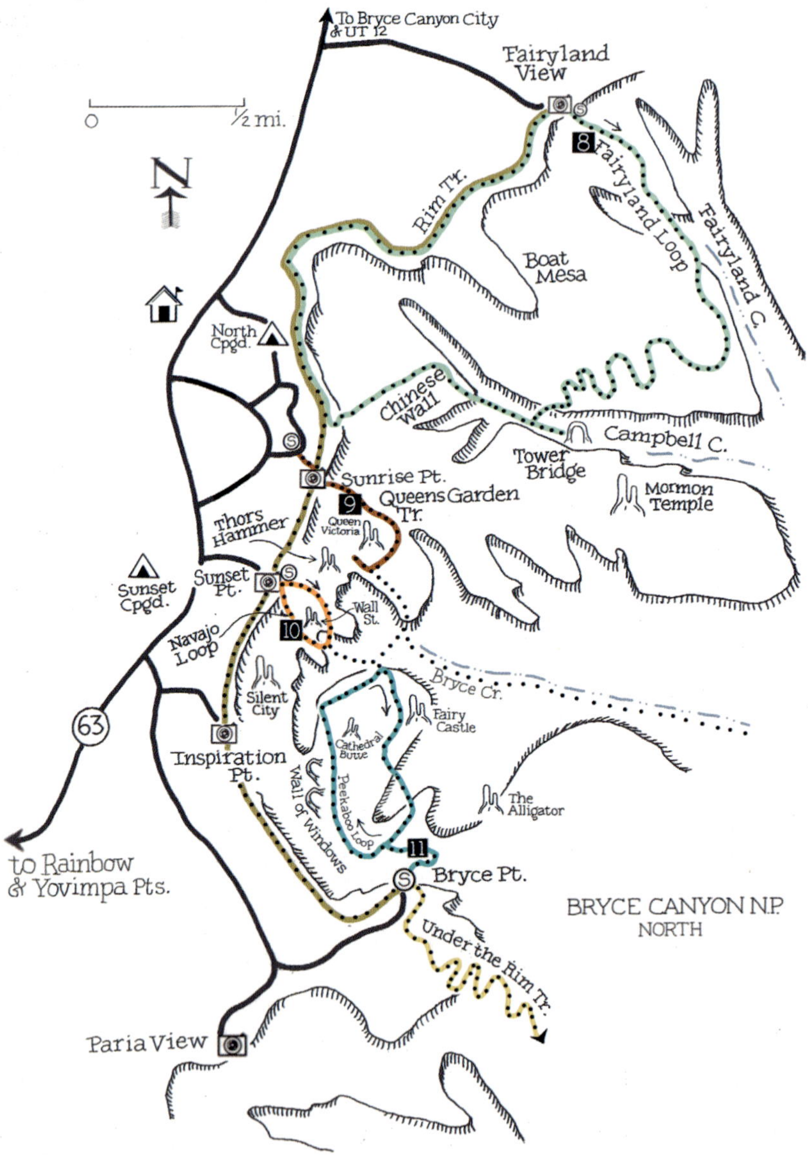

ON THE TRAIL: The park's most popular trail, the Navajo Loop gives access to the hoodoos at its heart. It can be combined with the Queens Garden Trail (see Hike 9) for a 3.5-mile loop by means of a connector.

The trail drops from the rim and almost immediately forks. Take the left fork and descend 525 feet on switchbacks to its base, enjoying close-up views of Two Bridges, The Pope, and **Thors Hammer**, a slender orange pinnacle capped by a mallet-shaped stone. Within 0.75 mile, the connector to the Queens Garden Trail joins on the left. Bear right to continue on the Navajo Loop. Rounding a bend, you thread through the narrow passageway of **Wall Street** before climbing back to the rim. Near the top, a spur visits an overlook of the **Silent City**.

11. Peekaboo Loop

Moderate 6.25-mile lollipop loop; allow 3 hours
Trekking poles recommended
Map: Trails Illustrated 219: Bryce Canyon National Park

GETTING THERE: From the park visitor center, drive south along the park road for 1.5 miles. Turn left here and continue for 2 miles, following signs for Bryce Point.
ON THE TRAIL: The Peekaboo Loop deters the casual visitor, whether because it is one of the park's more challenging hikes, with an elevation change of 1000 feet, or because horse parties also utilize this trail. Sublime scenery more than makes up for any unpleasantness along the way. (Watch your step!)

Peekaboo connects to the rim via trails leading down from Sunset, Bryce, and Sunrise Points; respectively, the round-trip mileages are 5.5, 6.5, and 7, all of which include 3.5 miles on the loop itself. You can start or end at any of these trailheads. Although the climb to Bryce Point is about 300 feet greater than to the others, the routing detailed here provides maximum enjoyment.

From Bryce Point, the trail takes off to the northeast, quickly arriving at a junction with the **Under the Rim Trail**. Turn left here. Pass through a tunnel and descend rapidly on switchbacks to meet the Peekaboo Loop at mile 1.5. Proceed clockwise on the loop. At mile 2, you approach the scenic crescendo of this trip: the **Wall of Windows**, a gossamer ridge of hoodoos festooned with arches. Go through another tunnel at about mile 2.75. Shortly thereafter, Cathedral Butte looms to your right.

The trail's low point comes at mile 3.5, where it joins a connector with the Navajo Loop. Turn right at the junction. As you climb through a wooded area, **Fairy Castle** dominates the scene around mile 4. Negotiate yet another tunnel and close the loop at mile 4.75. Catch your breath before ascending briskly to Bryce Point.

12. Under the Rim Backpack

Moderate 22-mile point-to-point; allow 3 days
Permit and vehicle shuttle or equivalent; trekking poles and water filter recommended
Map: Trails Illustrated 219: Bryce Canyon National Park

GETTING THERE: From the visitor center, drive south along the park road for 1.5 miles. Turn left and continue for 2 miles, following signs for Bryce Point. Your trip ends at the end of the park road.
ON THE TRAIL: The Under the Rim Trail offers Bryce Canyon's only backpacking opportunity. Many people, however, prefer to tackle the trail in segments. Connectors to the rim make this option eminently feasible. The trail extends from Bryce Point to Rainbow Point, with several connectors, each about a mile long, to the park road. Although much of the trail is through forested country and the Pink Cliffs are not always in view, there are numerous compensations, solitude and serenity among them.

The Wall of Windows, a scenic crescendo along the Peekaboo Trail (Hike 11)

Start by dropping almost 1000 feet to the **Hat Shop** at mile 1.5, a collection of salmon and tangerine needles with white erosion-resistant caps. Past here, continue descending to the right fork of Yellow Creek at mile 3. This is the lowest elevation on the route and the location of the first of several designated campsites.

Follow the creek upstream through scrubby terrain to a spot beneath Paria View. The trail undulates over the next few miles. Descend into Sheep Creek at mile 9 and the right fork of Swamp Canyon at mile 10. Sheep Creek usually contains flowing water. The **Sheep Creek Trail** climbs steeply through heavy timber to the rim, while the **Swamp Canyon Trail** offers an easier ascent.

The main trail gradually ascends Swamp Canyon until it intersects the **Whiteman Trail**, at roughly the trip's halfway mark (mile 11.5). This connector, which follows an old roadbed, meets the park road about 0.25 mile north of a picnic area.

From the Whiteman junction, the main trail levels out and winds through an aspen grove. It descends into the forest, following Willis Creek below Farview Point and

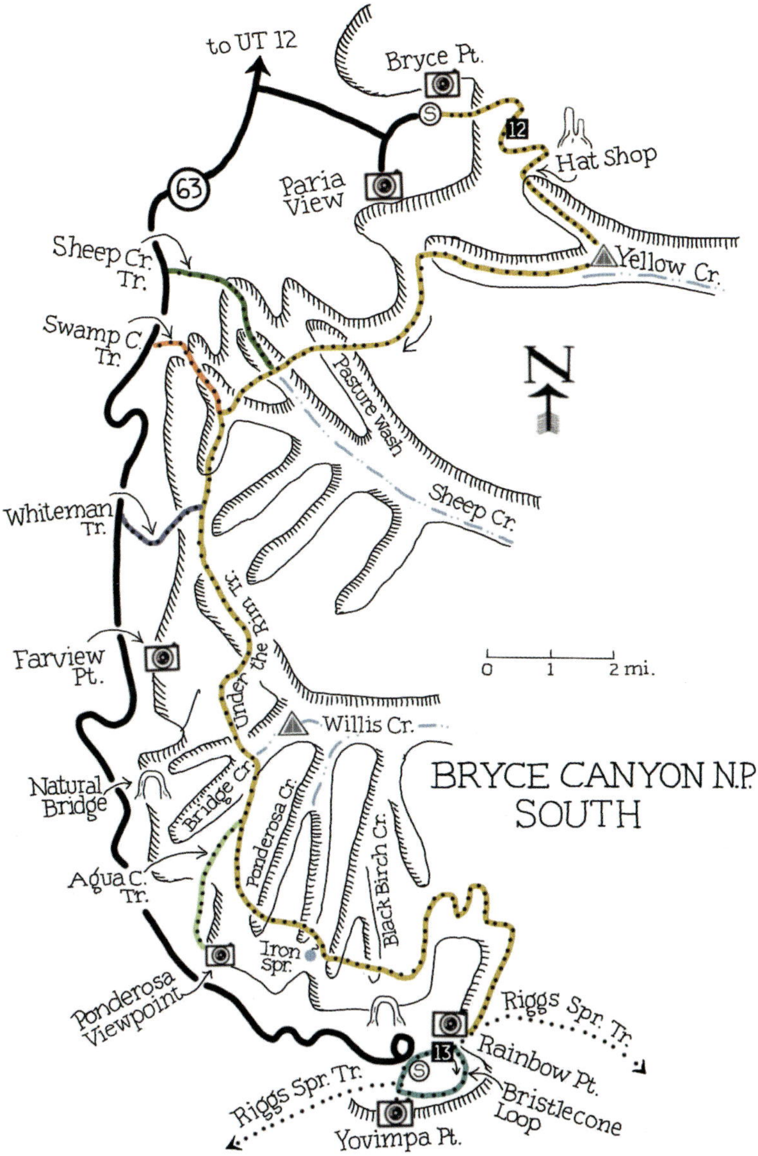

threading between the rim and an isolated battlement. An unnamed pass takes you into the Bridge Creek drainage. You may notice a window or two in the cliff wall. In a fire-scarred clearing, look toward the rim to pick out **Natural Bridge**. The 85-foot span is technically an arch, since its opening was not formed by running water.

At about mile 16, the **Agua Canyon Trail** branches off to the right. This well-engineered connector, which leads to Ponderosa Viewpoint, is longer and steeper than the others, but offers striking panoramas.

In the next few miles, cross many arms of Ponderosa and Black Birch Creeks. A saddle with a hoodoo at about mile 17.25, between two branches of Ponderosa Creek, provides an ideal rest stop. Soon after comes a level walk through forested country, memorable for an aspen glade. The orange, mineral-stained water flowing at about mile 18.5 is not potable. From here the trail laterals around a point before crossing the Black Birch drainage. Look up at the ramparts to spy another arch.

Now begins the long, final push to the rim. The altitude may make the climb tiring. But visually, this is the highlight of the trip, for you can see an extensive section of the Pink Cliffs as well as Navajo Mountain on the Arizona border. Eventually you attain a sharp ridge. Switchback through stands of conifers to Rainbow Point.

13. Bristlecone Loop

Very easy 1-mile loop; allow 30 minutes

Map: Trails Illustrated 219: Bryce Canyon National Park

GETTING THERE: Drive to Rainbow Point at the southern end of the park.

ON THE TRAIL: This trail connecting Rainbow and Yovimpa Points involves little elevation change as it passes through forested uplands, swinging out to a promontory with bang-up views.

14. Mossy Cave

Easy 0.75-mile out-and-back; allow 30 minutes

Map: Trails Illustrated 219: Bryce Canyon National Park

GETTING THERE: Located in a detached unit of the park, this trail begins east of Bryce Canyon City off UT 12, between mileposts 17 and 18.

ON THE TRAIL: From the parking area south of the highway, the route follows a stream, which it crosses on two bridges. After the second bridge, the trail forks. The left fork heads to Mossy Cave, an alcove sheltering a perennial spring. The right fork leads to a small waterfall and offers a good view.

KODACHROME BASIN STATE PARK

Explore a world of standing stone in one of Utah's most beloved state parks, which sports a first-rate campground. Almost 70 "sand pipes" rise from Kodachrome's valley floor. These chimney-like columns, unique in all the world, were produced by geothermal pressures and exposed as surrounding Entrada Sandstone eroded away. Some experts regard them as remnants of ancient geysers that gradually became choked with sediment. Enjoy short hikes on the **Sentinel Loop** (1.75 miles, with a more difficult return option on the Slickrock Cutoff); **Angels Palace Trail** (1-mile lollipop loop); and **Grand Parade Trail** (mile lollipop loop, featuring two box canyon spurs). The longer option outlined in Hike 15 examines sand pipes at close range.

On UT 12 drive east 12 miles from Bryce Canyon City (or 33 miles west from Escalante) to Cannonville. Pick up Cottonwood Canyon Road (County Road 400) here, and travel southeast 7.75 miles to a junction. Turn left to enter the park.

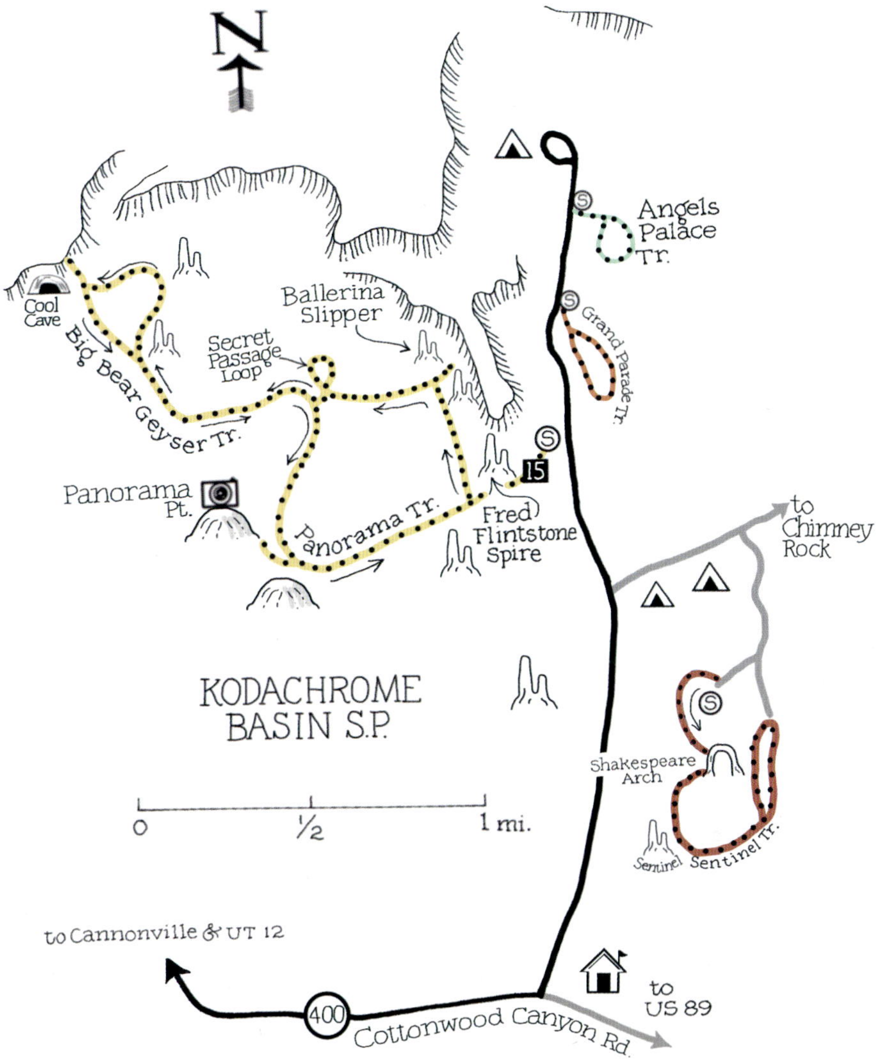

15. Panorama Loop

Easy 5.75-mile lollipop loop, including spurs; allow 3 hours
Map: Trails Illustrated 714: Grand Staircase, Paunsaugunt Plateau

GETTING THERE: The trailhead is about 1 mile north of the state park entrance on Cottonwood Canyon Road.

ON THE TRAIL: This memorable hike samples the best of what Kodachrome has to offer. On foot, head west about 0.25 mile to a junction. Turn right onto a spur to investigate the alcove called Old Indian Cave. Back on the main trail, continue for 0.5 mile to graceful **Ballerina Slipper** and then to formations known collectively as the Hat Shop. The trail is unchallenging as it crosses a flat toward the 0.25-mile loop to

Secret Passage, a short slot. From here you soon join the **Big Bear Geyser Trail**. Turn right and continue to a spur on the left, which ends at the park's largest sand pipe, **Mammoth Geyser**.

Just past here, intersect a short loop trail. Go right, passing the Big Bear Geysers, to the spur that traverses a slot canyon to Cool Cave. Returning to the main trail, close the loop after gentle ups and downs. Within 0.75 mile, rejoin the **Panorama Trail**, turning right. If you wish, drink in the view from the end of the spur to Panorama Point, a 125-foot climb, for an additional 0.5-mile round-trip. Returning to the main trail, continue 0.5 mile to **Fred Flintstone Spire** and from there 0.25 mile back to your vehicle.

GRAND STAIRCASE-ESCALANTE NATIONAL MONUMENT: WEST

For hikers seeking solitude and variety, the area southwest of Escalante is second to none. Several intriguing canyons can be accessed from Cannonville, 12 miles east of Bryce Canyon City or 33 miles west of Escalante on UT 12. Cottonwood Canyon Road (County Road 400), which is unpaved south of Kodachrome Basin, eventually intersects US Route 89. Branching off Cottonwood Canyon Road 2.5 miles south of Cannonville is Skutumpah Road (CR 500), also unpaved. As both byways are impassable when wet, check on their condition at the visitor center in Cannonville. Also bear in mind that the farther south you travel on Cottonwood Road, the more its condition may deteriorate; a four-wheel-drive or high-clearance vehicle is recommended for those sections.

The featured hikes are in or near Grand Staircase-Escalante National Monument, designated by President Bill Clinton in 1996.

16. Willis Creek

Easy 5-mile out-and-back; allow 2.5 hours

Map: Trails Illustrated 714: Grand Staircase, Paunsaugunt Plateau

GETTING THERE: From Cannonville, drive south 2.5 miles on Cottonwood Canyon Road (CR 400). Turn right onto Skutumpah Road (CR 500) and proceed 6 miles, descending to a wash. Park here.

ON THE TRAIL: Cross the road to begin. Within 100 yards the trail drops into the wash. In the first 1.5 miles, you squeeze through several short slots with cross-bedded sandstone walls, which get deeper as you progress downstream. The only significant obstruction is a low waterfall, bypassed on the right.

Beyond these narrow sections, look for a graceful double arch on the canyon's left wall. Just past this point, Averett Canyon enters, and Willis Creek changes its character. While ceasing to be a true slot, it remains a rather narrow and scenic gorge harboring upland tree species such as ponderosa pines and Douglas fir. Retrace your steps upon reaching the confluence with **Sheep Creek**.

17. Bull Valley Gorge

Difficult, with variable mileage and time depending on chosen exit route
Trekking poles, river shoes, and 30-foot rope recommended
Map: Trails Illustrated 714: Grand Staircase, Paunsaugunt Plateau

GETTING THERE: From Cannonville, drive south 2.5 miles on Cottonwood Canyon Road (CR 400). Turn right onto Skutumpah Road (CR 500) and proceed 7.75 miles to the bridge over Bull Valley Gorge. Park here.

ON THE TRAIL: This Navajo Sandstone defile contains numerous logjams and boulder jams in its upper reaches that pose a challenge for hikers. Because the gorge is so tight, its configuration changes with every flood. You can either day hike the upper canyon or construct a 15.5-mile backpacking loop with mellow Sheep Creek (where you follow a jeep road) and its tributary, Willis Creek (see Hike 16). Pack a water filter if you elect the latter option. Do not enter the canyon if rain threatens.

From the bridge, walk upstream a few hundred yards until it is safe to drop into the wash. Then reverse course, heading downstream. Almost immediately the canyon pinches in. As you near the bridge, look up to see the wreck of a jeep that plunged over the rim in 1954 and got wedged between the narrow cliffs, killing all three passengers.

Continue downcanyon as far as you like. Normally the gorge is dry, but occasionally downstream travel may be complicated by pools and mud. After the first few miles, when the gorge widens out, several opportunities to make a safe, if lung-burning, exit present themselves on the right. Once you top out, hug the rim to return to your car.

18. Lick Wash

Easy 8-mile out-and-back; allow 4 hours
Map: Trails Illustrated 714: Grand Staircase, Paunsaugunt Plateau

GETTING THERE: From Cannonville, drive south 2.5 miles on Cottonwood Canyon Road (CR 400). Turn right onto Skutumpah Road (CR 500) and drive 22 miles to the designated parking area.

ON THE TRAIL: This dry Navajo Sandstone canyon makes for a lovely stroll. Its narrows extend about a mile. Beyond that point, the canyon widens and deepens somewhat. Conifers line both the canyon floor and the benches above. At mile 4, beneath the swirling slickrock domes of No Mans Mesa, Lick Wash feeds into **Park Wash**. This is your logical turnaround point.

19. Grosvenor Arch

Very easy 0.25-mile out-and-back; allow 15 minutes
Map: Trails Illustrated 714: Grand Staircase, Paunsaugunt Plateau

GETTING THERE: From Cannonville, drive 15 miles down Cottonwood Canyon Road (County Road 400; 7.25 miles past the turnoff to Kodachrome Basin State Park). Turn left onto a marked spur.

ON THE TRAIL: This stately, cream-colored span with a double opening takes its name from Gilbert Hovey Grosvenor, one of the founders of the National Geographic Society. A paved trail leads to the base.

A conifer leans between the Navajo Sandstone walls of Lick Wash (Hike 18).

20. Cottonwood Narrows

Easy to moderate 2.25-mile loop; allow 1.5 hours
High-clearance or four-wheel-drive vehicle recommended
Map: Trails Illustrated 714: Grand Staircase, Paunsaugunt Plateau

GETTING THERE: From Cannonville, drive 19.25 miles south on Cottonwood Canyon Road (CR 400) to meet the **Cockscomb**, a colorful hogback that extends into Arizona. The road drops steeply into what locals call Candyland Valley. Park at the signed pull-out for Cottonwood Narrows North.

ON THE TRAIL: Scramble into the canyon and prepare to bliss out. Explore the upstream narrows, which continue about 300 yards, before proceeding downstream for the bulk of the hike. Although the drainage is mostly level and unproblematic to traverse, you encounter obstacles at the end, near two small windows in the Navajo Sandstone cliffs. Powerlines are strung overhead where the canyon rejoins the road at the Cottonwood Narrows South parking lot. Go left and walk the road back to your vehicle.

21. Hackberry Canyon

Moderate 12.5-mile out-and-back, with exposure and scrambling; allow 7 hours
High-clearance or four-wheel-drive vehicle recommended
Map: Trails Illustrated 714: Grand Staircase, Paunsaugunt Plateau

GETTING THERE: Take Cottonwood Canyon Road (CR 400) 31.25 miles south from Cannonville. Park in a lot on the right, signed for Lower Hackberry.

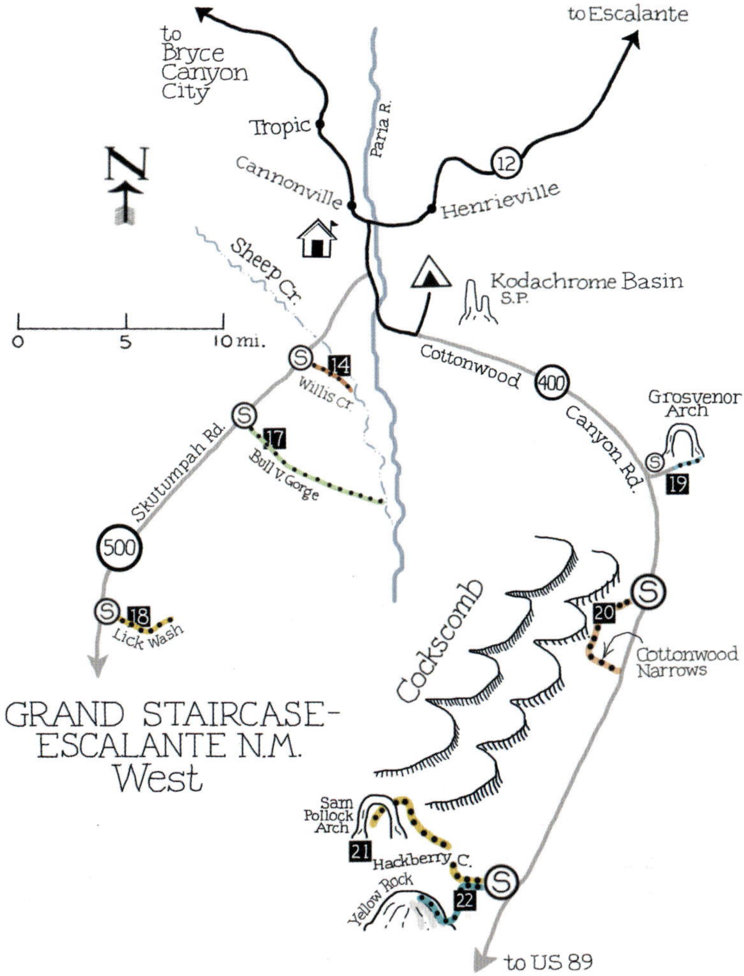

ON THE TRAIL: Hackberry enjoys nothing like the renown bestowed on the Paria River, into which it empties, yet it offers solitude and enjoyable hiking. The recommended route leads to Sam Pollock Arch, its crown jewel.

From the parking lot, approach the streambed. There is an evident trail even at the beginning. Note that two watercourses flow together here: Cottonwood, which parallels the road, and its tributary Hackberry, which emerges from the Navajo Sandstone section of the Cockscomb monocline. Bearing right, head north to enter Hackberry.

You quickly reach the narrows and must wade for at least 0.5 mile, as the canyon leaves little room on either bank. After about 0.75 mile, you enter the reddish, ledgy Kayenta Formation. Eventually the canyon widens enough to form benches. You can follow social trails to cut across meanders in the streambed. Before long the colorful Chinle Formation appears at river level. This soft rock weathers into low, banded hills that broaden the canyon still more.

At about mile 5, just beyond an old cabin, Sam Pollock Canyon comes in from the left, recognizable by a steep, boulder-choked profile. Initially, hiking up this tributary requires considerable scrambling. The harder test comes at about mile 5.5, where a cairned route leads upward through a break in the Kayenta. You must ascend here onto a nasty, exposed ledge to avoid a pour-off.

Beyond the pour-off, the trail returns to the sandy wash, where the walking becomes much easier. Plod on until you spot **Sam Pollock Arch**. The span boasts an opening in front, an echo-rich alcove behind, and a huge hole in its ceiling.

22. Yellow Rock

Difficult 3-mile out-and-back; allow 2 hours
High-clearance or four-wheel-drive vehicle and trekking poles recommended
Map: Trails Illustrated 714: Grand Staircase, Paunsaugunt Plateau

GETTING THERE: Take Cottonwood Canyon Road (CR 400) 31.25 miles south from Cannonville. Park in a lot on the right, signed for Lower Hackberry.

The two-toned slopes of Yellow Rock tower above Cottonwood Canyon.

ON THE TRAIL: From the parking lot, drop down to the streambed and turn left into broad **Cottonwood Wash**, which is frequented by cattle. Dodging cow pies, mush through sand about 0.25 mile to an unnamed box canyon on the right. Turn into this canyon and ascend rapidly, following a cairned route. Although exposure is not an issue, one glance at the steep, slippery slope may deter the faint of heart. The first pitch, involving 200 vertical feet of scree and loose dirt, is brutally steep. Curse words may fly until the grade abates near the top.

From here the hiker-made trail veers to the right. Shortly thereafter, Yellow Rock—a deeply saturated expanse of Navajo Sandstone—comes into view. Follow cairns to the left across a narrow ridge and then bear hard to the right beneath four snaggle-toothed protrusions. Past these fangs, ascend a rocky slope before swinging to the right toward Yellow Rock. Intersect the dome just below a prominent swirl reminiscent of Jupiter's Great Red Spot. Commit this intersection point to memory.

Traction on the slickrock mass is good all the way to the summit. From here look north to see a blindingly white, castle-like formation called **The Stupa**. Once you've had your fill, retrace your steps. A finger of rock on the horizon to the east will help orient your return.

GRAND STAIRCASE-ESCALANTE NATIONAL MONUMENT: SOUTH

This vast, rugged, often inhospitable region shelters some of the Southwest's premier hikes. Unlike most other national monuments, Grand Staircase-Escalante is administered by the Bureau of Land Management (BLM), the original custodian of nearly all public lands within the monument's borders. Its attractions are legion: deep, narrow canyons, hanging gardens, natural bridges and arches, unusual erosional forms, and stupendous views spanning vast distances. The canyons of the Escalante River comprise the beating heart of the monument.

Named for a Spanish padre *cum* explorer, the Escalante is a tributary of the Colorado. Placid and shallow most of the time, it was the last river in the continental United States to be "discovered," during Major John Wesley Powell's second expedition down the Green and Colorado Rivers, in 1872. Much of the river's lower end is now part of Lake Powell, the reservoir created by the 1963 completion of Glen Canyon Dam.

About 5 miles east of the town of Escalante off UT 12 begins historic **Hole in the Rock Road**, from which all hikes in this section originate. The unpaved, corrugated track parallels the Kaiparowits Plateau, and although it deteriorates significantly near the end, it is passable without a four-wheel-drive vehicle to the following trailheads. Most of the road and its environs, once included in the national monument, lie outside the current borders as redrawn by the Trump administration in 2017.

Hole in the Rock Road derives its name from a landmark event in Mormon history. In 1879, a party of two hundred pioneers sent to colonize southeastern Utah set off from Escalante over the open desert. Upon reaching sheer-walled Glen Canyon, they spent months excavating a "dugway" down a natural chute to accommodate their

Pea-sized accretions decorate colorful Zebra Slot.

wagons and livestock. Fording the river, they then made their way to the valley of the San Juan, where they established the settlement of Bluff before later relocating to present-day Blanding.

23. Zebra Slot

Moderate 5-mile out-and-back; allow 2.5 hours
Map: Trails Illustrated 710: Canyons of the Escalante

GETTING THERE: From the town of Escalante, drive east on UT 12 for 5 miles. Turn right onto washboarded Hole in the Rock Road, and prepare to be "shaken, not stirred." Travel 8 miles to reach a parking area on the right.

ON THE TRAIL: Recharge your batteries at horizontally striped Zebra Slot. The well-defined trail hugs the left side of attractive **Halfway Hollow**, which empties into Harris Wash. Pass through a cattle guard at mile 1. At mile 2, cross the shallow streambed and proceed to the red cliffs on the other bank. Turn left here, following the cliff-line into Zebra Wash. Have faith: Within a short distance the wide, sandy bed will slot up. Expect to wade across a small pool at the entry to the narrows and to chimney past a few obstacles before reaching the defile's end.

24. Harris Wash Backpack

Moderate 21.5-mile out-and-back; allow 2–3 days
Permit required; high-clearance or four-wheel-drive vehicle, river shoes, and water filter recommended
Map: Trails Illustrated 710: Canyons of the Escalante

GETTING THERE: From the town of Escalante, drive east on UT 12 for 5 miles. Turn right onto Hole in the Rock Road. Drive about 10.5 miles south on this road to the signed track for Harris Wash. Bear left here and bump along another 6.5 miles to the trailhead, just beyond a corral. Issue yourself a permit for overnight camping.

ON THE TRAIL: Harris Wash lacks the arches that make Coyote Gulch (see Hike 28) such a crowd magnet, but it is comparable in most other respects.

Begin by dropping down on a jeep track into the broad, gravel-filled streambed. Turn right, leaving the track, and walk down the sandy wash toward distant bluffs marking the gateway into the canyon. In years with normal precipitation, water may be flowing even at the start. After over an hour of slogging you enter **Glen Canyon National Recreation Area** at mile 2.5. A few bends beyond, you can detour into a scenic, if brushy, rincon. Indeed, brush will become your enemy as you penetrate deeper into the canyon. Although many benches have rough paths, they tend to be overgrown.

At mile 5, take note of a large cave on a tree-shaded bench. It shelters mineral deposits arranged in a bullseye pattern. Significant side-canyons enter at miles 6.5 and 7.25, but they are easy to miss if you are walking on the opposite bank. At mile 8.5, the first reliable landmark appears, a lush seep spring flowing from an undercut cliff to the right of the wash. You will encounter several more seeps in the next few bends. The wash broadens somewhat between here and the **Escalante River** at mile 10.75. Take note of a small granary on the left at the confluence.

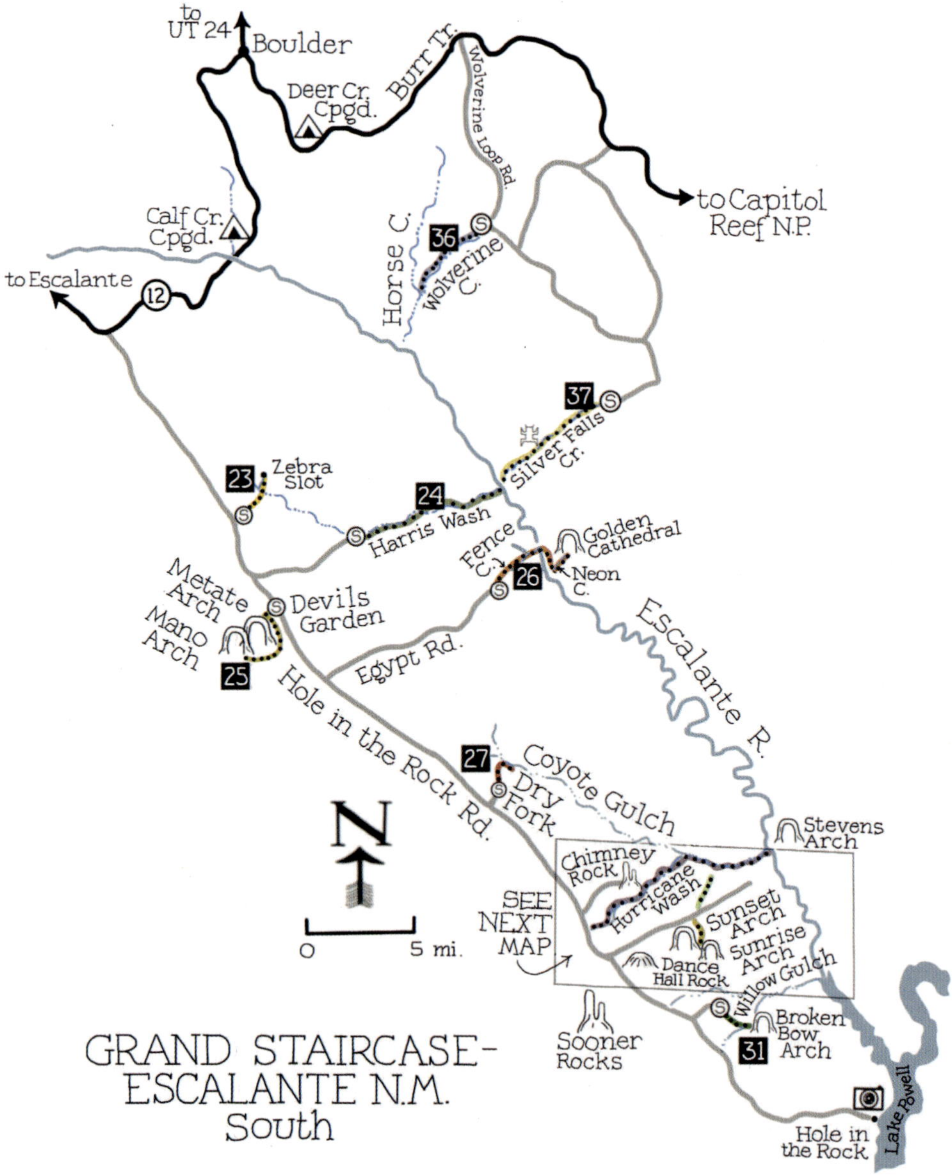

Only 0.25 mile upstream, **Silver Falls Creek** joins the Escalante from the east (see Hike 37). Those with energy to spare can hike up this gorge for 1.75 miles to see a pioneer inscription.

On your return, be careful not to overshoot the route to the parking lot, recognizable by the jeep track that crosses the wash.

25. Devils Garden

Easy wandering, with variable mileage; allow 1 hour

Map: Trails Illustrated 710: Canyons of the Escalante

GETTING THERE: From the town of Escalante, drive east on UT 12 for 5 miles. Turn right onto Hole in the Rock Road and continue for 12.5 miles. Take a signed spur road on the right for 0.25 mile to the parking and picnic area.

ON THE TRAIL: Kids of all ages delight in the strange goblins, arches, and erosional forms found in this day-use site. Although there are no official trails, you can wander at will through the hallucinatory landscape. **Mano and Metate Arches**, named for stone implements used by aboriginal peoples to pulverize grain, are a few hundred yards to the south of the picnic ground, and a shallow, sheer-walled red canyon starts less than 0.5 mile down the wash.

26. Golden Cathedral

Difficult 10-mile out-and-back, with routefinding; allow 6–7 hours

High-clearance or four-wheel-drive vehicle required; long pants, trekking poles, water filter, and river shoes recommended

Map: Trails Illustrated 710: Canyons of the Escalante

GETTING THERE: From the town of Escalante, drive east on UT 12 for 5 miles. Bear right onto Hole in the Rock Road. Proceed 16.25 miles to a spur on the left for Egypt Bench. Reset your trip odometer here. Follow the spur to Egypt Rd., a fork at mile 9 and turn right. Park at the mile 10 trailhead.

ON THE TRAIL: Avoid this area during bug season, when you may encounter gnats at the overlook, deerflies along the river, and mosquitoes in Neon Canyon.

Begin by negotiating a 450-foot descent, mainly on steep slickrock, to the rim of the South Fork of **Fence Canyon** at mile 1.5, aided by bootprints and unofficial cairns. Looking to the right, you will spot a trail on the canyon floor, and you may be tempted to follow false cairns leading down to it. Resist that temptation, which only invites trouble. Instead, continue along the rim, losing elevation slowly, until you reach a point directly above the confluence of two forks of Fence at mile 2, recognized by a jug-handle arch and a trio of caves. Here the cairned route takes a stab at a switchback on the right to deposit you at the bottom at mile 2.5, where you join the creekside trail mentioned above.

Upon reaching the Escalante River at mile 3, about 1000 feet vertical below the trailhead, prepare for your first ford. Enter the river and skirt a headland on your right, being sure to stay on the same side of the river. Here pick up a clear trail that escorts you through what otherwise would be an impenetrable thicket. Arriving at a second ford, cross the river, surmounting steep banks. You will remain on the left bank for the remainder of the inbound trip. At about mile 3.75, check out a petroglyph panel beneath an alcove on the left, comprising both older and newer contributions. Just before entering **Neon Canyon**, the first side-canyon on your left at mile 4, wade around another headland, again remaining on the left bank.

Soon you come upon a campsite amid cottonwoods at Neon's mouth. Drop down and follow the canyon upstream, ascending about 250 feet over the next mile. You are

Seep springs feed a refreshing pool below the Golden Cathedral.

likely to encounter stagnant pools and luxuriant stands of poison ivy, hence the recommendation to cover your limbs. Just before the canyon boxes up you will encounter two boulder jams in rapid succession; skirt the second on the left. Into the mystic! You have arrived at superlative **Golden Cathedral** grotto, with its triple opening, hanging gardens, and reflective pool. Although adrenaline junkies sometimes rappel through this Wingate Sandstone formation, for mere hikers this is the end of the line. Bask in the afterglow on your return.

27. Dry Fork of Coyote Gulch

Moderate 4.25-mile out-and-back; allow 3 hours
Map: Trails Illustrated 710: Canyons of the Escalante

GETTING THERE: From the town of Escalante, drive east on UT 12 for 5 miles to Hole in the Rock Road. Turn right here and continue south for 26.5 miles. Go left at the sign for Dry Fork. Proceed, bearing left at the Y, to the parking lot at road's end on the canyon rim.

ON THE TRAIL: This exciting hike visits three slot canyons, one of which contains highly unusual erosional patterns. From the parking area, a cairned route leads down into a side-canyon of Dry Fork. Upon reaching the wash bottom, detour left to visit a short, picturesque narrows section. Then turn around and walk downstream.

The first slot on the left past this intersection is **Peek-a-Boo Gulch**. Since it is a hanging canyon, you will need to scramble up a 15-foot dry-fall, aided by foot- and handholds chipped into the rock. Once inside this natural fun house, a double bridge, Swiss cheese holes, and spiral-staircase turns greet you. Ascending slightly, you top out after 0.25 mile and must retrace your steps.

To visit **Spooky Gulch**, continue downstream in Dry Fork for about 0.5 mile to the next side-canyon on the left. Walk up the wash to the slot. Spooky Gulch is tight in the extreme, so remove your pack and ease yourself through sideways. After about 0.25 mile, you arrive at a 6-foot pour-off, which requires free-climbing skills to ascend. Return the way you came.

If you like, you can stroll farther down Dry Fork, though tumbleweeds and chockstones may impede forward progress.

28. Coyote Gulch Backpack

Moderate 26-mile out-and-back; allow 3–4 days
Permit required; water filter and river shoes recommended
Map: Trails Illustrated 710: Canyons of the Escalante

GETTING THERE: From the town of Escalante, go east on UT 12 for 5 miles. Turn right onto Hole in the Rock Road. Drive 34 miles south down to the Hurricane Wash Trailhead. Park on the right, just past the cattle guard.

ON THE TRAIL: This hike takes you near the Escalante River's mouth at Lake Powell. In Coyote Gulch, you'll be walking through shallow water most of the time.

From the parking lot, follow an old four-wheel-drive road down **Hurricane Wash**, picking up a trail at mile 1.75. After a level, sandy stretch the Navajo Sandstone cliffs gradually rise and cottonwoods begin to appear. The wash empties into Coyote Gulch at mile 5.5. Turn right to walk downstream.

At mile 7, **Jacob Hamblin Arch** looms above the canyon. Seep springs line the canyon's left side, and nearby campsites deserve their popularity.

At mile 8.5 you arrive at a rincon. Either shortcut across the bench or simply continue to follow the streambed. Just 0.5 mile farther, pass under **Coyote Natural Bridge**, with its 100-foot span. Beyond this point, you encounter several obstacles. At mile 10.75, skirt a boulder jam and waterfall on the left. Soon, **Cliff Arch** comes into view. Twin 15-foot waterfalls appear at mile 11.25. Bypass the first of these by means of a trail on the right. To get around the second, hike along a ledge on the right side of the canyon for about 100 feet before carefully lowering yourself down. Circumvent a final, smaller waterfall easily on the right. Several perennial springs occur between this point and the Escalante confluence.

The canyon continues to deepen and narrow as you leave the Kayenta Formation and enter the Wingate Sandstone layer. Less than 0.5 mile short of the river, progress is blocked by a boulder jam. Bypass it on a path to the right, staying as low as possible. This route leads across a sandbank to a steep slickrock slope. Eventually you arrive at a ledge several feet above the canyon floor. Makeshift log ladders assist your descent.

Approaching the river at mile 13, spot **Stevens Arch** upstream, on the east bank of the Escalante. Unless the level of Lake Powell is uncharacteristically high, you should be able to splash upstream with no problem. About 0.5 mile north of the confluence is a sandy bank, where you can make a camp. **Stevens Canyon**, 0.5 mile farther upstream, contains a beautiful grotto about 1 mile from the river, though pools may hinder your passage. Double back to your car.

29. Coyote Gulch Overlook

Moderate 5-mile out-and-back; allow 3 hours
Medium-duty vehicle required; trekking poles recommended
Map: Trails Illustrated 710: Canyons of the Escalante

GETTING THERE: From the town of Escalante, drive east on UT 12 for 5 miles and turn right onto Hole in the Rock Road. Proceed 35.7 miles to Fortymile Ridge Road. Turn left here and continue about 4.75 miles to Water Tank/Jacob Hamblin Trailhead on the left, up a steep, rocky spur.

ON THE TRAIL: Begin by mushing through soft, beach-quality sand toward a low red mesa. Following cairns, swing around the mesa to the left and hop a saddle. After crossing another sandy expanse, you come to a sea of slickrock. Descend about 600 feet, following cairns, to the rim of **Coyote Gulch**. Across the gulch are two deep amphitheaters separated by a rocky spine. Jacob Hamblin Arch, not visible from here, is on the left side of the horseshoe bend. From a rocky knob you can see the canyon floor 100 feet below. A safety rope may be affixed here to assist hikers wishing to drop

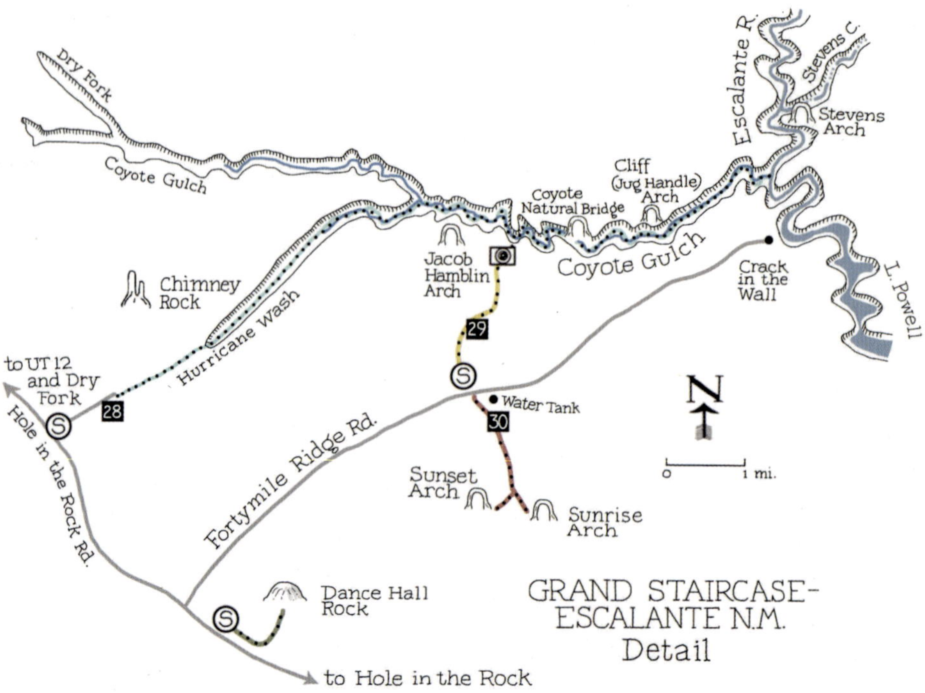

down the precipitous chute, though it is advisable to bring your own rope if you dare to attempt the descent. People without climbing skills and equipment should content themselves with savoring the view.

NEARBY: Beyond the Water Tank, Fortymile Ridge Road deteriorates sufficiently to warrant a four-wheel-drive vehicle. Stay left at a fork. At its end is the trailhead for another difficult shortcut into Coyote Gulch, **Crack in the Wall**. A cross-country route leads in a northeasterly direction toward the rim. The 2.5-mile route requires you to downclimb a vertical slit, as advertised, before surfing an enormous dune to the canyon floor, 700 feet below the rim. Since the sand hill would be exhausting to ascend, hikers who begin here typically exit at Jacob Hamblin Arch, aided by a safety rope.

30. Sunset Arch

Easy 2.5-mile out-and-back, with some routefinding; allow 1.5 hours
Medium-duty vehicle required
Map: Trails Illustrated 710: Canyons of the Escalante

GETTING THERE: From the town of Escalante, drive east on UT 12 for 5 miles to intersect Hole in the Rock Road. Go right here and proceed 35.7 miles south to Fortymile Ridge Road. Turn left and continue about 4.75 miles to Water Tank/Jacob Hamblin Trailhead on the left, up a short, rutted spur. Park here. The trail to Sunset Arch is to the right, on the south side of the road.

Cross-bedded brainrocks lead the way to Sunrise Arch.

ON THE TRAIL: From the Water Tank parking lot, descend the rutted spur back to Fortymile Ridge Road and turn left. In about 25 yards you arrive at a water trough on the right, where cattle typically congregate. From the trough, head cross-country toward a mesa with prominent red cliffs to your southeast. Meet an arroyo and follow along its rim on the left, walking in the direction of **Sooner Rocks**, a collection of large white domes to the south near Hole in the Rock Road. Notice a butte straight ahead that may call to mind a teakettle or a snapping turtle. **Sunset Arch**, which frames Navajo Mountain, is in this formation. Clamber up a low ridge to access it. Visible from Sunset Arch, and easily reachable, is smaller **Sunrise Arch**, about 0.25 mile to the southeast.

NEARBY: Farther south on Hole in the Rock Road, about 1 mile past the turnoff to Fortymile Ridge Road, you can explore enchanting **Dance Hall Rock**, on the left. In 1880–81, Mormon pioneers used this slickrock massif for recreational purposes during the months they spent excavating the Hole in the Rock passage to the Colorado. Follow the marked trail and circle around Dance Hall to the left. Locate an obscure path on the right leading gently upward. Climb onto the dome and bear about 30 degrees to the southeast. In about 0.25 mile, notice what looks like a Dance Hall mini-me, sporting tafoni and a large alcove. Near its base are some "keeper" potholes, many of which have been colonized by deciduous trees.

31. Willow Gulch

Moderate 5-mile out-and-back; allow 3 hours
Medium-duty vehicle and river shoes recommended
Map: Trails Illustrated 710: Canyons of the Escalante

GETTING THERE: From the town of Escalante, travel east on UT 12 for 5 miles and turn right onto Hole in the Rock Road. Drive south for 43 miles to Road 276, branching off to the left. Take this rocky, marginal track 1.5 miles to its end.

ON THE TRAIL: One of the premier short hikes in the Escalante region, this trip features a narrow, watery canyon and an exquisite arch carved through a Navajo Sandstone fin. (See map, page 68.)

The descent begins near a register box. The path goes past **The Mortar Board**, a pedestal rock resembling a graduation cap, before heading down a sandy slope into a tributary of Willow Gulch. Follow the wash downstream after taking a few minutes to admire a beautiful set of narrows upstream. The canyon tightly slots up for a short distance. Bypass this obstacle by means of a path that ascends to the right. After yet another section of narrows, the wash joins **Willow Gulch** at mile 1, amid a cottonwood grove. Turn left, heading downstream.

From here on you encounter seep springs that ensure at least an intermittent water flow. Beavers have exploited these sources, and at times the combination of dams and willow thickets may slow you down. Trails on the banks allow you to avoid the worst of it, though frequent stream crossings may prove necessary.

At mile 2, after a big bend in the canyon, enormous **Broken Bow Arch**—named for an Indian bow once found beneath it—commands center stage. This spot has it all, offering shady pools and a dramatically undercut Kayenta Formation ledge complete with hanging gardens. You can scramble up to the arch with little difficulty and inspect it at close range.

Past the arch the canyon narrows, with every twist and turn bringing fresh delights. The level of "Glen Canyon Reservoir" (a.k.a. Lake Powell) will determine how far you can explore. But you should be able to continue at least to the confluence with **Fortymile Creek** at mile 2.5. Obstacles in Fortymile may preclude making this hike a loop for those without superior climbing skills.

GRAND STAIRCASE-ESCALANTE NATIONAL MONUMENT: EAST AND VICINITY

The hikes in this section branch off UT 12 east of Escalante, a drive of jaw-dropping beauty. It traverses an ocean of petrified dunes before ascending toward Boulder Mountain on a narrow neck separating Calf Creek on the left and Boulder Creek on the right. From vantage points along **Boulder Mountain** you can peer down upon the Circle Cliffs and Waterpocket Fold. Inquire at the Interagency Visitor Center in Escalante about permits and shuttles, if needed.

32. Lower Calf Creek

Easy 6-mile out-and-back; allow 2.5 hours
Binoculars recommended
Map: Trails Illustrated 710: Canyons of the Escalante

GETTING THERE: From the town of Escalante, drive east on UT 12 for 14.5 miles. Turn left into Calf Creek Recreation Area, parking at the picnic ground. The trailhead is a short distance up the road on the left.

ON THE TRAIL: This little Shangri-La features an incomparable 125-foot waterfall. Proximity to a streamside campground makes it an immensely popular family destination. Plan on an early start, and avoid weekends, when parking spaces may be scarce.

Walk to the rear of the campground to access the trail, on your left. Mostly over sand, it runs along the bank of perennial Calf Creek with its high Navajo Sandstone cliffs. Total elevation gain is about 250 feet. Look for a pictograph panel across the canyon at mile 1.5. The waterfall forms an idyllic perennial pool. Leafy trees provide shade, hanging gardens add allure, and cool mists refresh body and soul. Soak up negative ions before heading back.

33. Upper Calf Creek

Moderate 2-mile out-and-back; allow 1 hour
Map: Trails Illustrated 710: Canyons of the Escalante

GETTING THERE: From the town of Escalante, drive north on UT 12 for about 20 miles. Turn left onto a dirt road between mileposts 81 and 82. Follow this short, rough track for 100 yards to the parking area.

ON THE TRAIL: The trail descends a no-nonsense slope, following occasional cairns, to the inner rim of Calf Creek. The first half of the trail is over slickrock, while the

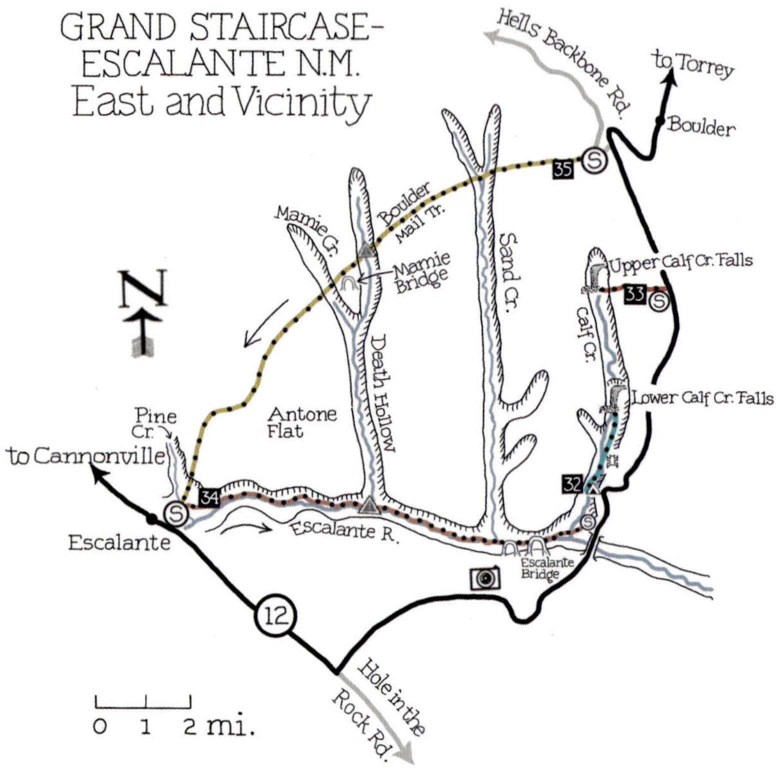

rest is mostly over sand, for a total elevation loss of over 600 feet. Near the creek, the trail divides. Cautiously follow the right fork to view the top of the falls and a series of upstream pools. Then return to the left fork, which plummets to the base of the waterfall. The pool formed by the waterfall is situated in a shady glade framed by wildflowers in season.

34. Upper Escalante Backpack

Moderate 15-mile point-to-point; allow 2 days
Avoid if flash floods threaten or water level exceeds knee-deep
Permit and vehicle shuttle or equivalent required; trekking poles, river shoes, and water filter recommended
Map: Trails Illustrated 710: Canyons of the Escalante

GETTING THERE: With two vehicles, drive east from the town of Escalante on UT 12 for 14 miles to the bridge near the mouth of Calf Creek. Leave one car here. Returning to the town of Escalante, locate the cemetery on the north side of the highway. Turn right onto a rough dirt road, which soon curves to the left and ends at a parking area. Stop short of the parking lot if need be. Register for camping at the trailhead.

ON THE TRAIL: From the trailhead, walk about 200 yards to a fence. Pass through a hiker maze to enter the Wilderness Study Area. The river portal lies just ahead, and **Pine Creek** enters at mile 0.75. The banks support stands of cottonwoods, willows, and Russian olives. Initial progress is rapid as you cut across looping meanders on well-worn paths. At about mile 2.5 you reach the **Great Alcove**, an undercut on the left. Past this point, the Navajo Sandstone cliffs rise, with the river's course becoming more sinuous and the vegetation more luxuriant. **Death Hollow**, a major tributary, joins from the north at mile 6.75. The confluence makes a good place to camp. Draw water to purify from this and other side streams in preference to the river, which carries a heavy load of sediment.

Beyond Death Hollow, it becomes impossible to stay dry by rock-hopping; you have no recourse but to wade. Where social trails lead up onto the benches, exits and entries from the river tend to be steep and muddy. The best alternatives take you well back from the river's brushy tangles, affording excellent views of the sheer cliffs, now approaching 1000 feet high. Look for a small freestanding arch along the rim at about mile 7.25.

Gradually, the canyon widens a bit. You pass the mouth of **Sand Canyon**, another major tributary, at mile 11.5. Not as inviting as Death Hollow, it can be buggy and marshy. Past here, abundant water and large cottonwoods create a verdant environment. At about mile 12, look for a sizable unnamed arch on the right; an additional 0.5 mile of walking puts you in sight of 100-foot-long **Escalante Natural Bridge**, which spans a drainage on the right side of the canyon. The bridge is easily approached from a spur.

Beyond this point, the main canyon continues to open up. The last 2 miles are quick and easy, with excellent social trails speeding you across wide benches. Ford the river one last time to reach the parking lot.

35. Boulder Mail Trail Backpack

Difficult 15-mile point-to-point; allow 2 days
Permit and vehicle shuttle or equivalent required; trekking poles, water filter, and long pants recommended
Map: Trails Illustrated 710: Canyons of the Escalante

GETTING THERE: With two vehicles, drive east from the town of Escalante on UT 12. Just past the high school, turn left onto the cemetery road, then go right on a dirt track running parallel to the highway. This track curves left and deteriorates as it descends toward a parking circle. Leave one vehicle here.

Continue in the second vehicle east on UT 12 for about 22 miles until you come to Hells Backbone Road, 3 miles south of Boulder between mileposts 83 and 84. Go left here, and take an immediate left onto McGath Bench Road, a dirt track. Within 0.5 mile you arrive at the parking area, just beyond a landing strip.

ON THE TRAIL: In the early 20th century, postmen delivered mail between the towns of Escalante and Boulder by mule train. The trip described here, which reprises that historic route, is memorable for dazzling expanses of Navajo Sandstone.

On foot, follow the road 1 mile to a BLM signboard. The cairned trail begins here, on the right. It soon drops down to cross the **Sand Creek** drainage at mile 2.75. Hug the right side of the canyon for about 0.25 mile. A cairn indicates where you exit up a draw, toward a slickrock dome sporting udder-like hoodoos. In this vicinity, follow

Overlooks reveal a Navajo Sandstone vastness along the Boulder Mail Trail.

an old telegraph line, which will accompany you for most of the hike. The trail attains Slickrock Saddle Bench at mile 5, where you enjoy mouthwatering views of **Death Hollow**, far below. Death Hollow takes its name from a hapless mule that fell into it. Cross-bedded alabaster rock as far as the eye can see supplies plenty of magic.

Soon when the trail forks, go right, descending steeply to reach the canyon floor at mile 5.75. Reliable water and well-groomed, shady campsites abound at the junction, but so does poison ivy, why it is wise to wear long pants. Although you can explore Death Hollow upstream as far as you wish, be prepared to wade. A swimming hole at mile 1.5 is a popular destination.

It is possible to hike downstream from this point for 7.75 miles to the junction of Death Hollow and the Escalante River, but that is a challenging route, especially in high-water years, and therefore is not described here. Instead, from the camping area, continue downstream for 0.5 mile. A large cairn marks the point where you scramble out of Death Hollow, on your right. Cross a saddle and descend to **Mamie Creek**, a Death Hollow tributary, at mile 8. Typically, seasonal pools are present. The trail follows the creek downstream for about 100 yards before climbing up and out. If you wish, you can drop your pack and walk about 0.75 mile farther downstream (left) to visit unusual **Mamie Natural Bridge**.

Back on the main route, cross an unnamed side-canyon and proceed to **Antone Flat**, a plateau dotted with pinyons and junipers, at about mile 10. Ascend on slickrock to an overlook of the peaceful river valley at about mile 11.75. From here, switchback down a slickrock slope about 1000 vertical feet to **Pine Creek** at mile 13.25. The trail becomes indistinct and easy to lose. Follow the creek downstream (left) to the Escalante River at mile 14. Turn right, following the river upstream for a short distance and passing through a cattle guard. A trail on the left returns you to your vehicle.

NEARBY: Just north of the charming hamlet of Boulder on UT 12, **Anasazi State Park Museum** allows you to tour reconstructed remnants of Neolithic dwellings.

36. Wolverine Canyon

Easy 9-mile out-and-back; allow 4 hours
High-clearance vehicle recommended
Map: Trails Illustrated 710: Canyons of the Escalante

GETTING THERE: Drive east from the town of Escalante on UT 12 to the town of Boulder. There, turn right at a sign marking the start of the so-called Burr Trail. Drive east on this road for 19 miles. Turn right onto the Wolverine Loop Road, resetting your

A hiker splashes through the Wingate Sandstone narrows of Wolverine Canyon.

trip odometer. Where the road forks at about mile 5, go left. Reach the parking area on the right at mile 10.

ON THE TRAIL: Follow a good trail that continues for 2 miles to where the canyon forks. Continue straight ahead, dodging cow chips as you amble down the wash. Maroon-colored Wingate Sandstone walls soon rise and pinch in. (See map on page 68.) At mile 2.5, come to a major alcove on the right, and its little brother around the next bend. The canyon narrows significantly at mile 3, with slickrock benches lining the base of the 400-foot cliffs. At mile 3.75, notice a "no vehicles" sign on the left. You can continue for another 0.75 mile to the junction with (lackluster) **Horse Canyon** or turn around here to abbreviate the trip.

NEARBY: **Little Death Hollow Canyon**, accessed at mile 7 off the Wolverine Loop Road, at times can be highly challenging, filled with deep pools and numerous obstacles. Adventurous souls sometimes combine it with Wolverine Canyon to make a loop.

37. Silver Falls Creek Backpack

Moderate 16-mile out-and-back; allow 2 days
High-clearance or four-wheel-drive vehicle required
Map: Trails Illustrated 710: Canyons of the Escalante

GETTING THERE: Drive east from Escalante on UT 12 to the town of Boulder. Take a right onto the historic road known as the Burr Trail and drive east 19 miles. Turn right onto the Wolverine Loop Road. Zero out your trip odometer and drive 8 miles to reach the track signed for Silver Falls/Moody Creek. Drive 2.25 miles down this track, turning right at the fork near its end, and park by a corral.

ON THE TRAIL: Contrary to what its name suggests, **Silver Falls Creek** has no cascades, only canyon walls shiny with moisture. Its shadeless upper reaches can be hot in summer. (See map on page 68.)

From the corral, follow a jeep track past hat rocks and colorful Chinle badlands for 1.75 miles to the boundary of **Glen Canyon National Recreation Area**. At mile 3, arrive at the confluence with the creek's north fork. A towering Wingate Sandstone monolith at mile 5 marks the location of seasonal Emigrant Spring. Within the next 0.5 mile, a rockfall creates a boulder garden, and intermittent flowing water begins. At mile 6, scan the right wall for a historical attraction, the **G. B. Hobbs Inscription**, dating from 1883. Enter the Kayenta Formation at mile 7, marked by a small arch. Another mile brings you to the **Escalante River**, your turnaround point.

NEARBY: **Harris Wash** (see Hike 24) lies almost directly across the river from the mouth of Silver Falls Creek. Intrepid backpackers sometimes combine these two hikes for a long, multiday trip. Be advised that such an excursion necessitates a lengthy car shuttle.

CHAPTER 2
DESERT REEFS

This chapter highlights two monoclines in south-central Utah—the San Rafael Reef and Waterpocket Fold—and the seductive canyons that slice through those uplifts. From hubs in Green River and Torrey, hikers can visit two national parks (Canyonlands and Capitol Reef), two state parks (Goblin Valley and Fremont Culture), and vast areas of national park quality that merit legal protection. Scenic drives presenting opportunities for short walks round out the chapter.

Hubs: Green River and Torrey, Utah

Green River (population 1000) was once a uranium mining center. Today, rafting enthusiasts flock here to battle the fierce rapids of Desolation and Gray Canyons farther upstream on the Green and to drift downstream through the placid canyons of Labyrinth and Stillwater. Hikers delight in the town's proximity to the San Rafael Reef and Swell. Take time to visit its excellent **River History Museum**.

Tiny **Torrey** (population 250), near the junction of UT 24 and UT 12, offers restaurants and lodgings disproportionate to its size, owing to its proximity to Capitol Reef. Settled by Mormon ranchers and farmers, the hamlet has an attractive downtown that is replete with historic buildings and shady deciduous trees. Bear in mind that grocery selections here are quite limited.

SAN RAFAEL SWELL

Westbound from Green River, Interstate 70 makes a beeline for the dramatically tilted **San Rafael Reef**. Resembling the backbone of a stegosaurus, the Reef is the business end of the San Rafael Swell, a massive kidney-shaped bulge created when subterranean forces deformed overlying strata. The highway cuts through the Reef, snaking up **Spotted Wolf Canyon**. The Swell is drained by the San Rafael River in the north and Muddy Creek in the south, each of which has created an impressive gorge.

1. Black Dragon Canyon

Very easy 0.5-mile out-and-back; allow 30 minutes
Map: Trails Illustrated 712: San Rafael Swell

GETTING THERE: From Green River, drive west on I-70. At milepost 147, turn right onto a good unpaved road. Pass through a livestock gate and continue for approximately a mile until you arrive at a wash, signed for Black Dragon Canyon. Park here.
ON THE TRAIL: This lovely drainage slices through the Reef before emptying into the San Rafael River. About 0.25 mile up the canyon, behind a fence, a pictograph panel decorates the right wall. The most unusual figure does resemble a dragon, although

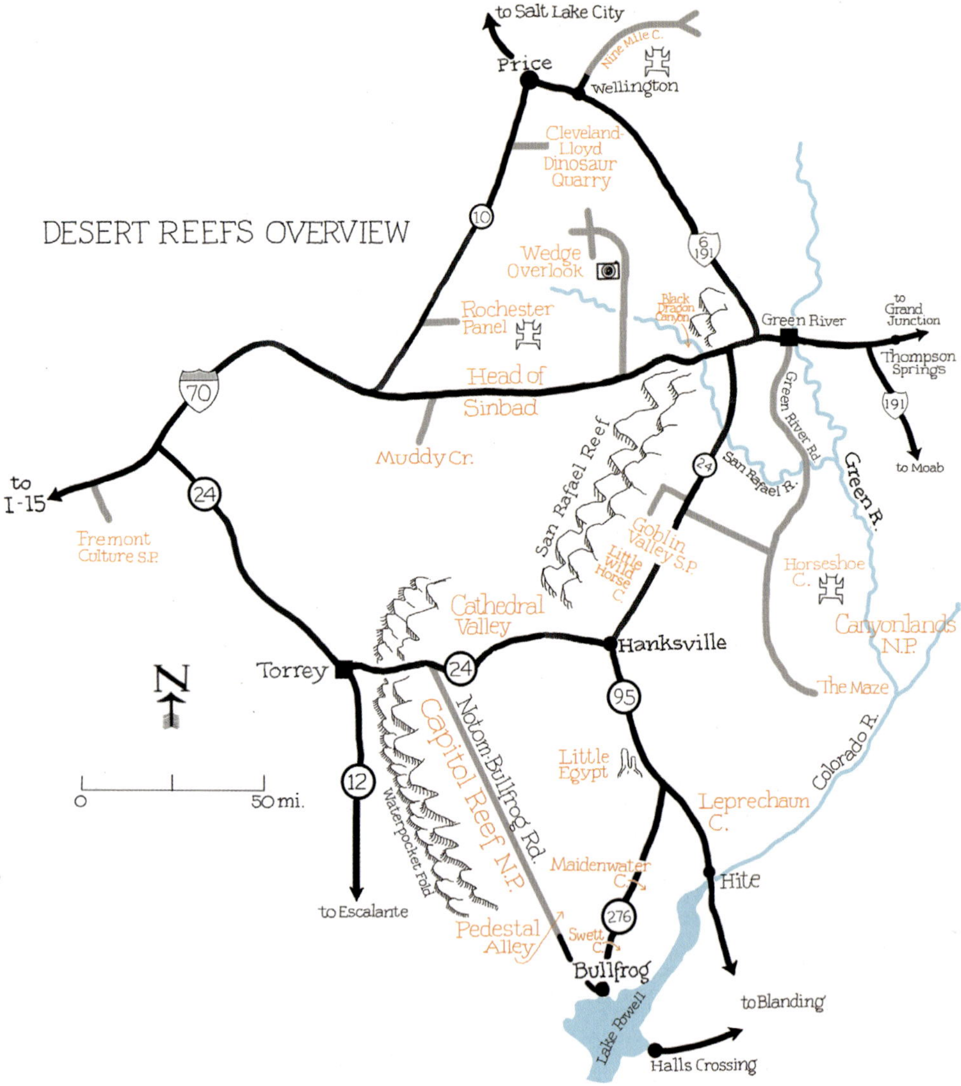

it is red rather than black. Another may remind you of Tolkien's Gollum. A quartet of vase-shaped shamans rounds out the grouping. Beyond the pictographs, the canyon widens. It can be hiked for several miles on a jeep road. (See map on page 85.)

NEARBY: To see more indigenous rock art, head east of Green River on I-70 near the whistle-stop of Thompson Springs. Exit here, turning north onto CR 159. Proceed about 4 miles to the junction of **Sego and Thompson Canyons**. The three major **panels (Ute, Fremont, and Desert Archaic)** are found to the left of the road, with two more about 100 yards upcanyon on the right.

A spectral human figure alongside an enigmatic animal in Black Dragon Canyon

2. Little Grand Canyon

Easy 7-mile out-and-back; allow 3 hours
Map: Trails Illustrated 712: San Rafael Swell

GETTING THERE: From Green River, drive west on I-70 for 30 miles to exit 131, marked for Temple Mountain. Turn right (north) onto a gravel road, which eventually enters the drainage of Buckhorn Wash amid starkly beautiful castles and monoliths. Continue north until you near the bridge over the San Rafael River, 19 miles from I-70. About 100 yards shy of the bridge, locate a short dirt road on your left, which ends at a parking lot.

ON THE TRAIL: The hike offers a taste of the Little Grand Canyon. During the spring runoff, small craft can run the stretch from the Fuller Bottom put-in to the take-out at the bridge in under a day, stopping en route to appreciate Virgin Springs Canyon and enchanting sidelights. With a car shuttle, the gorge can be backpacked point-to-point, though complicated logistics recommend this shorter alternative.

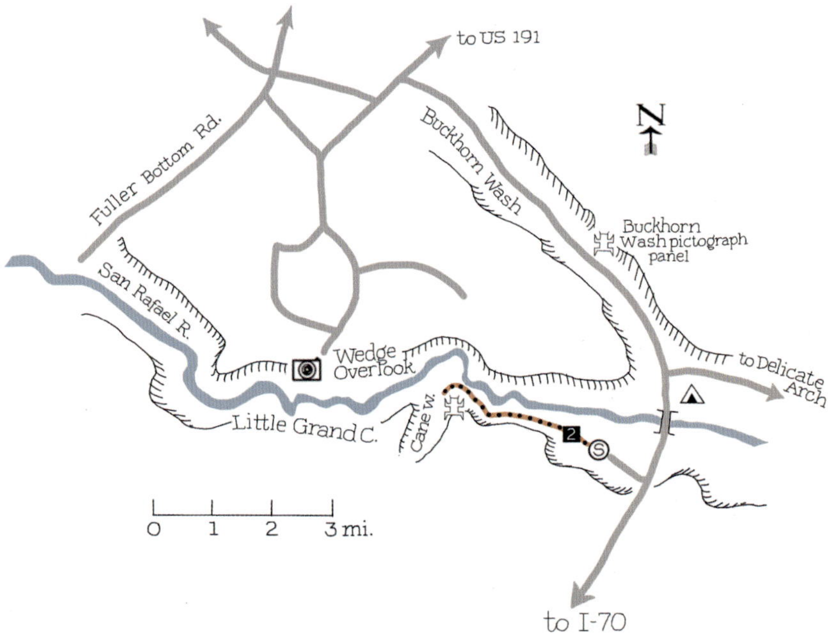

From the parking lot, follow an old mining track that leads to the riverbank. At mile 0.75, enter **Sids Mountain Wilderness Study Area**. The path follows the left bank to your destination, Cane Wash, which is almost directly beneath the Wedge Overlook (see the Nearby entry, below).

A small pictograph hides under an overhang at the mouth of **Cane Canyon**. This is the turnaround point. Although it is possible to go farther, the route deteriorates markedly and may require stream crossings. Look for petrified wood adjacent to the trail on your return, as well as a small arch on the right.

NEARBY: Check out the extensive **Buckhorn Wash pictograph panel**. From the bridge over the San Rafael River where you parked, drive north 4 miles. The panel is on the right. Once badly vandalized, the life-sized Barrier Canyon–style figures have been restored to their original glory.

The other must-see venue in this neighborhood is **Wedge Overlook**. About 5.5 miles north of the Buckhorn Wash pictograph panel, go left at a T junction and drive 2 miles to a dirt track, also on the left. In 6 miles, the track ends at the overlook. The last mile can be rough for passenger cars, so you may want to walk that stretch. However you get there, the view into the 1000-foot-deep gorge is sure to amaze.

3. Delicate Arch

Moderate 10-mile out-and-back; allow 5 hours
High-clearance or four-wheel-drive vehicle required
Map: Trails Illustrated 712: San Rafael Swell

GETTING THERE: From Green River, head west on I-70 for 30 miles to exit 131, signed for Temple Mountain. Turn right (north) onto a gravel road and drive 19 miles (see map for Hike 2), reaching a bridge over the San Rafael River. Cross the bridge and continue a short distance to the campground. Turn right here, as though accessing the campground, but then take an immediate left onto Mexican Mountain Road, which parallels the river. Window Blind Peak soon dominates the scene to the right.

Beyond the gate at mile 7.25, cross a hoodoo-lined wash and enter colorful badlands. A kiosk at mile 9.5 marks the trailhead for the watery **Upper Black Box**, a sunless slot in which unlucky and/or ill-prepared hikers have lost their lives. The road deteriorates as you bounce along past spectacular temples. Go through a second gate at mile 12. Just before the road's end at mile 14.25, park in a clearing on the right. From the San Rafael bridge, allow an hour for the drive.

ON THE TRAIL: Of approximately fifty spans found in the Swell, **Delicate Arch** may be the most visually arresting. Wow factor aside, it has little in common with its famous namesake in Arches National Park (see Chapter 3, Hike 31), being composed of Wingate rather than Entrada Sandstone, sporting a jug handle rather than a parabolic shape, and promising solitude rather than throngs of pilgrims. Indeed, you are far more likely to encounter cows here than people.

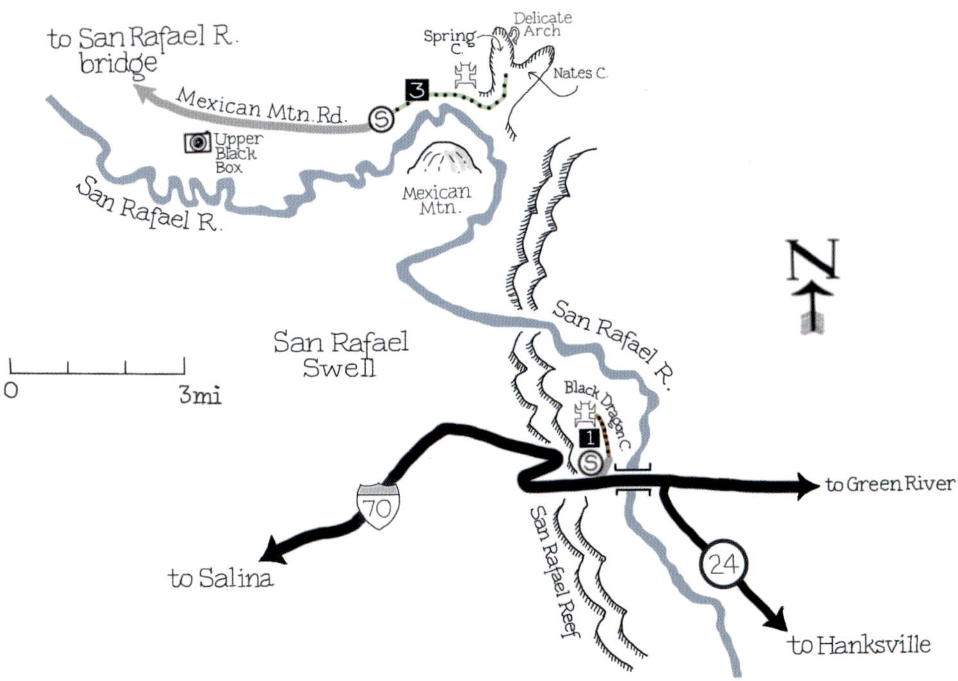

Gossamer Delicate Arch may not be long for this world.

On foot, descend the badly eroded roadbed to the river. At mile 2, where the river bends sharply to the right, the road seems to disappear. Turn left here into a side-canyon and proceed about 100 yards. A large cairn on the right marks a short, steep path that reconnects with the road. The road climbs to a saddle before descending to an airstrip directly under **Mexican Mountain**, which looms over the confluence of the San Rafael River and Spring Creek.

Follow the airstrip to a wind sock at mile 3. An unofficial trail cuts a hypotenuse into **Spring Canyon**, circling below a field of whimsically eroded boulders. Two boulders contain petroglyphs that are easier to spot on the return trip.

Immediately before dropping into Spring Canyon, pause to inspect a commemorative plaque. As you proceed, expect to encounter pools and occasional stretches of running water; in one short section, bushwhacking may be necessary. Hiker-made paths enable you to crosscut meanders. The inaccessible, wafer-thin arch is high on the cliffs of Spring Canyon, at the junction with its tributary, Nates Canyon. Its north side offers the best vantage point.

4. Head of Sinbad

Easy; distance negligible; allow 1 hour
Map: Trails Illustrated 712: San Rafael Swell

GETTING THERE: From Green River, drive 30 miles west on I-70 to exit 131. Go south through an underpass and onto the graded dirt road signed for Temple Mountain.

Reset your trip odometer. In 4 miles, turn right at a fork and proceed to a T intersection at mile 5. Bear right here and also at mile 6.75. At mile 9, you reach a second I-70 underpass. Just north of here, the road forks. Each fork offers special attractions.

ON THE TRAIL: The Head of Sinbad, an extensive limestone outcrop that has eroded into gold-and-white buttes, represents the scenic climax of the central San Rafael Swell. Among its attractions are a major arch and a memorable pictograph attributed to the Desert Archaic culture.

For **Dutchman Arch**, turn left at the fork referenced above. In 0.25 mile, go left again. The arch is clearly visible 0.5 mile down this track. Climb in, on, around, and through this impressive span.

To access the rock art, take the right fork near the second underpass, turning right again at mile 1.5. About 0.25 mile farther, find the **Head of Sinbad panel**, tucked under Locomotive Point Butte behind a split rail fence. The well-preserved pictograph features snake-handling shamans.

5. Eagle Canyon

Moderate 3.5-mile out-and-back; allow 2 hours

Map: Trails Illustrated 712: San Rafael Swell

GETTING THERE: From Green River, drive 30 miles west on I-70 to exit 131. Go under the highway through a viaduct and head south on a good dirt road in the direction of Temple Mountain. When you reach the first fork, turn right, driving past a stock pond.

At mile 9.75, after crossing a cattle guard, take a short detour on the right to inspect the reddish **Lone Warrior** pictograph. To do so, drive about 0.5 mile down a dirt road, bearing left at each intersection. Two areas are protectively fenced off; both enclosures contain pictographs, with the warrior figure occupying the second.

Returning to the Temple Mountain Road, follow signs to **Swaseys Cabin**. Park here.

ON THE TRAIL: Before starting the hike, examine the small, windowless cabin tucked under Broken Cross Butte. Brothers who ran cows in the Swell built and occupied this structure a century ago. From the cabin, follow a trail for a few hundred yards to Refrigerator Cave, where the Swaseys stored their food. Then drop back down to the road.

The track descends gently but steadily into a side-canyon of Eagle Creek. Since it is suitable for ORVs (off-road vehicles) and dirt bikes, don't be surprised if you have company, especially on weekends during the high season.

Reaching Eagle Creek takes only 45 minutes. Turn right and walk downstream for about 0.5 mile to 100-foot-high **Eagle Canyon Arch** with its jug-handle opening.

6. The Chute of Muddy Creek

Moderate 15-mile point-to-point; allow 1–2 days

Vehicle shuttle or equivalent required; trekking poles and river shoes recommended; carry water because Muddy Creek is highly alkaline

Map: Trails Illustrated 712: San Rafael Swell

GETTING THERE: Far off the beaten track, this trip requires a car shuttle. Driving two vehicles west from Green River, leave I-70 at exit 131. Zero out your trip odometer and head southwest on the good dirt road, Temple Mountain Road, following the signs toward Swaseys Cabin. At about mile 4, go left at a T intersection and a mile farther, go left again. Continue for 5 miles to a marked junction, where you turn right.

Intersect the Reds Canyon Loop Road at mile 13.5. Go left on the loop and proceed southwest about 9 miles to Hidden Splendor Road. Follow this road to its end near an airstrip for **Hidden Splendor mine**, once a productive source of uranium. Leave one vehicle here.

In the second vehicle, backtrack to rejoin the Reds Canyon Loop Road. Turn left, following the loop for 6.5 miles to **Tomsich Butte** and **Hondoo Arch**, in the towering Wingate cliffs. Park alongside the canyon. Since Muddy Creek is highly alkaline, carry ample drinking water.

ON THE TRAIL: The Chute is carved out of the Moenkopi Formation and Cedar Mesa Sandstone by Muddy Creek, which joins the Fremont River at Hanksville. Throughout its length, walking is straightforward and unobstructed. During the spring runoff, people sometimes float the creek on a day trip, but it affords wonderful hiking at other times of year.

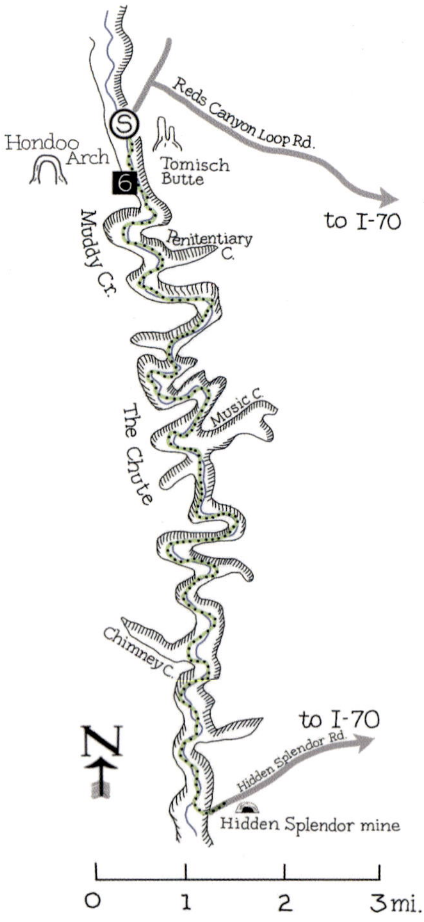

For about the first mile, follow an old prospecting road on the right bank. Thereafter, splash through the stream for the better part of the journey. The water never is likely to be above your knees, though the canyon can harbor deep holes and quicksand, especially around bends.

Around mile 2, **Penitentiary Canyon** enters from the left, and Muddy Creek starts pinching in. Near **Music Canyon** at mile 7.25, you reach the incomparable **Chute.** It consists of two sets of narrows, the second even deeper and more impressive than the first. Because of flash flood danger, there are no safe campsites in the vicinity. After about an hour of hiking, before the second slot ends, a photogenic logjam about 25 feet overhead provides eloquent testament to their fury.

Exiting the narrows, continue to **Chimney Canyon** on the right at mile 12.5, which can be explored fully only by hikers with technical equipment and skill. Leave the canyon at mile 15, where a dirt track leads to the Hidden Splendor parking lot and your first vehicle.

7. Rochester Panel

Easy 0.75-mile out-and-back; allow 1 hour
Map: Trails Illustrated 712: San Rafael Swell

GETTING THERE: From Green River on I-70 west, exit at milepost 91. Drive northeast on UT 10, through the town of Emery. Turn right at about mile 16 onto an unpaved road, then turn right in under a mile, heading south. About 3 miles farther, take another right at a four-way intersection, following signs for about 0.75 mile to Rochester Panel Rock Art Site. The trailhead is near the point where Muddy Creek enters the Swell.

ON THE TRAIL: The route contours below a cliff face and onto a peninsula. Although many rock faces are decorated, the most unusual panel features a rainbow accompanied by lightning and precipitation. Where the path forks, go right, staying high, to view more antiquities.

NEARBY: In the vicinity is **Cleveland-Lloyd Dinosaur Quarry**. From the Rochester Panel, go back to UT 10 and turn right (north), driving about 30 miles to the small town of Huntington. Just a mile or so past Huntington, turn right, following signs on unpaved roads for 13 miles to the pit-type quarry.

Although less interesting than its counterpart in Dinosaur National Monument on the Utah-Colorado border (described in Chapter 3), Cleveland-Lloyd has the advantage of receiving fewer visitors, so you are likely to enjoy a private orientation at the visitor center. The quarry boasts the world's largest concentration of dinosaur bones, particularly from carnivorous species such as the allosaurus. As elsewhere, the fossil remains are embedded in the Late Jurassic era's Morrison Formation, which often contains uranium deposits as well.

A short walk from the quarry visitor center takes you to two structures housing pit-type graveyards. If no one is at work excavating the site, the interiors of the buildings may be quite dark. The quarry is open daily from Memorial Day to Labor Day and Friday through Sunday in the spring and fall.

8. Fremont Culture State Park

Moderate 1.5-mile lollipop loop; allow 1 hour
Map: USGS: Marysvale Canyon

GETTING THERE: Take I-70 west from Green River to exit 17, following signs for the state park. Locate the **Alma Christensen Trail** 0.25 mile west of the visitor center.

ON THE TRAIL: Kid-friendly Fremont Culture State Park was established to protect ancient Fremont pit houses, petroglyphs, and other pre-Columbian artifacts that were unearthed when the highway was routed near Clear Creek Canyon. Its attractive streamside campground has conglomerate bluffs that merit closer inspection.

The interpretive trail, named after one of the area's early pioneers, ascends steeply 200 feet to a canyon viewpoint. On top, the trail becomes a loop, which you follow counterclockwise. Stop to visit a reconstructed wickiup, a form of brush shelter. The loop winds through pinyon and juniper forest along the rim.

NEARBY: An easy, 1.5-mile nature loop begins at the visitor center. The **Rim Rock Trail**, from which more rock art can be enjoyed, requires a guided tour.

SCENIC DRIVE: NINE MILE CANYON

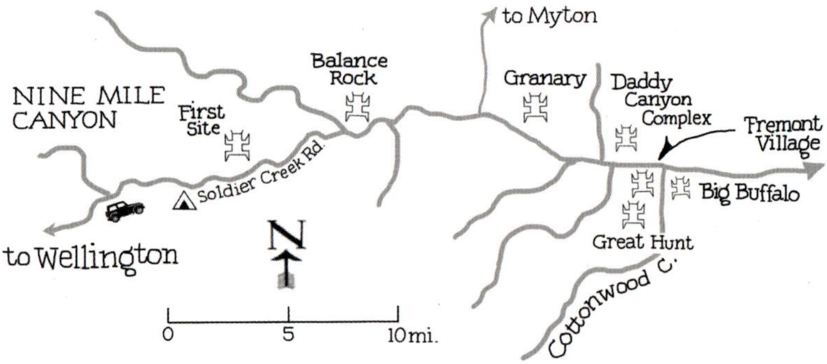

A tributary of the Green River, **Nine Mile Canyon** cuts through the **Book Cliffs**, the world's longest escarpment. The 100-mile round-trip drive on secondary roads offers many opportunities to stretch your legs while appreciating an abundance of rock art.

To get there, first find the junction of Interstate 70 about 4 miles west of Green River with northbound US Route 6/191, which parallels the San Rafael Reef. At the south end of Wellington, between mileposts 249 and 250, turn right onto the seasonally maintained Soldier Creek Road. Paved for the first 12.25 miles, this byway turns to gravel and climbs to a pass in the aspen belt before dropping down into the canyon. A signboard at mile 21 marks the official entry point.

The Fremont hunters and gatherers who roamed the Book Cliffs in pre-Columbian times left an ample record of their presence. The masterpiece panels cluster near the road's end. En route, visit the less impressive First Site (mile 26.25) and Balance Rock (mile 32). When you reach an intersection at mile 39, go straight to view the **Daddy Canyon Complex** on the left (mile 43.75), and the splendid **Big Buffalo** and **Great Hunt** panels on the right (at miles 45.75 and 46, respectively).

Range Creek is another Book Cliffs canyon studded with archeological treasures. Unknown to the public until quite recently, its existence was divulged by a rancher who had kept it a secret for years before deeding land to the state of Utah. Although seeing the canyon to best advantage requires a private tour, you can explore downstream on your own as far as you wish.

Reaching the Range Creek trailhead requires a four-wheel-drive vehicle. From Nine Mile Canyon, return to Wellington and turn southeast on US 6. Drive 8.5 miles to a junction with UT 124. Turn left (south) here and continue 7.75 miles. Soon the road turns to gravel. At mile 8.75, bear left at a fork. Follow signs 9 miles farther to the parking lot. Pass through a gate to begin hiking.

SAN RAFAEL REEF

From Green River, go west on Interstate 70 for 9 miles to exit 149 and turn south onto lonely UT 24, which parallels the San Rafael Reef all the way to Hanksville. To the west, a series of short, narrow slots have penetrated the Reef's dominant rock layer, Navajo Sandstone. To the east, the arid and featureless San Rafael Desert gives little hint of the tranquil canyons of the Green River that beckon just beyond. Numerous hiking opportunities await on either side of the highway.

9. Eardley Pool

Moderate 5-mile out-and-back; allow 3.5 hours
High-clearance or medium-duty vehicle required
Map: Trails Illustrated 712: San Rafael Swell

GETTING THERE: From Green River, go west on I-70 for 9 miles to exit 149 and turn left onto UT 24. Drive south to milepost 147, turning right onto a dirt road. At mile 1.5 the road dips down to ford Straight Wash. The creek is usually shallow; check its depth before proceeding. The road may contain rough spots just past this point, and also at mile 2.5. It curves north for a while, then turns sharply right at mile 3.25, heading directly for the base of the Reef. Continue to the road's end just shy of mile 3.75 and park near the canyon mouth.

ON THE TRAIL: This hike is ideal on a calm day (for perfect reflections) in a low-water year (for viewing the pool's prismatic bathtub rings). Begin by dropping down into **Straight Wash** and turning left. Look for a petroglyph panel 100 yards up the canyon on the right. Ubiquitous cow pies on the banks and rocky cobbles in the streambed may put you off, but trust me, it's worth it. The wash emerges from the Reef at mile 1 into an open area.

Ignore side-canyons that branch left and right, heading instead toward the formidable brown cliffs to the west. Nearing them, ascend a low slickrock ramp. Happily, all evidence of ungulates ends here. The wash enters a zone of boulders—not terribly challenging—and makes a 90-degree bend to the left at mile 1.5. Expect more boulder-hopping over the next 0.5 mile.

At mile 2, an abandoned uranium mine penetrates a saddle directly ahead. Here the wash veers 90 degrees to the right. Parallel the soaring cliffs for about 0.5 mile until you come to a prominent gash on the right. This is Eardley Canyon, possibly marked by a mudhole at its mouth. Turn into Eardley and boulder-hop for about 250 yards to a magical mystery pool enclosed by a sheer slickrock bowl. The grotto, with its sacramental vibe, is one of the great beauty spots of the Southwest. Above the pour-off, the canyon gets technical.

10. Wild Horse Canyon

Easy 6-mile out-and-back; allow 3.5 hours
Map: Trails Illustrated 712: San Rafael Swell

GETTING THERE: From Green River, go west on I-70 for 9 miles to exit 149. Pick up UT 24 and drive south for 25 miles. Near milepost 136 turn right on Temple Mountain

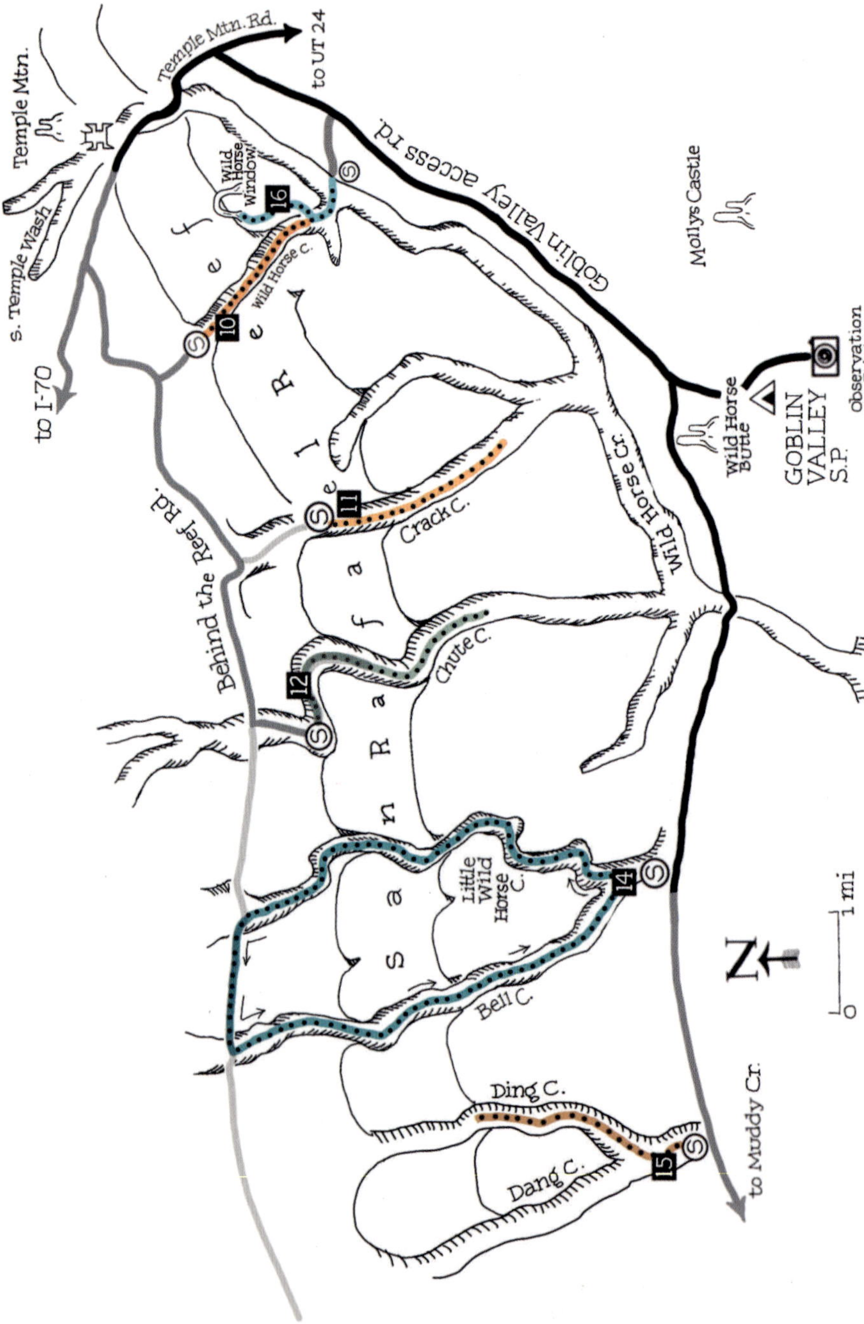

Temple Mtn.
Temple Mtn. Rd.
to UT 24
S. Temple Wash
to I-70
Wild Horse Window
16
Wild Horse C.
10
Goblin Valley access rd.
Mollys Castle
Observation Point
Wild Horse Butte
GOBLIN VALLEY S.P.
Wild Horse Cr.
11
Crack C.
Behind the Reef Rd.
S a n R a f a e l R e e f
12
Chute C.
Little Wild Horse C.
14
Bell C.
N
0
1 mi
Ding C.
Dang C.
15
to Muddy Cr.

Road. Go straight at the junction with the Goblin Valley access road, stopping along South Temple Wash 0.75 mile past the junction to admire a Fremont **pictograph panel** on the right. The pavement ends here.

At mile 7.25 on Temple Mountain Rd., turn left onto Behind the Reef Road, normally suitable for all vehicles as far as Chute Canyon. Magnificent views of **Temple Mountain**—a prime source of uranium for the Manhattan Project of the 1940s—and the top of the San Rafael Reef greet visitors at this junction. Proceed 1.5 miles, then go left onto the track down Wild Horse Canyon. Continue 0.25 mile to the signed trailhead or, with a high-clearance vehicle, 0.75 mile farther to the canyon's head. The former option adds 1.5 miles (45 minutes) to the hike.

ON THE TRAIL: Although the scenery may not knock your socks off, this pleasant stroll provides relative solitude as you descend imperceptibly through the Wingate, Kayenta, and Navajo strata, encountering an impressive fault and three short sets of narrows. At mile 1, bypass the first narrows on the left. At mile 2, skirt the second set on the right, following a cairned path. The last narrows, carved out of salmon-colored Navajo Sandstone, contain no obstacles. Where they end, the canyon opens up. Extend your hike if you wish with a side trip to **Wild Horse Window** (see Hike 16).

11. Crack Canyon

Moderate out-and-back, up to 7 miles; allow up to 3.5 hours
Map: Trails Illustrated 712: San Rafael Swell

GETTING THERE: From Green River, head west on I-70 for 9 miles to exit 149 and turn south onto UT 24. Continue for 25 miles. Near milepost 136 turn right on Temple Mountain Road and reset your trip odometer. At mile 6.5 the pavement ends.

At mile 7.25 on Temple Mountain Rd., turn left onto the Behind the Reef Rd., which is also unpaved. Drive for 4.25 miles to reach the entrance of the canyon. Park here.

ON THE TRAIL: A jeep track extends south into the canyon for about 0.75 mile. As it slices through the Reef, the canyon exposes the Navajo and Kayenta Formations. Both strata contain colorful sets of narrows. Though very short, the Navajo narrows, loaded with tafoni ("Swiss cheese" solution holes), feature a charming subway-type overhang. The Kayenta narrows, much longer and deeper, begin about 2 miles down the canyon. Dry-falls and other obstacles make these tricky to negotiate, so people who find such features challenging may wish to stop here.

12. Chute Canyon

Easy 5-mile out-and-back; allow 2.5 hours
Map: Trails Illustrated 712: San Rafael Swell

GETTING THERE: From Green River, go west on I-70 for 9 miles to exit 149. Here, turn south onto UT 24 and continue for 25 miles. Near milepost 136 turn right on Temple Mountain Road. Go straight at the junction with the Goblin Valley access road, stopping along South Temple Wash 0.75 mile past the junction to admire a Fremont pictograph panel on the right. The pavement ends here.

At mile 7.25 on Temple Mountain Rd., turn left onto Behind the Reef Road, normally suitable for all vehicles as far as Chute Canyon. Drive for 6 miles down Behind the Reef Road to reach the canyon.

ON THE TRAIL: Because Chute and Crack Creeks are neighbors, you may be tempted to combine them into a long loop. But since that option involves a dusty trek down Wild Horse Creek and nearly 2 miles of road-stomping north of the Reef, investigating each canyon separately proves a more sensible option. With no obstructions or tight narrows, Chute makes for an easy walk. A jeep track extends a long way into the canyon before climbing out to the west. Turn back where the narrows end.

GOBLIN VALLEY STATE PARK AND VICINITY

The goblins of this magical place are carved out of cocoa-brown Entrada Sandstone and capped by the greenish-white Curtis Formation. The area initially bore the name of Mushroom Valley for its strangely eroded, toadstool-shaped mudstones.

GETTING THERE: From Interstate 70 west of Green River, go south on UT 24 for 25 miles to milepost 136. Turn right, toward enchanting Temple Mountain, reminiscent of a fairy-tale castle. In about 5 miles, bear left at a signed junction. Continue 7 miles to the entrance station. Follow the park road to its end at the sheltered overlook of Observation Point.

ON THE TRAIL: From the overlook, pick up a path descending along a ridgeline to the right. After about 50 yards, the trail peters out and you're left to follow your inclinations in this otherworldly setting. Most visitors content themselves with exploring the large basin closest to the observation deck, known as Valley 1, but don't miss Valleys 2 and 3, cities of stone marked by prominent sage-green mounds. Less open and more rugged, these zones require moderate scrambling.

Aside from free-form hiking, Goblin Valley offers four official trails. The **Entrada Canyon Trail** (easy 1.25-mile point-to-point) connects Observation Point to the campground. The **Curtis Bench Trail** (easy 2-mile out-and-back) dead-ends at an overlook of the remote Henry Mountains, the last major range in the Lower 48 to be "discovered." Combine two remaining trails (Hike 13) for more of a wilderness experience.

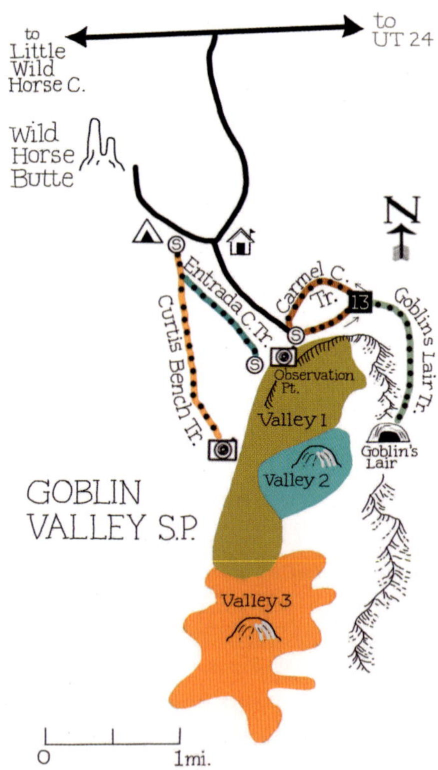

Mushroom rocks seen through a natural window in Goblin Valley State Park

13. Carmel Canyon and Goblins Lair

Moderate 2.5-mile lollipop loop, with scrambling; allow 1.5 hours
Trekking poles recommended
Map: Trails Illustrated 712: San Rafael Swell

GETTING THERE: From I-70 west of Green River, go south on UT 24 for 25 miles to milepost 136. Turn right here, toward Temple Mountain. In about 5 miles, bear left at a signed junction. Continue 7 miles to the Goblin Valley entrance station. Drive to Observation Point overlook at the end of the park road. Park at the covered pavilion. On its left, locate the start of the Carmel Canyon Trail near an outhouse and kiosk.

ON THE TRAIL: Amid badlands, the trail drops down into Carmel Canyon on your right. At the signed junction at mile 0.5, turn right toward **Goblins Lair**. Cairns and poles mark the route, which heads south paralleling the cliffs. Near the end of the spur, at mile 1.5, ignore the social trail forking left in favor of the improbable-looking path on the right, which climbs steeply to a shoulder where you can peek into the lair. Pick your way over boulders to descend into the spooky pit, worthy of the Brothers Grimm, and admire its rooftop skylights.

Reverse course to the junction with the Carmel Canyon Trail and turn right to resume the loop. The route passes below **Three Kings** butte and enters **Carmel Canyon**, which becomes ever-narrower. Where the canyon forks, go straight (left). Shortly thereafter you encounter a few minor obstacles on your way back to the parking lot. If these prove too much, backtrack a bit and follow one of many shallow side washes to the park road.

14. Little Wild Horse and Bell Canyons Loop

Moderate 7.5-mile lollipop loop, with scrambling; allow 4 hours
Map: Trails Illustrated 712: San Rafael Swell

GETTING THERE: From I-70 west of Green River, go south on UT 24 for 25 miles to milepost 136. Turn right and drive about 5 miles to a junction signed for Goblin Valley State Park. Bear left and continue 7 miles. Just before reaching the park's entrance station, bear right at a fork. From here, drive 5.75 miles to the parking area on the right side of the road.

ON THE TRAIL: Extensive narrows make Little Wild Horse Canyon a visual and tactile delight. Its southern end joins Bell Canyon, to produce an exciting loop that *Backpacker* magazine has dubbed "the best day hike in Utah." Because the sun penetrates the deep slots only around noontime, temperatures remain cool most of the way. Do not enter if rain threatens, since few exit routes are available. (See map on page 92.)

Start by walking in the wash. Past a grove of cottonwoods, skirt two pour-offs on the left in quick succession to reach a fork. Bell Canyon takes off to the left. Turn right into **Little Wild Horse**.

Before long, you reach the twisty Navajo Sandstone narrows that continue, on and off, for about two-thirds of the way up the canyon. At times, you must turn sideways and remove your day pack to proceed. You also may have to jump or wade across small pools. Where the canyon opens out, you encounter minor chockstones and dry-falls.

After about 3.5 miles, you meet a jeep road. Turn left, following the road west over a pass to the head of **Bell Canyon** at mile 4.75. Upper Bell is narrower, prettier, and shadier than upper Little Wild Horse, and a rough dirt track extends almost as far as its narrows section. You encounter some obstructions near the top and an 8-foot pour-off near the confluence, which you can detour on the left. Closing the loop, return to your car.

15. Ding Canyon

Difficult 3-mile out-and-back; allow 2 hours
Map: Trails Illustrated 712: San Rafael Swell

GETTING THERE: From I-70 west of Green River, turn left onto UT 24 and travel south for 25 miles to milepost 136. Turn right here. In about 5 miles, bear left at a junction signed for Goblin Valley State Park and continue 7 miles. Just before the state park's entrance station, bear right at a fork. Follow this road 7 miles to reach the canyon mouth.

ON THE TRAIL: A jeep track leads up this high-octane drainage to the junction with its cutely named companion, **Dang**, on the left. (See map on page 92.) You can continue

You easily can touch both walls of narrow Little Wild Horse Canyon at the same time.

up Ding almost to the head, though it takes ample skill and imagination to negotiate pour-offs. Near the top is a slickrock ramp festooned with potholes. Only experienced canyoneers with technical equipment should attempt Dang, which contains major obstacles and possible deep pools.

16. Wild Horse Window

Moderate 2.5-mile out-and-back, with routefinding; allow 1.5 hours
Map: Trails Illustrated 712: San Rafael Swell

GETTING THERE: From I-70 west of Green River, go south on UT 24 for 25 miles to milepost 136. Turn right, toward Temple Mountain. In about 5 miles, bear left at a junction signed for Goblin Valley State Park. Drive 0.5 mile to a good dirt road on the

Dusk falls over the goblins.

right. Follow this track for about 0.5 mile. Just before the track starts to descend, park at either of two obvious pull-offs on the right.

ON THE TRAIL: The window—actually a pothole arch—is clearly visible from the road, although it assumes the appearance of an enormous cave. Orient yourself by studying its position from the parking lot. (See map on page 92.)

Begin by dropping down to **Wild Horse Canyon** on a rudimentary path. Turn left here and follow the wash as it meanders around a point, ignoring the side-canyon that branches off to the left. A set of narrows starts where the wash swings north. Instead of entering the narrows, ascend the slickrock bench on the right to an old roadbed, which soon curves around to the right. Leave the roadbed just before it veers left below a low cliff at about mile 0.5. Follow cairns and footprints, gradually ascending a slickrock flat toward a sandy valley. In the valley, head due north. At mile 1, enter a box canyon with low white walls on either side. Along with a neighboring alcove, the handsomely sculpted arch decorates its end.

CANYONLANDS NATIONAL PARK: MAZE DISTRICT AND VICINITY

The Green and Colorado Rivers converge near Spanish Bottom, forming a Y that divides Canyonlands National Park into three separate districts: the Island in the Sky to the north, the Needles District to the east, and the Maze to the west. (For the Island in the Sky and Needles Districts, consult Chapter 3.) The Maze receives by far the least visitation, with its distance from civilization, lack of amenities, and difficult dirt roads conspiring to scare people off. Of those who do enter the district, many arrive by boat rather than car. The three hikes featured below are all accessed from UT 24, whose northern terminus is at Interstate 70 west of Green River. The first—a detached unit of the Maze District—is relatively well-known; the second, near but not actually in the national park, is largely unknown; and the third presents physical and logistical challenges.

17. Horseshoe Canyon

Moderate 7-mile out-and-back; allow 4 hours

Map: Trails Illustrated 205: Maze District/Canyonlands National Park

GETTING THERE: From Green River head west on I-70 to UT 24. Drive south for 25.5 miles to a signed junction for the Maze District. Turn left and proceed on this dirt road, which is impassable when wet, for 24 miles. At the fork here, go left onto the Green River Road and continue 5 miles, following signs. Then turn right onto another marked dirt road. Proceed about 2 miles on this spur to reach the lip of the canyon. The last mile or so may be rough for passenger cars.

Alternatively, you can access the spur to Horseshoe Canyon on the unpaved Green River Road. In downtown Green River, turn south onto Broadway St. Reaching the railroad tracks, go left onto Green River Ave. and follow signs to the airport. At a major fork near mile 3, the road to the airport veers off to the right. You turn left here onto Green River Rd. (a.k.a., South Lower San Rafael Rd.). Impassable when wet, this road initially parallels the **San Rafael River**, crossing it at mile 23.5. The San Rafael

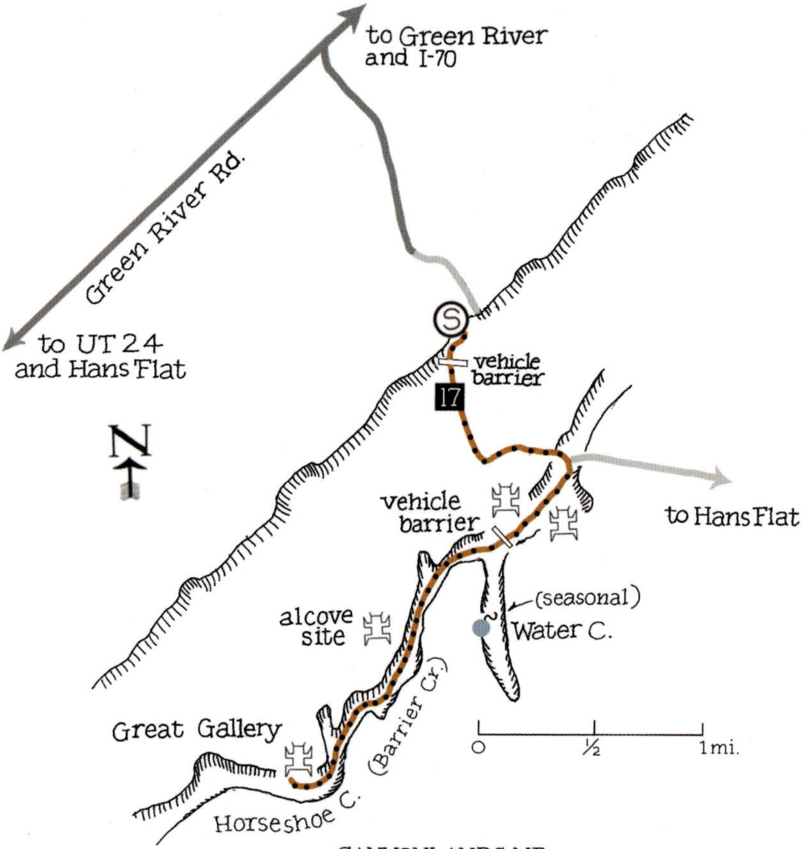

CANYONLANDS N.P.
Horseshoe Canyon

flows into the **Green** just east of this bridge. Continue south on Green River Rd. to mile 42, where you intersect the marked spur for Horseshoe Canyon, a left turn.

ON THE TRAIL: Horseshoe Canyon, which feeds into the Green River, owes its renown to several major league pictograph panels, including the 200-foot-long Great Gallery—the Louvre of the Southwest.

From the parking area, an abandoned jeep road leads toward the canyon floor. Cairns mark the 1.5-mile descent. Near the top are an abandoned trough and water tank. Notice a prominent three-toed dinosaur track along the trail here. About halfway down, where the roadbed has collapsed, you intersect the trail constructed to replace it.

At the bottom, turn right and proceed upcanyon. Within 0.5 mile, look for two pictograph panels, one on each wall. Beyond a vehicle barrier you pass Water Canyon, on the left. From here it is a leisurely stroll to the **Great Gallery**, 1.75 miles farther on the right.

Archaeologists attribute the life-sized pictographs to Desert Archaic nomads, who roamed the area thousands of years ago. The figures, with their small heads and elongated, jug-shaped or trapezoidal bodies, probably had religious significance. The

Polychromes in Horseshoe Canyon (formerly Barrier Canyon) often depict shamans with trapezoidal bodies.

most remarkable depicts a spectral white being known as the **Ghost King**. On your return trip, stop at a large alcove on the left, about halfway back to the vehicle barrier, to inspect a fourth panel that regrettably has been vandalized.

18. Colonnade Arch

Moderate 2.5-mile out-and-back, with routefinding; allow 2 hours
High-clearance vehicle required
Map: USGS: Bowknot Bend
GPS coordinates: 38.3510°N, 110.0436°W

GETTING THERE: From I-70 west of Green River, take UT 24 south for 25.5 miles. Turn left onto an unpaved road (impassable when wet) signed for the Maze District. Continue for 24 miles to intersect the unpaved Green River Road, also impassable when wet. Turn left at this junction and travel 10.25 miles to another intersection. Here turn right onto a spur leading to **Keg Knoll**, a low dome about 2 miles distant. Expect to encounter rocky stretches as you contour around it. Continue for another 2.5 miles, arriving at a Y. Turn left and proceed for about 125 yards to a slickrock flat outlined with boulders. Park here.

Alternatively, you can access the Keg Knoll spur road by heading south from downtown Green River on Broadway St. Reaching the railroad tracks, go left onto Green River Avenue and follow signs to the airport. At a major fork near mile 3, turn left (a right would take you to the airport) onto Green River Rd., a.k.a. South Lower San Rafael Rd. Impassable when wet, this road initially runs parallel to the San Rafael River before crossing it at mile 23.5. The confluence of the San Rafael and the Green is just east of this bridge. Continue driving south on Green River Rd. until you reach the Keg Knoll spur at about mile 36.75. Turn left here and proceed as directed above.

ON THE TRAIL: This multichambered span on the rim of Labyrinth Canyon near stunning Bowknot Bend ranks among the most remarkable on the Colorado Plateau, but finding it poses some navigational challenges. Not only is it far-flung, requiring a long drive on unpaved roads; it is also off-trail, and therefore unsuitable for hikers without proven routefinding ability.

Before starting out, take time to study the topo, on which Colonnade (a.k.a. Five Hole)—located just west of some massive meanders of the Green River—is identified simply as "Natural Arch." It adorns the rim of the northern lobe of tiny **Twomile Canyon**. Keeping this bit of information in mind should help you to locate the arch.

From the parking lot, cairns lead toward a deteriorated jeep track. Follow it about 0.25 mile to a wooden fence and pass through a hikers' gate. The track ends amid a sea of slickrock about 0.25 mile beyond the fence.

At this point, marked by a significant cairn, strike off toward the rim of the southern lobe of Twomile Canyon, bearing left as you descend on progressively lower terraces. Within about 0.25 mile look for a trio of cairns running parallel to the rim. Remaining on the level of those cairns, continue across the rolling slickrock. In yet another 0.25 mile, the cairns resume and become rather numerous, rounding a corner and leading down to the arch, which occupies the transition zone between the Navajo and Kayenta strata. Note that the arch is visible only from the side of the slickrock mass facing the river. A smaller arch is twinned alongside. Total elevation loss from the end of the jeep track to the arch is about 150 feet.

The name Colonnade seems apt, as the arch has an air of antiquity about it, calling Roman aqueducts to mind. With care, you can climb on top from the back, where you enjoy sublime views into the canyon of the Green. To the south, off the cairned route, other curiosities beckon, including an unnamed natural bridge and a freak of nature sometimes called the Crocodiles Teeth.

19. The Maze

Difficult 33-mile or longer out-and-back, with routefinding and scrambling; allow 4 days

Permit required; trekking poles, 50 feet of rope, water filter, and headlamps recommended

Map: Trails Illustrated 205: Maze District/Canyonlands National Park

GETTING THERE: These directions apply to the recommended, third option described below. From its junction with I-70, drive south 25.5 miles on UT 24. Turn left onto a decent, if tooth-rattling, dirt road and follow signs 46 miles to **Hans Flat Ranger Station**. After securing your permit, continue to the North Point Road. Park here.

ON THE TRAIL: Intricate, branching canyons and peerless rock art define the main unit of Canyonlands' Maze District. Despite the superlatives that attach to it, no one would describe the Maze as easy to access. Of three main ways to do so, all involve logistical headaches, not the least of which is locating reliable supplies of water.

One option involves hiring a jet boat in Moab to motor you two hours down the Colorado River to Spanish Bottom, just below the confluence with the Green. Here you pick up the **Doll House Trail** (1.25 strenuous miles, one way), which ascends 1100 feet to that splendid collection of needles. Cairned routes and dirt tracks facilitate touring other parts of the Maze.

A second option entails negotiating rough roads in a four-wheel-drive vehicle from either Hite on UT 95 or Hans Flat Ranger Station. Both contain expert-level sections that have been the ruin of many a poor jeep. Typically, motorists park at either Maze Overlook or Chimney Rock Camp. A designated 8.75-mile loop from the latter traverses the bighorn sheep habitat of Petes Mesa before dropping into the Horse Canyon drainage.

A third option, the one detailed below, combines a drive on a decent unpaved road with a 14-mile slog to Maze Overlook, with its to-die-for panorama.

Starting out on North Point Road, walk through wooded uplands for about a mile to the **North Trail Canyon** trailhead. In the first 0.5 mile, you descend gently to a slickrock terrace. Thereafter the path drops precipitously 1500 feet.

In the next 3.5 miles the canyon narrows and levels out. The wash bottom may contain deep sand. Junctions with jeep roads mark the halfway point. Just south of here is perennial spring Big Water. Bear right at the first junction and left at the second. You can make good time while road-walking between the **Horse Canyon** system and the many-armed monster of **Elaterite Butte**.

About a mile past the butte, you arrive at **Maze Overlook**, where a vast and dazzling spectacle unfolds. Two designated campsites hug the rim. Horizontally striped sandstone canyons with curving walls extend from here to the Green River. On a promontory straight ahead, four massive slabs of Organ Rock Shale capped by White Rim Sandstone, collectively known as the **Chocolate Drops**, survey the scene.

To the left of the overlook, locate the **Maze Overlook Trail**, a cairned route that begins near the white-capped **Nuts and Bolts**. This 1-mile trail careens 650 feet to the floor of **South Fork Horse Canyon**. In a few places, a rope proves helpful in lowering packs. Exposed ledges, slickrock slides, narrow clefts, and two sets of Moki steps create a jungle-gym experience that is not for the faint of heart. Shade and water welcome tired hikers on the floor of the labyrinth.

Possibilities for exploration are endless. The easy 3-mile out-and-back stroll to the **Harvest Scene** pictograph (GPS coordinates: 38.2199°N, 109.991°W) is a must. From the base of the overlook trail, walk north down the South Fork for about 0.5 mile. Bear right at the first junction and proceed upstream 0.5 mile to the second, in an area known informally as Pictograph Fork.

Turn right here, following cairns beneath the east side of the Chocolate Drops. In about 0.5 mile, you come to an isolated minaret presiding over a broad open area. Clearly, Archaic Desert peoples would have regarded this as a place of power. Scour the cliffs to your right to find the polychrome Harvest Scene panel, featuring a parade of colorfully dressed shamans. The most memorable figure grasps a sheaf of rice grass; a bird flies into its hand from the left, while a rabbit emerges on the right.

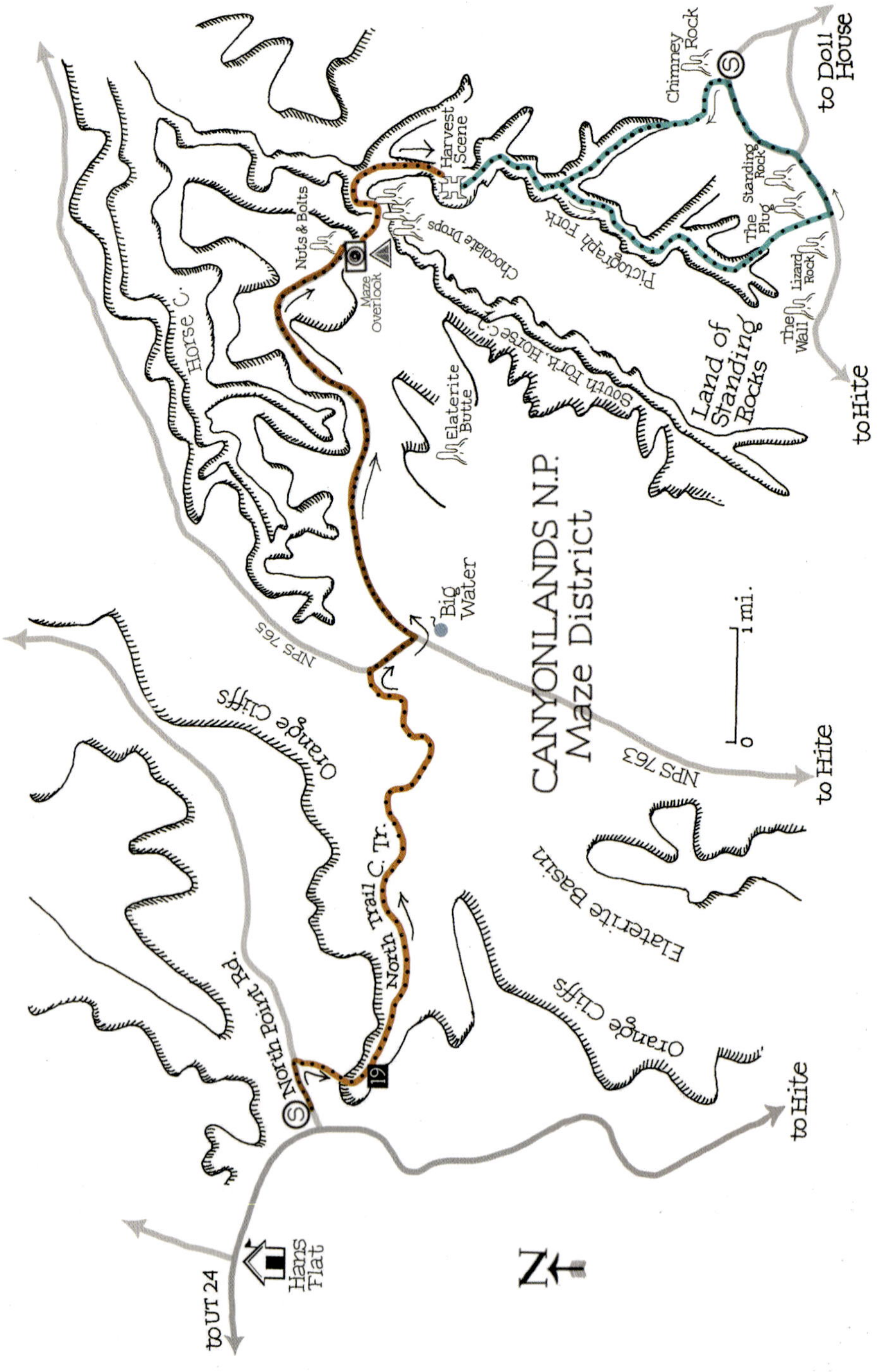

CANYONLANDS N.P.
Maze District
Horse C.
Nuts & Bolts
Maze Overlook
Harvest Scene
Chocolate Drops
Pictograph Fork
Chimney Rock
to Doll House
The Standing Rock
The Plug
Lizard Rock
The Wall
Land of Standing Rocks
South Fork Horse C.
Elaterite Butte
to Hite
Big Water
NPS 765
NPS 763
1 mi.
0
Orange Cliffs
North Trail C. Tr.
North Point Rd.
19
Elaterite Basin
to Hite
to Hite
Hans Flat
to UT 24
N

From here, proceed farther upcanyon if you wish to the **Land of Standing Rocks**. About 1.5 miles past the panel is a fork. The right fork leads to **Lizard Rock** and **The Plug**, while the more popular left fork skirts some minor obstructions on its 2.25-mile journey to **Chimney Rock**. The road heading southeast from Chimney Rock ends at the Doll House, 3.5 miles distant.

One last tip: Packing headlamps enables you to hike the jeep road portion of the trip in the cool of night. If you have the flexibility, you may even want to plan your visit to coincide with the full moon. In season, a profusion of fragrant evening primrose provides extra motivation for a nighttime excursion.

AROUND LAKE POWELL

For hikes in this section, take UT 24 south from Interstate 70 or east from Torrey to Hanksville, where you pick up UT 95 toward Blanding.

20. Little Egypt

Easy freestyle exploring; allow 1 hour
Map: USGS: Raggy Canyon

GETTING THERE: In Hanksville, pick up UT 95 south. At mile 20.5, turn right onto an unpaved road. Soon you will see a sign indicating that you are on the Bull Creek Pass Scenic Byway. Drive 1.5 miles to a track on the right. Park at its end.

ON THE TRAIL: Those with an appetite for goblins will delight in this geologic site, featuring hoodoos of ochre Entrada Sandstone framed by the Henry Mountains. Drop down from the parking lot. The largest hoodoo, which could be called "Cleo's Asp," presides over the second bay.

21. Leprechaun Canyon

Moderate 2-mile out-and-back; allow 1 hour
River shoes recommended
Map: USGS: Turkey Knob

GETTING THERE: From Hanksville, follow UT 95 south for 28 miles (2 miles past the junction with UT 276). Turn left onto a dirt track. Park about 50 yards down the track on the left, taking care to avoid sand traps.

ON THE TRAIL: One of the so-called **Irish canyons** (Lucky Charms, Shillelagh, etc.) emptying into **North Wash**, Leprechaun is the sweetest little hike that nobody, aside from hard-core rock climbers, has ever heard of. It offers a trifecta of treats.

The first 0.5 mile requires bushwhacking through thickets. Bear right where the canyon forks. From here on out, anticipate one OMG moment after another. The first attraction is "Fatso's Misery," perhaps the narrowest slot that individuals of average girth can negotiate. To access it you must either crawl under or climb over a chockstone. From there you need to contort your body to pass through the defile. Most hikers will not want to attempt ascending the steep slot where it ends.

Therefore, backtrack to the slot's beginning and bypass it by means of a slickrock mass on the canyon's east side. Drop back down to the floor above the slot. Just past a large boulder in the center of the canyon, enter a short subway section. That undercut gives way to the Stygian depths of **Belfast Boulevard**, a spooky tunnel that boxes up at its end. On the return, pause to investigate an "inscription chamber" in the very short east fork, between the narrows and the subway.

NEARBY: Half a mile northwest of Leprechaun is the more challenging **Blarney Canyon**. A short way in, avoid an obstacle on the left. At about mile 0.5 is a skinny 10-foot pour-off with a chockstone that large people may be unable to negotiate. Past here, where the canyon forks, seasonal pools commonly develop.

22. Hog Springs

Moderate 2-mile out-and-back; allow 1 hour

Map: USGS: Hite North

GETTING THERE: In Hanksville, pick up UT 95. Shortly past milepost 33, park at the picnic area on the right.

ON THE TRAIL: The main attraction here is a plunge pool formed by a waterfall about 1 mile up reed-choked Hog Canyon. An abundance of social trails can cause confusion, especially where the Kayenta Formation canyon forks at about mile 0.5. Take the right fork to visit the idyllic grotto. Go no farther unless you're packing a machete.

NEARBY: Back at UT 95, walk southeast for about 200 yards to an enormous alcove. Cross the wash and pick up a short trail ascending to the alcove's deepest recess. On the cliff face to the left, stop to admire the Barrier Canyon–style **Moki Queen** pictograph.

23. Maidenwater Canyon

Difficult 6-mile out-and-back or 7-mile loop, with exposure, routefinding, and scrambling; allow 5–6 hours

Headlamps required; trekking poles, river shoes, and water filter recommended

Map: Trails Illustrated 213: Glen Canyon National Recreation Area

GETTING THERE: From Hanksville, follow UT 95 south for 26 miles to the junction of UT 276, which extends past the stunning Henry Mountains and Little Rockies toward Lake Powell's Bullfrog Marina. Turn right onto UT 276 and continue 9.5 miles to the main (south) fork of Maidenwater Canyon. Park at a small pullout on the left.

Sun-kissed cliffs reflected in the pools of lower Maidenwater Canyon

ON THE TRAIL: Maidenwater is a Navajo Sandstone slot with many challenging obstacles, including perennial pools in its lower end. The hike works as either an out-and-back or a loop with neighboring Trail Canyon. Each plan has its virtues and shortcomings. Speaking in favor of the former is that Trail Canyon lacks the grandeur and drama of Maidenwater. Speaking in favor of the latter is that some of Maidenwater's obstacles may prove tricky to ascend. Inquire locally about existing conditions before setting forth.

From the southwest end of the highway bridge, descend steeply into the canyon by means of a boulder-choked ravine. Illuminate your headlamp and enter the long, dark tunnel blasted out of the sandstone by highway engineers. The tunnel floor is far from smooth and contains a gigantic pothole with serious potential to injure anyone unlucky enough to fall into it. Emerging into the light, proceed downstream, where you encounter obstructions almost immediately. At about mile 0.75, veer left to bypass a pour-off. At mile 1, stop to explore the middle fork, which comes in on the left. Just beyond this point you arrive at a 30-foot pour-off. A trail on the left, which is cairned but exposed, circumvents it.

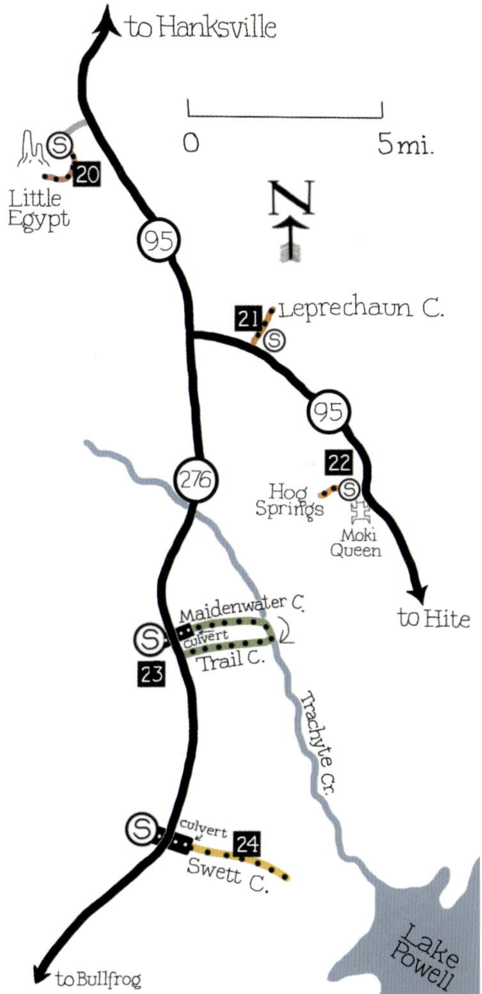

As the canyon slots up, the impediments continue, fast and furious, abating only when you reach the first of many perennial springs at mile 1.5. From here on out, the hike is pure pleasure. Water soon fills the canyon from wall to wall, requiring hikers to wade. Enter a 200-yard "subway" section around mile 2. At about mile 2.75, arrive first at a small cascade and then at a picturesque pool. The canyon snakes around to its confluence with **Trachyte Creek** at mile 3.

For the loop, turn right (downstream) into Trachyte, a broad canyon with ample evidence of grazing. At mile 3.5, turn right into misnamed **Trail Canyon**, the first drainage on the right. Trail has water in its lower reaches but should not involve wading. Alas, there is no trail here. Expect instead a slow, tiring slog over cobbles. Near the end, follow the leftmost fork for easy access to the highway along the rim.

24. Swett Canyon

Moderate 8-mile out-and-back, with scrambling; allow 4 hours
Trekking poles recommended
Map: Trails Illustrated 213: Glen Canyon National Recreation Area

GETTING THERE: From Hanksville, follow UT 95 south for 26 miles to UT 276. Turn right here and continue 13.5 miles to a bridge. There is no designated parking; pull off the road on the bridge's southwest side.

ON THE TRAIL: Swett Canyon empties into the northernmost arm of Lake Powell. Two handsome sets of narrows decorate its upper reaches. The canyon floor is rocky, with occasional boulders.

Pick your way down a brushy slope on the southwest side of the road and pass through an enormous culvert under the highway to enter the Navajo Sandstone narrows. Almost immediately, work around two minor hindrances, the only ones in this part of the hike. Milk Canyon, a tributary, comes in at a scant 0.5 mile. At mile 2, the Navajo narrows end near a slide-rock "arch." In the Kayenta Formation, a boulder field slows your progress. Immediately thereafter, at about mile 3, come the ruddy Wingate Sandstone narrows that are Swett's claim to fame. They continue for about a mile, ending just past a side-canyon on the right, amid likely pools. Turn around here.

CAPITOL REEF NATIONAL PARK: NORTH

At Hanksville, UT 24 doglegs west toward Torrey, passing prominent **Factory Butte** (best appreciated from milepost 104.5) before winding through the starkly beautiful **Caineville Badlands**. Unlike the Goblin Valley hoodoos, which are messy and irregular in form, these badlands exhibit an austere, fractal geometry. It will come as no surprise that a Mars research station is based nearby.

Much more inviting for most people is Capitol Reef. Known to Navajos as "the land of the sleeping rainbow," the park is a hiker's dream, with intricate canyons, arches, spires, and domes. One of the largest domes, composed of Navajo Sandstone, resembles the Capitol Building in Washington, DC. The park has an elongated profile. Its more popular section is located in the north around the abandoned hamlet of Fruita, while a remote panhandle extends almost to Lake Powell.

The dominant landform is the 100-mile-long **Waterpocket Fold**, a rugged ridge warped and uplifted 60 million years ago by subterranean pressures. Many canyons bite into the Fold, exposing its tilted strata. Traveling from east to west through these gorges, you move forward in geologic time, beginning with the Chinle Formation and passing through the majestic Glen Canyon Group: Wingate Sandstone, the Kayenta Formation, and Navajo Sandstone. Throughout the region, small "pockets" in the rock collect rainwater. The Fremont River, named for explorer John C. Frémont of Civil War fame, drains the area.

Between 800 and 1200 CE, Fremont Indians lived along the river, and their carvings are amply in evidence; a large grouping of **petroglyphs** clusters around a marked pullout 1.25 miles east of the visitor center. In later centuries, the area was frequented by Ute and Paiute Indians, law-evading polygamists, and members of Butch Cassidy's outlaw gang, the Wild Bunch. The valley was settled by pioneers who planted orchards that the Park Service still maintains, and in season visitors

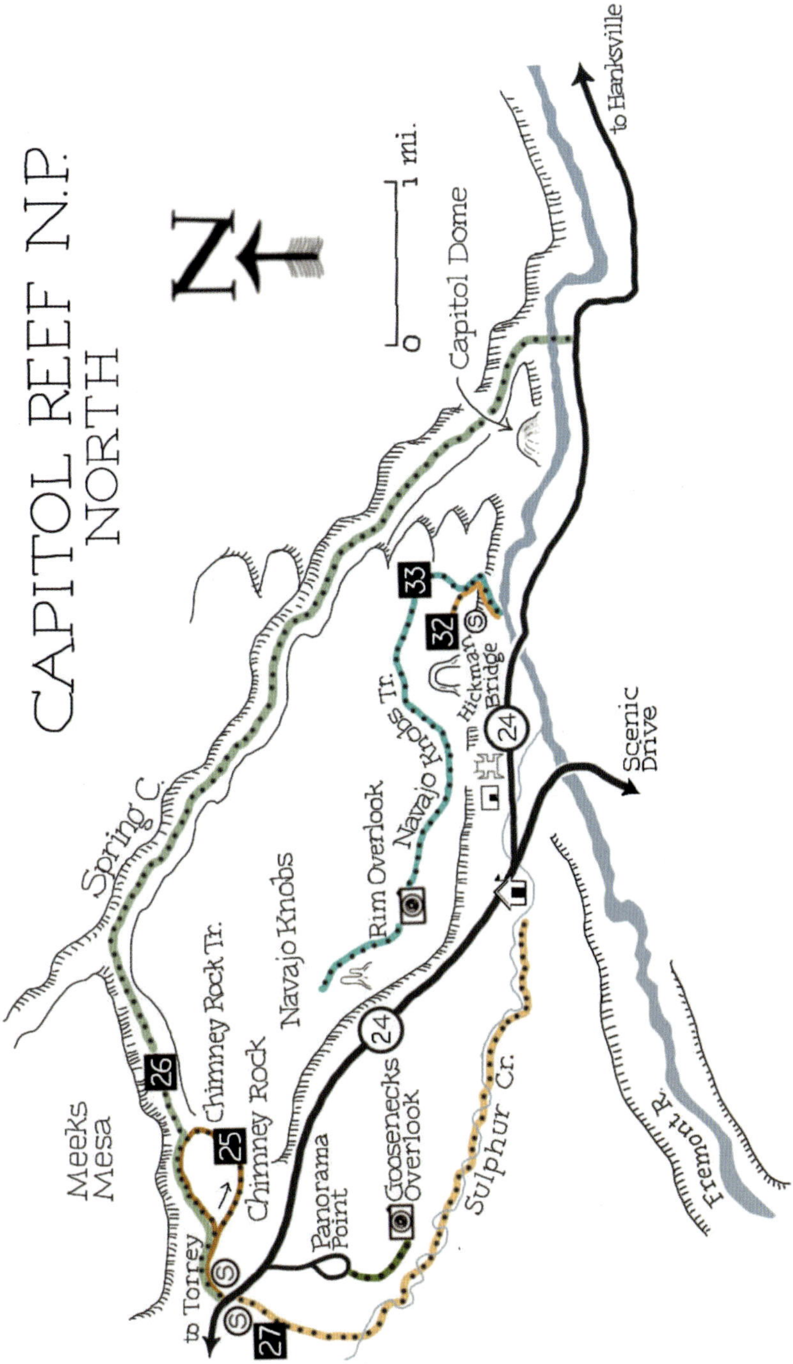
CAPITOL REEF N.P.
NORTH
N
0
1 mi.
to Hanksville
Capitol Dome
Spring C.
33
32
Hickman Bridge
Navajo Knobs Tr.
Rim Overlook
Navajo Knobs
24
Scenic Drive
Chimney Rock Tr.
26
25
Chimney Rock
Meeks Mesa
Panorama Point
Goosenecks Overlook
Sulphur Cr.
Fremont R.
to Torrey
27

may pick and purchase fruit. The leafy campground provides a comfortable base for adventure.

25. Chimney Rock

Moderate 3.5-mile lollipop loop; allow 2 hours
Map: Trails Illustrated 267: Capitol Reef National Park

GETTING THERE: From Torrey, take UT 24 east for about 5.5 miles. Turn left into the Chimney Rock parking lot.

ON THE TRAIL: The trail forks after 0.25 mile. Turn right and ascend several hundred feet to a mesa top. Here you are treated to glorious views of **Chimney Rock**, a Moenkopi pillar with a cap of Shinarump Sandstone. After a flat stretch, the trail heads east to another mesa. Mummy Cliff commands the scene. Crossing over to the back of the second mesa, descend sharply to meet the trail to Spring Canyon (see Hike 26). At the junction, turn left. The trail crosses a low saddle before dropping down to the parking lot.

26. Spring Canyon

Difficult 10-mile point-to-point; allow 6 hours
Vehicle shuttle or equivalent required; trekking poles and river shoes recommended
Map: Trails Illustrated 267: Capitol Reef National Park

GETTING THERE: On UT 24, drive east from Torrey about 12 miles. Leave one car at the pullout near milepost 83. The mouth of Spring Canyon, where the hike concludes, is 100 yards east of this point, obscured by brush. Drive your other vehicle 6.75 miles west on UT 24 to the Chimney Rock parking area, on the right. Start the hike here.

ON THE TRAIL: Spring Canyon runs parallel to the axis of the Waterpocket Fold for several miles before finally cutting through it. The route through this remarkable gorge is slightly downhill and relatively shady as it snakes toward the Fremont River. Because you will have to ford the river at the end of the journey, check its depth before setting forth, and scout out an exit point on the bank.

The trip begins on the Chimney Rock Loop (Hike 25), which climbs a set of switchbacks. At about mile 1, the trail forks; go left here. Soon you meet the other end of this loop. Take another left, descending into **Chimney Rock Canyon** on a marked route. Between here and the junction with Spring Canyon at about mile 3, pass several side-canyons to your left.

If you were to turn left (upstream) at the confluence, within 1.25 miles you would reach a large amphitheater on the right containing a seep that creates a refreshing pool and gives Spring Canyon its name. However, this itinerary has you turning right (downstream) instead. Expect a fair amount of boulder-hopping in the next few miles.

At about mile 4, you encounter two pour-offs. Avoid the first by utilizing a trail on the left. Exposure and unstable soil mandate caution. After dropping back into the wash, take time to inspect the narrows. The second pour-off also is bypassed on the left.

Capitol Reef (a.k.a. Waterpocket Fold)—not a marine formation, but a geologic impediment to travel

Beyond the pour-offs, a side-canyon enters from the right at mile 4.5 amid box elders and cottonwoods. Detour to avoid a rockfall when another significant side-canyon comes in from the left. In another mile or so, two major side-canyons appear on the right; look for an arch here, high on the canyon wall.

Soon after, at about mile 6.5, you start encountering intermittent water. The last third of this hike delivers the biggest payoff, affording glimpses of the looming Navajo Sandstone domes for which the park is known. Near the **Fremont River**, the canyon is choked with reeds and brush that may obscure the trail. Pick a shallow spot to ford the stream. Climb to the opposite bank and execute the short road-walk west to your waiting vehicle.

27. Goosenecks

Difficult 5-mile point-to-point; allow 3 hours

Vehicle shuttle or equivalent required; trekking poles and river shoes recommended

Map: Trails Illustrated 267: Capitol Reef National Park

GETTING THERE: From Torrey, drive east on UT 24 for 8 miles to the junction with the main park road, known as the **Scenic Drive**. The visitor center is immediately south of the junction. Leave one car here. In the other, backtrack 3 miles west on UT 24 and pull into the Chimney Rock parking lot, on the right. The Sulphur Creek Goosenecks trailhead is directly across the highway.

ON THE TRAIL: Check the weather forecast before starting out, since the narrow canyon is no place to be caught in a storm. Avoid this trip, too, if the water is cold or its level is high.

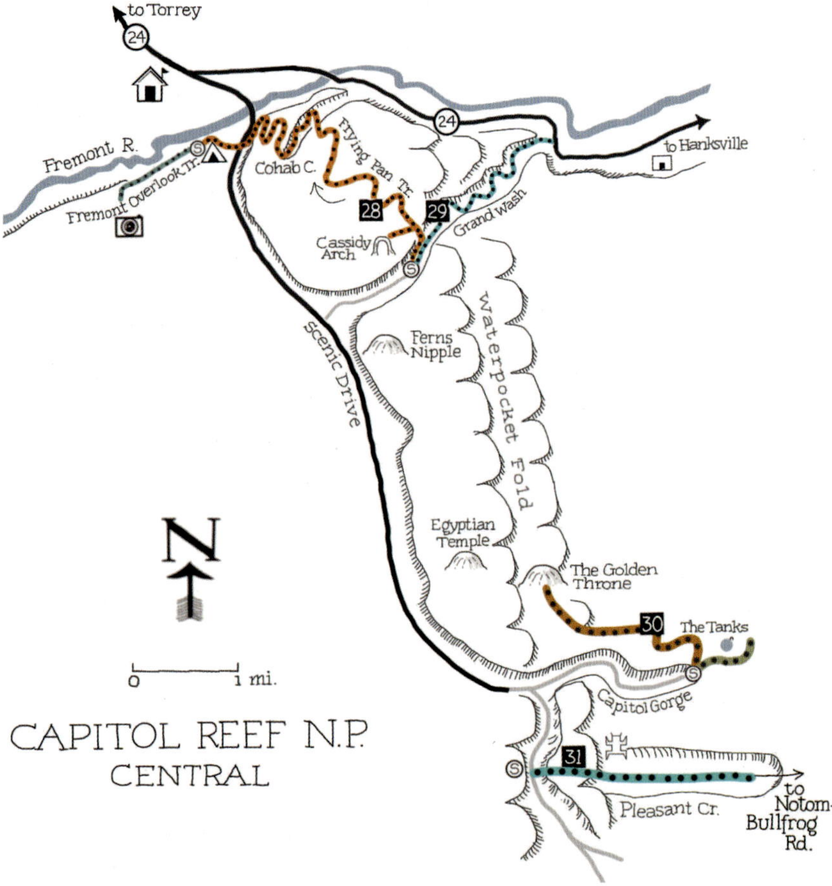

The route begins by dipping into a side-canyon of Sulphur Creek. A minor obstruction should pose little difficulty. After about 0.75 mile, you meet **Sulphur Creek**. Here the canyon is shallow, with a hardpacked dirt floor, and you can make good time. As the creek cuts into older, uplifted rock layers, the canyon narrows considerably, and you soon enter the goosenecks, where the streambed doubles back on itself repeatedly. If you look up and to your left, you may spot tourists on the observation platform at **Goosenecks Overlook**, reached from UT 24 by a short pathway.

About 0.5 mile beyond this point, your progress is impeded by a series of obstacles, mainly falls, of which the first two present the greatest challenge. Carefully skirt each on the right bank. If water is flowing in the wash, it may be deeper here. When the canyon widens out again, about 0.75 mile past the first of the falls, travel becomes quicker and easier.

Dodge the final obstruction, a waterfall, on the left at mile 4. Just past the waterfall, a side-canyon comes in on the right; stay in the main channel. A few more meanders bring you within sight of the highway bridge. Go left on a cairned trail to the visitor center.

28. Frying Pan Trail

Moderate 6.25-mile point-to-point, including Cassidy Arch spur; allow 3.5 hours

Vehicle shuttle or equivalent required

Map: Trails Illustrated 267: Capitol Reef National Park

GETTING THERE: Take UT 24 east from Torrey for 8 miles. Turn right onto the Scenic Drive (main park road) and continue 1 mile to the campground, on the right. Leave one car here. Then continue south on the Scenic Drive for 2.5 miles to the spur for **Grand Wash**. Turn left here. The parking area is at the end of this 1.25-mile spur.

ON THE TRAIL: The Frying Pan Trail traverses the slickrock terraces of the Kayenta Formation overlooking the park. Because some sections may be oven-like in summer, it is advisable during that season to begin the trip in early morning.

At 0.25 mile, your trail branches off to the left, climbing briskly about 900 feet to the canyon rim. Shortly after you top out, a 0.5-mile spur trail laterals left to **Cassidy Arch**, a muscular span named for outlaw Butch Cassidy.

Back at the main trail, go left. Climb a few hundred feet more, winding through eroded pinyon and juniper uplands. After leveling out for a short distance, the trail descends to cross the shallow arm of a canyon and then ascends a low pass before dropping into the **Cohab Canyon** drainage, about 3 miles beyond the junction with the Cassidy spur.

Upon entering Cohab Canyon, turn left, proceeding upcanyon to its head. This narrow chasm, with its pockmarked rock walls and even narrower side slots, was once a refuge for Mormon polygamists, or "cohabitationists," trying to evade federal marshals. From the canyon's end, the trail drops steeply in the next mile, snaking down a precipitous cliff to the Scenic Drive and campground.

NEARBY: The **Fremont Overlook Trail**, a moderate 2.25-mile out-and-back, that starts at the west end of Campground B, ascends 475 feet to a ridge. Views of the river canyon slicing through Boulder Mountain reward you on top.

29. Grand Wash

Easy 2.25-mile point-to-point; allow 1.5 hours

Vehicle shuttle or backtrack required

Map: Trails Illustrated 267: Capitol Reef National Park

GETTING THERE: With two cars, leave one at the terminus of the hike, located 4.5 miles east of the visitor center on UT 24. Drive the other vehicle back toward the visitor center. Proceed south on the Scenic Drive for 3.5 miles to the spur for Grand Wash. Turn left here. The parking area is at the end of this 1.25-mile spur.

ON THE TRAIL: A sheer-walled canyon with short but unusually beautiful narrows, Grand Wash has carved through the Waterpocket Fold. For the first 0.25 mile, a trail parallels the streambed on the right, but most of the way you just walk in Grand Wash. Because the 500-foot-deep canyon has few exit routes, do not enter it when rain threatens. At about mile 1.25, the narrows begin; at some points the canyon is a mere 15 feet wide. After another mile, the canyon opens up somewhat, and you soon reach the highway.

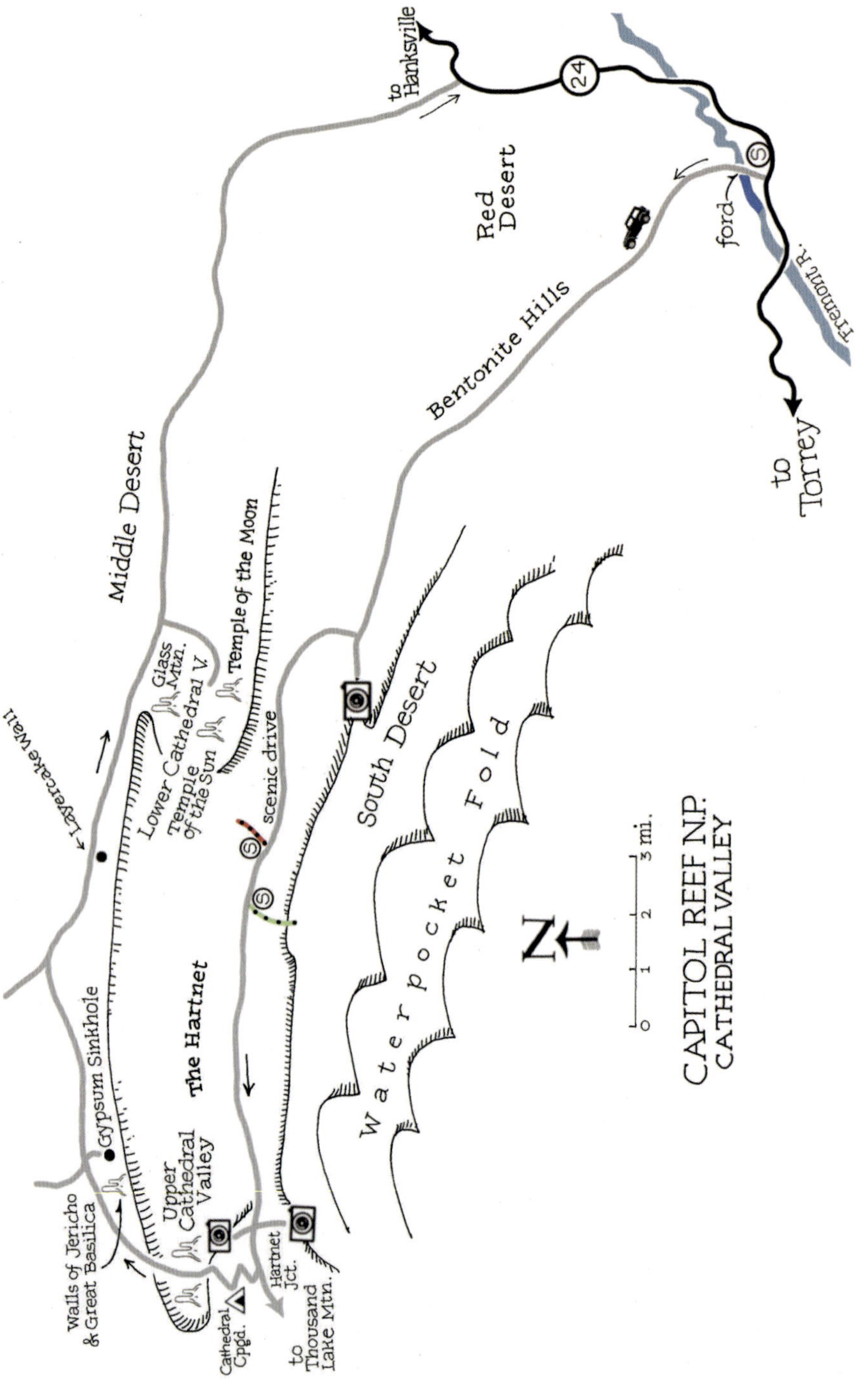
CAPITOL REEF N.P.
CATHEDRAL VALLEY
to Hanksville
24
Red Desert
ford
Fremont R.
to Torrey
Bentonite Hills
Middle Desert
Temple of the Moon
Glass Mtn.
Lower Cathedral V.
Temple of the Sun
scenic drive
South Desert
Waterpocket Fold
Layercake Wall
Gypsum Sinkhole
The Hartnet
Upper Cathedral Valley
Walls of Jericho & Great Basilica
Cathedral Cpgd.
Hartnet Jct.
to Thousand Lake Mtn.
N
0 1 2 3 mi.

Short side-canyons branching east from Grand Wash merit investigation. Especially enjoyable are **Bear Canyon**, which intersects the main canyon just before the narrows, and an unnamed slot at the heart of the narrows, where the wash bends sharply left.

SCENIC DRIVE: CATHEDRAL VALLEY LOOP

This spectacular 49-mile loop leads to the remote northern sector of Capitol Reef National Park, frequented more by cowboys than tourists. Allow yourself a full day to enjoy the drive. Along the way, several short hikes allow you to stretch your legs.

From Torrey, drive east 22 miles on UT 24. At a sign indicating the Fremont River ford, turn left. Test the rocky-bottomed stream for depth before crossing. The mileages given below do not include optional side trips on spurs. Inquire about local conditions, and avoid the area in the event of rain, since the unpaved roads are impassable when wet.

For the first several miles, you travel through the rainbow-hued **Bentonite Hills**. This area, with its barren, claylike mounds, is geologically younger than other sections of the park, part of the uranium-bearing Morrison Formation. The Henry Mountains dominate the southern horizon.

About 12 miles from the UT 24 turnoff, a 1-mile spur on the left leads to an overlook of the **South Desert** basin, bounded on the west by the Waterpocket Fold. Spurs at miles 27 and 27.5 provide other viewpoints.

Immediately thereafter, reach Hartnet Junction and turn right to switchback down to **Upper Cathedral Valley**. The road traverses rough, rocky terrain as it flanks Thousand Lake Mountain, passing a primitive campground. At the bottom of the switchbacks are some fluted Entrada Sandstone pyramids. Here begins the most scenically compelling part of the trip, which continues as you descend gradually toward Lower Cathedral Valley.

Pass the **Walls of Jericho** and the **Great Basilica** on your right at mile 31. At a junction 2 miles down the road, continue straight ahead. The **Layercake Wall**, with torte-like horizontal banding, is on the right about a mile after you cross the irregular park boundary. At mile 36, a worthwhile spur on the right ends at the **Temples of the Sun and Moon** and sparkling **Glass Mountain**, composed of gypsum. About 4 miles beyond the spur, notice a small arch. At mile 49 you reach the end of the loop at UT 24. Look for a granary in a shallow alcove between highway mileposts 90 and 91.

Miter-shaped Towers of the Sun and Moon preside over upper Cathedral Valley.

30. Golden Throne

Moderate 4-mile out-and-back; allow 2 hours
Map: Trails Illustrated 267: Capitol Reef National Park

GETTING THERE: From Torrey, drive 8 miles east on UT 24 to the Scenic Drive. Go south (right) here, passing the visitor center, and continue for 8 miles to a Y. At the Y, turn left onto the unpaved road down Capitol Gorge. Take this road 2.5 miles to its end and park in the lot. (See map on page 112.)

ON THE TRAIL: Beginning near the picnic shelter, the trail ascends 1100 feet to a viewpoint below the base of a saffron dome. The climb, although initially steep, takes advantage of natural sloping ledges of slickrock and compressed dirt. It hugs the rim of Capitol Gorge, digging in toward the north several times to head side-canyons. At the top, hikers enjoy magnificent views of the Navajo Sandstone formations that define this part of the park. In late afternoon, the Golden Throne seems to glow with an inner flame.

NEARBY: From the picnic shelter at the end of the parking lot, a very easy trail (2 miles out-and-back) leads down Capitol Gorge to **The Tanks**, water-filled potholes that gave welcome refreshment to early pioneers and their stock animals. Halfway in, migrants recorded their names on the smooth sandstone cliffs. A diminutive natural bridge marks the trail's end.

31. Pleasant Creek

Moderate 7.5-mile out-and-back; allow 4 hours

Medium-duty vehicle required; river shoes and trekking poles recommended

Map: Trails Illustrated 267: Capitol Reef National Park

GETTING THERE: Travel 8 miles down the Scenic Drive (main park road) from the visitor center. At the junction with the spur to Capitol Gorge, turn right onto a dirt road. Arrive at the parking lot on the right in 2.75 miles, just before the road meets the stream. Cross the road to locate the trailhead. It is also possible to access Pleasant Creek from the east, from a dirt track off the Notom-Bullfrog Road, about 6 miles south of UT 24. (See map on page 112.)

ON THE TRAIL: As its name suggests, this canyon—one of the few that cuts completely through the Waterpocket Fold—offers a delightful way to spend an afternoon. It features Navajo Sandstone domes comparable to those seen along UT 24. But since the trip involves sixteen stream crossings, wearing amphibious shoes will avert the time-consuming tedium of taking your shoes and socks off to dry your feet.

At mile 0.25, pause to inspect a fenced-off petroglyph panel on the canyon's left wall. The first ford soon follows. Between miles 1.5 and 2.5, the canyon narrows. Where it opens up again, washes enter from both sides and Pleasant Creek makes a horseshoe bend to the left. Turn around upon reaching a fence near the park's east boundary.

32. Hickman Bridge

Moderate 2-mile out-and-back; allow 1.5 hours

Map: Trails Illustrated 267: Capitol Reef National Park

GETTING THERE: From Torrey, drive east on UT 24 for 10.5 miles. Park in the large lot to the left of the highway. (See map on page 109.)

ON THE TRAIL: Hickman Bridge bears the name of a local man instrumental in securing federal protection for the area. The trail follows the river a short distance before climbing rapidly about 400 feet to the canyon rim. Where the trail splits, at mile 0.25, take the left fork, which drops into a shallow wash before reaching the 130-foot-long Kayenta Formation bridge at mile 1. Highlights along the way include an ancient granary, a pit house, and two small natural bridges, not to mention striking views of **Capitol Dome** and **Pectols Pyramid**. On the far side of Hickman Bridge, a short loop ascends for a better view before dropping back to the main trail.

33. Navajo Knobs

Moderate 9-mile out-and-back; allow 4–5 hours

Map: Trails Illustrated 267: Capitol Reef National Park

GETTING THERE: From Torrey, head east on UT 24 for 10.5 miles. Park in the large lot on the left. (See map on page 109.)

ON THE TRAIL: Although this cleverly designed trail involves a 2500-foot climb, the ascent follows gently tilted ramps. Take the Hickman Bridge Trail for 0.25 mile, climbing to a fork amid lava boulders. Go right here. After crossing a wash, the trail slowly and steadily ascends. At about mile 1, arrive at another signed junction. The main trail continues to the right, but you can detour first onto the short spur to the left to a Hickman Bridge viewpoint.

Returning to the main trail, turn left. Head a few shallow side-canyons while climbing toward **Rim Overlook**, at mile 2.25. Past here the trail drops to round a large bay before topping a ridge, where **The Castle** comes into view. Descend to the midpoint of a large flat, and then start a big climb on slickrock toward the Navajo Knobs. A cairned route helps you scramble atop one of them.

CAPITOL REEF NATIONAL PARK: SOUTH AND VICINITY

The southern end of Capitol Reef, a panhandle tracking the east side of the Waterpocket Fold, is laced with canyons matching any in the Southwest for visual appeal. Access them from the lightly used, mostly unpaved **Notom-Bullfrog Road**, which joins UT 24 just past the park boundary and continues to Lake Powell. The Park Service maintains a small, primitive campground at mile 22.

34. Lower Muley Twist

Out-and-back or semi-loop of variable difficulty and distance, with exposure, routefinding and scrambling for Cutoff Trail option; allow up to 2.5 days

Permit required if camping; vehicle shuttle or equivalent required for semi-loop; trekking poles recommended for Cutoff Trail

Map: Trails Illustrated 267: Capitol Reef National Park

GETTING THERE: From Torrey, take UT 24 east for 17.5 miles. Turn right here and drive 32.5 miles down the Notom-Bullfrog Road to its intersection with the Burr Trail. With two cars, continue south for 2.25 miles and turn right onto a 0.5-mile spur to The Post. Leave one car here. Backtrack to the Burr Trail junction and turn left. Find the trailhead 2.5 miles up the Burr Trail, at the top of the Waterpocket Fold switchbacks. If you have only one vehicle, park here.

ON THE TRAIL: This drop-dead gorgeous canyon received its name from pioneers who declared it sinuous enough to "twist a mule." Running parallel to the axis of the Waterpocket Fold, the gorge is chiseled out of the Navajo, Kayenta, and Wingate formations. Although the entire canyon offers outstanding hiking, the **Cutoff Trail** allows for the option of a 6.5-mile semi-loop. But a short out-and-back is much easier, particularly with only one vehicle. With only one vehicle, you would need to hitchhike or road-walk 4.25 miles back to your car. Keep in mind that the canyon contains no reliable water. Also, because flash flooding poses a danger, check the forecast.

From the trailhead, descend into the canyon and enter the reddish Kayenta Formation. About 2 miles down Muley Twist, a large side-canyon comes in from the right. Bear left here. At mile 4, a sign on the left marks the very difficult Cutoff Trail.

If you have opted for a semi-loop day hike, take the Cutoff, which ascends a tributary to the crest of the Fold. From here on, the strenuous, exposed track favors slickrock. Because the way forward is not always predictable, be sure to locate cairns in sequence before proceeding. You will traverse far to the right, sometimes climbing unexpectedly or passing through notches in the low domes near the top of the Reef.

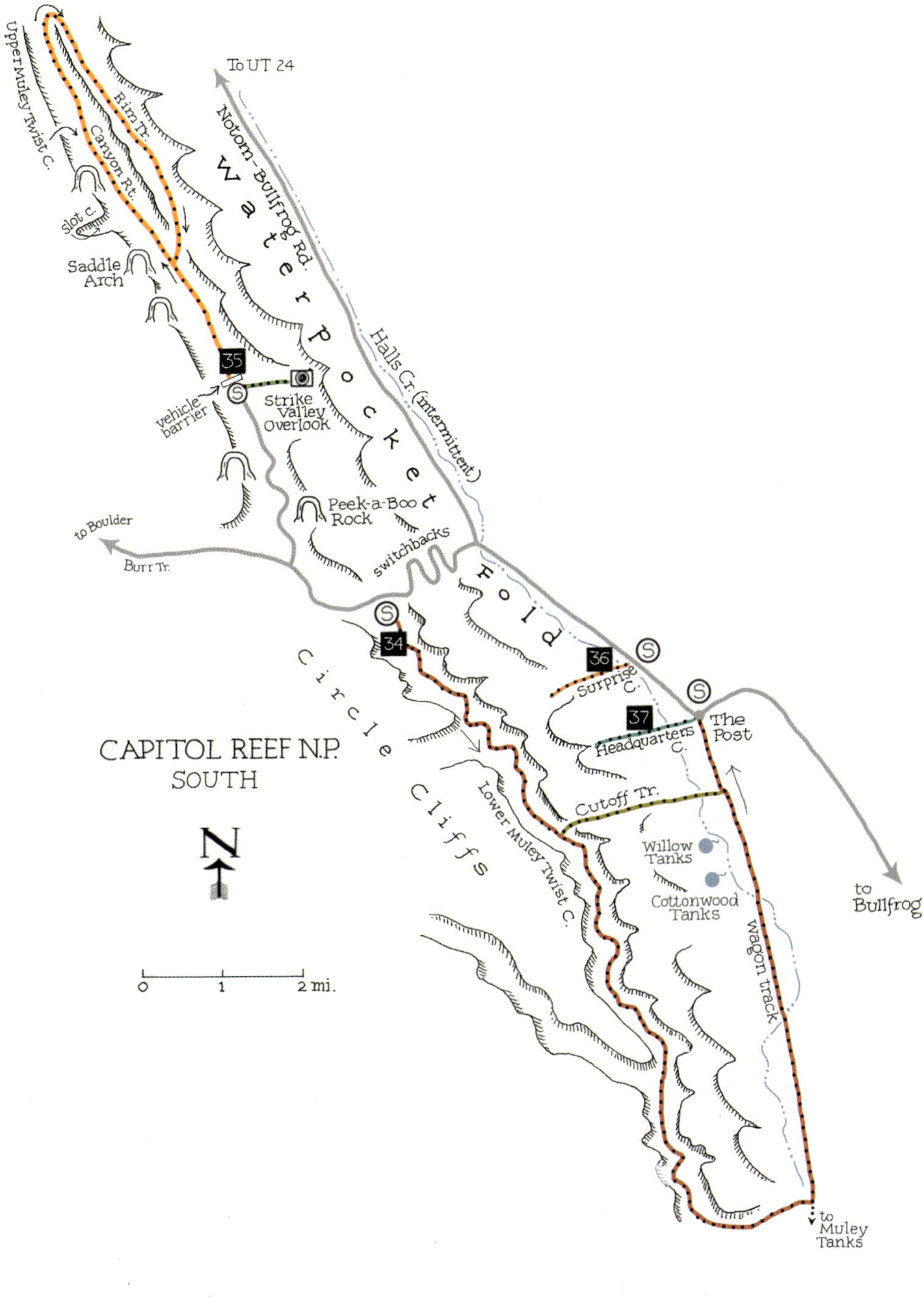

To UT 24
Upper Muley Twist C.
Rim Tr.
Canyon Rt.
Slot C.
Saddle Arch
Notom-Bullfrog Rd.
Waterpocket Fold
Halls Cr. (intermittent)
35
vehicle barrier
Strike Valley Overlook
Peek-a-Boo Rock
to Boulder
Burr Tr.
switchbacks
34
36
Surprise C.
37
Headquarters C.
The Post
Circle Cliffs
CAPITOL REEF N.P.
SOUTH
N
Lower Muley Twist C.
Cutoff Tr.
Willow Tanks
Cottonwood Tanks
to Bullfrog
wagon track
0
1
2 mi.
to Muley Tanks

Eventually, the trail plunges back into the Kayenta Formation. At the bottom it crosses a wash to arrive at a spur road 2 miles from the start of the Cutoff. Turn left here, passing a corral, and proceed 0.5 mile to reach The Post.

Those electing the longer backpack trip should follow Muley Twist 8 more miles to its end. The serpentine canyon slices deeply into the Kayenta and Wingate layers, older strata than the white Navajo Sandstone looming above. After delighting in immense overhangs in the next few miles, you arrive at a major drainage entering from the right. This tributary showcases nature's handiwork, featuring stripes of desert varnish, pockmarked cliffs, and hat-wearing gremlins. It can be explored easily for about 1.5 miles, until a dry-fall and set of narrows impede further progress.

Back in Muley Twist, a long, golden cliff dominates the left bank. At about mile 10, a smaller tributary comes in on the right. Slickrock benches offer excellent camping. Past this point are a number of amphitheaters. On the rear wall of the largest and southernmost of these, at a big bend, cattlemen from years gone by carved their names. Although grazing has not been allowed here for decades, overabundant cow pies from an earlier period make this an unappealing place to spend the night. Happily, there are nicer spots between here and the canyon's 90-degree turn toward the Reef. The walls pinch in, opening up again near the junction with **Halls Creek** at mile 12.

At the junction, turn left, following a deteriorated wagon track toward The Post, 5.5 miles distant. If your water is low, detour 0.5 mile to the south and refill at **Muley Tanks**, reliable pools that nourish a grove of cottonwoods.

About 0.5 mile before The Post, reach the east end of the Cutoff Trail. Either return to your car via this challenging route, revisiting the northern 4 miles of Lower Muley (for a grand total of 23 miles), or proceed to The Post, walking along the road back to your car if necessary (for a total of 22 miles).

NEARBY: If you turn south after exiting the Waterpocket Fold, you can extend the hike by about 2 miles round-trip to visit the **Hamburger Rocks**, near Muley Tanks. This sandstone oddity also can be reached by a longer route from Halls Overlook (see Hikes 38 and 39).

35. Upper Muley Twist

Difficult 9.5-mile lollipop loop from vehicle barrier, with exposure and scrambling; allow 1–2 days

Permit required if camping; high-clearance or four-wheel-drive vehicle and trekking poles recommended

Map: Trails Illustrated 267: Capitol Reef National Park

GETTING THERE: Take UT 24 east from Torrey for 17.5 miles. Turn right here onto the Notom-Bullfrog Road and continue 32.5 miles to its intersection with the Burr Trail. Turn right (west) and proceed 3.5 miles to the turnoff for Upper Muley Twist. Turn right again. In 3 miles, the highly scenic access road, which passes a trio of natural arches, ends at a vehicle barrier. After the first 0.5 mile, this road requires a high-clearance vehicle. Otherwise, you must add 5 more miles onto your hike, in which case an overnight backpack option is advisable.

ON THE TRAIL: This feast of a hike regales you with unsurpassed vistas both within the canyon itself and along the crest of the Waterpocket Fold. The first hour of walking beyond the barrier is nearly flat, making this a suitable day trip for nearly all age and ability groups. Directly opposite brick-red **Saddle Arch** at mile 2, a sign on the right indicates the start of the **Rim Trail**, a cairned route to the top of the Fold. Those who are spending the night should consider establishing camp on one of the benches near Saddle Arch. That option allows you to complete most of the trip carrying only a day pack with water and other essentials.

Between Saddle Arch and the upper end of Muley Twist, several more arches come into view. At mile 2.5, a slot opens on the left; chockstones complicate exploration of its interior. Back in the main canyon, skirt a petite set of narrows within another 0.5 mile by ascending slightly up the right bank. After about 100 yards, drop back to the wash and follow it for the next mile.

At a sharp bend to the right, a small jug-handle arch appears directly ahead. The true narrows start 0.25 mile beyond this point, or 4 miles from the vehicle barrier. Leave the canyon floor and climb steeply up the right bank, following a difficult but clearly delineated route. The route stays high above the chasm for the next 0.75 mile. Watch your footing, especially around sheer drop-offs.

Once the narrows end, the trail returns briefly to the stream level. Proceed to the Rim Trail, which begins immediately after a small chute. The cairned trail to the rim seems nearly vertical at times, necessitating a hand-over-hand climb.

At the top is a prominent Navajo dome with a tall sign reading, "Canyon Route." From here you must travel south a couple of miles freestyle. The route is generally uncairned, so take your bearings by closely observing the landmarks you saw from below. On the sheer ridges between domes, passage is often hazardous. But you may be energized by the world-class tableau to the east, incorporating Strike Valley, the Henry Mountains, and Halls Creek.

Near Saddle Arch, the Rim Trail route descends to the canyon through an obvious break in the cliffs. The descent is not hard, but spotting the unobtrusive sign that marks its beginning may be. At the bottom, go left to return to the vehicle barrier.

NEARBY: From the trailhead at the vehicle barrier, enjoy a 0.75-mile out-and-back jaunt on the easy **Strike Valley Overlook Trail**.

36. Surprise Canyon

Moderate 2-mile out-and-back; allow 1 hour

Map: Trails Illustrated 267: Capitol Reef National Park

GETTING THERE: From Torrey, go east for 17.5 miles on UT 24, then turn right onto the Notom-Bullfrog Road. Drive 34.25 miles down this road and park at the trailhead, on the right.

ON THE TRAIL: This memorable trail enters a box canyon that bites deeply into the Fold. Cross **Halls Creek** at the 0.25-mile mark and climb over a sandy hill. At 0.5 mile you reach the mouth of Surprise Canyon and cooler, shadier walking. The canyon narrows at mile 1, bounded by 500-foot-high cliffs. Near its end are two overhangs, one on each side. Hikers confident in their friction-climbing abilities can ascend a

Top: Brimhall Double Bridge from Halls Overlook; *bottom*: Orange alcove reflected in pools of Halls Creek Narrows

25-foot pour-off and continue farther in the rubble-strewn wash, but most will prefer to beat a retreat here.

37. Headquarters Canyon

Easy 3-mile out-and-back; allow 2 hours
Map: Trails Illustrated 267: Capitol Reef National Park

GETTING THERE: From Torrey, head east on UT 24 for 17.5 miles to the junction with the Notom-Bullfrog Road. Turn right here and drive south 36 miles to a parking area to the left of the road. Cross the road to reach the trailhead. (See map on page 119.)
ON THE TRAIL: This attractive slot features hanging gardens and interesting potholes. The route hugs the left side of a fence, then follows cairns toward the mouth of the wash, climbing over a small hill. Enter the canyon at mile 0.5. At mile 1, where it narrows briefly, bushwhacking may prove necessary. About 0.5 mile farther, ascend a slickrock ramp for about 100 yards. At the top is a steep chute that might tempt experienced rock climbers. The canyon boxes up about 25 yards past this obstacle.

38. Brimhall Double Bridge

Difficult 4.5-mile out-and-back, with exposure and scrambling; allow 3 hours
High-clearance or four-wheel-drive vehicle required; trekking poles and river shoes recommended
Map: Trails Illustrated 267: Capitol Reef National Park

GETTING THERE: Check on the status of Brimhall Canyon before starting out. Ideally, you want the canyon to be dry for this hike, since deep pools may render it impassable.

From Torrey, go east on UT 24 for 17.5 miles. Turn right onto the Notom-Bullfrog Road. Drive south on this road for about 45.5 miles to a T intersection. Turn right here to remain on the Notom-Bullfrog Road. In about 1.5 miles, come to a Y. Bear right to reach awe-inspiring **Halls Overlook**, 2.5 miles farther. This road can be rough, especially near its end. Park as close to the overlook as your vehicle allows. The span is visible across the canyon.
ON THE TRAIL: Because exquisite Brimhall Double Bridge involves a long drive and a difficult trek, it receives far fewer visitors than many of Capitol Reef's other attractions. Gnats at the overlook and deerflies in the gorge can be pesky in late spring and early summer.

The trail cuts boldly down the top part of the cliffs and then traverses north for several hundred yards before plunging to the floor of cottonwood-lined **Halls Creek** at mile 1.25. Watch your footing on the loose rubble. Most likely, your legs will feel like spaghetti as you bottom out. Turn left here and proceed down the wash. A sign points the way. Beware of quicksand after heavy rains.

The bridge commands the head of **Brimhall Canyon**, the first side-canyon on the right. Entering it, proceed about 0.25 mile. Where the canyon veers sharply right, you encounter the first of several obstacles, a slope requiring a short friction climb. Within a few hundred yards, at another hard-right turn, comes the second obstacle, a boulder field. Here the canyon constricts, and pools may

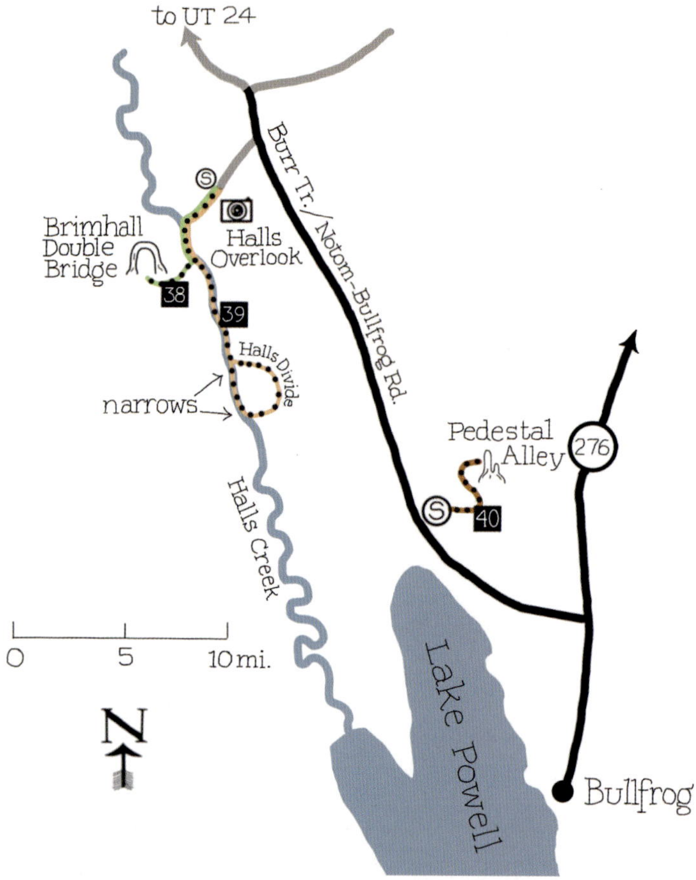

require wading or even swimming. The final obstacle is a dry-fall that cannot be climbed by ordinary mortals; avoid it by ascending a steep scree hill on the right.

Drop back into the canyon and walk in the brushy wash bottom. Exercising care, you can work your way under the bridge from the left side.

39. Halls Creek

Moderate out-and-back with optional loop, up to 22.5 miles; allow 2–3 days
Permit and high-clearance or four-wheel-drive vehicle required; trekking poles and river shoes recommended
Map: Trails Illustrated 267: Capitol Reef National Park

GETTING THERE: From Torrey, drive east on UT 24 for 17.5 miles to meet the Notom-Bullfrog Road. Turn right here and continue for 45.5 miles to a T intersection. Turn right to stay on the Notom-Bullfrog Road. In about 1.5 miles, you arrive at a Y. Go right at the Y to Halls Overlook, 2.5 miles farther. The rocky spur deteriorates markedly near its end.

ON THE TRAIL: This hike delivers solitude and scenic grandeur in equal portions. It is best attempted in the fall, when temperatures are cool and water levels low.

From Halls Overlook, descend precipitously down the rubble slope into Halls Creek at mile 1.25. Turn left, walking downstream. Cut meanders by using social trails on the benches.

At about mile 2.5, the spectacular **Red Slide** formation appears on your right, adorned with curious toadstools. It steals the show for the next 1.5 miles. Below the slide, you may find water-filled potholes, or "tanks," in short side-canyons on the right. The scenery remains unmatched as you pass between Halls Mesa and the Navajo Sandstone cliffs of the Waterpocket Fold, and the hiking is straightforward, barring possible quicksand.

Just before you enter **the narrows** at mile 9, a good campsite beckons. The onset of the narrows, where the creek cuts into the Fold, is abrupt and dramatic. In wet years, deep pools may impede your progress. The dark passage extends about 3 miles. When it ends, either retrace your steps through the gorge or take a 1.5-mile shortcut over **Hall Divide**, which loops back to the start of the narrows on a historic wagon route.

40. Pedestal Alley

Moderate 3-mile out-and-back; allow 1.5 hours

Map: Trails Illustrated 267: Capitol Reef National Park

GETTING THERE: From Torrey take UT 24 east for 17.5 miles. Turn right here onto the Notom-Bullfrog Road. Drive about 60 miles south on this road, following signs for Bullfrog Marina, until you reach the marked trailhead on the left (4.75 miles northwest of UT 276). Park across the road, on the right.

ON THE TRAIL: The cairned trail in **Glen Canyon National Recreation Area** drops into a shallow wash after a few hundred yards. Trudge through sand to an area containing a few stunted pedestals at the base of a Summerville Formation peninsula at about mile 0.75. Take note of a chimney of rock atop the peninsula on the left. Your destination awaits on the opposite side of that chimney. To get there, the trail first swings sharply left, passing a sandstone cigar halfway up a cliff, and then ricochets back to the right. The end is marked by a metal post. Work your way into the canyon to commune with the pinnacles.

CHAPTER 3
REDROCK

With hubs in Grand Junction, Colorado, and Moab, Utah, this chapter explores the fractured landscape on the east side of the Green and Colorado Rivers. Featured areas include Arches, Canyonlands, and Black Canyon of the Gunnison National Parks, Colorado and Dinosaur National Monuments, and two state parks. Aside from hiking, this area offers opportunities for high-adrenaline recreation, from mountain biking and four-wheeling to rock climbing and rafting.

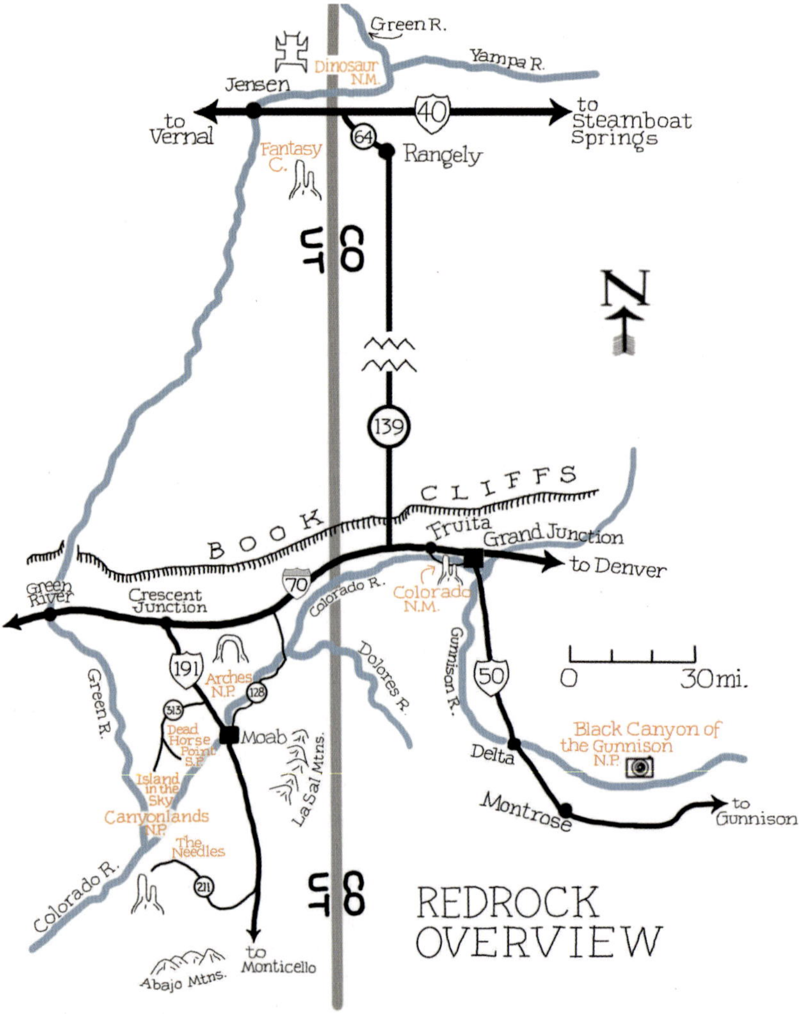

Hubs: Grand Junction, Colorado, and Moab, Utah

The sprawling energy hub of **Grand Junction** (population 62,000) differs from most other communities profiled in this chapter, in both size and the range of its services. Situated on the western flank of the Rockies, but within easy reach of the desert, it lies at the junction of two mighty rivers, the Gunnison and the Colorado, formerly known as the Grand. Alluvial soil here nurtures a thriving wine industry.

Once the epicenter of a uranium boom, **Moab** (population 5500) has transitioned away from an extractive economy over the last few decades. With its tourist sector on hyperdrive, the town attracts close to two million visitors per year, and its name is virtually synonymous with wilderness adventure. Like Grand Junction, Moab is one of just a handful of communities along the banks of the Colorado River, which remains ensconced in formidable canyons for most of its journey.

BLACK CANYON OF THE GUNNISON NATIONAL PARK

Dropping farther in less than 50 miles than the lazy Mississippi River does in 1500, the **Gunnison River** roars down from the high peaks of the Rockies, having scoured out a yawning abyss over the ages. At their narrowest point, the canyon walls stand merely 40 feet apart.

Black Canyon poses a challenge for hikers because of both its sheer verticality and its unforgiving igneous rock. The inner canyon's topography makes it suitable for only the most fit, fearless, and experienced individuals, and all travel below the rim requires a permit. For these reasons, most visitors content themselves with driving or hiking to photogenic overlooks.

To reach the **North Rim** from Grand Junction, drive south on US Route 50 to Delta, turning left onto CO 92. Just past Crawford, turn right, following signs. The last 6 miles are on Black Canyon Road, which has a good gravel surface.

For the more developed **South Rim**, which is open year-round, drive south on US 50 to Montrose. Turn left here, continuing on US 50 until you intersect CO 347. Follow that road 5 miles to the park entrance.

No bridge over the canyon connects the rims. Allow 2.5 hours to drive between them.

1. Chasm View

Very easy 0.25-mile loop; allow 30 minutes
Map: Trails Illustrated 245: Black Canyon of the Gunnison

GETTING THERE: From the North Rim visitor center, continue to the campground at the west end of the park road. The trail begins here.

ON THE TRAIL: Pick up an informative brochure at the trailhead before proceeding counterclockwise around the loop. Reach the vertiginous lip of the gorge at marker 5, where the rims are merely 1100 feet apart. You can hear the raging river 1700 feet below, and may spot climbers scaling the formidable cliffs. Looking downstream, enjoy views of the **Painted Wall**, famed for its pink-and-white crystalline intrusions. Canyon views continue at markers 6 and 7.

2. Exclamation Point

Easy 3-mile out-and-back; allow 1.5 hours
Map: Trails Illustrated 245: Black Canyon of the Gunnison

GETTING THERE: Pick up the North Vista Trail on the left side of the North Rim visitor center.

ON THE TRAIL: Winding through forested country, the path heads side-canyons on its way to one of the few physical features in America that derives its name from a punctuation mark. A sign indicates the start of the 75-yard spur to the overlook. Directly opposite the park's signature formation, the Painted Wall, the overlook treats you to a rare, straight-on view of the river.

Turn around here, or continue another 2 miles on the North Vista Trail to **Green Mountain**, an 850-foot climb.

3. Deadhorse Trail

Moderate 5-mile lollipop loop; allow 2 hours
Map: Trails Illustrated 245: Black Canyon of the Gunnison

GETTING THERE: Drive east from the North Rim visitor center on the park road about 4 miles. Park at Kneeling Camel Viewpoint. The trail begins about 25 yards farther down the road, to the left.

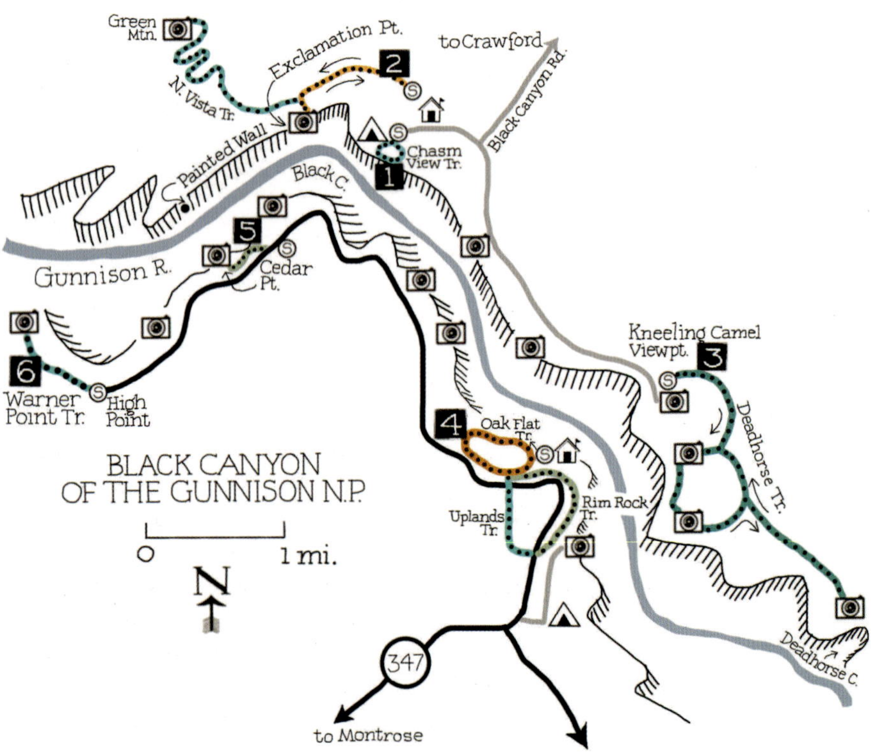

Black Canyon's Painted Wall is the tallest cliff face in Colorado.

ON THE TRAIL: This foot and pack trail extends to an overlook of Deadhorse Canyon and the east end of the gorge. Start out on a gravel roadbed leading to an abandoned ranch. The track, now dirt, contours down a hill, passing a corral and stock pond. Here it turns into a regular path.

Shortly thereafter, at mile 1, you arrive at the start of the 0.75-mile loop, which climbs to secluded overlooks along the Black Canyon rim. Look sharp for the continuation of the trail beyond the second of these. Reconnect with the main trail at mile 1.75. A right takes you to **Deadhorse Canyon** at mile 3. On the return, stay on the main trail instead of retracing the loop. In the fall, enjoy the chaparral and scrub oaks along the way, which blaze with color.

4. Oak Flat Loop

Moderate 2-mile loop; allow 1 hour

Map: Trails Illustrated 245: Black Canyon of the Gunnison

GETTING THERE: Park at the South Rim visitor center and locate the trailhead immediately to the west.

ON THE TRAIL: The trail descends through timber to a series of vantage points. The hike's preferred direction is counterclockwise. At about the halfway mark the **Gunnison Route** into the forbidding inner canyon takes off to the right (wilderness permit required). Toward the end of the loop is another junction, with the **Uplands Trail**.

NEARBY: Access the **Rim Rock Trail** (an easy 2-mile out-and-back) on the east side of the visitor center. Link with the Uplands Trail for an easy 4-mile loop.

5. Cedar Point

Easy 0.75-mile out-and-back; allow 30 minutes

Map: Trails Illustrated 245: Black Canyon of the Gunnison

GETTING THERE: From the South Rim visitor center, drive west about 4 miles to the pullout for Cedar Point. Park here.

ON THE TRAIL: The highlight of this trail is the view it affords of the Painted Wall, the tallest cliff face in Colorado, with a vertical rise of 2700 feet. The wall, composed primarily of gneiss, contains pink veins of pegmatite.

6. Warner Point

Moderate 2-mile out-and-back; allow 1 hour

Map: Trails Illustrated 245: Black Canyon of the Gunnison

GETTING THERE: From the South Rim visitor center, drive to High Point (8300 feet) at the west end of the scenic road. Park here.

ON THE TRAIL: The Warner Point Trail begins by descending, sometimes on stairs, in the direction of the **Uncompahgre Valley**. It then veers to the right and climbs toward a vertiginous overlook of the gorge, nearly 2775 feet below—the canyon's deepest point. The river bends sharply north before exiting its canyon near the town of Delta.

DINOSAUR NATIONAL MONUMENT AND VICINITY

Straddling the Colorado-Utah border, the park protects a vast hinterland around the confluence of the Green and Yampa Rivers. Its big draw is the quarry, where the petrified bones of dinosaurs, crocodiles, and turtles are embedded in a Morrison Formation cliff. For many visitors, the backcountry remains an afterthought. But it should not be, since the topography is second to none. However, its fractured nature complicates motorized travel. Because the park's few roads don't connect, you must drive long distances to travel between trailheads.

From Grand Junction, drive west on Interstate 70 and then north on CO 139 for 89 miles to Rangely. Turn left onto CO 64 and proceed 19 miles to intersect US Route 40. The **Canyon Visitor Center** (seasonal) is located 2 miles east of Dinosaur, Colorado, on US 40. To reach the **Quarry Visitor Center**, which is open year-round, drive west about 25 miles to Jensen, Utah, and turn right on UT 149.

7. Harpers Corner

Easy 2-mile out-and-back; allow 1.5 hours

Map: Trails Illustrated 220: Dinosaur National Monument

GETTING THERE: From the Canyon Visitor Center, travel north on Harpers Corner Road for 32 miles to its end. (See map on page 133.)

ON THE TRAIL: The monument's premier hike delivers unforgettable views of the deep-walled canyons of the **Green and Yampa Rivers**, which meet at **Echo Park**. It follows an undulating finger of land that drops 2000 feet on each side, ending at a fenced overlook. The Green comes in from the north and the Yampa from the east; **Steamboat Rock** blocks views of their confluence, and faulting has tilted the rock layers to a nearly vertical plane.

8. Desert Voices and Sound of Silence Loop

Moderate 5.5-mile lollipop loop; allow 3 hours

Map: Trails Illustrated 220: Dinosaur National Monument

GETTING THERE: From the Quarry Visitor Center, drive east on UT 149 to the spur for Split Mountain Campground. At the end of that spur, park in the large lot. Find the trailhead to the left of the boat ramp access road.

ON THE TRAIL: Combining two loops, this hike affords rapturous views of **Split Mountain**. Start out on the **Desert Voices Loop**, which follows Cottonwood Wash. Interpretive signs line the path. Take the right fork where the trail splits at mile 0.25 and ascend 150 feet to a low pass. Near the top is a 0.25-mile connector to the Sound of Silence. Reaching that trail, turn left. Descend a slickrock slope and a steep, rocky embankment to arrive at another junction. The left fork leads to the official **Sound of Silence** trailhead along the park road. Stay right here, following Red Wash.

When the wash passes through a notch in the cliffs, the trail enters a shallow ravine on the right. The branching drainage twists up through badlands to a bench. Remain on

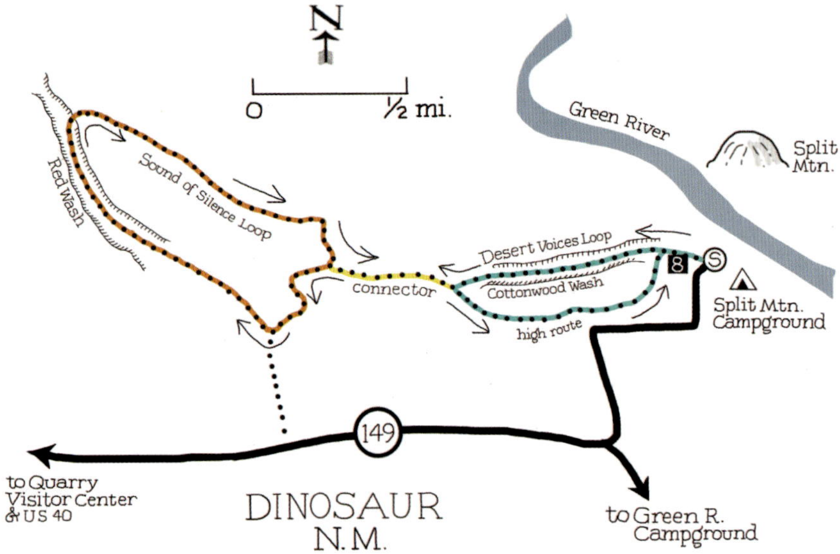

the bench for 0.5 mile before climbing to meet the connector. Go left on the connector and continue to the junction with the Desert Voices Trail. Turn right, walking high above Cottonwood Wash. The trail descends to the wash to finish the hike.

9. Jones Hole

Easy 8.5-mile out-and-back; allow 4 hours
Map: Trails Illustrated 220: Dinosaur National Monument

GETTING THERE: From the Quarry Visitor Center, drive toward Jensen on UT 149. Crossing Brush Creek, turn right on 3500 South. In 5 miles, turn right at a fork. Four miles farther, turn right at another fork, and then right again onto Diamond Mountain Road. In 18 miles, Diamond Mountain Road veers left; continue straight ahead here onto Jones Hole Road. Follow this road to its end at a Federal Fish Hatchery. Park in a small lot on the left.

ON THE TRAIL: This hike has something for everyone: a trout stream, a waterfall, rock art, and big canyon views. It begins unprepossessingly, passing through the industrial-scale hatchery. Entering a shady forest, it parallels **Jones Creek** as the watercourse rushes to its rendezvous with the Green River. At mile 1.75 the trail crosses a bridge to the right bank, where it will remain for the rest of the trip. About 100 yards past the bridge, the trail splits briefly; take the right fork, ascending on steps to view pictograph panels from the Fremont culture. The most unusual figures are Bart Simpson look-alikes.

Just beyond the panels, you come to some campsites and a sign that marks the route to 25-foot-high Ely Falls, a 0.5-mile out-and-back detour. Back on the main trail, continue to **Whirlpool Canyon** on the Green. This is a day-use-only area except for rafting parties.

10. McKee Spring Petroglyphs

Easy 0.25-mile loop; allow 30 minutes

Map: Trails Illustrated 220: Dinosaur National Monument

GETTING THERE: From the Quarry Visitor Center, take UT 149 toward Jensen. Turn right onto 3500 South. In 5 miles, take the right fork at a Y. Four miles farther, turn right onto the Island Park Road (impassable when wet). Just after you enter the national monument, park in a lot on the left.

ON THE TRAIL: The trail ascends toward the rim to a series of superb Fremont panels, all on dark brown rock. The shaman figures have characteristic linebacker shoulders and headdresses, and carry what appear to be shields. Walk back up the road about 150 yards to find a smaller but equally outstanding masterpiece to the left of a curve.

NEARBY: Farther down the Island Park Road is a spur to a small primitive campground at Rainbow Park. A mile past here, **Island Park Overlook** presents a bird's-eye perspective on one of the river's most scenic zones. Time your visit to catch the early morning fog rising from the water.

Talented prehistoric artists carved petroglyphs in and around what is now Dinosaur National Monument.

11. Dry Fork Petroglyphs

Easy cumulative 1-mile out-and-backs; allow 1.5 hours
Binoculars recommended
Map: USGS: Dry Fork Creek

GETTING THERE: From UT 121 in Vernal, drive north one block on 500 West. Curve left onto 500 North and continue on to 3500 West at mile 3.5. Turn right here and follow signs to **McConkie Ranch** at mile 10, parking in the designated lot. Sign the guest register and pay a small entrance fee.

ON THE TRAIL: The ranch's owners allow the public to tour two extensive sets of Fremont petroglyph panels on the Navajo Sandstone cliffs above Dry Fork Creek. To reach the first set, ascend on the trail that begins just to the left of the parking lot (avoid the rugged trail on the right). The panels, depicting enormous big-shouldered shamans, improve in artistic quality as you proceed along the escarpment. To reach the second set, cross the road and open the gate to a cow pasture. The trail follows the fenceline to skirt private property, passing through additional gates. Find the rock art along the cliffs to the left of the trail. The last and best panel here, the **Three Kings**, is inaccessible at the top of the formation, so bring binoculars if you have them.

12. Fantasy Canyon

Easy 0.25-mile loop; allow 1 hour

Map: USGS: Red Wash SW

GETTING THERE: Visit the BLM office in Vernal at 170 South 500 East to obtain a map and an up-to-date weather forecast, as some of the roads are impassable when wet. Then drive 4 miles southeast on US Route 40 from Vernal to Naples, where you pick up UT 45 heading south.

Zeroing out your trip odometer, drive about 20.25 miles, crossing the Green River and passing countless drill rigs. Turn right at a large corral onto Glen Bench Road.

The surreal dreamscape of Fantasy Canyon, set among oil pumpjacks

Proceed 12.5 miles to a water disposal facility. Reset your trip odometer and turn left, following signs. At the first junction (about mile 2.25) go right at the Y; at the second (mile 3.25), go right again; at the third (mile 3.75), go left; and at the fourth (mile 4), go right to reach the parking area.

ON THE TRAIL: In the midst of the **Uinta Basin**'s oil and gas fields lies a quirk of geology. Only a few acres in size, Fantasy Canyon is a bizarro world of weathered rocks that must be seen to be believed. A rudimentary loop through these fragile, delicate formations, which resemble gargoyles, stalagmites, or bleached-out corals, starts at the picnic area. The BLM has assigned names to many features, but you may be tempted to invent your own. (See map on page 133.)

COLORADO NATIONAL MONUMENT AND VICINITY

Colorado National Monument occupies a mesa on the **Uncompahgre Plateau**, which erosion has cut into a series of sheer canyons and isolated sandstone towers. Up to 2000 feet higher than the surrounding desert, it offers broad views of the Grand Valley and the Book Cliffs.

Trails of varying lengths either hug the rim or drop down from the scenic drive. Many were built in the early 20th century by John Otto, a wilderness enthusiast who sought federal protection for these cliffs and buttes. Because of the park's vertical topography, having two cars at your disposal enables you to complete point-to-point trails between the park road and the valley. Alternatively, you can access such trails from below. Bighorn sheep are sometimes spotted in this area.

To reach the **east entrance station** from Grand Junction, take exit 28 off Interstate 70 for 24 Road, which becomes Redlands Parkway. Turn left onto CO 340 (Broadway Rd.), then right onto Monument Road. The spectacular 23-mile scenic drive traverses the park before rejoining CO 340 on the outskirts of Fruita. This marvel of engineering owes to the effort of the Civilian Conservation Corps in the 1930s. The visitor center and attractive campground are near its west end. The **west entrance station** can be accessed from exit 19 for Fruita off I-70.

13. Serpents Trail

Moderate 1.75-mile point-to-point; allow 1 hour
Vehicle shuttle or backtrack required
Map: Trails Illustrated 208: Colorado National Monument/McInnis Canyons

GETTING THERE: Drive to the east entrance station. This hike has two trailheads, one at the Devils Kitchen pullout 500 feet past the east entrance station and the other a mile farther up, where the park road enters a tunnel. With two vehicles, start at the tunnel end to avoid a big climb.

ON THE TRAIL: This memorable trail parallels Rim Rock Drive as it follows the incredibly crooked bed of the original road into the national monument. From the tunnel, it descends 775 feet to the lower pullout on dozens of wiggly switchbacks.

NEARBY: From the lower pullout, an easy 1.25 mile out-and-back trail ascends 300 feet to the **Devils Kitchen** rock garden.

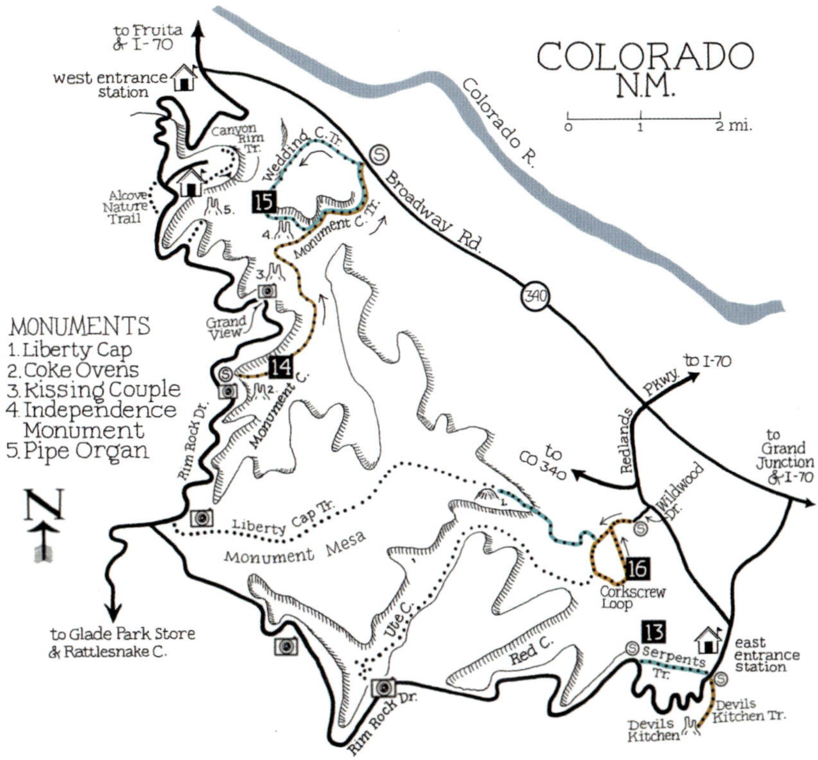

14. Monument Canyon

Moderate 6-mile point-to-point; allow 3 hours

Vehicle shuttle or equivalent required; trekking poles recommended

Map: Trails Illustrated 208: Colorado National Monument/McInnis Canyons

GETTING THERE: The trail starts at the Upper Monument Canyon parking lot, which is located 3.75 miles east of the visitor center along Rim Rock Drive. It terminates at the Lower Monument Canyon parking lot, near milepost 5 on CO 340 (Broadway Rd.). With two vehicles, set up a shuttle system; otherwise, opt for an out-and-back to Independence Monument from either the top or the bottom (see Hike 15).

ON THE TRAIL: Initially coinciding with a pathway to the bulbous **Coke Ovens** formation, the trail soon branches off to the right, plunging into **Monument Canyon**. It rounds **Kissing Couple** butte to meet **Independence Monument** at mile 3.5, which is 850 feet below the rim. From here, descend on the left side of the cliffs, sometimes aided by stairs. You will pass through an extensive boulder garden formed as the Wingate Sandstone cliffs weathered before entering an igneous Precambrian zone. A billion years separate these strata; during that time the intervening rocks eroded away, creating an "unconformity." A butte resembling a sinking ship looms to your right. Reaching the canyon floor, look for petroglyphs in an alcove on the right. Turn left and follow a fence around suburban development about 0.25 mile to the parking lot. The total descent is 1450 feet.

The Coke Ovens formation scrapes the sky along Monument Road.

15. Wedding and Monument Canyons Loop

Moderate 5-mile loop; allow 2.5 hours
Trekking poles recommended
Map: Trails Illustrated 208: Colorado National Monument/McInnis Canyons

GETTING THERE: From Colorado National Monument's west entrance station in Fruita, head east on CO 340 (Broadway Rd.). The marked trailhead is near milepost 5. Parking is limited here and the lot fills quickly.

ON THE TRAIL: This loop allows you to visit the area around 450-foot-high Independence Monument from the bottom. Just minutes from the parking lot, the trail forks; go right and descend slightly, passing a fence that cordons off suburban development. At mile 1, turn left to enter **Wedding Canyon**. The rocky, unmaintained trail ascends steeply on the left side, with occasional mild exposure, before topping out at mile 2. About 0.25 mile farther comes the junction with the **Monument Canyon Trail**. Turn left here and descend 600 feet to return to the parking lot (see Hike 14).

16. Corkscrew Loop

Moderate 3.25-mile lollipop loop; allow 2 hours
Optional, difficult 1.5-mile out-and-back to Liberty Cap; allow 1 hour extra
Trekking poles recommended
Map: Trails Illustrated 208: Colorado National Monument/McInnis Canyons

GETTING THERE: In Grand Junction, take exit 28 off I-70 for 24 Road, which merges into Redlands Parkway. Cross CO 340 (Broadway Rd.) and continue to the junction with Wildwood Drive. Turn left here. Proceed 0.5 mile to the Wildwood Trailhead parking lot, on the right.

ON THE TRAIL: From the parking lot, walk north for 0.5 mile to intersect the loop, which you should plan to hike in a counterclockwise direction. The route ascends a fracture separating a pale sandstone hogback and a dark Precambrian bench. Continue to a trail junction at the top of the basement rocks, just below the red cliffs of **Monument Mesa**, for a total climb of 650 feet.

To visit the **Liberty Cap**, an off-white mound of Wingate Sandstone resembling hats fashionable during the French Revolution, turn right at the junction and climb an additional 450 feet to the mesa top. If the formation, which is visible from below, disappoints, the intimate views into Ute Canyon from a nearby overlook most assuredly will not. Backtrack to rejoin the loop.

From the junction, intersect to the **Ute Canyon Trail** in 0.25 mile. Turn left here. Descend the bench on a set of tight switchbacks that give the Corkscrew Loop its name. At the base of the cliffs, the trail swings left toward the parking lot. It meets several unofficial paths that also will take you there.

NEARBY: Gluttons for punishment can combine the Liberty Cap and Ute Canyon Trails in a moderate 10.5-mile semi-loop starting and ending along the scenic drive and using the connector mentioned above. A car shuttle between the trailheads is recommended.

Nine massive Entrada Sandstone arches beautify the Rattlesnake Canyon rim.

17. Rattlesnake Canyon

Moderate 4.5-mile out-and-back; allow 3 hours
High-clearance or four-wheel-drive vehicle required
Map: Trails Illustrated 208: Colorado National Monument/McInnis Canyons

GETTING THERE: From either entrance station of Colorado National Monument, take Rim Rock Drive to the signed turnoff for Glade Park Store, opposite the Liberty Cap trailhead (about 11.5 miles). Turn south here. In under 0.25 mile, go right; 0.5 mile farther, at a fork, take whichever of two access roads happens to be open, a circumstance that changes seasonally. Both roads are impassable when wet. From here it is about 13 miles to the parking area and trailhead. High-clearance vehicles can make it most of the way, though the last 2 miles cry out for four-wheel drive.

ON THE TRAIL: Except for the grueling drive, it doesn't get much better than this: a series of enormous Entrada Sandstone arches, all less than a mile apart in the **Black Ridge Canyon National Conservation Area**.

From the parking lot, the cairned trail switchbacks about 400 feet in the first 0.25 mile to the base of an escarpment, where it joins the **Pollock Bench Trail** coming in from Fruita (a 14-mile out-and-back). Turn left to contour around the escarpment. Within another 0.75 mile the so-called "parade of arches" unfolds as you pass several majestic spans in quick succession. A tributary of the Colorado, Rattlesnake is perched above mellow **Ruby Canyon**, a favorite of flatwater rafting enthusiasts.

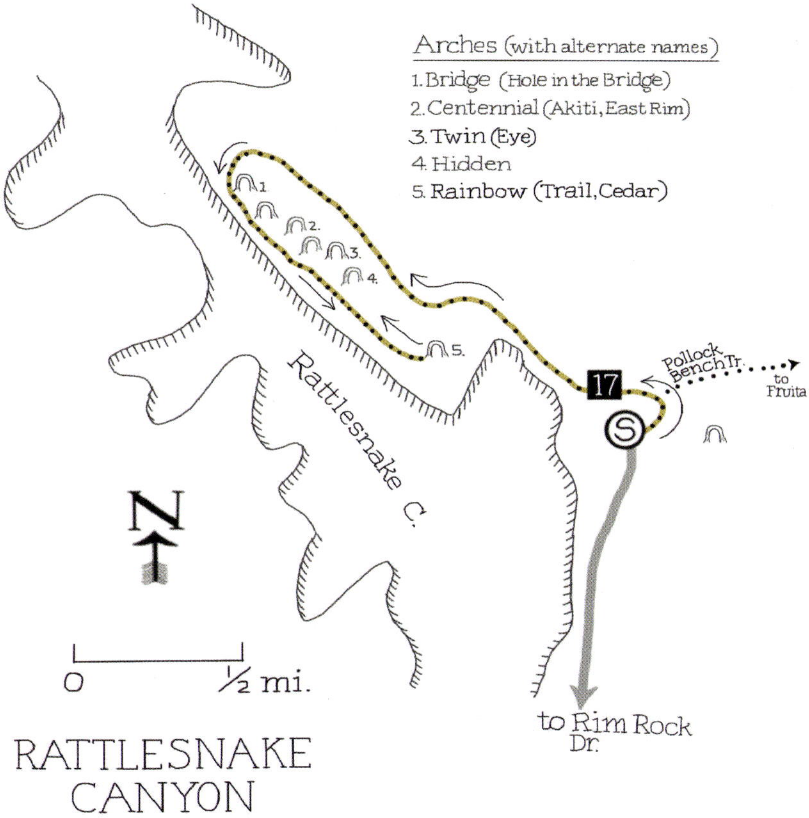

Reaching the last major arch, you can either clamber up through it (class 4 terrain) to the mesa top where your car is parked or retrace your steps. The former option cuts about 1.5 miles off the hike but is not for the nervous hiker; a 50-foot security rope is recommended. The latter option enables you to spot another good-sized arch, located one bay past the Pollock Bench junction.

COLORADO RIVER: NORTH OF MOAB

Between Grand Junction and Moab, the Colorado River carves a series of magnificent canyons, including placid Horsethief and Ruby, turbulent Westwater, and **Professor Valley**, featured here. Containing both flat- and whitewater sections, the run through Professor Valley is the bread and butter of Moab-based rafting companies.

From Grand Junction, head west on Interstate 70, which parallels the desolate-looking **Book Cliffs**, the longest escarpment in the world at 250 miles. Take exit 204 to UT 128, a classic among desert roads. After traversing a bleak plateau, this scenic byway dips to cross the river. Next to the modern **Dewey Bridge** stand the remains of its one-lane wooden predecessor, which was consumed by fire in 2008. Soon the

Bighorn sheep abound on the lower slopes of Colorado National Monument.

cloud-covered **La Sal Mountains** come into view. The road follows the river to Moab, 47 miles from I-70. Many official campgrounds line the river's east bank.

Whether by car or boat, the trip provides a textbook lesson in Four Corners geology. Most of the way, Chinle slopes and Wingate cliffs predominate, dipping beneath the earth's surface just north of Moab, to be succeeded by Navajo Sandstone bluffs.

All trails described below are reached easily from Moab, this chapter's other hub. Just look for mile markers along UT 128, north of town.

18. Fisher Towers

Moderate 4.5-mile out-and-back; allow 2.5 hours
Map: Trails Illustrated 500: Moab North

GETTING THERE: From Moab, take US Route 191 north for about 3 miles to UT 128. Turn right here, driving though the river canyon north of town. Around milepost 21 the brick-colored Fisher Towers loom. Locate a dirt road to the right, which ends in 2 miles at a parking lot and primitive campground.

ON THE TRAIL: The trail starts to the right of a kiosk. After crossing a shallow canyon, it gradually ascends, snaking alongside a series of fluted monoliths composed of

Moenkopi Sandstone atop Cutler mudstone and conglomerate. Iron oxides account for the tint of the rock. Knockout views prevail along the entire route. To the west is Professor Valley; to the south are the maroon cliffs of labyrinthine **Onion Creek**. The base of the tallest free-standing monolith in the US, the **Titan** (900 feet), is a mile up the trail. These pinnacles have become popular with climbers, despite the crumbly rock of which they are composed. Often you can spot adventurers scaling the ethereal **Ancient Art** pinnacle, lower down.

Not far past the Titan, negotiate a downclimb with the aid of a short metal ladder. Once the trail tops out after a 975-foot ascent, it swings right onto a promontory. The grand finale is a panoramic overlook of Onion Creek and environs. Sage-green gypsum hills (known as the "Gypsqueeze") frame the chocolate hoodoos that line the creek, making them pop.

NEARBY: To visit **Onion Creek narrows**, take the four-wheel-drive-vehicle road heading east off UT 128 at milepost 20, signed for Onion Creek, which fords the usually

The collapse of this E.T. doppelgänger in 2014 offers a textbook lesson in topographic impermanence.

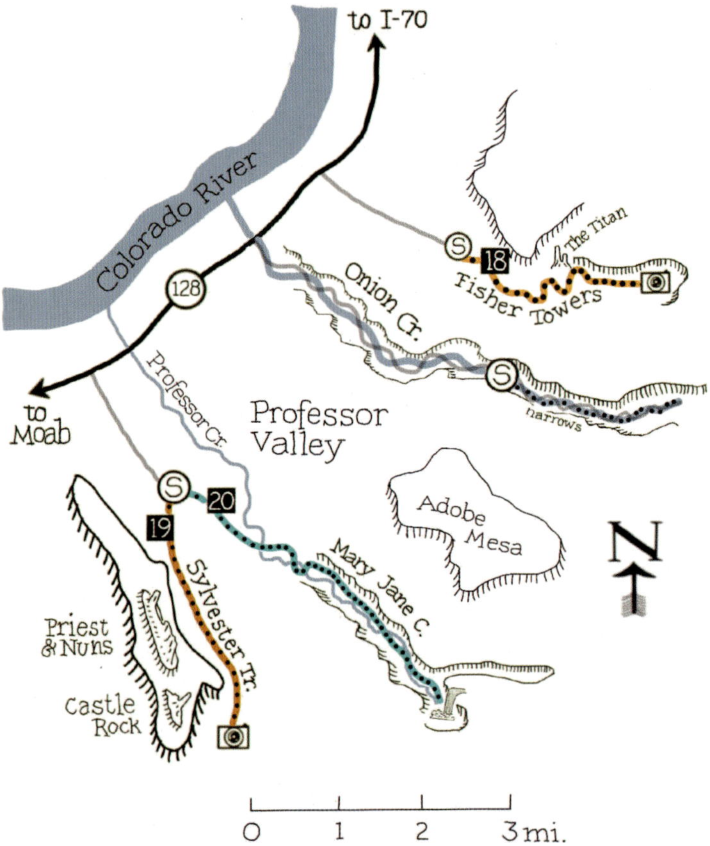

shallow creek numerous times. Enter the narrows on foot from a pullout at mile 3, shortly before the road crosses a bridge, and exit after about a mile, when the road rejoins the canyon floor.

The **Amphitheater Trail**, a moderate 2.75-mile loop, starts across UT 128 from Hittle Bottom Campground near milepost 23. Hike in a counterclockwise direction, taking time to explore a narrow canyon before the trail swings sharply left to scale a ridge.

19. Sylvester Trail

Moderate 6.5-mile out-and-back; allow 3 hours
Map: Trails Illustrated 500: Moab North

GETTING THERE: From Moab, take US Route 191 north for about 3 miles. Turn right onto UT 128. Just north of milepost 18, turn right onto a dirt road signed "Ranch Road, Dead End." Drive for 2 miles to a parking area. The road deteriorates somewhat in the last 0.25 mile but almost any vehicle should be able to go the distance. A kiosk marks the start of the trail.

ON THE TRAIL: The trail takes its name from Professor Sylvester Richardson, who homesteaded here with his wife, Mary Jane, in the 1880s. Professor Valley, the wide amphitheater that defines this part of the river canyon, also pays homage to him.

Prolific mule ears provide foreground interest to the Priest and Nuns buttes.

Winding through the brick-red Cutler Formation, the well-engineered trail passes beneath iconic Wingate Sandstone buttes called the **Priest and Nuns** on its 800-foot ascent to the aerie between **Castle Rock** (a.k.a. Castleton Tower) on the right and **Adobe Mesa** on the left. The first mile is largely flat, with multiple crossings of a Professor Creek tributary. The second mile traverses rolling terrain.

The climb begins in earnest after you cross a fenceline at mile 2. Expect some trail erosion and mild exposure as you near the top. You often see, or more likely hear, rock climbers in this vicinity. Although the maintained trail ends at an overlook that may disappoint those who hoped to peer into Castle Valley, it delivers bang-up views of the La Sal Mountains, which look their best when dusted with snow. From here, unmaintained paths descend to intersect jeep tracks to the south. Beware of scree as slippery as ball bearings on the return trip.

20. Mary Jane Canyon

Easy 9-mile out-and-back; allow 4.5 hours
River shoes recommended
Map: Trails Illustrated 500: Moab North

GETTING THERE: From Moab, take US Route 191 about 3 miles north to the junction of UT 128. Turn right here and proceed about 18 miles. Here, turn right (east) onto a dirt road signed "Ranch Road, Dead End." Drive for 2 miles to a parking area. The road deteriorates somewhat in the last 0.25 mile. A kiosk marks the start of the trail.

ON THE TRAIL: The hike up Mary Jane Canyon (a.k.a. Professor Creek), which ends at a double waterfall, allows exploration of one of the few non-technical slots in the Moab area. Because the route follows a streamcourse, the hike is best reserved for the low-water season of autumn, when the cottonwoods turn gold.

From the parking lot, head north, bypassing the first branch of the stream and crossing a low ridge to enter the second. Turn right to follow the canyon upstream and be treated to intimate views of the spires that separate Professor and Castle Valleys. At about mile 4 the canyon narrows. The twin falls, separated by a chockstone, are located where the canyon boxes up.

21. Morning Glory Bridge

Moderate 4.5-mile out-and-back; allow 2.5 hours
Map: Trails Illustrated 500: Moab North

GETTING THERE: From Moab, drive north about 3 miles on US Route 191. Turn right onto UT 128 and continue for 3 miles to the marked parking lot for the **Grandstaff Trailhead**, on the right side of the road.

ON THE TRAIL: Formerly known as Negro Bill, this lush canyon derives its name from William Grandstaff, a cowboy of African American and Native American descent who lived here in the late 19th century. The trail begins to the left of the perennial stream. Consult the map corresponding to the Slickrock Bike Trail (Hike 46, page 168).

At about mile 1.75, where the canyon curves left, leave the main drainage and enter the second side drainage on the right. The path ends at a chamber housing **Morning Glory Bridge**, a vaulting 250-foot Navajo Sandstone span. Underneath, find a small pool created by a seep spring. Beware of poison ivy, which thrives in this moist, shady environment. Ambitious hikers can explore farther up the main canyon, which extends for some 10 miles toward its origins in the La Sal Mountains.

NEARBY: Immediately north of the Grandstaff parking lot on UT 128, locate the **Porcupine Rim** trailhead. This shared-use pathway connecting the river corridor with the Sand Flats area is popular with mountain bikers. Initially paralleling the river, it gradually ascends on ledges, providing cross-canyon views into Arches National Park.

COLORADO RIVER: SOUTH OF MOAB

Two roads hug the banks of the Colorado River after it cuts across Moab Valley. The Potash Road (UT 279), on the river's west side, ultimately connects to the white-knuckle Shafer Trail, which slithers up to the Island in the Sky. Kane Creek Boulevard parallels the river to the east before ascending Kane Creek, a Colorado tributary. Invigorating trails strike off from each of these roads.

22. Poison Spider Loop

Moderate 3-mile loop, with scrambling; allow 2 hours
Map: Trails Illustrated 501: Moab South

GETTING THERE: From Moab, drive north on US Route 191 about 1.5 miles past the bridge over the Colorado River. Turn left onto UT 279 and reset your trip odometer. At mile 2.75, the road enters **The Portal**, where the river abandons Moab (a.k.a. Spanish) Valley to entrench itself again in a deep canyon. Beyond several pullouts for viewing petroglyphs, you will see a sign for the Poison Spider Trailhead on the right at mile 5.75. Park at the far end of the lot.

ON THE TRAIL: This trip offers myriad attractions. Begin at a kiosk near the outhouse. Paint splotches and occasional cairns mark the route. Almost immediately you arrive at a junction. Turn right and ascend to the base of the cliffs to inspect dinosaur tracks and petroglyphs. Then continue left to rejoin the main stem of the trail. You soon reach a small jug-handle arch. To its left, iron rungs drilled into the slickrock help you ascend to the next level. This move may prove challenging to some.

At about mile 0.5, the trail comes within spitting distance of the Poison Spider jeep road, which you later will follow back to the parking lot. For now, continue on a northward trajectory, alternating between surfaces of rock and sand. The trail curves right at mile 1 to enter a canyon, which narrows to form a rocky chute. Soon, you spot **Longbow Arch** on the left. The trail goes slightly past it before doubling back underneath. The span, a wall-arch, measures 100 feet across.

Retrace your steps until you arrive at the point closest to the jeep road. Veer right a bit to drop down to it. As the road winds down the cliff, feast your eyes on the canyon of the Colorado River and the **Behind the Rocks Wilderness Study Area** on its opposite bank.

23. Corona and Bowtie Arches

Moderate 3-mile out-and-back; allow 2 hours
Map: Trails Illustrated 501: Moab South

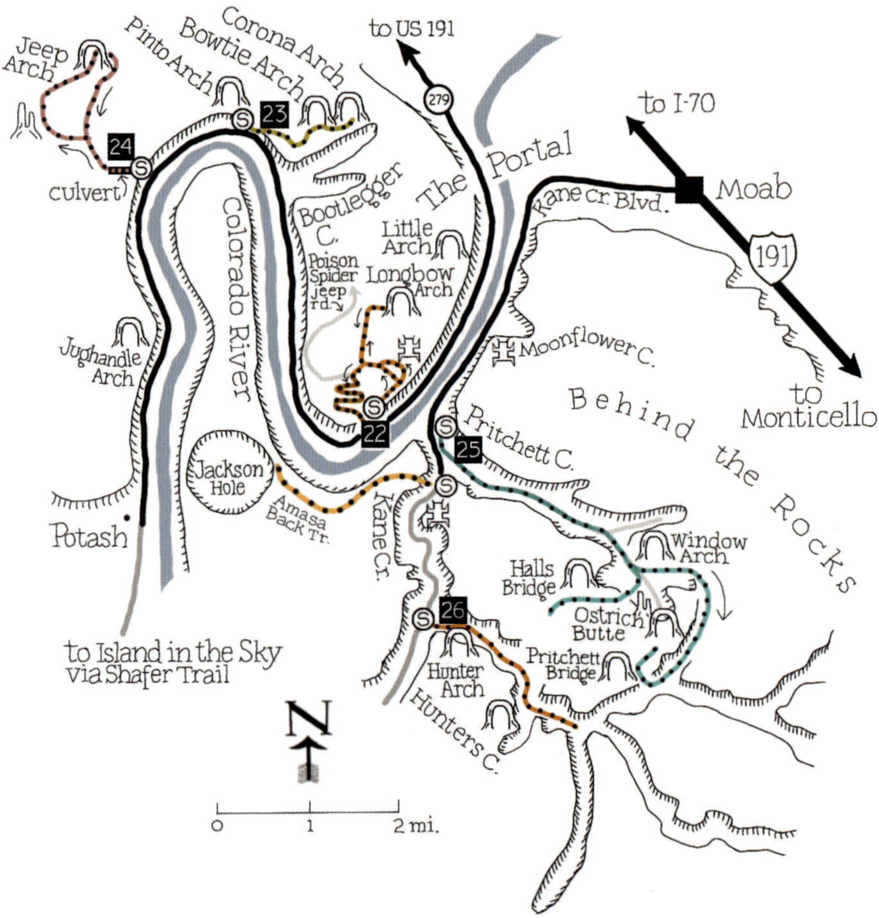

GETTING THERE: From Moab, drive north on US Route 191 about 1.5 miles past the bridge over the Colorado River. Turn left onto UT 279. Drive 10 miles to a parking lot on the right.

ON THE TRAIL: Formed from the weathering of a fin, Corona is also known as Little Rainbow because it resembles famous Rainbow Bridge on the Utah-Arizona border (see Chapter 6, Hike 38). Nearby Bowtie Arch is the cherry on top.

The extremely popular trail ascends a steep embankment to cross railroad tracks. **Pinto Arch** is remotely visible in the distance to your left. Beyond the tracks, pass through a hiker maze. The trail goes to the right of a shallow gorge, climbing gradually while heading left toward golden cliffs. It contours to the right and rounds a bend. At a small scallop in the cliff, wire cables, carved-out footholds, and a ladder help you negotiate rough spots.

From the top of the ladder, two gigantic spans come into view. **Bowtie** is the "potty" arch at the midpoint of the amphitheater, while **Corona** dominates the bowl's far end. Poetry in stone, **Corona** measures almost 150 feet across. Dizzying views into Bootlegger Canyon are yours from its base.

24. Jeep Arch

Moderate 4-mile lollipop loop, with scrambling; allow 2.5 hours
Map: Trails Illustrated 501: Moab South

GETTING THERE: From Moab, drive north on US Route 191 about 1.5 miles past the bridge over the Colorado River. Turn left onto UT 279. Drive for 10.25 miles, stopping at a pullout on the left.

ON THE TRAIL: Culvert Canyon's Jeep Arch provides an attractive alternative to the Corona-Bowtie trail when (as often) the latter is overrun. You gain about 500 feet of elevation on the cairned loop.

Begin by passing through an enormous culvert. On the culvert's far end, a path on the left ascends briskly to railroad tracks used to transport potash from mine to market. Walk along the tracks for a short distance, then cross them to meet a cairned trail leading to a slickrock bench above the canyon. From here you enjoy wonderful views across the river toward the Navajo Sandstone domes of Behind the Rocks WSA.

Continue to climb gradually to the 1.25-mile mark, where a sign indicates the start of the loop. Here the trail forks. You will return to this fork later by means of the lower route. For now, take the higher route on the left, scrambling steeply toward the

Hikers admire the view through Jeep Arch.

base of a sandstone tower that resembles a chess piece. Drink in expansive vistas from the pass. At this point your natural inclination may be to follow the ramp on the right side of the tower, but doing so would lead you astray. Instead, locate cairns that direct you across a valley toward another ridge.

When the trail curves around to the right at mile 1.5, Jeep Arch comes into view, the genesis of its name immediately obvious. A path to the left of the span winds between boulders to reach its opening at mile 1.75. Wide ledges on either side of the arch provide a relaxing perch. On the far side of the arch, drop down to pick up the ledgy lower trail at mile 2.75 to complete the loop.

25. Pritchett Canyon

Moderate 11-mile out-and-back, with routefinding and scrambling; allow 6 hours

Map: Trails Illustrated 501: Moab South

GETTING THERE: From downtown Moab, drive south on US Route 191 for about a mile and turn right at a traffic light onto Kane Creek Boulevard, which soon parallels the Colorado. Follow this road for about 4.5 miles, parking opposite the canyon mouth. The owner of the land at the mouth charges a modest entry fee.

ON THE TRAIL: Cutting through the bread-loaf domes of **Behind the Rocks**, Pritchett Canyon owes much of its charm to three major arches. On weekends in season, you may encounter thrill-seekers trying to negotiate one of Moab's most notorious jeep trails.

Begin by walking a dirt track toward the canyon's head, passing several side-canyons on the left. At about mile 2, the road forks. The main trail bears right, but a 0.25-mile detour down the left fork reveals a small natural bridge.

At about mile 3, the road crosses a weathered fin separating two branches of the canyon. **Window Arch**, with its huge triangular opening, occupies this fin. As you drop back down, the road forks again near distinctive **Ostrich Butte**.

To visit Halls Bridge, turn right here and then take another right, passing the roads that access Pritchett Canyon's upper reaches. The route you want heads back downcanyon a short distance, closely following the rim. When it ends, pick up a faint path into the left fork of the first side-canyon on the left. The path can be dicey, especially where it ascends a slickrock slot to avoid a pour-off. Continue on for a few hundred yards until muscular **Halls Bridge** (really an arch) appears in the fin to your right. You can climb up the cleft at the head of the side-canyon and cautiously work your way beneath the arch from the back.

Hikers with excellent orienteering skills can proceed cross-country over slickrock terraces to Pritchett Bridge, but the more common route involves backtracking to the jeep road between the Ostrich and Window Arch. Follow this road up the canyon to a pass, and then descend into upper **Hunters Canyon**, which runs parallel to a massive escarpment. In the valley, after approaching an isolated obelisk and a small arch, the road crosses a wash twice, forking at the second crossing. Go right here and follow the spur to its end under the cliffs. Pritchett Bridge, one of the region's largest spans, appears on the ridge to the right.

A cairn indicates the obscure footpath that ascends through a notch behind a split column of sandstone. Once on top of the mesa, bear right, contouring around the base of the cliff into a hanging side-canyon. Within the next 0.25 mile you spot a cave and a pothole arch. The trail peters out except for an occasional marker. Continue straight ahead. Near the far end of the hanging side-canyon, **Pritchett Bridge** peeks out from behind a slickrock mass. Climb the slope to get underneath this classically beautiful span. Follow the side-canyon to an overlook of Pritchett Canyon.

NEARBY: A bit farther down Kane Creek Blvd., at mile 6, is the start of a multi-use trail to **Amasa Back**, a thumb of land jutting out into the middle of the river. Park here or at the large lot on the right at mile 5.5. Before setting out, look across the canyon to locate a prominent alcove. A unique **owl petroglyph** sits just to the left of its base. You can access the panel from a dodgy path that departs a few switchbacks after the initial stream crossing and veers right after topping out. Back on the main trail, a gradual climb of about 1000 feet presents jaw-dropping views of the La Sal Mountains and the domes of Behind the Rocks.

26. Hunters Canyon

Easy 6-mile out-and-back; allow 3 hours
Map: Trails Illustrated 501: Moab South

GETTING THERE: From downtown Moab head south on US 191 and turn right onto Kane Creek Boulevard. Continue about 8 miles to a parking area at its sandy mouth.

ON THE TRAIL: The narrow, watery gorge of **Hunters Canyon** contains several spans, including unusual **Hunter Arch** at 0.5 mile and an unnamed beauty up a significant side-canyon on the right at about mile 2. Past this point, progress is hampered by heavy brush. Hikers who persist will reach a pour-off 3 miles above the canyon mouth, complete with a pool and a small natural bridge.

ARCHES NATIONAL PARK

Located about 4 miles north of Moab off US Route 191, the slickrock nirvana that is Arches occupies a rolling plateau above the canyon of the Colorado. It is celebrated for fins and towers, balanced rocks, petrified sand dunes, and over two thousand spans and windows, all formed by the action of ice, water, and gravity on Entrada Sandstone. An 18-mile scenic drive bisects the park, providing access to this treasure trove. A seasonal timed-entry system has been in effect since 2022; consult the park website for current information.

27. Park Avenue

Easy 1-mile point-to-point; allow 30 minutes
Shuttling vehicles or backtracking required
Map: Trails Illustrated 211: Arches National Park

GETTING THERE: The trail starts at an overlook to the left of the road 2 miles past the visitor center and concludes at the Courthouse Towers pullout, to the right of the road about 1.25 miles farther on. With two cars, position one at each end of the hike.

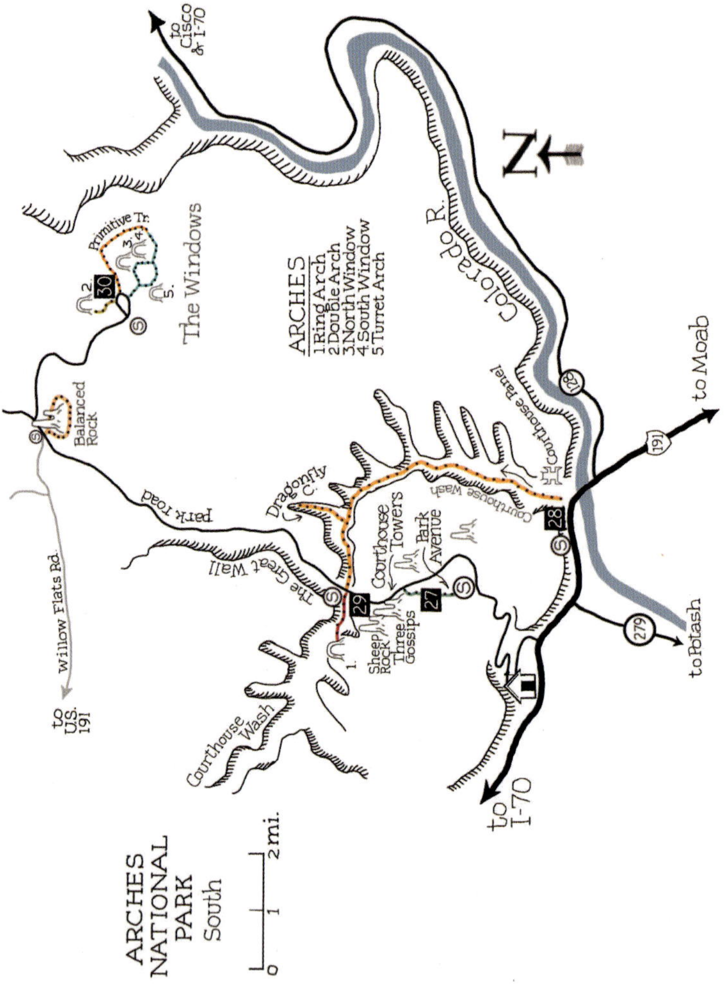

ON THE TRAIL: This leisurely stroll introduces visitors to the wonders of Arches National Park. Descending 325 feet toward Courthouse Wash and its massive buttes, you walk between cliffs topped by wafers of Entrada Sandstone reminiscent of Egyptian bas-relief. **Nefertiti Rock** and "the Fudgesicle" greet you near the top of the hike on the left, while **Sheep Rock**, the **Three Gossips**, and **the Organ** anchor the lower end.

28. Lower Courthouse Wash

Moderate 6.5-mile point-to-point, including spur, with exposure; allow 3 hours

Shuttling vehicles or equivalent required; trekking poles and river shoes recommended

Map: Trails Illustrated 211: Arches National Park

GETTING THERE: Using two vehicles, drive north from Moab on US Route 191, crossing the Colorado River bridge and passing the mouth of Courthouse Wash. About 0.25 mile beyond that point, locate a large parking area on the right, but keep driving. Because the route through the canyon is easier to follow from the bottom, take both vehicles into the park. Leave one vehicle at the hike's terminus at the bridge over Courthouse Wash, about 4.5 miles from the visitor center. Then, using the second vehicle, return to the US 191 parking area to begin the hike.

ON THE TRAIL: Relatively few visitors explore this serene canyon with its lush, perennial watercourse. Its crescendo occurs in the fall, when frost has killed off insects and turned the cottonwoods a lustrous gold.

Follow a sidewalk to the canyon mouth. Pick up an intermittent trail that begins on the far side of the creek, heading upstream between orange Navajo Sandstone cliffs. Cross the creek at mile 0.25 to avoid a beaver pond. About 0.75 mile in, bypass a marshy area that may contain quicksand by means of a faint, exposed trail above the left bank. Be extra careful here!

The canyon widens in the next few miles, becoming easier to negotiate. You will pass three side-canyons on the right at half-mile intervals starting at about mile 3. Shortly thereafter, the canyon forks, with the main stem of Courthouse on the left and black-walled **Dragonfly Canyon** on the right. Take time to explore this exceptional slot for about 0.5 mile until it boxes up. You may spot climbers rappelling down the pour-off at the canyon's head.

Returning to Courthouse Wash, continue hiking for about 0.75 mile, skirting more beaver dams that have created shallow pools. Where the canyon widens and bends to the left, look for an unofficial trail up a steep embankment on the opposite side, which will cross a sandy area and take you to your car near the Courthouse Towers formations of Sheep Rock and the Three Gossips. If you should miss this cutoff, continue to the bridge over the wash and exit on the far side.

NEARBY: Between the bottom of Courthouse Wash and the Colorado River bridge, look for the **Courthouse Panel** on the cliff face paralleling the highway. Bighorn sheep frequent this area.

29. Ring Arch

Moderate 4-mile out-and-back, with routefinding; allow 2 hours
Map: Trails Illustrated 211: Arches National Park

GETTING THERE: From the Arches visitor center, follow the park road 4.5 miles to the bridge over Courthouse Wash. Park at the large pullout on the left.

ON THE TRAIL: One of the park's loveliest spans, Ring Arch receives little press, probably because it lacks an official trail. The hike works best in early spring, before the willows leaf out.

Begin on a social trail on the northwest side of the bridge (not the one signed with a climbing symbol). Within about 0.25 mile the trail passes a boulder field before crossing the drainage. When the path fades out, veer farther left into an overflow channel, which contains less brush.

The arroyo walls quickly deepen. At about mile 1.25 the cliffs on your right sport a pair of "eye sockets." A few minutes thereafter, enter a substantial side-canyon on the left and follow it about 0.5 mile, first over sand and later over slickrock. Where the slickrock bottom ends, climb out of the by-now shallow wash on the right side and spot the arch straight ahead. Work your way underneath on the left for a superior view.

30. The Windows

Easy cumulative 1.5-mile loop and out-and-back; allow 1.5 hours
Map: Trails Illustrated 211: Arches National Park

GETTING THERE: Reach the popular Windows section by turning right onto a paved spur road 9 miles from the visitor center.

ON THE TRAIL: Short, well-groomed paths lead to several major arches. The trail to **Double Arch** is an out-and-back, but your visit to the others can be completed as a loop. Start by ascending on stairs to the **North Window**. Scramble gingerly up the rocks on the left behind the span, if you wish, for a "framed" view of **Turret Arch**.

Past North Window, pick up the spur to Turret Arch before returning to the main trail, which descends to **South Window**. Here it meets a cairned Primitive Trail back to the parking lot. This trail rounds the cliffs, enabling you to view both windows

Delicate Arch frames the snowcapped La Sal Mountains. *(photo by Bryce Hinchman)*

from the back side. Preferring slickrock, the route remains fairly level, except where it crosses a steep, low ridge.

NEARBY: To the right of the park road just before the Windows spur, an easy 0.25-mile trail encircles **Balanced Rock**. At both of its ends, the trail is paved.

31. Delicate Arch

Moderate 3-mile out-and-back; allow 2 hours
Map: Trails Illustrated 211: Arches National Park

GETTING THERE: From the visitor center, drive 11.5 miles north on the park road to a signed junction. Turn right and proceed about 1.5 miles to the parking lot.

ON THE TRAIL: This freestanding beauty perfectly frames the La Sal Mountains. For that reason, it originally was known as Landscape Arch, but a cartographer confused the two names, and the changes stuck. Because Delicate Arch is the park's signature feature, expect to join a veritable conga line of pilgrims along this trail.

The trail begins near **Wolfe Ranch**, a pioneer cabin. Crossing a bridge over **Salt Wash**, it twists through Morrison Formation badlands to the base of a massive slick-rock ramp. Ascend briskly, following cairns. At the top, the trail enters a gully, which it follows to a ledge of Entrada Sandstone on the right. Contouring up this ledge toward a large "potty" arch, it passes a window that affords a tantalizing glimpse of the iconic span. **Delicate Arch** occupies a steep-sided bowl just around the corner. It is easy to work your way underneath.

On the return, detour to visit a Ute **petroglyph panel** near the Salt Wash bridge. For a different perspective on the arch, drive past the Wolfe Ranch parking area to the end of the spur road and continue on foot to a viewpoint.

32. Fiery Furnace

Moderate 2-mile loop, with routefinding and scrambling; allow 3 hours
Permit required; ranger-led tour recommended
Map: Trails Illustrated 211: Arches National Park

GETTING THERE: The parking circle is off a short spur to the right of the park road at about mile 14.5.

ON THE TRAIL: The route through this redrock labyrinth is all but impossible to describe. While some people hike the **Furnace** independently, aided by occasional trail markers, visitors are well-advised to take a guided tour on their first time through. Even if you manage not to get lost amid narrow passageways and exposed perches, you are likely to miss special attractions, including massive **Surprise and Skull (a.k.a. Twin) Arches** and two charming natural bridges. For many, traversing the Furnace's chutes and ladders is the highlight of a trip to Arches, though claustrophobes and acrophobes alike may prefer to sit this one out.

33. Four Arches Loop

Easy 3.5-mile lollipop loop; allow 2 hours
Map: Trails Illustrated 211: Arches National Park

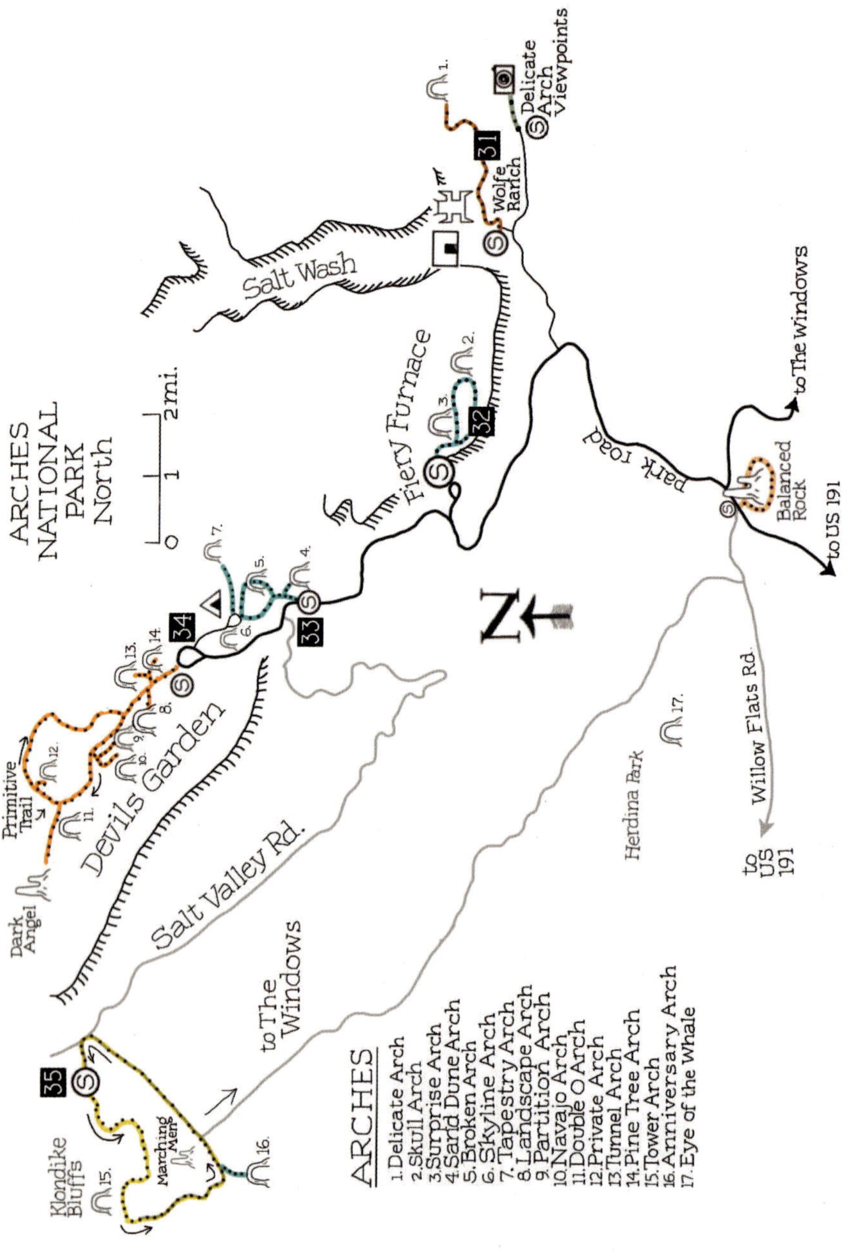

GETTING THERE: Travel 16.5 miles up the main road from the visitor center. Park in the lot on the right, marked for Sand Dune Arch.

ON THE TRAIL: Winding through the upper Fiery Furnace is a route connecting four distinctive spans. Near the start, a short spur on the right passes through fins to delightful **Sand Dune Arch**, which has dunes at its base. Returning to the main trail, cross the meadow. At the first intersection, veer to the right (later you will return on the left-hand trail) and continue to **Broken Arch**, named somewhat misleadingly after its characteristic fracture. Clamber through the opening to the other side to continue the hike.

At about mile 2.5, take a spur on the right to **Tapestry Arch**, located in a fin. With care you can work your way underneath the arch. Its walls, as you might notice, are coated with streaks of desert varnish. Back on the main path, you reach the campground at mile 3. To inspect **Skyline Arch**, turn right onto the campground road and walk to the rear of the amphitheater where rangers give nightly talks in season.

Backtrack down the campground road, locating the continuation of your trail between campsites 51 and 52. The path leads up and through a scenic fin canyon on its way to the meadow, where it closes the loop.

34. Devils Garden

Moderate 5-mile out-and-back or 6-mile lollipop loop, plus spurs, with exposure and scrambling; allow 3–4 hours

Map: Trails Illustrated 211: Arches National Park

GETTING THERE: Drive to the end of the park road and park in the large lot. A kiosk marks the trailhead.

ON THE TRAIL: This much-traveled network of trails gives access to seven major arches. The hike offers several variations. Most people turn around at Landscape Arch. Wide and well-groomed to this point, thereafter the route becomes more challenging by several orders of magnitude, involving traverses of slickrock domes and occasional exposure.

From the trailhead, walk between tall fins to intersect a spur on the right at mile 0.5. The spur soon divides, with one fork leading to **Pine Tree Arch** and the other to **Tunnel Arch**. All spurs along the route come highly recommended.

The main trail leads to enormous but fragile **Landscape Arch** at mile 1: the world's fifth longest, at 290 feet across. Rockfalls have forced the Park Service to fence off the zone beneath it. Originally known as Delicate Arch, Landscape received its current name as the result of a mapmaker's blunder.

From here, carefully ascend a rugged slickrock fin, following cairns. On the right, notice debris from Wall Arch, which collapsed in 2008. A worthwhile 0.25-mile spur to the left goes to both **Navajo and Partition Arches**.

Past the spur, the trail stays mostly on rock. Stop at the signed overlook for **Fin Canyon**, where you can pick out **Black Arch** in the distance. Directly underfoot lies yet another natural span. From here, the trail swings left, climbing atop fins. Carefully descending the last of these, continue up a sandy wash to **Double O Arch** at mile 2, consisting of a large opening stacked atop a smaller one.

At a nearby junction, two decisions confront you. First, you must choose whether or not to take a side trip (0.5 mile each way) to rocket-shaped **Dark Angel** monolith, visible on the horizon. Second, you must choose between retracing your steps to the parking lot or returning on the **Primitive Trail** through lovely Fin Canyon, which adds 1 mile to the trip. Except for a seasonal pool that must be avoided, this loop is only marginally more difficult than the regular route, with ladders or logs facilitating

Spindly Marching Men preside over the trail to Tower Arch.

steep descents; it hops several fins and provides access to **Private Arch** by means of a 0.25-mile spur. In its last mile the trail crosses an undulating sandy expanse before rejoining the main pathway near Landscape Arch.

35. Klondike Bluffs

Moderate 3.5-mile out-and-back or 6-mile loop; allow 2 hours for the out-and-back, 4 hours for the loop

Map: Trails Illustrated 211: Arches National Park

GETTING THERE: Reach this unspoiled destination from the park road by turning west onto dirt Salt Valley Rd. near Skyline Arch, 17 miles from the visitor center. The road, generally easy to navigate but impassable when wet, runs the length of its namesake **Salt Valley**. The turnoff to the Klondike Bluffs parking lot is about 8 miles up the road, on the left.

ON THE TRAIL: The trail begins just left of the parking lot. It rapidly ascends a bluff, treating hikers to glorious views of the Fiery Furnace and Devils Garden. Then it veers to the right between widely spaced rock walls, descending slowly toward a drainage. Look for an unnamed arch on the left near the low point.

Crossing the wash, the trail climbs a sandy hill past the **Marching Men** and then bears right and continues for about 0.25 mile. A signed spur on the left extends 0.25 mile to **Tower Arch Road**, a jeep track. At this junction, **Tower Arch** comes into view in a fin. An enormous pinnacle next to the arch lends its name to the noble span. On the arch's abutment is an inscription carved by Alexander Ringhoffer, a founding father of what was then Arches National Monument. Just 100 yards to the south, in another fin, is an unnamed double arch.

Either return the way you came or loop back on Tower Arch Road, adding 2.5 miles to the trip. The latter option allows you to visit **Anniversary Arch** (GPS coordinates: 38.46305°N, 109.4051°W). To reach this double span, follow the cairned trail to the jeep road. Turn left and walk down the road about 1.25 miles to where it descends and turns sharply left. Almost immediately the road begins to climb steeply over slickrock. Just before reaching the slickrock, enter a shallow wash on the right. After about 30 yards, the wash bends to the left and an obscure tributary enters on the right. Go up the tributary, where you will find a clear social trail leading directly to Anniversary Arch (about 0.25 mile round trip from the jeep road). The arch cuts through a fin that sports what looks like a graduation cap. If you walk around the fin, you can appreciate the arch from the other side as well. When finished there, return to the jeep track and proceed to its junction with the Salt Valley Road. Go left and follow signs to the Klondike Bluffs parking lot.

CANYONLANDS NATIONAL PARK: ISLAND IN THE SKY DISTRICT AND VICINITY

Rugged and magnificent, Canyonlands is three parks rolled into one. This preserve, which is divided into separate zones by the confluence of the Green and Colorado Rivers, includes some of the wildest land in the Lower 48. It has everything an adventurer could want, including turbulent whitewater, ancient rock art, canyons studded with ruins and arches, hair-raising jeep roads, and sweeping vistas of spires, buttes, and goosenecks.

The Island is joined to the rest of the plateau by a narrow isthmus. This high, rolling mesa, dotted with pinyons and junipers, drops precipitously to the **White Rim**, a terrace almost 1000 feet above the Green and Colorado Rivers. Trails are off either the main park road or a spur to the west near its end.

From Moab, drive 9 miles north on US Route 191 to the intersection of UT 313. Turn left here to access all trails in this section. About 10 miles farther you reach a fork. Take a left for Dead Horse Point State Park (4 miles) and a right for Canyonlands' **Island in the Sky** (4.5 miles).

36. South Fork of Sevenmile Canyon

Easy 4-mile out-and-back; allow 2 hours

Maps: Trails Illustrated 212: Canyonlands National Park/Island in the Sky or USGS: Merrimac Butte

GETTING THERE: From Moab, drive 9 miles north on US Route 191 to the intersection of UT 313. Drive south on UT 313, which follows the main fork of Sevenmile Canyon. At mile 2.5, locate a small pull-off on the right. Park here and pick up a short, steep trail on the other side of the road that leads toward the South Fork.

Winter comes to Dead Horse Point (Hike 37).

ON THE TRAIL: Rock art aficionados will enjoy three unique Barrier Canyon–style panels in a shallow, plain-vanilla canyon that otherwise is noteworthy only as a tumbleweed graveyard. After dropping down from the road, bear right and proceed along a fence to the hiker's maze against the cliffs. Just past the maze take note of some standard-issue petroglyphs on the right wall before descending into the sandy wash. All the good stuff is on the canyon's left side.

At mile 0.5, you come to a cottonwood grove on the left where the canyon pinches in. Immediately past the grove is a short drainage. Walk up this drainage to its end, clambering up boulders, to see the first collection of pictographs, about 15 feet above you on a narrow, exposed ledge.

Continue up the South Fork. A major side-canyon enters from the left at mile 1. Look for a social trail leading to a shallow, ground-level alcove on the left at mile 1.5. The alcove has a deeper recess on its right side. This recess houses the second panel, featuring a petroglyph that may depict fish bones.

At mile 2, a second major side-canyon comes in from the right. It has a gigantic, clefted boulder at its mouth. A mirror image boulder lies just opposite on South Fork's left side. Behind that boulder is a wide ledge about 15 feet above the canyon floor. Climb onto this ledge and follow it to the right for about 50 yards. The third panel is just above this point, near a rockfall. It consists of a lone polychrome figure that epitomizes stylistic elegance.

Shortly past this panel the canyon is roped off. A tall, vase-like anthropomorph adorns the left wall.

NEARBY: On the cliffs adjacent to the parking lot, find two more rock art panels at about eye level: the **TV Sheep** petroglyphs on the right and the faint **Intestine Man** pictograph on the left.

Continue driving south on UT 313. Ascending the switchbacks, stop at **Monitor and Merrimac Overlook**, which affords commanding views of a pair of Entrada Sandstone buttes. From a large pullout on the right at the foot of the switchbacks, 0.5 mile beyond the mouth of South Fork, experienced route-finders can hike cross-country to these buttes, then execute a figure-eight on the slickrock around them.

37. Dead Horse Loop

Easy 4-mile loop, plus spurs; allow 2 hours
Map: Trails Illustrated 212: Canyonlands National Park/Island in the Sky

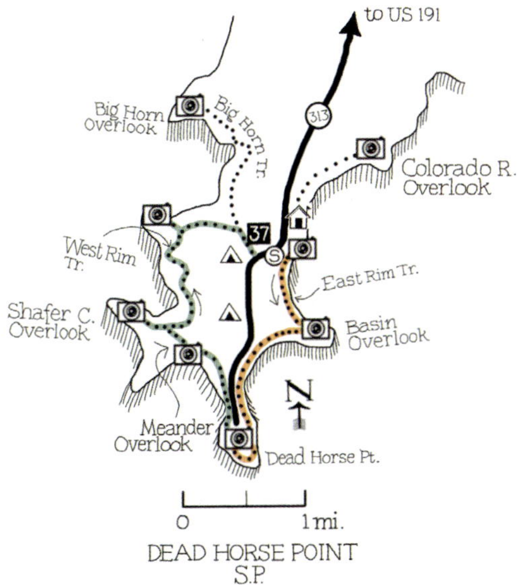

GETTING THERE: From Moab, drive north on US 191 for 9 miles to intersect UT 313. Turn left here. Continue 10 miles to a fork. Turn left, staying on UT 313, and enter **Dead Horse Point State Park**. The hike begins behind the visitor center.

ON THE TRAIL: Dead Horse Point, jutting out over the erosional basin of the Colorado River, connects to the main body of the mesa by an isthmus barely 30 yards wide. According to local legend, the point got its name when wild mustangs were rounded up there and accidentally left to die. The vista from the point, especially at sunset, is one of the most mesmerizing in all the Southwest, with the Colorado River executing a bowknot bend just below.

Dead Horse Point State Park offers a well-appointed campground and numerous short, easy trails popular among both hikers and mountain bikers. Reserved for foot traffic are the **Big Horn Overlook Trail** (2.5 miles out-and-back) and the East and West Rim Trails. These latter two extend from the visitor center to Dead Horse Point and back, for an invigorating loop.

Start out on the **East Rim Trail**, which hugs the edge of the mesa as it heads for Dead Horse Point, 1.5 miles distant. The terraced, turquoise pools visible far below are associated with a potash processing plant near the river. In the vicinity you can see the Long Canyon jeep track, connecting the Potash Road with the Shafer Trail. After feasting your eyes at **Dead Horse Point**, pick up the **West Rim Trail**, which returns you to the parking lot. Spurs along the way lead to overlooks.

38. Lathrop Trail

Difficult 12-mile out-and-back; allow 6–7 hours
Trekking poles recommended
Map: Trails Illustrated 212: Canyonlands National Park/Island in the Sky

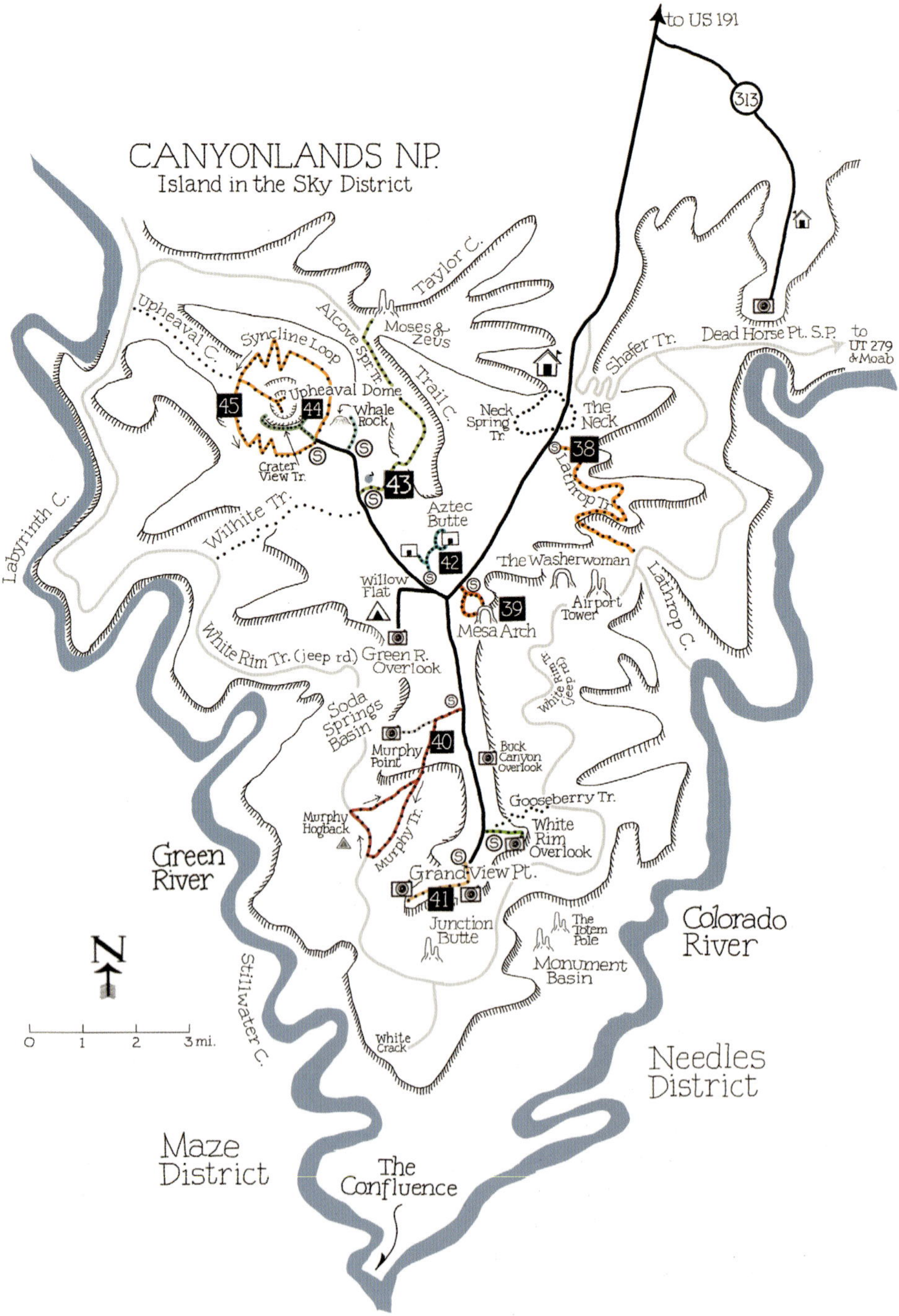

CANYONLANDS N.P.
Island in the Sky District
to US 191
313
Dead Horse Pt. S.P.
to UT 279 & Moab
Shafer Tr.
Taylor C.
Moses & Zeus
Alcove Spr. Tr.
Trail C.
Upheaval C.
Syncline Loop
Upheaval Dome
Whale Rock
Crater View Tr.
45
44
43
38
42
39
40
41
Neck Spring Tr.
The Neck
Lathrop Tr.
Lathrop C.
Wilhite Tr.
Aztec Butte
Willow Flat
The Washerwoman
Airport Tower
Mesa Arch
Labyrinth C.
White Rim Tr. (jeep rd)
Green R. Overlook
White Rim Tr. (jeep rd)
Soda Springs Basin
Murphy Point
Buck Canyon Overlook
Gooseberry Tr.
Murphy Hogback
Murphy Tr.
White Rim Overlook
Grand View Pt.
Green River
Junction Butte
The Totem Pole
Monument Basin
Colorado River
Stillwater C.
White Crack
Needles District
Maze District
The Confluence
N
0 1 2 3 mi.

GETTING THERE: From Moab, drive 9 miles north on US Route 191 to the intersection of UT 313. Turn left. About 10 miles farther you reach a fork. Take the right fork, and drive 4.5 miles to reach Canyonlands' Island in the Sky. From the Island in the Sky visitor center, drive 1.75 miles south. Park at the signed trailhead on the left side of the road.
ON THE TRAIL: The Lathrop Trail is the first of many that descend from the mesa top to the White Rim Trail, a favorite dirt road of mountain bikers and four-wheelers. Although shadeless and waterless, the Lathrop Trail has less elevation change than its counterparts and offers better views than most.

Start by crossing **Grays Pasture**, passing Navajo Sandstone domes on the way to the rim at mile 1.5. Descending somewhat, the trail contours to the right until reaching a rockslide that produced a break in the Wingate cliffs at mile 2.5. Although the trail's tight switchbacks appear intimidating, they were constructed to allow safe passage through the slide. At the bottom of the Chinle Formation, the trail follows a deteriorated prospecting road, passing an old mine on the left (dangerous: do not enter!) at mile 4.5. It then arrives at Moenkopi terraces that afford big views of a bend in the river. The whole area has a Grand Canyon feel about it.

At about mile 5.5, the trail leaves the jeep track and drops into a shallow wash. From here it is about another 0.5 mile to the White Rim Trail. The stunning **Airport Tower** butte defines this area. Individuals with backcountry permits may continue down **Lathrop Canyon** all the way to the river, for an extra 8 miles round trip. Allow 3 or 4 days for that adventure.

39. Mesa Arch

Very easy 0.5-mile loop; allow 30 minutes
Map: Trails Illustrated 212: Canyonlands National Park/Island in the Sky

GETTING THERE: From Moab, drive 9 miles north on US Route 191 to the intersection of UT 313. Turn left. About 10 miles from that junction, you reach a fork. Go right here, and drive 4.5 miles to reach Canyonlands' Island in the Sky. From the visitor center on the main park road, drive 5.75 miles south to a parking area on the left.
ON THE TRAIL: Walk counterclockwise on the nearly level loop trail to **Mesa Arch**, composed of Navajo Sandstone. The famous arch is poised on the edge of a 500-foot drop-off into Buck Canyon, which cuts down another 700 feet to the White Rim. It frames **The Washerwoman**, a distinctive butte enclosing a small window. At dawn, the arch attracts photographers like flies, so expect to wait in line to take your shot.

40. Murphy Trail

Difficult 10.75-mile lollipop loop; allow 6 hours
Trekking poles recommended
Map: Trails Illustrated 212: Canyonlands National Park/Island in the Sky

GETTING THERE: From Moab, drive 9 miles north on US Route 191 to the intersection of UT 313. Turn left. About 10 miles from that junction, you reach a fork. Bear right, and drive 4.5 miles to reach Canyonlands' Island in the Sky. From the visitor center, drive south on the park road 8.5 miles. Turn right onto a dirt road signed for **Murphy Point** overlook. Park here.

ON THE TRAIL: The trail begins by following the jeep road. Where it forks, bear left (a right would take you to Murphy Point) and continue to its end at mile 1. Strike out toward the rim of the canyon and cut across Kayenta Formation ledges, dropping about 100 feet to a break in the Wingate cliffs. The next mile of trail, though carefully constructed, traverses rocky, precipitous terrain. Low masonry walls minimize the risk of injury, and a footbridge helps you across a chasm. Plunging through the Wingate in a knee-busting 750-foot descent, the trail deposits you at its base. At the fork, go left; you'll return via the other path.

The trail follows the canyon bottom for a few miles, slowly descending until it intersects the **White Rim Trail**, a jeep road that contours around the base of the Island in the Sky. Turn right here and road-walk to the top of **Murphy Hogback**. Anticipate outstanding views, particularly as you peer into Soda Springs Basin to the north.

Next, leave the jeep road to rejoin the Murphy Trail. From here to the cliff base, the trail is level and the scenery sublime. Take a rest before tackling the grueling climb back to the rim.

41. Grand View Trail

Easy 2-mile out-and-back; allow 1 hour

Map: Trails Illustrated 212: Canyonlands National Park/Island in the Sky

GETTING THERE: From Moab, drive 9 miles north on US Route 191 to the intersection of UT 313. Turn left here. About 10 miles from that junction, you reach a fork. Take the right fork, and drive 4.5 miles to reach Canyonlands' Island in the Sky. Drive to the tip of the Island and park in the spacious lot.

ON THE TRAIL: At the southernmost edge of the Island is **Grand View Point**, whose name is no exaggeration. Views here, while similar to those from Dead Horse Point, are much vaster in scope. The Green and Colorado Rivers—although not visible from the overlook—snake along 2000 feet below, and on a clear day you can pick out landforms up to 100 miles distant. As far as the eye can see, virtually all this land is public, and therefore (presumably) protected from development. The rock layers, from top to bottom, include the Entrada, Navajo, Kayenta, and Wingate strata as well as the Chinle, Moenkopi, Cutler, and Honaker Trail Formations.

To the right of the overlook, a well-worn trail descends one level below the rim and follows a wide slickrock bench to the end of the peninsula. **Junction Butte** lies immediately to the south, and the intricate canyons, fins, and standing rocks of Canyonlands' Maze District are almost palpable.

NEARBY: Just north of Grand View Point is the trailhead for **White Rim Overlook**. A very easy 1.5-mile out-and-back hike on a finger of sandstone affords views into the shutterbugs' delight of **Monument Basin**. The basin sports rows of chocolate-colored Organ Rock Shale pinnacles wearing erosion-resistant White Rim Sandstone "hats." The skinniest of these is **The Totem Pole**.

42. Aztec Butte

Moderate 2-mile out-and-back; allow 1 hour

Map: Trails Illustrated 212: Canyonlands National Park/Island in the Sky

Moses and Zeus, towering Wingate Sandstone spires, reach for the sky.

GETTING THERE: From Moab, drive 9 miles north on US Route 191 to the intersection of UT 313. Turn left. About 10 miles from that junction, you reach a fork. Take the right fork, and drive 4.5 miles to reach Canyonlands' Island in the Sky. From the Island visitor center, drive south on the scenic drive to meet the spur road to Upheaval Dome. Turn right there and continue 1 mile to the parking area.

ON THE TRAIL: The trail forks at 0.25 mile. Take the right fork, which climbs 200 feet over slickrock to the top of Aztec Butte at mile 0.75. The final push, which requires scrambling, may prove challenging to some. Once on top, you intersect a short loop that rewards you with excellent views into Trail Canyon, as well as the chance to visit a small Fremont ruin. Although several other structures are located just below the rim on the butte's north side, this area currently is closed due to a rockfall hazard. The ruins explain the name of the formation: Early settlers wrongly assumed that canyon country's ancient masonry structures had been built by transplanted Mesoamericans.

Now retrace your steps back to the fork mentioned earlier. Follow cairns to the top of the lower mound, and then bear right along the rim until you see a rift. Just below this fracture, investigate a pair of photogenic granaries.

43. Alcove Spring

Moderate 10-mile out-and-back, with optional 1-mile extension; allow 5 hours
Trekking poles recommended
Map: Trails Illustrated 212: Canyonlands National Park/Island in the Sky

GETTING THERE: From Moab, drive 9 miles north on US Route 191. Turn left onto UT 313. About 10 miles from that junction, you reach a fork. Take the right, and drive 4.5

miles to reach Canyonlands' Island in the Sky. From the Island visitor center, drive south on the scenic drive to meet the spur road to Upheaval Dome. Turn right and continue for 3.5 miles where you park in a pullout on the right.

ON THE TRAIL: The least difficult of the descents from the Island (with an elevation change of 1300 feet), this trail offers an intimate perspective on two towering Wingate Sandstone buttes. From the parking area, walk down to a badly eroded roadbed. In 0.5 mile you pass the spring, emanating—as advertised—from a humungous alcove. When you bottom out, turn left, remaining on a bench for about a mile before reaching **Trail Canyon**. Turn left, walking downstream. At mile 5, you arrive at the junction with Taylor Creek, where the sculpted towers of **Moses and Zeus** come splendidly into view. If you continue 0.5 mile, you can circle them.

NEARBY: The difficult **Wilhite Trail** (12.25 miles round trip), which begins 1.25 miles south of the Alcove Spring Trailhead, is quite steep and eroded as it plunges 1600 feet to the White Rim. Only sure-footed hikers should attempt this hike.

44. Crater View (Upheaval Dome Overlooks)

Moderate 2-mile out-and-back; allow 1 hour

Map: Trails Illustrated 212: Canyonlands National Park/Island in the Sky

GETTING THERE: From Moab, drive 9 miles north on US Route 191 to UT 313. Turn left here. About 10 miles from that junction, you reach a fork. Go right, and drive 4.5 miles to reach Canyonlands' Island in the Sky. From the Island visitor center, drive south on the scenic drive to meet the spur road to Upheaval Dome. Turn right and continue 6 miles to the end of the spur road. Park here.

ON THE TRAIL: Note that the two names given in this hike name reflect a discrepancy between the Park Service signage and the topographic map. The trail climbs 200 feet in under 0.5 mile to an initial overlook of **Upheaval Dome**. Although it was once regarded as an eroded salt dome, most geologists now attribute the crater to a meteor impact. Walk along the rim of the 1000-foot-deep, mile-wide depression, marveling at the colorful, convoluted badlands at its center.

Past this first overlook, the trail veers left, becoming steeper and rougher. It plummets down a sandstone defile with the aid of hacked-in steps before reaching the second overlook at mile 1, which affords an even better view of the oddity.

NEARBY: Less than a mile back down the road, an easy 0.5-mile trail ascends the slickrock mass of **Whale Rock** with the aid of handrails. The lofty perch treats you to views of the dome's entire perimeter.

45. Syncline Loop

Difficult 11.5-mile loop, including spur into Upheaval Dome, with routefinding and scrambling; allow 6–7 hours

Trekking poles recommended

Map: Trails Illustrated 212: Canyonlands National Park/Island in the Sky

GETTING THERE: From Moab, drive 9 miles north on US Route 191 to the intersection of UT 313. Turn left here. About 10 miles from that junction, you reach a fork. Take the right fork, and proceed 4.5 miles to reach Canyonlands' Island in the Sky. From the

Island visitor center, drive south on the scenic drive to meet the spur road to Upheaval Dome. Turn right and continue 6 miles to the end of the spur road. Park here.

ON THE TRAIL: This turbo-charged trail provides access into Upheaval Dome through its outlet, Upheaval Wash. Backpackers can continue down the wash to Labyrinth Canyon on the Green (an extra 6 miles round trip).

Both ends of the Syncline Loop begin a short distance up the Crater View (a.k.a. Upheaval Dome Overlooks) Trail. Turn right onto the loop. After a long, fairly level stretch, the trail drops steeply through **The Breach**, a wide gap between Navajo Sandstone cliffs.

Reaching **Syncline Valley**, you arrive at a field of enormous Wingate boulders that have fallen on the trail near the top of the Chinle Formation. Following cairns, carefully pick your way around these obstructions. Then rapidly descend an enormous pour-off. Watch your step on the loose, slippery scree. You may find springs at both the top and the bottom of this drop. Continue to the junction with a spur trail on the left, which follows a wash into **Upheaval Dome**. Here again, cairns guide hikers around minor obstructions. After about 1.75 miles, the wash forks amid unearthly badlands. Both forks deserve exploration.

Back at the junction, the Syncline Loop dips to the floor of **Upheaval Canyon**. Within several hundred yards it intersects a major side-canyon on the left, which you enter in preparation for the tough 1300-foot climb to the Island. Your efforts are compensated with Green River views that improve with every step. Mercifully, the trail levels off in the last mile.

SPANISH VALLEY

The city of Moab occupies the north end of Spanish Valley. Rather paradoxically, the Colorado River does not follow Spanish Valley but slices across it, imprisoned in deep gorges on either side. The featured hikes, all of which overlook the valley and/or the river canyon, illustrate the variety that the area has to offer.

46. Slickrock Bike Trail

Moderate 10.25-mile lollipop loop; allow 5 hours

Map: Trails Illustrated 501: Moab South

GETTING THERE: In downtown Moab, turn east off US Route 191 onto 300 South. Follow this street to a T intersection with 400 East and bear right. In two blocks, turn left onto Mill Creek Drive, which intersects Sand Flats Road. Proceed up Sand Flats Road for about 2 miles. The trailhead and parking lot are on the left, 0.5 mile beyond the entrance booth for **Sand Flats Recreation Area**. Fees apply.

ON THE TRAIL: Although designed originally for motorcyclists and used now primarily by mountain bikers (advanced skills mandatory!), this trail offers opportunities for hiking on petrified dunes of Navajo Sandstone. Avoid it on weekends, holidays, and during the "high season" of spring and fall.

The main route for both hikers and bikers is indicated by white dashes painted on the slickrock. More challenging alternate routes are marked by black diamonds. To

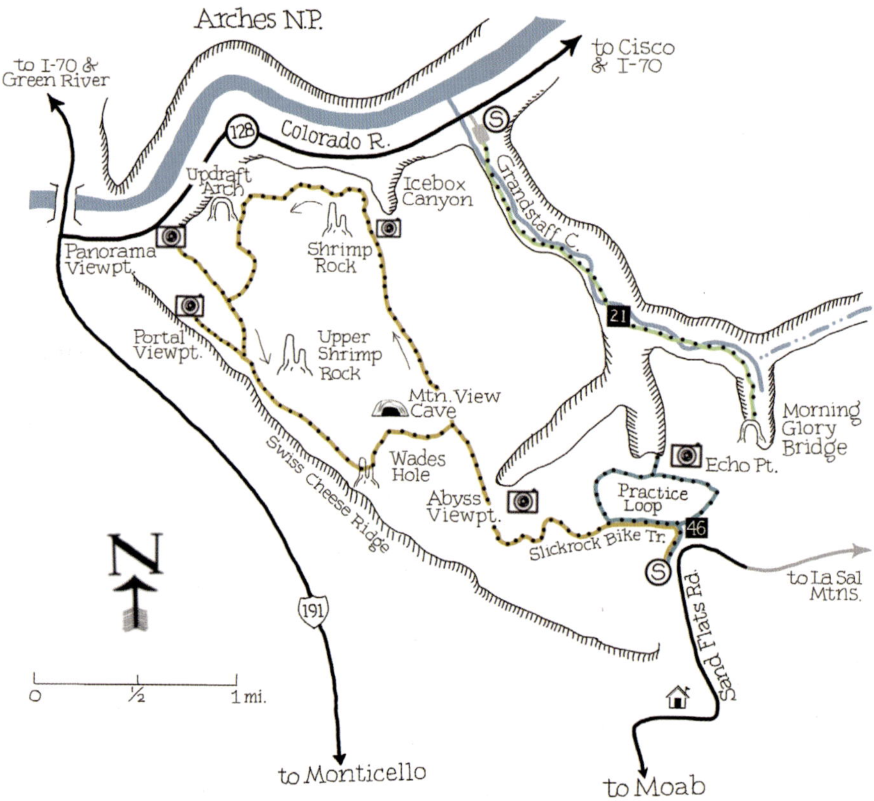

stay clear of bicyclists, who typically have a tough time of it, keep to the right side of the line.

In 0.25 mile the trail splits; a 2-mile **Practice Loop** takes off to the right. Its highlight is **Echo Point**, overlooking a side-canyon of the Grandstaff system, formerly called Negro Bill. The main trail continues to dizzying **Abyss Viewpoint** and soon forks again. Take the right fork and proceed to **Shrimp Rock**, an oddly shaped butte on the edge of Icebox Canyon. This rock, visible from the river, gets its name from a nearby pool containing fairy shrimp and other tiny critters.

Three short spurs nearby lead to two spectacular overlooks, the Portal and Panorama Viewpoints. The main trail swings south to close the loop near Wades Hole.

47. Hidden Valley and Moab Rim

Difficult 6.25-mile point-to-point, with routefinding; allow 3.5 hours
Vehicle shuttle or equivalent required; trekking poles recommended
Map: Trails Illustrated 501: Moab South

GETTING THERE: To set up a shuttle, drive two vehicles south a few blocks from downtown Moab on US Route 191 and turn right at a traffic light onto Kane Creek Boulevard. Follow this road for about 2.75 miles to a marked pullout about 150 yards past a cattle guard. Park one vehicle here.

In the second vehicle, return to US 191 in Moab, then drive 3 miles south to Angel Rock Road. Turn right here. You soon come to a T intersection. Turn right onto Rimrock Lane, and continue to the parking lot at its end.

ON THE TRAIL: Behind the Rocks, administered by the BLM, is a slickrock wonderland of domes, fins, and arches. Jeep roads provide good access to the most picturesque spots, and cross-country backpacking opportunities for skilled orienteers abound. Although the featured hike requires that you shuttle vehicles, you can hike partway in from either end.

From the Rimrock Lane trailhead, ascend briskly on rocky switchbacks. Topping a saddle at mile 0.5, you enter **Hidden Valley**, a serene sanctuary nestled between Navajo Sandstone cliffs that seems light-years away from the bustle of town. You are likely to see a flock of chukar partridges here. The trail climbs gradually to a pass at mile 2.5. The total ascent thus far is 700 feet. Linger to peer into the heart of Behind the Rocks and to hunt for petroglyphs in the cliff face high above on your right. This would be a good stopping point for hikers without two vehicles.

Leaving the pass, the trail drops down into a maze of slickrock to intersect the **Moab Rim Trail**, a major jeep road, in about 0.25 mile. Follow this road as it bends to the right, passing spurs that lead to viewpoints. The road descends a sand hill and then climbs steadily, skirting stately fins and domes.

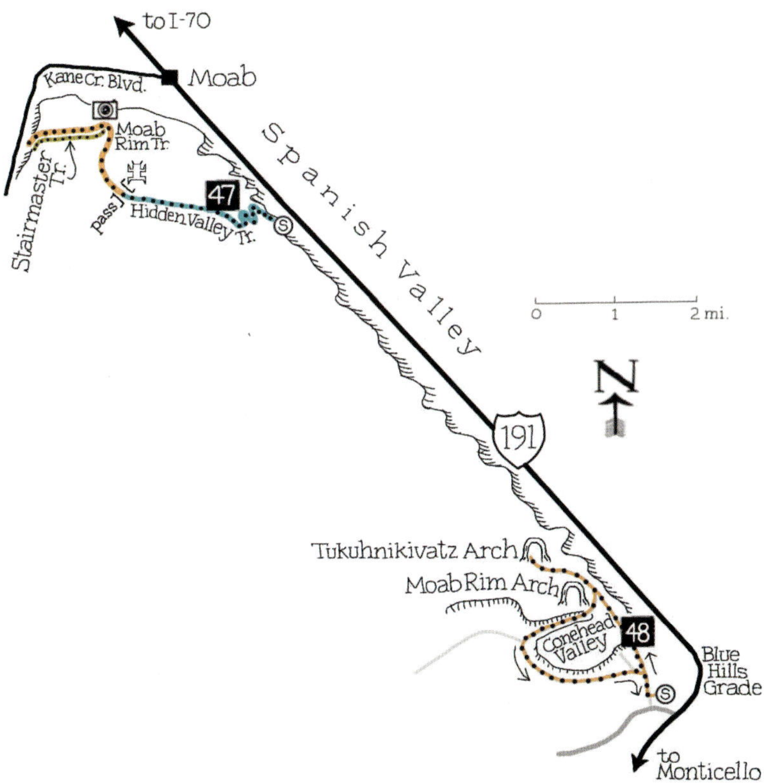

The Moab Rim Trail, shared by hikers and four-wheelers, drops vertiginously to the Colorado River.

Near the crest, at mile 4.25, you attain a dramatic overlook of Moab and Spanish Valley. From here the road contours along the top of the cliffs toward the river. It then plunges 950 feet on Kayenta Formation ledges. Rather incredibly, this route between the rim and the river is a mecca for four-wheel-drive-vehicle enthusiasts. As you descend toward the parking lot, look for scrapes, dents, and oil stains left where jeeps have bottomed out on challenging ledges. Running parallel to the Moab Rim Trail for its last 0.75 mile is the **Stairmaster Trail**, designed for hikers who would prefer not to compete with motorized vehicles.

48. Coneheads

Moderate 4-mile lollipop loop, with exposure, routefinding, and scrambling; allow 2 hours
Trekking poles recommended
Map: Trails Illustrated 501: Moab South

GETTING THERE: From Moab, drive south on US Route 191 to the top of a grade just past milepost 113. Locate a marked dirt road on the right, the BR (Behind the Rocks) jeep trail. Although this track soon deteriorates, its initial section does not require high clearance. In 0.5 mile, turn right at a fork and park along the shoulder.

ON THE TRAIL: This fascinating dome-bounded area marks the southern end of Behind the Rocks. Excellent day hiking possibilities present themselves on the rough jeep tracks that honeycomb this wild area.

Hike north along the jeep road. The area that some locals call Conehead Valley, clearly visible as an array of tapered pinnacles, is about a mile distant. Continue straight ahead past intersecting jeep tracks until you reach a Y junction and a fenced-off Wilderness Study Area. You will return later on the left fork, but for now go right, paralleling the fence. Enjoy out-of-this-world views toward the La Sal Mountains as you walk past upper Conehead Valley and **Moab Rim Arch**, 0.5 mile farther on. Climb up under the arch if you wish.

The road dead-ends at a turnaround circle. An unusual arch on the horizon is your next destination. At the circle, pick up a social trail on the left. It follows a small wash and then scrambles rapidly up a side-canyon, skirting to the left of some pour-offs. At the top, go left about 25 yards to locate the curious span named for the mountain peak it frames: **Tukuhnikivatz** ("land where the sun shines longest").

Backtracking to the circle and beyond, proceed to the upper end of **Conehead Valley**. Although there is no trail to guide you, it is easy to drop into the valley. Pick up a jeep road here. As the road leaves the valley's lower end, it climbs aggressively up a sand hill. From the top you can spy all three of southern Utah's mountain ranges: the La Sals, Abajos, and Henrys. The road loops back to the Y mentioned above. Turn right to return to your car.

NEARBY: About 35.5 miles south of Moab off US 191 is the turnoff to the west for **Canyon Rims Recreation Area**, which leads to three vertiginous vantage points above the Colorado River: Needles, Canyonlands, and Anticline Overlooks. Reaching Canyonlands Overlook requires a high-clearance vehicle. Near Anticline Overlook, the **Trough Springs Trail** (5-mile out-and-back, rated moderate) descends 1100 feet to Kane Creek.

CANYONLANDS NATIONAL PARK: NEEDLES DISTRICT

The Needles constitutes one of three districts of Canyonlands National Park. Although as easy to access as Island in the Sky, it receives far fewer visitors—a pity, because the area offers hiking opportunities second to none.

Travel south on US Route 191 from Moab about 42.5 miles, passing distinctive **Church Rock** on the left. Just beyond that butte, turn right (west) onto UT 211. The road drops into the **Indian Creek** drainage, which it follows to the park entrance, 34 miles from the turnoff. Rock climbing is popular along the sheer cliffs to the right. On your left as you approach the park, admire the **Six-shooter Peaks**, classic Chinle Formation slopes topped by slabs of Wingate Sandstone. You also pass **Davis and Lavender Canyons**, the upper arms of which are studded with arches and ruins (permits required), as well as numerous BLM campgrounds.

Short of the Needles on UT 211, about 10 miles west of US 191, stop at enchanting **Newspaper Rock**, called Tse Hane ("rock that tells a story") by members of the Navajo tribe. This Wingate Sandstone slab is decorated with two millennia of petroglyphs contributed by diverse cultures, ranging from prehistoric Desert Archaic, Anasazi, and Fremont to present-day Navajo and Ute.

49. Slickrock Loop

Easy 2.75-mile lollipop loop; allow 1.5 hours
Map: Trails Illustrated 210: Canyonlands National Park/Needles/Island

GETTING THERE: From the visitor center, take the park road west to Squaw Flat Campground. Before you reach the campground, the road forks. Stay to the right here, then turn right onto the scenic drive. The trailhead is near the end of the drive, on the right.

ON THE TRAIL: If you are in the mood for a short hike that packs a wallop, the Slickrock Trail delivers big-time. Four spurs offer sweeping panoramas of the Needles

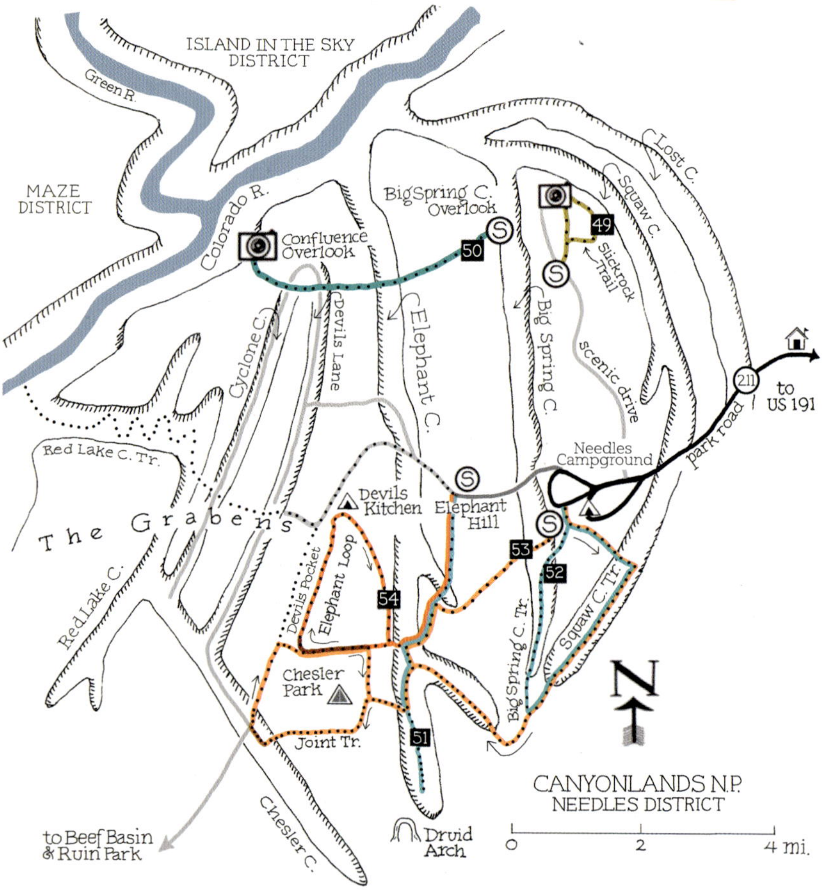

District, the Six-shooter Peaks, Grand View Point on the Island in the Sky, and Ekker and Elaterite Buttes in the Maze District across the river. From the parking lot, pick up the stem of the lollipop, following cairns. At mile 0.5, turn right, proceeding counterclockwise around the loop. Don't miss superb viewpoint #2, located about a mile in, overlooking Little Spring Canyon. Bighorn sheep frequent the area.

50. The Confluence

Moderate 10-mile out-and-back; allow 5 hours

Map: Trails Illustrated 210: Canyonlands National Park/Needles/Island

GETTING THERE: From the visitor center, drive west on the park road to Needles Campground. Before you reach the campground, the road forks. Stay to the right. Turn right onto the scenic drive and follow it 3.5 miles to its end.

ON THE TRAIL: Best reserved for the cooler months, this otherwise ordinary hike culminates in a sweeping view of the confluence of the Colorado and Green Rivers.

The trail crosses Big Spring Canyon and enters the lower reaches of Elephant Canyon. From a ridgetop near the halfway point, feast your eyes on the needles around

Chesler Park. Descend to cross **Devils Lane** and **Cyclone Canyon**, two of the "grabens" (sunken fault-blocks) that define the west end of the Needles District. In the latter, pick up a jeep road and follow it a short distance to its end. **Confluence Overlook** is 0.5 mile farther on, at the top of a rise. The Green River, coming in from the northwest, is indeed noticeably greener than the Colorado, which carries a heavy load of silt. Inside the V of their union lies the Island in the Sky, while the Maze District looms directly to the west.

51. Druid Arch

Moderate 11-mile out-and-back, with routefinding and scrambling; allow 6 hours or overnight

Permit required if camping; trekking poles and water filter recommended

Map: Trails Illustrated 210: Canyonlands National Park/Needles/Island

GETTING THERE: From the visitor center, where you should check with rangers about water availability, drive west on the park road to Needles Campground. Before you reach the campground, the road forks. Stay to the right. Continue to an intersection. Turn right here toward **Elephant Hill**, 3 miles distant on a good, if narrow, dirt road. Park in the lot.

ON THE TRAIL: Nature imitates art in this majestic span with its twin Stonehenge-like openings. The trail takes off from the south side of the parking lot. It ascends about 150 feet to a gently rolling plateau, aided by stairs of rock. A level stretch follows, offering 360-degree views of the surrounding needles. Favoring slickrock, the trail contours around "elephants' feet" and intersects a path to Needles Campground. Ignore that path, continuing straight ahead to stay on the main trail. In rapid succession, it squeezes through two joints before descending on stairs to the floor of **Elephant Canyon** at mile 2.5.

Here you arrive at a major junction. The trail you've been on continues to Chesler Park, but you turn left instead, walking upstream. A sandy bottom soon gives way to rocky benches, and the scenery improves as the canyon closes in. Side trails coming in at miles 2.75 and 3.25 cut across the canyon to connect Needles Campground with Chesler Park.

From here on out, you follow a ledgy route that rewards decent navigational skills. Although you cross the streambed occasionally, most of the time you remain on or above the left bank as the canyon narrows. After passing some small pools, follow cairns around a pour-off. You encounter minor obstacles here. A ladder has been installed to dodge one of them. The last push to 200-foot-high **Druid Arch**, which is only visible end-on from below, requires scrambling up a talus slope. Carefully contour around its base to the other side for an equally hypnotic vantage point.

52. Squaw Flat Loop

Moderate 7.5-mile loop; allow 4 hours

Map: Trails Illustrated 210: Canyonlands National Park/Needles/Island

GETTING THERE: From the visitor center, drive west to Needles Campground and park near the trailhead.

ON THE TRAIL: This hike combines the Squaw Canyon and Big Spring Canyon Trails into a delightful and invigorating loop. Excellent signage makes the route a breeze to follow.

From Needles Campground, the trail forks almost immediately. Go left here toward Squaw Canyon. Climb two low Cedar Mesa Sandstone ridges on the way to a second junction at 1.25 miles. Turn right, hiking up **Squaw Canyon**. At the mile 3 junction, bear right and enter a side-canyon. Turn right at mile 4 and climb briskly to a slickrock pass between the Squaw and Big Spring systems.

After catching your breath, carefully descend to the floor of **Big Spring Canyon**, walking sometimes in the bed of the wash and sometimes on the bank. At mile 6.75 you reach an intersection. Make a hard right onto **Big Spring Canyon Trail**. As you leave the wash, this trail crosses two ridges on its way back to your starting point.

53. Chesler Park Backpack

Moderate 19-mile loop; allow 2–3 days
Permit required
Map: Trails Illustrated 210: Canyonlands National Park/Needles/Island

Magnificent Druid Arch (Hike 51) recalls England's Stonehenge.

GETTING THERE: From the visitor center, drive to Needles Campground A. Park here near the Squaw Flat trailhead. Check with rangers about water availability; there may be pools near the official campsites in upper Elephant Canyon near Druid Arch (see Hike 51), but most likely nowhere else.

ON THE TRAIL: Chesler Park—a grassy meadow surrounded by spindly Cedar Mesa monoliths—is one of the Southwest's crown jewels. Start on the **Squaw Canyon Trail**, which merges with the **Big Spring Canyon Trail** at mile 3.75. Bear right onto the Big Spring Canyon Trail. The trail, which soon seems to disappear on a sandstone bench, actually is cleverly routed through a fracture between two fins. Logs jammed into this joint ease your passage. Hop a saddle into a tributary of the Elephant Canyon system, aided by ladders.

Bear left upon reaching **Elephant Canyon** at mile 5.75. At mile 6.25, near campsite EC3, pick up the trail on the right that ascends to enchanting **Chesler Park**. Here, at mile 7.25 you begin a clockwise loop around its perimeter that eventually returns to this point. Go left near campsite CP2 to access the **Joint Trail** at mile 8, which follows a narrow fissure between towering sandstone walls. The passageway occasionally opens into cool, dark chambers. When it ends at mile 8.75, turn right onto a jeep road, which you follow for 0.5 mile. Then turn right at the next two trail junctions (miles 10.25 and 11.5, respectively) to close the loop at mile 12.75.

Now turn left to backtrack to the floor of Elephant Canyon, which you reach at mile 13.75. From here go left, walking downstream 1.25 miles to a junction. Turn right here, climbing out of the canyon and passing through two small joints. At the next junction (mile 15.5), turn right and follow signs back to Needles Campground.

54. Elephant Loop

Moderate 10.5-mile lollipop loop; allow 5–6 hours
Map: Trails Illustrated 210: Canyonlands National Park/Needles/Island

GETTING THERE: From the Needles District visitor center, drive west on the park road toward the Needles Campground. Just before you reach the campground, the road forks. Bear right and continue to Elephant Hill, which is 3 miles distant on a good, if narrow, unpaved road. Park in the lot.

ON THE TRAIL: This scenic trip visits Chesler Park and the Devils Pocket graben (sunken fault-block). The trail begins at a kiosk to the rear of the parking lot. Assisted by stairs, it ascends 150 feet to a plateau. Favoring slickrock, the trail affords excellent views of surrounding needles as well as the more distant Six-shooter Peaks. Go right at the mile 1.5 junction with a trail leading to Needles Campground. From here, the trail passes through two slots and descends on steps to a side-canyon of Elephant Canyon. At mile 2.5 you reach the Elephant Canyon floor, intersecting the trail to Druid Arch (Hike 51), which heads upstream.

Go straight ahead at this intersection. The trail ascends, hugging a side-canyon. When the side-canyon forks, turn right, continuing to climb. At mile 2.75, you arrive at a junction. The trail to the right, marked for Devils Kitchen, is the one on which you will return later to close the loop. But for now, ascend steeply to a lookout above needle-encircled **Chesler Park**. Descending from the pass, proceed for a short distance, reaching yet another junction at mile 3, this one signed for Devils Kitchen. Turn right here.

Exit Chesler Park by means of a low pass with views of the remote Henry Mountains. Descending to a bowl, you reach a signpost at mile 4.25. Turn right here, continuing toward **Devils Kitchen**. Soon the trail drops down through a notch, assisted by logs. It takes a sharp right turn and heads for a pass through the needles. On the other side of the pass is the **Devils Pocket**. Cross its lush meadow to reach **Devils Kitchen Camp** at mile 5.5, adjacent to a jeep road.

Rather than following the jeep road, the trail jogs sharply to the right. Expect many ups and downs in the next few miles. You will pass through a few joints, the last of which has a low ceiling. Skirting back around the needles that delimit the boundary of Chesler Park, the trail contours around slickrock benches to close the loop at mile 7.75. Go left here to return to Elephant Hill.

55. Peekaboo Arch

Moderate 10-mile out-and-back; allow 5 hours

Map: Trails Illustrated 210: Canyonlands National Park/Needles/Island

GETTING THERE: From the visitor center, drive to Needles Campground, and park in the lot. Find the trailhead here.

ON THE TRAIL: This is one of the most scenic and imaginatively designed hikes in the Needles District, which is saying a lot. At a fork a short distance from the campground, turn left onto the **Squaw Canyon Trail**. Walk 1 mile to the junction with the trail signed for Lost Canyon and Peekaboo Spring. Go left here, climbing out of a draw and then up a steep slickrock pass at mile 2. Descend sandstone ledges into the **Lost Canyon** drainage, following cairns and utilizing a ladder. Then head downstream to a junction with the **Lost Canyon Trail** at mile 2.5. Take a left at this fork onto the Peekaboo Trail.

The trail traverses sandstone rims on its way to Salt Creek. It heads numerous side-canyons and passes through a window in a fin near a small jug-handle arch. Eventually it descends a long ladder through a cleft to a sandy bench above Salt Creek. Veering right, it mimics a big bend in the creek to end below a Fremont rock art panel, adjacent to **Peekaboo Arch**. You can clamber up to the arch if you wish. Return as you came.

56. Salt Creek Backpack

Moderate 28.5-mile point-to-point; allow 4 days

Permit and vehicle shuttle or equivalent required; water filter, trekking poles, and binoculars recommended

Map: Trails Illustrated 210: Canyonlands National Park/Needles/Island

GETTING THERE: As described here, this loop requires two vehicles. First, leave one at the Cave Spring parking area just west of the visitor center, following signs. (A short loop trail starts here.) Then drive the second vehicle east on UT 211 about 15 miles. Near historic Dugout Ranch, now administered by the Nature Conservancy, turn south onto Beef Basin Rd. (County Road 104) in the direction of Beef Basin. Take

Iconic Angel Arch with the Molar in the foreground

this decent unpaved road for approximately 12.5 miles, bearing right at mile 3.5. The road follows the North Cottonwood Creek drainage in the Abajo foothills. Your hike begins 0.25 mile beyond prominent **Cathedral Butte**, off a spur on the right. This spur, not to be confused with a jeep road immediately before it, dead-ends after 100 yards. A sign points to the trailhead.

ON THE TRAIL: Studded with ancient Indian ruins and pictographs, the verdant Salt Creek drainage boasts numerous arches, including enormous Angel Arch, one of the park's signature formations. In the upper canyon, you can camp only at designated sites, which provide bear-proof containers for food storage. Below the confluence with Angel Arch Canyon, off-trail camping is unrestricted, but desirable sites are few and far between. Check on water availability when you obtain your permit.

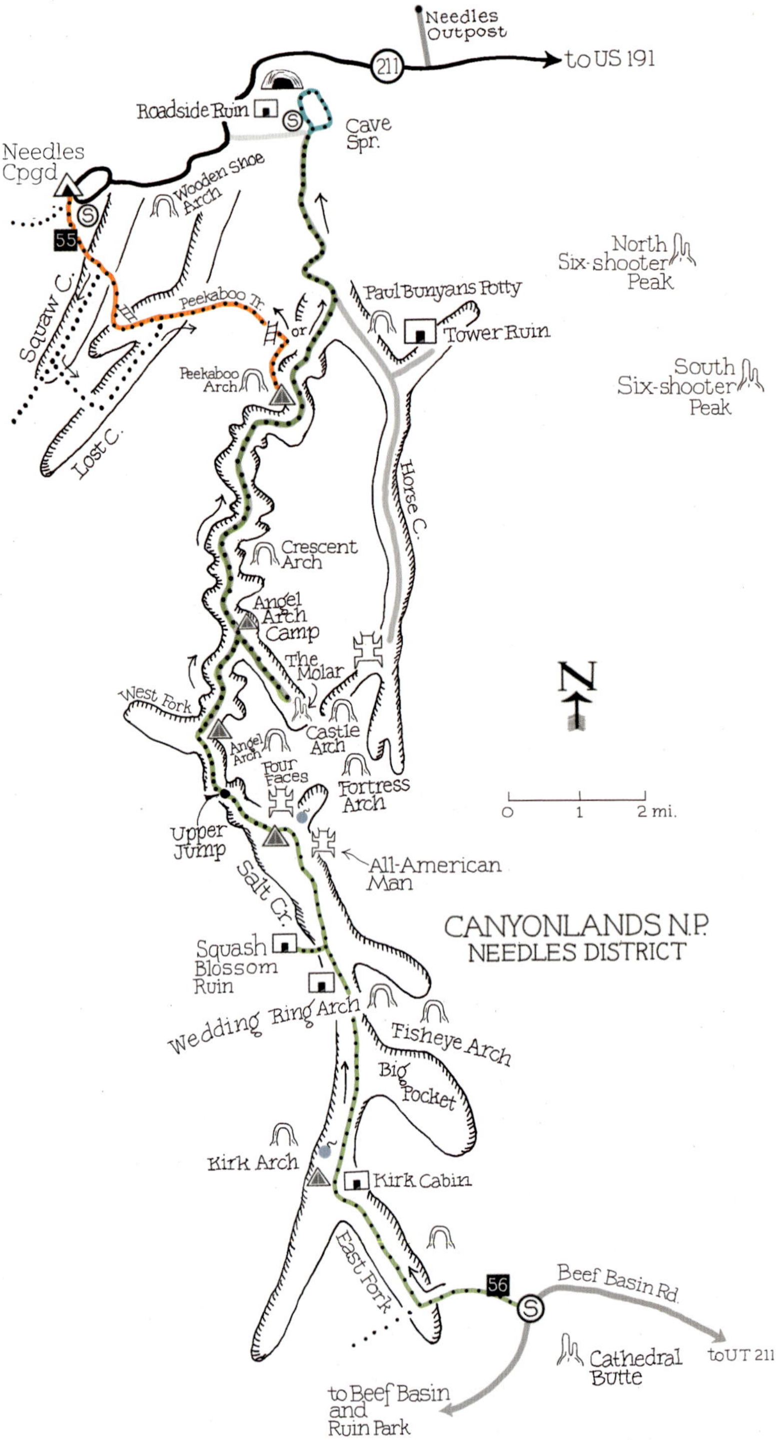
Needles Outpost
211
to US 191
Roadside Ruin
Cave Spr.
Needles Cpgd
Wooden Shoe Arch
55
Squaw C.
Peekaboo Tr.
or
Paul Bunyans Potty
Tower Ruin
North Six-shooter Peak
South Six-shooter Peak
Peekaboo Arch
Lost C.
Horse C.
Crescent Arch
Angel Arch Camp
The Molar
West Fork
Castle Arch
Angel Arch
Four Faces
Fortress Arch
Upper Jump
All-American Man
0
1
2 mi.
Salt Cr.
CANYONLANDS N.P.
NEEDLES DISTRICT
Squash Blossom Ruin
Wedding Ring Arch
Fisheye Arch
Big Pocket
Kirk Arch
Kirk Cabin
East Fork
56
Beef Basin Rd.
Cathedral Butte
to UT 211
to Beef Basin and Ruin Park

In its first 2 miles, the trail drops 1000 feet to the floor into the East Fork, passing through the Chinle, Moenkopi, and Organ Rock Shale strata. It levels out as you enter the white and rose-colored sandstone of the Cedar Mesa Formation, through which you will be traveling for the rest of the trip.

Around mile 3, you come to a nearly impenetrable marshy thicket where it is easy to lose your way. To minimize bushwhacking, stay far to the right of the canyon. Within a mile, reach the confluence with the main fork of Salt Creek. There should be potable water near **Kirk Cabin** at about mile 4, erected by a Mormon pioneer in the 1890s. In this vicinity are two natural arches, some distant cliff dwellings, and a pair of designated campsites.

Within a half mile of the campsites, you will spot **Kirk Arch** to your left. The first major side-canyon on the right, **Big Pocket**, comes in at about mile 5. Look for an accessible ruin here, near a diamond-shaped rock to the right of the trail. Directly across Salt Creek, pause to inspect **Big Ruin**, a large, inaccessible cliff dwelling. Just beyond Big Pocket, a short spur trail on the right leads to spectacular **Wedding Ring Arch**.

Back on the main trail, continue another 0.5 mile and follow a short spur on the left to **Squash Blossom Ruin**, a small but enchanting granary site. The squash specimens here are descended from plants introduced hundreds of years ago by Ancestral Puebloan farmers. At about mile 6.5, explore some cool, echo-filled grottoes on the left. The trail next veers to the right of the canyon and at mile 7 passes directly under a cave housing two masonry structures as well as a whimsical Fremont pictograph, the **All-American Man**.

Just beyond the cave, the trail ascends a steep ravine, emerging on the north side of a fin. Within 0.25 mile you come to a major spring. Past the spring, a spur on the right visits a small ruin complex containing another wonderful pictograph panel, the **Four Faces**. A designated campsite is near, just 0.25 mile shy of **Upper Jump** waterfall and pool.

From here it is 3.5 miles to the final designated campsite, at the mouth of Salt Creek's West Fork. To get to this campsite, continue up the trail. The canyon narrows; willow thickets retard your progress, and you cross the streambed several times. Eventually, the trail attains a sandy bench to the right of the canyon. Above the bench is an extensive ruin. You can easily scramble up to it. If you reach the final campsite without having spotted this complex, it is well worth a 0.25 mile backtrack.

Continue on 2.5 miles to the marked junction with Angel Arch Canyon, at mile 13. Angel Arch Camp is nearby, on the right. The 3.5-mile out-and-back trip to **Angel Arch** is easier if you drop your packs near the junction. En route, look for ruins on the left side of the canyon. Before the canyon boxes up, a spur on the right leads past a well-named formation called **The Molar** to a superb view of the arch, one of the most sublime spans in all of canyon country.

Back on the main trail (henceforth an abandoned track), **Crescent Arch** comes into view at mile 17.25. From here to Peekaboo Camp at mile 25, you're in the sinuous canyon's bliss-out zone. Don't miss the spur ascending to **Peekaboo Arch**. Just before the spur on the left are several rock art panels. More pictographs await at the arch itself.

The Four Faces pictographs sport matching necklaces.

Continuing through the arch, drop down to the other side of the canyon and proceed downstream, passing **Horse Canyon** on the right at mile 26, a magnificent tributary that houses several major arches and archaeological sites. Save that canyon for another trip. From here it is 2.5 miles to Cave Spring. In the late spring and early summer, you may find yourself swatting insects as you slog through deep sand. It is tempting to try to cut this leg of the hike by using a four-wheel-drive vehicle below Peekaboo Camp. But be warned that driving on this rough, unmaintained road risks a budget-busting tow. Inquire about its condition at the visitor center.

CHAPTER 4
TABLELANDS

This chapter describes hikes on Utah's Cedar Mesa as well as the high country across the border in Colorado. From hubs in Blanding, Utah, and Cortez, Colorado, it includes the Bears Ears area, Mesa Verde National Park, Natural Bridges National Monument, and Canyons of the Ancients National Monument. The area contains an extremely high concentration of pre-Columbian archaeological sites erected by the Anasazi (Ancestral Puebloan) people.

Hubs: Blanding, Utah, and Cortez, Colorado

Nestled beneath the Abajo Mountains, **Blanding** (population 4000) was established by Mormon pioneers. The town's ultrawide streets and ban on the sale of alcohol are obvious legacies of that heritage. Local Utes, whose reservation south of here dates from the early 1920s, exert a subtler influence. Don't miss **Edge of the Cedars State Park**, home to a restored pueblo with a "great kiva" as well as the largest collection of prehistoric pottery in the Four Corners region.

Cortez (population 9000) is a natural gateway community, poised geographically between deserts and mountains and culturally between the "Anglo," Hispanic, and Indian worlds. Taking its name from the famous conquistador, the town counts farming and ranching as its economic pillars. The massive bulk of **Sleeping Ute Mountain** dominates the landscape, which is drained by tributaries of the San Juan River. Free Native American dances are held nightly in season at the **Cortez Cultural Center.**

BEARS EARS NATIONAL MONUMENT

All hikes in this section are accessed from scenic UT 95, 4 miles south of Blanding off US Route 191. The road cuts through the **Comb Ridge** hogback, which extends from the Abajo foothills to northeastern Arizona. Because of the radical uplift that occurred here, the formation's east and west sides display totally different rock layers. West of Comb Ridge are the **Bears Ears**, a pair of reddish buttes that lent their name to one of America's newest national monuments. Hiking and camping permits, required for most backcountry travel, can be obtained through the BLM office in Monticello or at Kane Gulch Ranger Station on UT 261, about an hour west of Blanding.

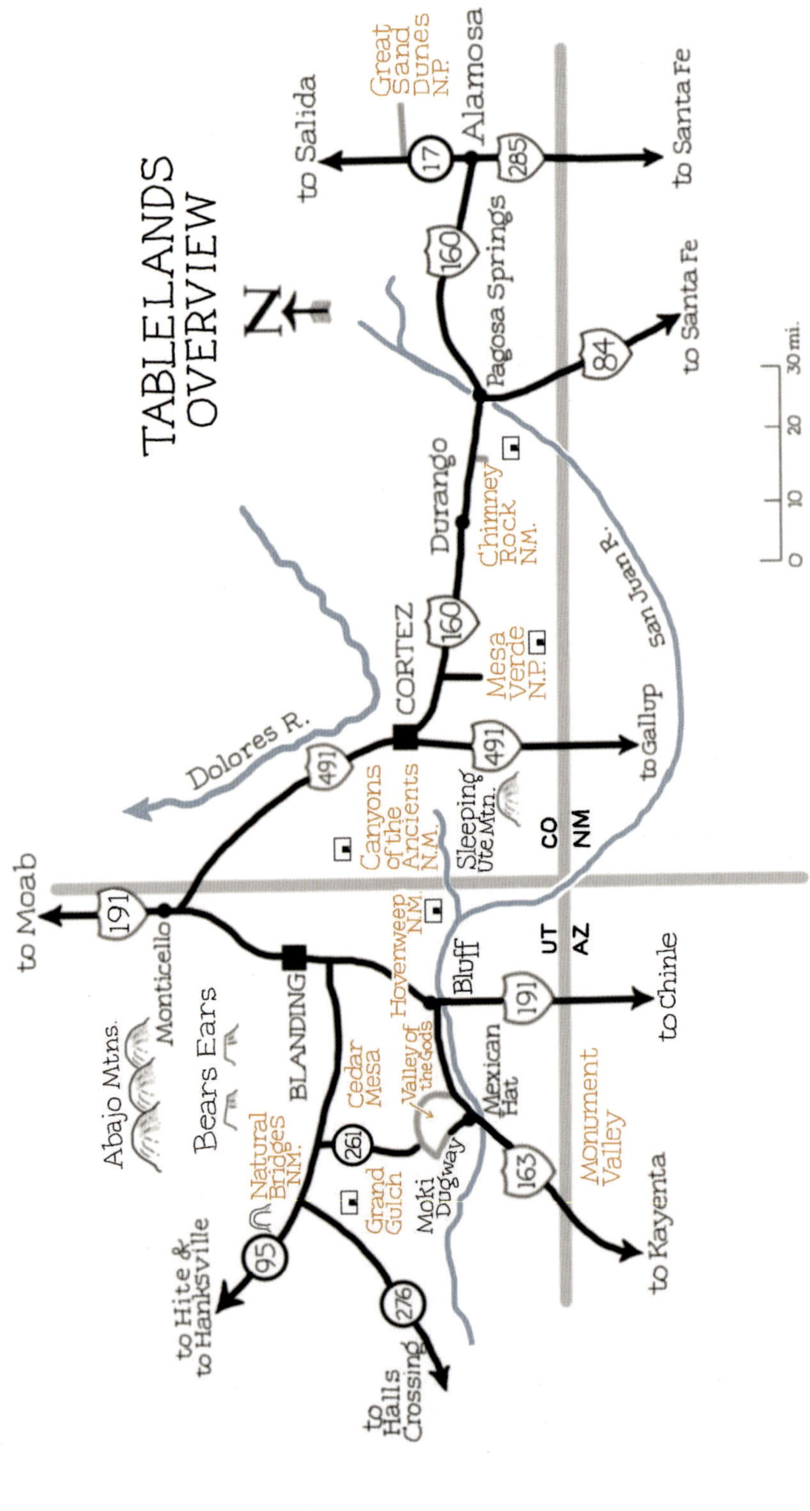
TABLELANDS OVERVIEW
N
to Salida
Great Sand Dunes N.P.
Alamosa
17
285
to Santa Fe
160
Pagosa Springs
to Santa Fe
84
Durango
Chimney Rock N.M.
0
10
20
30 mi.
San Juan R.
CORTEZ
160
Mesa Verde N.P.
Dolores R.
491
491
to Gallup
Canyons of the Ancients N.M.
Sleeping Ute Mtn.
CO
NM
to Moab
191
Monticello
BLANDING
Hovenweep N.M.
UT
AZ
Bluff
191
to Chinle
Abajo Mtns.
Bears Ears
Cedar Mesa
Valley of the Gods
Mexican Hat
Monument Valley
Natural Bridges N.M.
261
Moki Dugway
163
Grand Gulch
95
to Kayenta
to Hite & to Hanksville
276
to Halls Crossing

1. Tower House

Easy 0.5-mile out-and-back; allow 1 hour
Map: Trails Illustrated 706: Grand Gulch/Cedar Mesa Plateau

GETTING THERE: From its junction with US Route 191 south of Blanding, drive 6.25 miles west on UT 95 to Cottonwood Canyon Road. Turn right here. At a fork about 1 mile down this good unpaved road, turn left onto County Road 228 and proceed 4 miles. Turn left onto a spur to the parking area.
ON THE TRAIL: Walk down the cairned trail to a hoodoo capped by a balanced rock, which marks the drainage containing the ruin. Follow the slickrock rim until it seems safe to descend. The two-story ruin and its adjacent kiva occupy a well-watered alcove.
NEARBY: With a high-clearance vehicle, you can drive about 1.75 miles farther on CR 228 to a commanding perch above Comb Ridge.

2. Butler Wash Ruins

Very easy 0.75-mile loop; allow 30 minutes
Map: Trails Illustrated 706: Grand Gulch/Cedar Mesa Plateau

GETTING THERE: From US Route 191, drive west on UT 95 for about 10.5 miles. The ruins are located at milepost 111. Turn right and park in the designated lot.
ON THE TRAIL: A short loop leads to an overlook of a cliff dwelling, perched in an alcove across the canyon. The ruin contains four kivas: one constructed in the square Kayenta style and three in the round Mesa Verdean variety. Walk about 50 yards to the left of the overlook to see a natural bridge near the main building.

3. Mule Canyon

Easy 8-mile out-and-back; allow 4 hours
Permit required (obtain at trailhead); binoculars recommended
Map: Trails Illustrated 706: Grand Gulch/Cedar Mesa Plateau

GETTING THERE: Drive west on UT 95 for about 20 miles. Near milepost 102, reach the junction with an unpaved road (County Road 263) signed for Texas Flat. Turn right and in under 0.5 mile, where the road crosses the south fork of Mule Canyon, pull off to park.
ON THE TRAIL: Both forks of Mule Canyon are bedecked with ruins. The South Fork contains several, some of which are accessible.

For the first 0.5 mile, and occasionally thereafter, you must fight brush. During the summer monsoon season, pools and quicksand also may conspire to slow you down. As usual, the cliff dwellings occupy the south-facing canyon wall. The first, at mile 1, is the much-photographed **House on Fire Ruin**, with a roof that appears to be licked with flame. The next four sites—at miles 2, 2.5, 2.75, and 3.25, respectively—are unnamed. Of these the second and fourth are the most extensive, but visiting either requires a perilous climb. Don't miss **Wall Ruin** at mile 3.75, a multiroom structure with intact roof beams. Two more sites, the former small and the latter difficult to access, are located within the next 0.25 mile.
NEARBY: With a high-clearance or four-wheel-drive vehicle, you can drive to spectacular **Arch Canyon Overlook**. Continue up Texas Flat Road to mile 4.5. Bear right here

One of the Bears Ears, as reflected in a stock pond

and at mile 5.25. At mile 6, you come to an expanse of slickrock. Here the road hairpins quite improbably to the right. Deteriorating badly, it ends near the aerie at mile 6.25. Walk a short distance from here onto a tongue of rock, aided by metal steps. From here you can spot a large, low arch on the canyon's east wall.

Just 0.5 mile west of Mule Canyon on UT 95, visit **Mule Canyon Ruins**, a seven-hundred-year-old complex with twelve rooms, a restored kiva, and the remains of a tower.

4. Cave Towers

Easy 1-mile out-and-back; allow 45 minutes
Map: Trails Illustrated 706: Grand Gulch/Cedar Mesa Plateau

GETTING THERE: Drive west on UT 95 for about 20 miles from US Route 191. The pullout lies on the south side of the highway between mileposts 102 and 103, just opposite the turnoff for Mule Canyon. Park outside the gate.

ON THE TRAIL: Take a dirt track to its end, then follow the shallow wash for 100 yards to the rim of lower Mule Canyon to visit numerous sites, some multistoried. Although no trails connect the dwellings, navigation is straightforward. Look for granaries under the rim to the east.

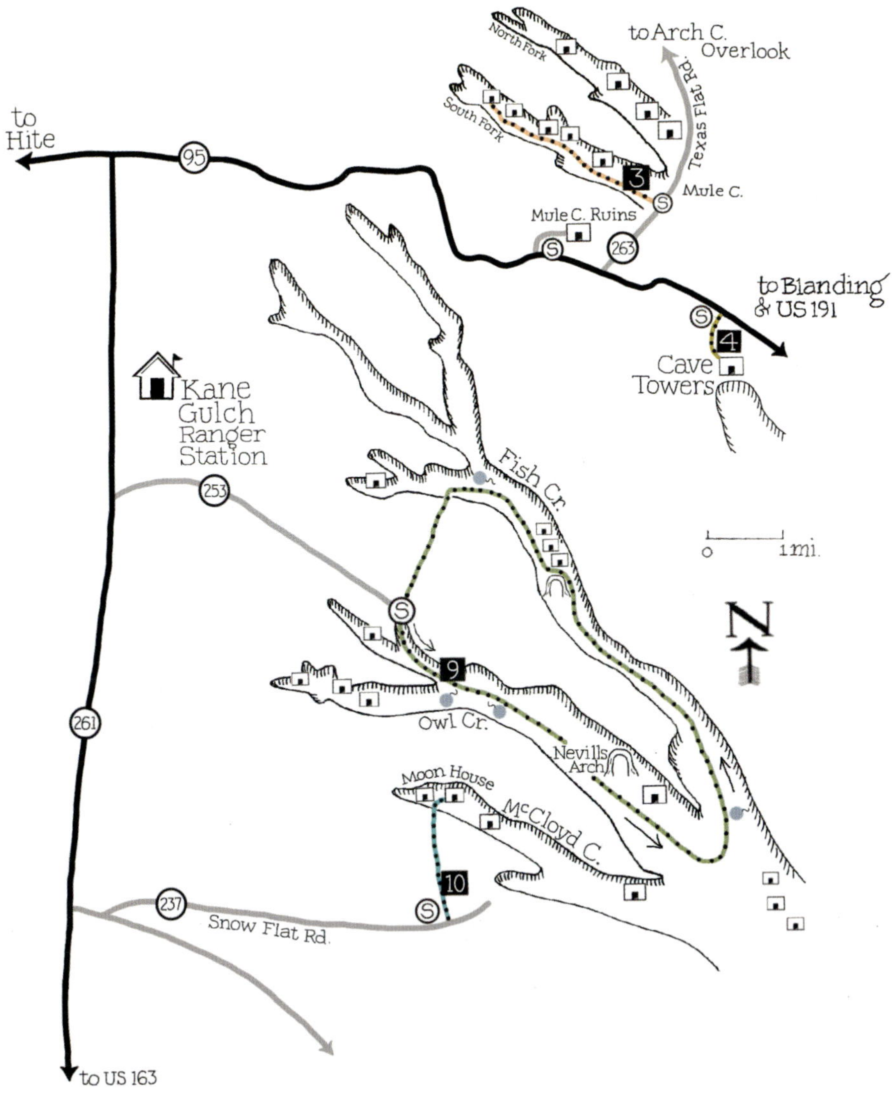

NATURAL BRIDGES NATIONAL MONUMENT

This national monument contains three spectacular spans, all bearing Hopi names. Bridges are relatively rare, and by any measure these rank among the largest in the world. Hewn from Cedar Mesa Sandstone, they were "discovered" by prospector Cass Hite in the 1880s, though the area long was known to local Indians. Because of its remoteness from human settlement, Natural Bridges was designated the world's first International Dark Sky Park in 2007. On clear nights, the Milky Way bursts forth in all its creamy brilliance. In season, rangers hold astronomy talks.

From the intersection of US Route 191 south of Blanding, drive about 35 miles west on UT 95 to UT 275. Turn north here to intersect the park road. Past the visitor center, that road is one-way.

5. Natural Bridges Loop

Moderate 8.25-mile loop; allow 5 hours
Optional car shuttle
Map: Trails Illustrated 703: Manti-La Sal National Forest

GETTING THERE: From the monument visitor center, go 2.75 miles down the park road to the Sipapu Bridge pullout. This is where the hike begins. If you have a second vehicle, you can drive it to the Owachomo Bridge pullout. Parking it there will allow you to shave 3 miles off the trip. In that case, simply drive the first vehicle back to the Sipapu Bridge pullout to begin the hike.

ON THE TRAIL: Although this loop can be executed in either direction, hiking counterclockwise minimizes elevation gain to the rim. Utilizing stairs, ladders, and handrails, the trail drops 500 feet from the overlook to the floor of White Canyon at mile 0.5. Halfway down, detour left past a small ruin to an excellent viewpoint.

Sipapu Bridge and its brethren are hewn from Cedar Mesa Sandstone.

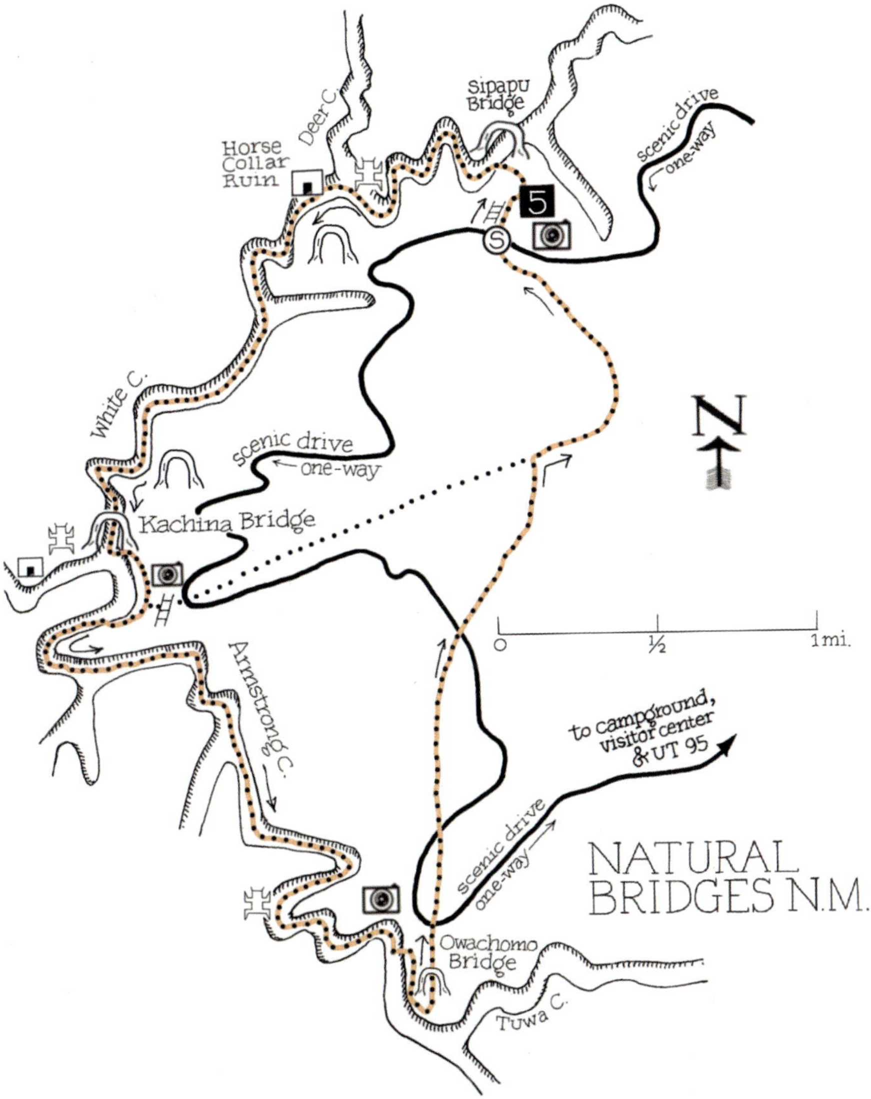

Vaulting over White Canyon, **Sipapu Bridge**—the grandest of the three, at almost 275 feet wide—derives its name from a travertine limestone formation on Arizona's Little Colorado River, which traditional Hopis regard as the portal through which their ancestors entered our world. In the underground ceremonial pits known as kivas, that passage is symbolized by a round depression in the floor. Turn left at the arch, heading downstream. Handprint pictographs adorn the junction with Deer Canyon. **Horse Collar Ruin**, a cliff dwelling, sits opposite a small arch. A seldom-used trail to the rim departs here.

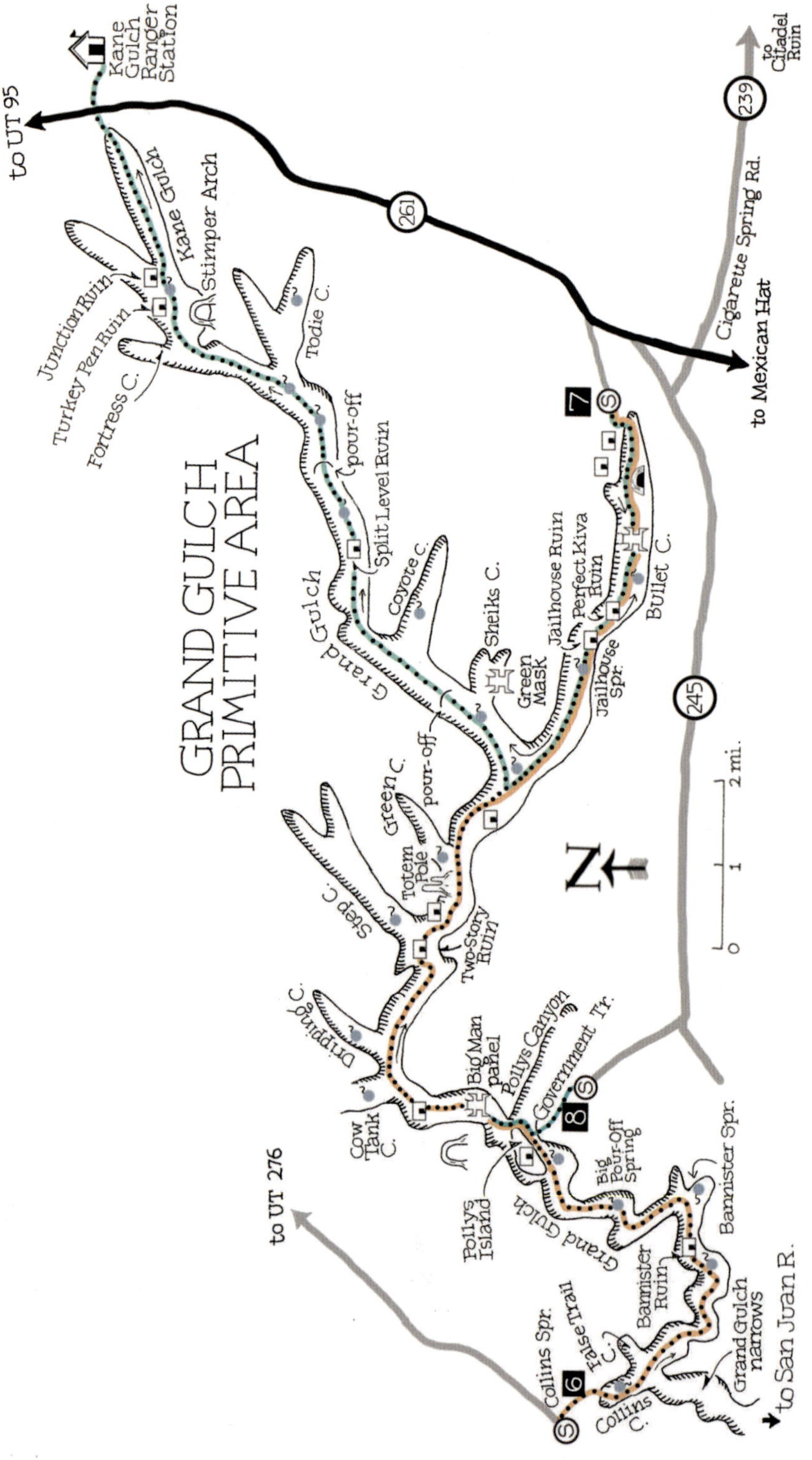

GRAND GULCH PRIMITIVE AREA
Kane Gulch Ranger Station
to UT 95
261
239
to Citadel Ruin
Cigarette Spring Rd.
to Mexican Hat
Kane Gulch
Stimper Arch
Junction Ruin
Turkey Pen Ruin
Fortress C.
Todie C.
pour-off
Split Level Ruin
Grand Gulch
Coyote C.
Sheiks C.
Green Mask
Jailhouse Ruin
Perfect Kiva Ruin
Jailhouse Spr.
Bullet C.
7
245
pour-off
Green C.
Totem Pole
Step C.
Two-Story Ruin
N
0 1 2 mi.
Dripping C.
Cow Tank C.
Big Man panel
Pollys Canyon
Government Tr.
8
Pollys Island
Big Pour-Off Spring
Bannister Spr.
Grand Gulch
Bannister Ruin
to UT 276
Collins Spr.
False Trail C.
6
Collins C.
Grand Gulch narrows
to San Juan R.

At mile 2.75, **Kachina Bridge**, the youngest of the trio, spans the idyllic junction of White and Armstrong Canyons. Pictographs decorate both abutments, with more rock art and small ruins located a short distance beyond the bridge. In Hopi cosmology, kachinas—the spirits of ancestors who supposedly transformed into clouds after they died—dwell in northern Arizona's San Francisco Peaks.

Go left from the arch, entering Armstrong Canyon. The trail ascends the left bank briefly to bypass some narrows before intersecting the path to the Kachina parking lot. Continue straight ahead here, dropping back into the canyon. At mile 3.75, where the wash snakes below an anvil-shaped undercut, look for a pictograph panel on the right.

The trail ascends to the left, remaining about 50 feet above the canyon floor. **Owachomo Bridge**—the oldest, smallest, and most eroded—comes into view around mile 5. Owachomo ("rock mound," an apparent reference to the knob that crowns the span) is adjacent to, rather than astride, Armstrong Canyon, having been carved by a different stream. Pass beneath the bridge and climb to the overlook at mile 5.25. Cross the park road to chill out on the 3-mile path through pinyons and junipers back to your vehicle.

GRAND GULCH PRIMITIVE AREA

Few canyons house as many unspoiled Anasazi (Ancestral Puebloan) artifacts as this lovely San Juan tributary, which extends over 50 miles from the river to its upper reaches in the shadow of the Bears Ears. Prior to the troubles that beset its inhabitants in the late 13th century, Grand Gulch may have been the most densely populated real estate in today's continental US. An abundance of entry and exit routes allows hikers to tailor trips to their wishes. Although day hikes can be rewarding, visitors can maximize their enjoyment by opting for point-to-point backpacks. Before setting forth, inquire about water availability at **Kane Gulch Ranger Station**, 4 miles south of UT 95 on UT 261. Reserve permits online several months in advance, or try for a walk-in permit on the morning of your desired hike.

6. Collins Spring to Bullet Canyon Backpack

Moderate 29.75-mile point-to-point; allow 4 days

Permit and vehicle shuttle required; high-clearance vehicles, water filter, and binoculars recommended

Map: Trails Illustrated 706: Grand Gulch/Cedar Mesa Plateau

GETTING THERE: Using two vehicles, drive to the **Bullet Canyon trailhead**. To get there, turn south off UT 95 onto UT 261 just east of Natural Bridges National Monument. Drive 10 miles to the marked turnoff. Go right onto the dirt road and continue 1 mile to its end. Park the first vehicle here. In the second vehicle, drive to the **Collins Spring trailhead**. Retrace your route to UT 95. Travel west on UT 95 past Natural Bridges and turn left on UT 276. Near milepost 83, turn east onto a dirt road and drive for about 6.5 miles to the canyon rim. Without a high-clearance vehicle, you may have to walk the last 2.5 miles.

These headless Grand Gulch pictographs exhibit an unusual, pointillist style.

ON THE TRAIL: This ambitious hike acquaints you with the best of what Cedar Mesa has to offer. You can lengthen it by 8 miles if you push on past Bullet Canyon to Kane Gulch.

From the Collins Spring trailhead, follow the trail 2 miles down **Collins Canyon** to its intersection with **Grand Gulch**. Careful map reading will prevent your being confused by False Trail Canyon, which joins Collins in this vicinity. If you want to detour to see the short but impressive **Grand Gulch narrows**, turn right, walking 0.25 mile downstream; otherwise, go straight ahead and amble up the canyon past a large slickrock platform. You may encounter shallow pools here.

A slickrock terrace at mile 4.25 offers ideal camping. At mile 4.5, you come to a spring just 0.25 mile below **Bannister Ruin** on the left. This two-tiered ruin contains an exposed horizontal beam and an intact but fragile kiva.

Head around the left side of **Big Pour Off Spring** at mile 8.75. Your next landmark is the junction with the **Government Trail** at mile 11.75. A good campsite awaits between this trail junction and **Pollys Island**, formed by a rincon of Grand Gulch; notice the ruin nestled up in the cliff on the left.

Look for the impressive **Big Man** pictograph panel 1.5 miles past Pollys Island, about 200 feet above the canyon floor on the right. The start of the 0.25-mile path leading up to it is marked by a cairn; climb a precipitous rocky draw to a cliff, and follow the cliff line to the left. Shortly before the viewpoint for this panel, a shady undercut on the left also shelters rock art. Water may be available up Cow Tank Canyon at mile 15.25 and in Dripping Canyon, 0.5 mile farther.

Just past Dripping Canyon is another terrace around mile 15.75 that could provide a suitable campsite. Few such sites exist between here and the Totem Pole. In fact, these next 4.25 miles, which involve considerable bushwhacking, are the most tedious of the trip. **Step Canyon**, at mile 18.5, has a small clearing that you can use as a base of explorations. The entire tributary deserves study. Anasazi sites abound, and you should persist until you locate **Two-Story Ruin**, hidden by brush on the left bank of the main canyon. Step has a reliable spring about 0.75 mile from its mouth.

The **Totem Pole**, an unmistakable pillar on the left at mile 20, signals the end of the difficult stretch. Relax among cottonwoods before proceeding to the **Bullet Canyon** junction, at mile 22.5. Although this section of trail contains continual ups and downs, you will be relieved to be done with the willows. Keep your eyes peeled for small ruins on both sides of the trail.

Turn right into Bullet Canyon. About 2.5 miles from the confluence, at mile 25 of the hike, Jailhouse and Perfect Kiva Ruins appear on the right. Across the canyon from **Jailhouse Ruin**, so-named for having a window with wooden crossbars, is a good campsite near a reliable spring. **Perfect Kiva Ruin** sports a reconstructed roof and a ladder leading to its interior. Between these sites and a slickrock ramp at mile 28, the canyon narrows and its floor becomes brushy. Pass a large cave on the right at mile 29. Rounding a bend at about mile 29.5, look up to view a square masonry tower on the rim. Shortly thereafter, climb out of the canyon on a steep trail to your left. To visit the square tower that you saw from below, detour left at a large cairn upon reaching the rim at mile 29.75.

NEARBY: Between mileposts 66 and 67 on UT 276, a pullout on the north side of the highway allows you to visit well-preserved **Castle Ruin**, a classic multiroom cliff dwelling.

7. Bullet Canyon to Kane Gulch Backpack

Moderate 23-mile point-to-point; allow 3 days
Permit and vehicle shuttle required; water filter and binoculars recommended
Map: Trails Illustrated 706: Grand Gulch/Cedar Mesa Plateau

GETTING THERE: Using two vehicles, drive to Kane Gulch Ranger Station, which is located 4 miles south of UT 95 on UT 261. Park the first vehicle here. Drive the second vehicle to Bullet Canyon by continuing 6 miles farther south on UT 261 to the marked turnoff to Bullet Canyon. Turn right and follow the dirt road 1 mile to its end.

ON THE TRAIL: The highlight of this trip is Perfect Kiva Ruin, the only place on Cedar Mesa where visitors may enter a kiva. When controversial explorer Richard Wetherill explored Grand Gulch in the 1890s, his party excavated this and other sites.

The Bullet Canyon Trail starts to the right of the parking area. Follow the rim a short distance. At a large cairn, descend to the canyon floor on a no-nonsense trail, turning right at the bottom. Less than a mile from the trailhead, pass a large cave on your left. Another mile brings you to a long slickrock ramp, below which hiking becomes tougher as the canyon narrows. The trail remains brushy for the next mile, but walking improves as the canyon widens out.

Jailhouse and Perfect Kiva Ruins are on your right at about mile 4.75. Jailhouse Ruin, with its small, barred window and striking white circular pictographs, is easier to spot. Perfect Kiva Ruin has a reconstructed roof and a ladder leading down to its interior. Across the canyon from the former is a good camping place amid cottonwoods. You can obtain water from a spring at mile 5.

Past this point, about 2.5 miles of rather effortless walking brings you to the confluence with **Grand Gulch**, where there is another, more heavily used campsite. Turn right, proceeding upstream. Be alert for ruins in alcoves throughout this area, especially on south-facing walls.

Sheiks Canyon at mile 8.5, on the right, is rich in rock art, the prime specimen of which is the **Green Mask** pictograph near a spring about 0.25 mile from the mouth. On the left at mile 12.75 is **Split Level Ruin**, one of Grand Gulch's major houses. **Todie Canyon**, 3 miles farther, boasts numerous archaeological treasures.

Past **Stimper Arch** are the significant pueblos of **Turkey Pen** and **Junction Ruins**, on the left at miles 18.25 and 19, respectively. The latter, housed in a football field–sized alcove, bears the inscription of John Wetherill (Richard's brother), the rancher-turned-explorer whose main claim to fame was his "discovery" of Rainbow Bridge (see Chapter 6, Hike 38). Junction Ruin marks the confluence of Grand Gulch with **Kane Gulch**, the tributary from which you exit the primitive area. Ascend 500 feet over 4 miles to the Kane Gulch parking lot and your waiting vehicle.

8. Government Trail

Moderate 9-mile out-and-back; allow 5.5 hours
High-clearance vehicle required
Map: Trails Illustrated 706: Grand Gulch/Cedar Mesa Plateau

GETTING THERE: Drive to the Kane Gulch Ranger Station, located 4 miles south of UT 95 on UT 261. From Kane Gulch Ranger Station, head south on UT 261 for 5.5 miles. Turn right onto County Road 245, which has a packed dirt surface. Turn right again at miles 2.5 and 5.5, remaining on CR 245. A rocky tertiary road branches off to the right at mile 7.5, paralleling Pollys Canyon. The parking lot is 1.5 miles down this road. Stop short of the end if the going gets too tough.

ON THE TRAIL: The Government Trail provides a relatively easy route into Grand Gulch and can be used as a launchpad for multiday trips.

Wide, unobstructed views of Navajo Mountain, the Bears Ears, and the Little Rockies are yours as you walk toward the rim of Grand Gulch. A post at mile 2 marks the path into the canyon. Directly across from this point is the isolated mesa of **Pollys Island**, named to honor a celebrated local archaeologist. Look for an inaccessible three-room ruin one ledge below the mesa top and, farther down, a granary. Nearby, two arches come into view, one on Pollys Island and the other near the mouth of Pollys Canyon.

From the overlook, the trail descends 700 feet to reach the floor of Grand Gulch at mile 3. To access the **Big Man** panel, turn right, proceeding upstream 1.5 miles past shady cottonwood groves. Marked by a large cairn on the right, a path ascends a precipitous rocky draw about 200 feet to a cliff. Follow the cliff-line to the left. The pictograph, about 0.25 mile from the initial cairn, represents two life-sized males and what appears to be a pregnant female.

CEDAR MESA AND VICINITY

Extending from Comb Ridge to Grand Gulch, the rolling plateau of Cedar Mesa sports pinyon and juniper vegetation. Its name derives from the junipers, which are known locally as cedars. Rock layers range from Navajo Sandstone, the youngest stratum, to the Honaker Trail Formation, the oldest; though buffy Cedar Mesa Sandstone is by far the most prevalent. A sampler of the area's archaeological wealth appears below.

The featured hikes are all off UT 261, which follows a ridgeline on rolling Cedar Mesa between the canyon systems of Grand Gulch to the west and the Comb Ridge area to the east. Both systems drain into the **San Juan River.** Hikes in this section explore some east side ruins. Obtain permits at Kane Gulch Ranger Station, 4 miles south of UT 95 on UT 261, or (for day use only) at fee-tubes near the trailheads.

9. Fish and Owl Creeks Backpack

Moderate 15.5-mile loop; allow 2 days
Permit required; water filter, trekking poles, and binoculars recommended
Map: Trails Illustrated 706: Grand Gulch/Cedar Mesa Plateau

GETTING THERE: From Blanding, drive south on US Route 191 for 4 miles to UT 95. Turn right (west) here and continue for 28 miles to its junction with UT 261. Go left (south) on UT 261 for 5 miles. Then go left onto a graded dirt road, following it 5 miles through a pinyon and juniper forest to its end.

ON THE TRAIL: These adjoining canyons boast numerous ruins, unusual rock formations, and a large arch. Check at Kane Gulch Ranger Station on water availability. (See map on page 185.)

From the parking area, follow the roadbed on the right 50 yards to a wash, which leads to the canyon rim. The first ruin sits near a dry-fall on the right. The cairned trail passes another ruin and pour-off before dropping into **Owl Creek** at mile 1.5. At the bottom, look for a spring at ground level. You may find pools over the next few miles.

Follow the wash downstream, passing **Nevills Arch** at mile 4.5 in a sandstone fin on the left. Owl Creek empties into Fish Creek at mile 6.75. The confluence makes a good place to camp. **McCloyd Canyon**, about a mile below the confluence, contains numerous ruins, including magnificent Moon House (see Hike 10).

Turn left at the confluence and walk up **Fish Creek**, which is even more inviting than Owl. It boasts more archaeological sites as well, though you must look carefully to find them. An open area 2.5 miles from the confluence is ringed by curious monoliths.

About 6 miles above the confluence, Fish Creek forks. Go left and continue 0.5 mile to a pour-off, where a spring gushes out of the canyon wall. The canyon narrows considerably past the fork, with heavy brush and boulders rendering progress more difficult. With an extra night to spare, camp on a slickrock terrace opposite the spring.

Immediately past the spring, a large cairn indicates the start of the brutal, nearly vertical climb out of Fish Creek (600 feet over 0.25 mile). The top rewards you with

A substantial overhang shelters atmospheric Moon House.

views of both canyons as well as the Bears Ears buttes. Pick up a 2-mile trail through the pygmy pinyon and juniper forest back to your vehicle.

10. Moon House

Moderate 4-mile out-and-back; allow 3 hours

Permit and high-clearance vehicle required; trekking poles and 30-foot safety rope recommended

Map: Trails Illustrated 706: Grand Gulch/Cedar Mesa Plateau

GETTING THERE: From its intersection with US Route 191 south of Blanding, turn right (west) onto UT 95 and proceed 28 miles to UT 261. Travel south on UT 261 for 10 miles. Turn left onto unpaved Snow Flat Road, which is rough in spots and impassable when wet. Before mile 0.5, go left at a fork. Follow the road for 8 miles to a kiosk. You can either park here (as is assumed in the write-up below), or turn left onto a sketchy two-track and continue to its end, thereby shortening the hike by 2 miles. For reference, consult the map corresponding to Mule Canyon (page 185).

ON THE TRAIL: Trot out the superlatives. This archaeological masterpiece in **McCloyd Canyon** will launch you into orbit. Visitation is limited to 20 persons per day. For reservations, contact the Monticello BLM (435-587-1510). Pick up your permit on the morning of the hike at Kane Gulch Ranger Station, 4 miles south of UT 95 on UT 261.

From the parking area, follow a two-track for 1 mile to the canyon rim and descend 400 feet along a steep, cairned trail. At about the halfway point, the route laterals to the right before resuming its downward course. The ruin, which occupies a south-facing alcove, comes into view. A sketchy 8-foot drop may alarm some hikers. Here a safety rope may prove reassuring, especially on the return. Beyond the drop, continue toward the canyon floor, passing between two immense boulders. Cross the canyon, then turn right and follow cairns up a slickrock slope to the **Moon House** ruin.

Inhabited circa 1250 CE, the complex extends for about 0.25 mile along a wide, flat ledge. The main ruin features a series of rooms lining an interior courtyard. A snake pictograph decorates the upper wall. Notice a large white circle accompanied by a string of small white dots, which may represent the moon and stars. For maximum enjoyment, explore the ledge in both directions.

11. Fallen Roof Ruin

Moderate 2.5-mile out-and-back, with routefinding; allow 3 hours
Permit and high-clearance vehicle required
Map: Trails Illustrated 706: Grand Gulch/Cedar Mesa Plateau

GETTING THERE: Four miles south of Blanding on US Route 191, turn right (west) onto UT 95. Drive 28 miles to the junction with UT 261. Turning left (south), drive 13 miles to intersect County Road 239, signed for Cigarette Spring. Go left on this unpaved road, which is impassable when wet. At mile 3.25, turn left onto a side track to park.

ON THE TRAIL: The trail winds through pinyons and junipers to the rim of a Road Canyon tributary at mile 0.25 before switchbacking to the canyon floor. The junction with **Road Canyon** is at about mile 1. Skirt a pool and pour-off, dropping down to the streambed between a monolith and a jumble of boulders. Turn right at the bottom, passing a second monolith. From here, pick out several uncommonly photogenic granaries interlinked on a ledge on the far side of the canyon. Ascend about 100 feet to the base of the second monolith and contour around to the right to visit them. As the ruin's name suggests, the ceiling of the alcove in which it is housed has partially splayed off, exposing the underlying rock. An optical illusion gives the ceiling a coppery appearance.

12. The Citadel

Moderate 4-mile out-and-back, with some exposure; allow 3 hours
Permit required; high-clearance or four-wheel-drive vehicle and a 30-foot safety rope recommended
Map: Trails Illustrated 706: Grand Gulch/Cedar Mesa Plateau

GETTING THERE: From its junction with UT 95, head south on UT 261 for 13 miles. Turn left onto the unpaved County Road 239 (impassable when wet), marked for Cigarette Spring. Issue yourself a permit at the fee station about a mile in. The road can be negotiated by passenger cars as far as mile 5.5. With a heavier-duty vehicle, continue to a fork at mile 6. Go left onto this miserable track and follow it 0.75 mile to its end.

ON THE TRAIL: The cairned trail to this extraordinary stronghold begins at a signpost to the right of the parking lot. For the first mile, it closely parallels the rim of many-armed Road Canyon, which showcases the layer-cake ledges characteristic of Cedar Mesa Sandstone. It then descends rapidly to the next level by means of a narrow crack on the right. Cairns simplify your passage to a still-lower level, about 150 feet below the rim. You emerge onto a causeway that leads to a promontory separating Road Canyon from one of its tributaries. Unless you fall at the extreme end of the acrophobe spectrum, crossing the 30-foot-wide isthmus should set off no alarm bells. The Citadel occupies the right side of the promontory, one ledge below its top.

Upon reaching the promontory, begin climbing while traversing slightly right toward some talus. A convenient slope leading upward through a break in the cliffs takes you directly below the ruin. Survey the boulders immediately in front of you to determine how best to negotiate the last 15 vertical feet. This is the point where a safety rope might prove useful. Your reward is an almost perfectly preserved set of rooms in the shadow of a colossal balanced rock. Around the corner are several

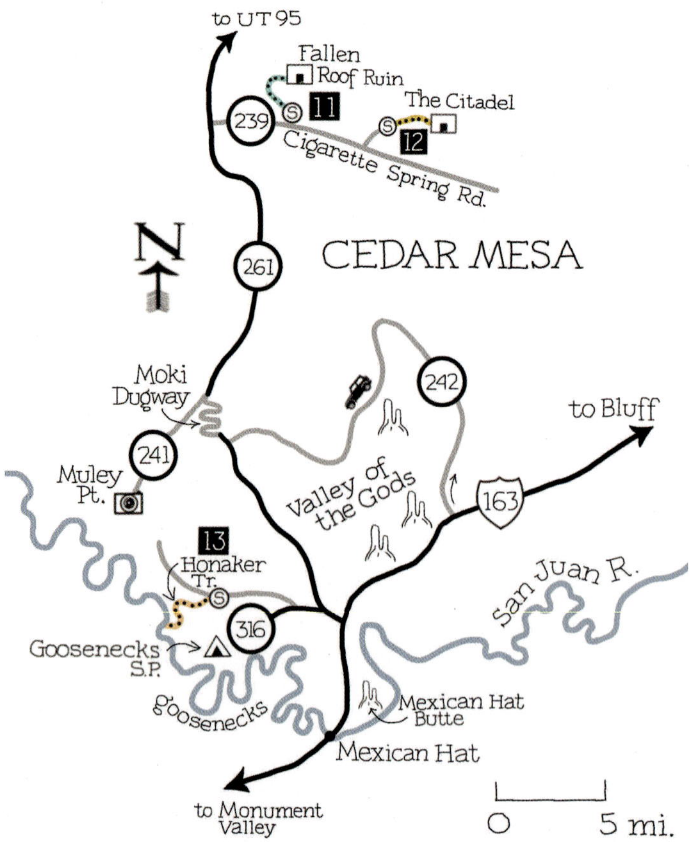

The ceiling of Fallen Roof Ruin appears to have a coppery glow.

additional structures, in varying degrees of deterioration. Defense from enemies clearly was uppermost in the minds of those who built the impregnable fortress.

NEARBY: From the parking lot, another cairned route leads to heavily damaged **Seven Kivas Ruin**, 1.5 miles distant, on the north side of the canyon.

If you backtrack to UT 261 and turn left, following that road south toward its terminus, you soon come to the rim of Cedar Mesa. Here the road executes a series of no-nonsense, hairpin bends down the 1200-foot escarpment. This thrilling part of the drive is known as the **Moki Dugway**, "Moki" for the Mormon pioneers' name for the Anasazi and "dugway" to indicate a route carved from solid rock. Trigger alert: The unpaved switchbacks here lack guardrails. At the top of the switchbacks, a good dirt road paralleling Johns Canyon leads to **Muley Point**, a spectacular aerie 2000 feet above the San Juan River. The buttes of Monument Valley are visible on the southern horizon.

The isthmus to the Citadel once boasted walls and armed defenders.

13. Honaker Trail

Moderate 4-mile out-and-back, with some exposure; allow 3 hours
High-clearance or four-wheel-drive vehicle and trekking poles recommended
Map: Trails Illustrated 706: Grand Gulch/Cedar Mesa Plateau

GETTING THERE: There are two ways to reach the trailhead. From Blanding, the most direct way is to drive south on US Route 191 for 25 miles or so to Bluff. Once the original Mormon settlement in southeastern Utah, the charming town has morphed into a thriving art colony and gateway to river trips on the San Juan. Pause briefly in town to admire the **Navajo Twins** buttes. A few miles past Bluff comes the intersection of US 191, which jogs to the left, and US 163. Go straight ahead here onto US 163 and continue south for approximately 37 miles to the junction of UT 261. Turn north onto UT 261 and drive 1 mile to the junction with UT 316, signed for Goosenecks State Park. Turn west (left) here onto UT 316. After 0.5 mile, go right onto a good dirt road and proceed 2.5 miles to a fork. Bear left at the fork and continue 1 mile to the top of a grade. Passenger cars should stop here (adding 1.5 easy miles to the hike); heavier-duty vehicles can proceed another 0.75 mile, parking by a large cairn to the right of the road.

Alternatively, if you are traveling directly from the area around Bears Ears and Cedar Mesa, take UT 261 south from UT 95 toward its end at US 163. About a mile north of Route 163, turn right (west) onto UT 316, signed for Goosenecks State Park, and proceed as above.

ON THE TRAIL: From the cairn, follow a dirt track about 100 yards to the canyon rim to yet another cairn, this one Olympic-sized. It marks the start of the somewhat rocky trail, which was expertly engineered by a prospector in the late 19th century. The trail's initial descent from the rim of the mesa utilizes a few tight switchbacks. Thereafter it features long, gentle traverses as it probes for breaks in the layer-cake walls. A series of four short, steep pitches commence after you reach a tongue at mile 1. From here the trail laterals far to the right before doubling back to end at a beach frequented by rafting parties. Although the rim is 1200 feet above the San Juan, the return leg of the hike seems easier because gravity no longer threatens to throw you off balance.

NEARBY: If you follow UT 316 to its end instead of turning right to access the Honaker Trail, you soon arrive at **Goosenecks State Park**. From the campground here, you receive breathtaking views of the goosenecks of the San Juan River.

A profitable 16.5-mile semi-loop drive through aptly named **Valley of the Gods** snakes between US 163 and UT 261. Although you can execute this scenic drive in either direction, it is better to start at the southern end of the loop along US 163, near milepost 29. Almost immediately upon accessing the loop, you must ford a shallow wash. Although this crossing is generally unproblematic, it would be wise to check its depth on foot before proceeding. The good unpaved road traverses a broad, open valley situated at the lower end of Lime Creek. Its characteristic formations are reddish-brown pyramids capped by round knobs. Among the more prominent are the Setting Hen, the Seven Sailors, and Scotchman Butte.

COMB RIDGE

Butler Wash, on the east side of the Comb Ridge monocline, offers an embarrassment of archaeological riches. Good dirt tracks, passable by regular vehicles, connect these marvels. All are off unpaved Butler Wash Road (County Road 262), which extends roughly between Blanding and the hamlet of Bluff, home to the **Bears Ears Education Center**. If driven carefully, the road is passable for all vehicles. Because the attractions in Butler Wash concentrate at the road's south end, plan to start there.

From Blanding, drive about 25 miles south on US Route 191 to Bluff, pausing to admire the Navajo Twins buttes. At milepost 39, the highway soon cuts dramatically through **Comb Ridge**. About 4 miles south of town, US 191 diverts to the left. Go straight ahead here onto US 163. Follow this highway for a mile. Across the road from an airstrip, turn right onto CR 262, passing through a gate. From here, follow the directions to your chosen trailhead. Hikes 14 through 17 all begin off this road on its left side.

Just south of Bluff is **Sand Island Recreation Area** on the banks of the San Juan. Rock art panels line the cliff. From here, private and commercial float trips launch for Mexican Hat and Clay Hills Crossing; permits are required.

14. Wolfman Panel

Easy 0.5-mile out-and-back, with scrambling; allow 30 minutes
Map: Trails Illustrated 706: Grand Gulch/Cedar Mesa Plateau

GETTING THERE: From Bluff, take US Route 191 south 4 miles to the junction of US 163. Go straight here, following US 163 for 1 mile, then turn right and pass through a

Aerial view of the San Juan River canyon near Mexican Hat

gate onto unpaved County Road 262. Reset your trip odometer here. Remain on CR 262, ignoring short tracks that branch off to the left and right. At mile 1, turn left onto a short, signed track to a parking area.

ON THE TRAIL: Strike off for the canyon rim. A cairned route descends a slickrock ramp to the cliffside pre-Columbian panel. Aside from the eponymous wolf mask, the unique figures include what appear to be a spinal column, thunderbird, squid, shield, and life-sized anthropomorph.

15. Procession Panel

Moderate 3-mile out-and-back, with routefinding and scrambling; allow 2 hours
Map: Trails Illustrated 706: Grand Gulch/Cedar Mesa Plateau

GETTING THERE: From Bluff, take US Route 191 south 4 miles to the junction of US 163. Go straight here, following US 163 for 1 mile. Then turn right onto County Road 262, passing through a gate. Reset your trip odometer here. Remain on CR 262, ignoring short tracks that branch off to the left and right. At mile 6.5, turn left down a short track and park where it ends.

ON THE TRAIL: The Procession Panel, near the crest of Comb Ridge, features 179 figures marching in lockstep. The route can be difficult to follow, both because it favors slickrock and because of some false cairns that may lead you astray. Avoid trouble by scouting the scene visually from the trailhead. Locate a ruddy cliff straight ahead on the skyline, about 650 feet above your present position. Immediately to its right is a defile separating the ridge from a white sandstone dome. The panel adorns the top of this dome, facing the ruddy cliff.

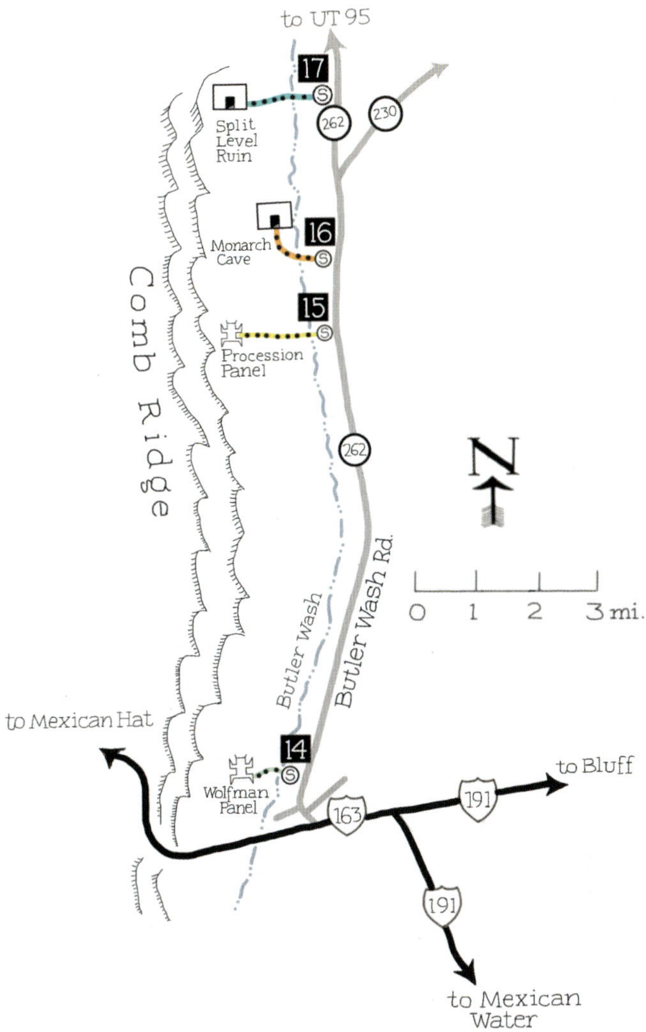

Begin by crossing three arroyos. Thereafter, the route favors slickrock. At mile 0.25 ascend the first of a few sandstone slopes and set a course for the defile. Skirting a pour-off, drop down into the drainage, then climb gradually to its head. The panel, etched into the dark desert varnish on the right, extends for several yards. To reach its base you must clamber up a talus field of boulders. Representations of bighorn sheep also figure prominently.

16. Monarch Cave Ruin

Easy 1.25-mile out-and-back; allow 1 hour

Map: Trails Illustrated 706: Grand Gulch/Cedar Mesa Plateau

GETTING THERE: From Bluff, take US Route 191 south 4 miles to the junction of US 163. Go straight here, following US 163. In 1 mile, turn right onto County Road 262, passing through a gate. Reset your trip odometer at the gate. Remain on CR 262, ignoring short tracks that branch off to the left and right. At mile 7, pull off onto a short track to the left.

ON THE TRAIL: Location, location, location! In Monarch Cave, local Anasazi picked an enchanting site to call home. From the parking lot, follow the trail across Butler Wash and into a shade-filled side-canyon on the right. Near its end is a small pool. The cliff dwelling, in an alcove about 125 feet above the streambed, soon comes into view. On your return, check out what may be the best vantage point, from a rocky bench on the right. You cannot reach that point safely from the ruin, so you must access it from the canyon floor.

17. Split Level Ruin

Moderate 2-mile out-and-back; allow 1.5 hours
Map: Trails Illustrated 706: Grand Gulch/Cedar Mesa Plateau

GETTING THERE: From Bluff, take US Route 191 south 4 miles to the junction of US 163. Go straight here, following US 163. In 1 mile, turn right onto County Road 262, passing through a gate. Reset your trip odometer at the gate. Remain on CR 262, ignoring short tracks that branch off to the left and right. At mile 8.25, you reach a junction with CR 230 immediately past a cattle guard. Go left here, remaining on CR 262, and continue for 1.25 miles. Turn left onto a dirt road and park.

ON THE TRAIL: The trailhead is marked by a tall signpost. Drop down to cross Butler Wash, where you intersect a two-track heading for a grove of cottonwoods near the base of Comb Ridge. Ignore a misleading, ill-positioned sign that seems to instruct hikers to turn right. Instead, leave the track here, continuing straight ahead for about 25 yards to a fork with another signpost. This one is accurate. The path to the right drops down into a wash and enters a channel on the right. Follow this path past an attractive alcove on your right. Here the ruin's inaccessible upper tier comes into view. Leave the wash upon arriving at a steep path on the right. Ascend and proceed along the base of the cliffs, first to rock art panels featuring a precision bull's-eye and then to the multiroom cliff dwelling. Expect to see cows, or evidence thereof, in the vicinity.

MONUMENT VALLEY TRIBAL PARK

Monument Valley, famed not only as a popular tourist destination but also as the backdrop for countless media events, sits astride the Utah-Arizona border. From Blanding, take US Route 191 south to Bluff, picking up US 163 about 4 miles south of town. Just shy of the town of **Mexican Hat**, stop near milepost 23 to appreciate the eponymous butte that resembles a man sporting a sombrero. Behind it looms **Raplee Ridge**, a severely tilted monocline through which the San Juan River carves a deep canyon. This colorful formation, with its gray, rust, and purple bands, is known locally as the Navajo Rug.

From Mexican Hat, cross the river to enter the Navajo Reservation. Approaching Monument Valley, stop at a pullout around milepost 13 to snap the classic photo. At the state line, turn left onto Monument Valley Road to enter the park. Fees apply for both driving and hiking. The unpaved road snakes down a few hundred feet to the valley floor and then circles mammoth Cutler Formation spires and buttes. Coming in all shapes and sizes, and looking fresh from each new angle, these plugs are all that remain of a high plateau subjected to millions of years of erosion.

Unfortunately, the road through the valley offers only a glimpse of its natural riches. To see more of them, arrange a guided tour. But visitors can enjoy the following trail on their own.

18. Wildcat Trail

Easy 3.75-mile lollipop loop; allow 2 hours
Permit required
Map: USGS: Mitten Buttes

GETTING THERE: Just past the tollbooth, park in the large lot by the visitor center. Register inside at the Information Desk. The trailhead is across the road.

ON THE TRAIL: This trail circles **West Mitten Butte**, one of the most recognizable features in the entire Southwest. Follow the wide, well-marked route down a gentle 200-foot slope to the valley floor.

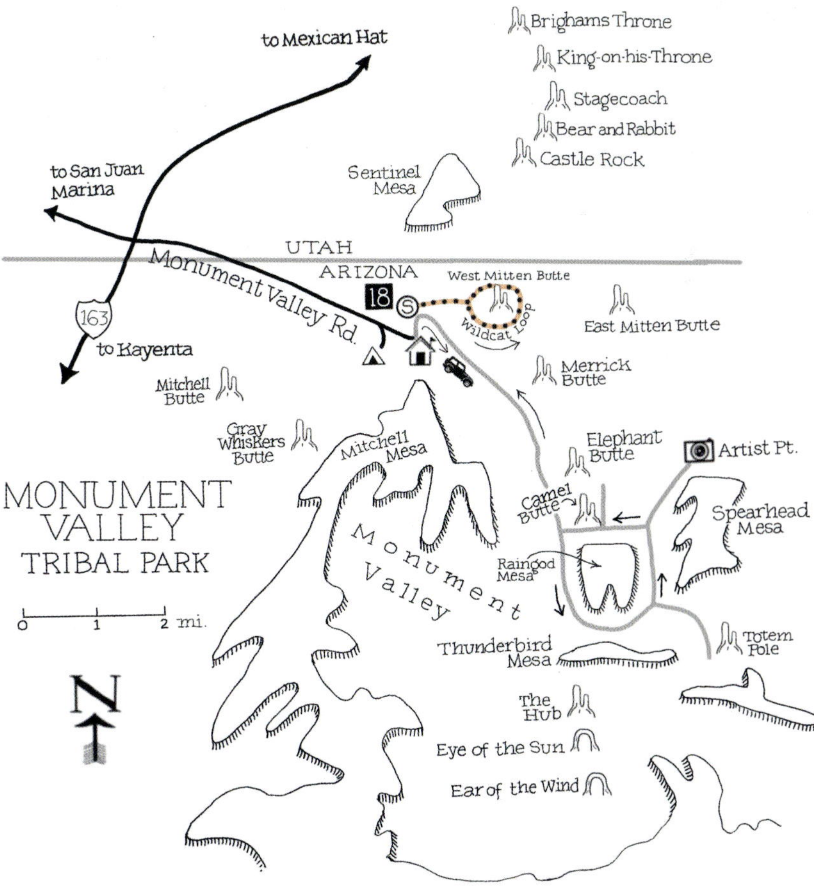

A new trail in Monument Valley encircles West Mitten Butte.

At the bottom, the trail forks. The preferred direction of travel is counterclockwise. You cross a shallow wash several times as you pass between the West and East Mittens and parallel **Sentinel Mesa**. After closing the loop, climb out of the canyon.

HOVENWEEP NATIONAL MONUMENT

Situated in pinyon and juniper country in the shadow of **Sleeping Ute Mountain**, Hovenweep—meaning "deserted valley" in Ute—consists of six prehistoric complexes along the Utah-Colorado border. The Hovenweep Anasazi, closely related to the residents of Mesa Verde, excelled in constructing stone and mud towers. All sites are at ground level rather than in cliffside alcoves. One of the complexes, **Cajon Mesa**, houses an ancient observatory. The campground and visitor center are based in the **Square Tower Ruins** complex, the most extensive of the lot. Like Natural Bridges National Monument, also featured in this chapter, Hovenweep recently was designated an International Dark Sky Park.

From Blanding, take US Route 191 south for 15 miles to UT 262. Turn left onto UT 262 and travel 8 miles to County Road 5099/401. Turn left onto CR 5099/401 and drive 16 miles. Go left here onto CR 413 at a sign for Hovenweep National Monument and continue 6 miles. Turn right onto the park entrance road.

From Cortez, head south on US 160 for 2 miles. Turn right onto McElmo Canyon Road (CR G). Travel 30 miles. Bear right on CR 5099/401 and continue 4 miles to the junction with CR 413/213. Turn right onto CR 413 and reach the park entrance road in 6 miles. Turn right here, and proceed to the visitor center.

19. Square Tower Ruins

Easy 2-mile lollipop loop; allow 1.25 hours
Map: USGS: Ruin Point

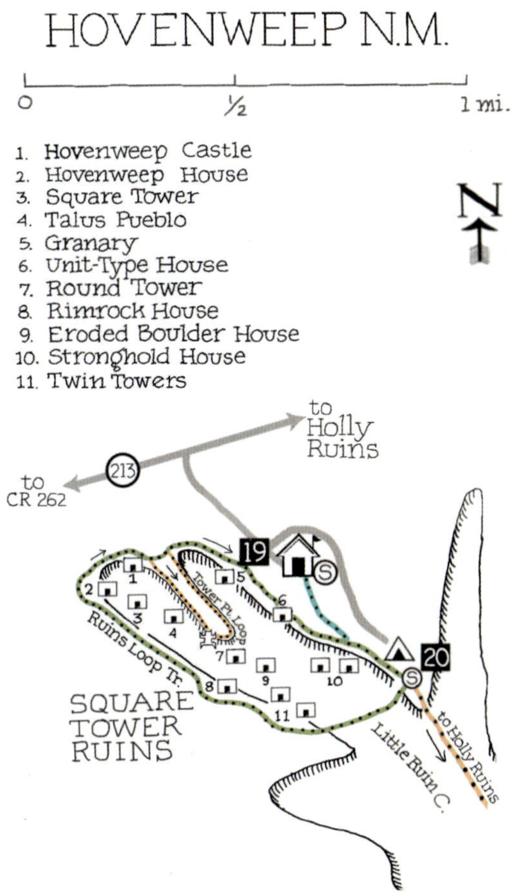

GETTING THERE: Begin the hike at the Hovenweep visitor center.

ON THE TRAIL: On this hike, which knits together two short trails, you explore the masonry structures of shallow Little Ruin Canyon, formed of Dakota Sandstone. A paved walkway from the visitor center leads to Stronghold House, where you intersect the unpaved loop. Turn right onto the **Rim Trail**, following it to the junction with the **Tower Point Trail**. Go left here onto a finger of land that delivers views of many structures, some located within the canyon and some positioned on the mesa top.

After 0.25 mile, the path circles back to reconnect with the Rim Trail. Turn left to continue. You soon pass **Hovenweep Castle**, arguably the most impressive building in this unit of the monument, and **Square Tower**, from which it derives its name. The trail heads the canyon and continues on its south side, the highlight of which is the **Twin Towers**. It soon switchbacks down to cross the canyon and link up again with the spur that returns you to the visitor center.

20. Holly House

Easy 8-mile out-and-back with shuttle option; allow 4 hours
Map: USGS: Ruin Point

GETTING THERE: This hike works well as an out-and-back from site 10 in the campground, though with two vehicles (preferably high clearance) you can execute a point-to-point option. To do so, drive both vehicles to the park entrance. Turn right onto Route 2422 and continue 4 miles. Bear right onto a dirt road signed for Canyons of the Ancients National Monument and follow signs to Holly Ruins, 1.75 miles distant. Leave one vehicle here and in the other return to the Square Tower complex. Park in a small lot at the rear of the campground.

ON THE TRAIL: The little-used path leads up **Keeley Canyon** to the mesa top occupied by Holly Ruins, just across the Colorado state line.

The trail descends to the canyon floor through a small joint. The otherwise well-marked route sometimes follows the wash and sometimes hugs the bank in its gentle progress toward the head of the canyon. In about 3 miles, you come to a small ruin on private land.

Soon the trail ascends to the left, passing through another slot on its way to the mesa top. After leveling out, it turns right and proceeds to the complex, whose major buildings include Great House, Boulder House, and Tilted Tower. Admire how the residents made creative use of boulders to anchor their structures.

NEARBY: About 0.5 mile north of Holly Ruins along the dirt road referenced above are two more units of Hovenweep National Monument. A cairned trail heading east first visits the D-shaped Horseshoe complex at mile 0.25. About 0.25 mile farther is the smaller and less interesting Hackberry site. Allow 45 minutes for the easy, 1-mile out-and-back.

CANYONS OF THE ANCIENTS NATIONAL MONUMENT AND VICINITY

Tucked under Sleeping Ute Mountain, Canyons of the Ancients protects more than six thousand archaeological sites in southwestern Colorado. Public access is limited to three areas: Lowry and Painted Hand Ruins and the stellar complex at Sand Creek.

21. Sand Creek

Moderate 7.75-mile lollipop loop; allow 4 hours
Map: USGS: Battle Rock

GETTING THERE: From Cortez, take US Route 160 south for 2 miles. Turn right onto McElmo Canyon Road (County Road G). At about mile 14, locate a small slickrock parking area on the right. The trailhead is marked by a kiosk.

ON THE TRAIL: Sand Canyon and East Rock Creek Canyon are studded with cliff dwellings, and their elaborate network of trails, serving mountain bikers and horse parties as well as hikers, can confuse the unwary. Of the many available options, the route featured here highlights the best of what the area has to offer. Along the way, Sleeping Ute Mountain is your almost-constant companion.

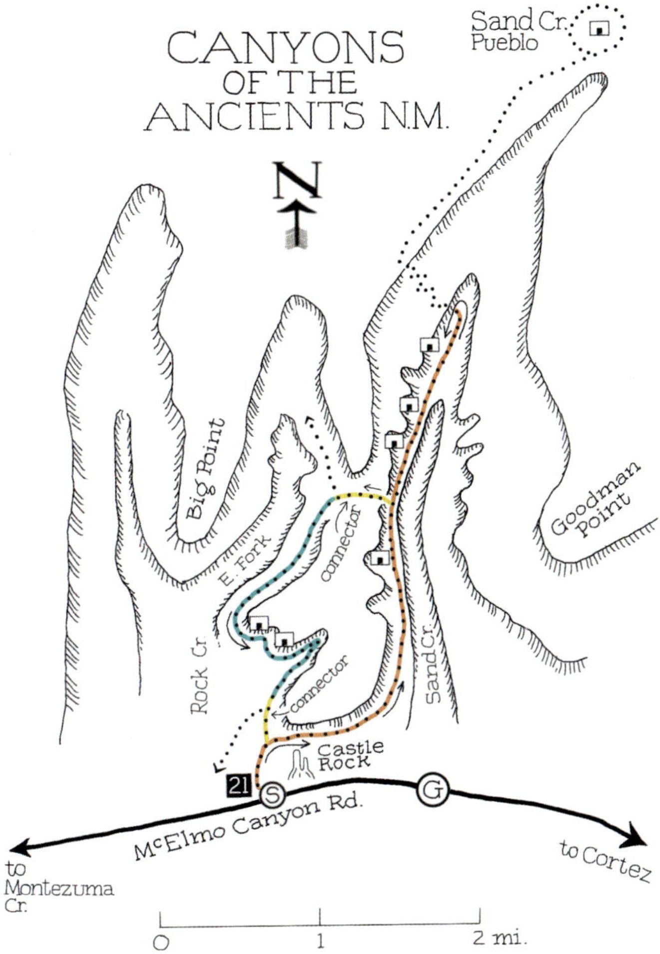

Begin by ascending a slickrock slope and bypassing **Castle Rock**, which is on the right. Within 0.25 mile you reach the junction of a connector to East Fork Rock, on which you will later return. Go right here, following the contours of **Sand Creek**. Well-marked spurs lead to archaeological treasures and scenic overlooks alike. Quickly, it becomes apparent that virtually every deep, south-facing alcove contains a ruin. Most are inaccessible.

At mile 1.5 you reach a signed trail that later will take you over the ridge separating Sand Canyon from East Fork Rock. But in order to see two of the best-preserved sites, press on past that intersection for about 1 mile to the point where the trail starts a steep 700-foot ascent on switchbacks to the mesa top. The large **Sand Creek Pueblo**, which occupies that mesa top, is in such a state of disrepair that it has little to recommend to non-archaeologists.

Therefore, instead of ascending the switchbacks, reverse course here, turning right onto the ridge trail connector to East Fork Rock mentioned earlier. This connector,

0.75 mile in length, gains about 200 feet in elevation as it crosses over to **East Fork Rock Creek**. When it ends at a T intersection, go left, descending on an abandoned jeep track that runs parallel to the canyon wall. A mile farther on, arrive at another junction, this time with the connecting trail that will eventually return you to the slickrock slope on which the hike began. Turn left here and regain some lost elevation, aided at times by steps. The mile-long trail hugs the cliffs, and you can identify additional ruins after it bends around one of the canyon's scalloped bays. When the connector ends, go right to return to the parking lot.

22. Painted Hand Ruin

Moderate, 0.5 miles round-trip; allow 1 hour
Map: USGS: Pleasant View

GETTING THERE: From Cortez, drive 18.5 miles north on US Route 491 to Pleasant View. Turn left onto County Road CC. At mile 9, where the pavement ends, CR 10 branches off to the left. Drive 12.5 miles down CR 10 until you reach the turnoff for Painted Hand Ruin. The parking area is about a mile down a dirt road, near the rim of a shallow tributary of Cross Canyon.

ON THE TRAIL: The 0.5-mile loop trail scrambles down some boulders and winds past three small structures, one of which—Trail Tower—is cylindrical. The site is named for two pictographs located in a rock shelter.

NEARBY: If you continue north on US 491 almost to Dove Creek (35 miles from Cortez), an unpaved road ends in 10.25 miles at tranquil **Dolores River Overlook**.

23. Lowry Ruin

Very easy stroll, with negligible distance; allow 30 minutes
Map: USGS: Pleasant View

GETTING THERE: From Cortez, drive 18.5 miles north on US Route 491 to Pleasant View. Turn left here onto County Road CC and proceed 9 miles, the first 6 of which are paved. Turn left onto a signed access road and continue a few hundred yards to the pueblo entrance. The pavement ends at mile 4.25. At mile 5.5, CC 10 branches off to the left. At this junction, continue right on CR CC and drive 3.5 miles. The access spur is on the left.

ON THE TRAIL: Lowry is a true gem, with forty rooms, eight kivas, and a great kiva erected in the late 11th century. The pueblo, which once housed up to one hundred residents, soared three stories high. By studying the style of masonry construction used here, archaeologists have concluded that the pueblo was established by Anasazi based in New Mexico's Chaco Canyon (see Chapter 5), perhaps as a colony or trading center.

24. Escalante and Dominguez Pueblos

Easy 1-mile out-and-back; allow 30 minutes
Map: USGS: Dolores East

GETTING THERE: From Cortez, drive east a short distance on US Route 160 to intersect CO 145. Turn left onto CO 145 toward Dolores and continue 10.5 miles, following signs to the Anasazi Heritage Center.

Lowry Ruin is one of just a few open to the public in Canyons of the Ancients.

ON THE TRAIL: The **Anasazi Heritage Center,** a museum that rivals Edge of the Cedars in quality, serves as headquarters for Canyons of the Ancients. Dominguez Pueblo is directly adjacent to the center, while a paved nature trail ascends to Escalante Pueblo. The ruins derive their names from the Spanish padres who encountered them on their failed quest to pioneer a route from Santa Fe to the missions of California.

MESA VERDE NATIONAL PARK

Mesa Verde National Park is an easy drive from Cortez. Take US Route 160 east for 10 miles, then turn right onto the main park road. The visitor center is located at this intersection.

Despite the throngs that it attracts, this celebrated park is a treat to visit, for it contains many of the largest, most thoroughly excavated and restored cliff dwellings in the United States. The dominant rock stratum, Cliff House Sandstone, weathered to produce the alcoves that the Anasazi (Ancestral Puebloans) found ideal for home building. To date, almost six hundred cliff dwellings have been identified. The sites are clustered on two mesas. **Chapin Mesa** remains open year-round, with curtailed services off-season, while **Wetherill Mesa** opens only during summer. At all cliff dwellings, visitors must be accompanied by a ranger on duty. Cliff Palace and Balcony

House on Chapin Mesa and Long House on Wetherill Mesa only can be accessed by official tours; fees apply. Make reservations at the visitor center off US 160. Because of high demand, it is advisable to stay overnight near Cortez so you can arrive at the visitor center when it opens. Alternatively, if you are in the area, you can purchase tickets a day in advance. During summer, rangers occasionally offer guided walks for small groups to ruins normally closed to the public, such as Mug House, Spring House, and Oak Tree House. These trips can be reserved online.

Mesa Verde ("green table") was inhabited beginning about 550 CE and abandoned—for reasons that probably included drought, resource depletion, and intergroup hostilities—prior to 1300. Compared to Hovenweep and other Anasazi clusters described in this chapter, Mesa Verde is a bustling tourist center, complete with snack bars and a colossal campground.

Aside from cliff dwellings, the park contains two other types of structures: earthen pit houses, dating to the Basketmaker culture that prevailed before about 750 CE, and mesa-top masonry dwellings such as those at **Far View.** During most of their period of occupancy, the Anasazi lived on the mesas, which they farmed.

The cliff dwellings appear to have been built for defensive reasons. Of these, the crescent-shaped, 130-room **Spruce Tree House**, which contains a reconstructed kiva, is the most accessible, reached by a paved trail that switchbacks from the museum. Illustrious **Cliff Palace** was found by ranchers Richard Wetherill and Charles Mason in 1888 while rounding up stray cattle during a snowstorm. The site, containing 150 rooms and 23 kivas, is believed to have accommodated about one hundred people. Enter by means of steps and ladders. Near the far end of the alcove, paintings adorn one of the rooms.

Smaller **Balcony House** may have had a special ceremonial purpose, since access was carefully limited. Touring the site requires ascending a 32-foot ladder and crawling through a 12-foot tunnel. Nearby is an easy 1-mile round-trip trail to **Soda Canyon Overlook**, from which Balcony House is visible in the distance. (See map on page 212.)

On Wetherill Mesa, all hikes begin at an information kiosk at the road's end. Beautiful **Long House**, with 150 rooms and 21 kivas, features an exceptionally large plaza. It takes 2 hours to complete the moderate 2.25-mile circuit. Because rangers are stationed at **Step House** during visiting hours, the dwellings here can be toured independently; allow 1 hour for the 1-mile loop. In the vicinity are easy trails to the **Badger House Community**, a pit-house site, and an overlook of the **Nordenskiöld Site #16**, a cliff dwelling. Each of these walks, which can be done in tandem, is about 2 miles out-and-back.

Although Mesa Verde is not a hiker's park, a few other short trails are open to visitors. Two of these—Petroglyph Point and Spruce Canyon—start near Spruce Tree House; hiking either trail requires a permit. Three others, including the Knife Edge, commence at the park's colossal campground and are unrestricted.

Guided half- or full-day tours of spectacular sites on the **Ute Mountain Ute Reservation**, adjacent to the park, can be arranged at Towaoc, south of Cortez off US 160/491 (see the entry for the Ute Mountain Ute Tribal Park in the Contact Information section at the back of this book).

The calm between the tours at Cliff Palace

25. Knife Edge

Easy 3-mile out-and-back; allow 1.5 hours
Map: USGS: Wetherill Mesa

GETTING THERE: From the visitor center along US Route 160, take the park road south 4 miles. Turn right into Morefield Campground. Drive to the northwest end of the campground and locate the trailhead near the **Lone Cone** formation.

ON THE TRAIL: This popular trail follows the bed of the original road through the park. Level nearly all the way, it hugs the rim of a cliff for its entire route, offering unobstructed vistas of Sleeping Ute Mountain, the Montezuma Valley, and the snow peaks of the southern Rockies.

26. Petroglyph Point

Moderate 2.75-mile loop; allow 1.5 hours
Permit required
Map: USGS: Wetherill Mesa

GETTING THERE: From the visitor center off US Route 160 east of Cortez, take the park road south for 15 miles to a major junction. Turn left here toward Chapin Mesa. Continue 5 miles to the parking lot for Spruce Tree House and the park museum, where you obtain your permit.

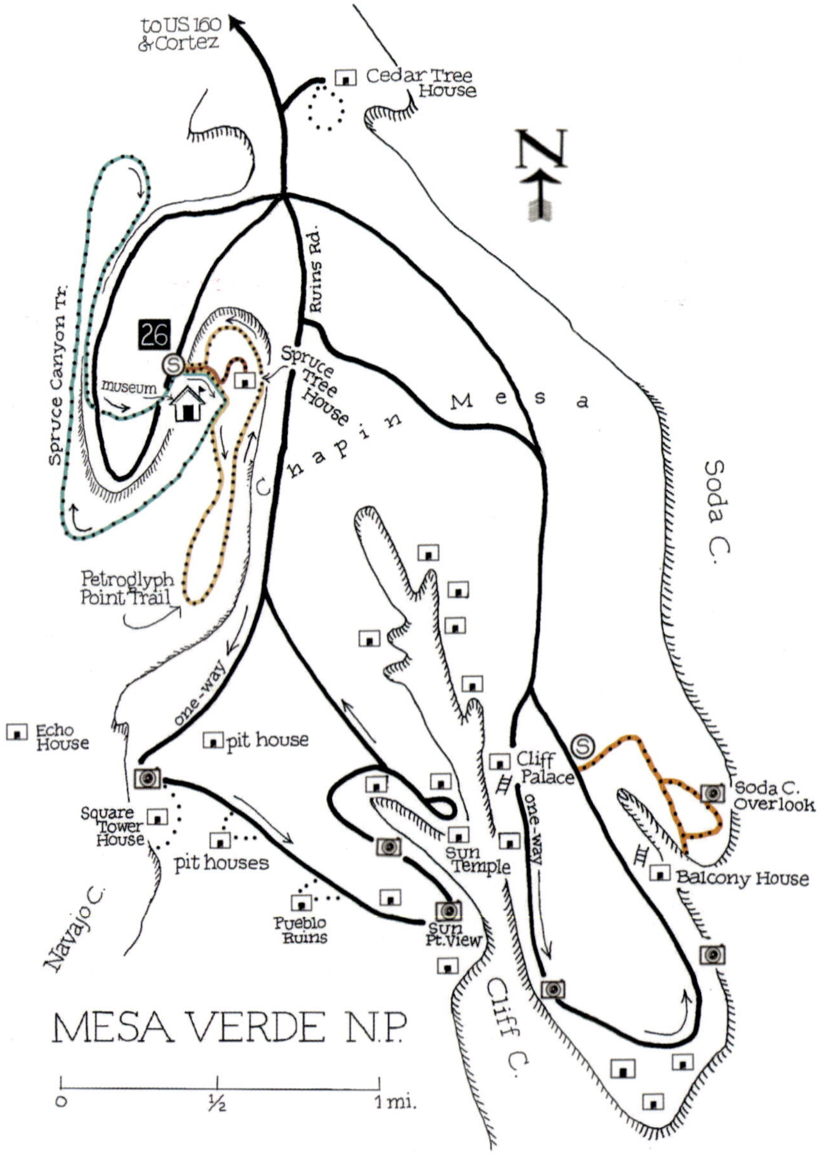

ON THE TRAIL: Descend the switchbacks leading toward Spruce Tree House. Near the bottom, turn right. Almost immediately, the trail splits. Take the left fork.

The first half of the route stays one level below the canyon rim, arriving at an excellent rock art panel before climbing stairs to the mesa top. From an overlook on the way up, scan for **Echo House**, a cliff dwelling in an alcove across the canyon. The trail traces the lip of Chapin Mesa, passing directly above Spruce Tree House.

NEARBY: To access the **Spruce Canyon Trail** (a moderate 2-mile walk, also requiring permits), go right at the fork mentioned above. The loop follows the canyon floor before climbing back to the rim.

FARTHER EAST

East of Mesa Verde, two other national treasures beckon. Either of these places is also within range of Santa Fe, New Mexico, one of the hub cities for Chapter 5.

27. Chimney Rock National Monument

Moderate 1-mile tour; allow 2 hours
Map: USGS: Chimney Rock

GETTING THERE: From Cortez, drive east on US Route 160 about 70 miles to CO 151. Turn south to reach the spur to **Chimney Rock National Monument**. In season, guided tours depart four times daily; fees apply.

ON THE TRAIL: Chimney Rock, one of the easternmost Anasazi settlements, occupies a mesa commanded by rocky twin pinnacles. The first half of the tour, on a very easy paved path, visits a partially excavated village containing pit houses and a great kiva. By far more scenic and interesting is the second half, which ascends a rocky trail to a Chacoan great house just below the buttes. Some archaeologists believe the great house was built for astronomical purposes. The moon rises directly between the buttes every 18 years and then seems to reverse its course, a phenomenon known as the lunar standstill.

28. Great Sand Dunes National Park

Moderate to difficult freelance exploration; allow 1 hour or more
Map: USGS: Liberty

GETTING THERE: From Cortez, follow US Route 160 east to Alamosa. Turn left on CO 17. In 12 miles, just past Mosca, turn right and proceed to the park.

ON THE TRAIL: These dunes, the highest in North America, were created when ancient deposits of sea sand piled up at the foot of the precipitous Sangre de Cristo ("blood of Christ") Mountains. From the Dunes parking area, cross seasonal Medano Creek and strike off cross-country, following ridgetops in order to avoid trudging through deep, soft sand. Allocate 4 or 5 hours round trip if you plan to visit **Star Dune**, 775 feet high. During summer, when the ground temperature can soar to 150°Fahrenheit, plan to hike in the early morning or evening and be sure to wear sturdy, closed-toe shoes.

Replica of a striking kiva mural, Coronado State Monument

CHAPTER 5
PUEBLOS

Albuquerque and Santa Fe serve as hubs for the hikes described in this chapter, which will appeal to those interested in the ancient artifacts and modern lifeways of Native Americans. These hikes visit dwellings erected by the Anasazi (Ancestral Puebloan) people as well as towns occupied today by their descendants. Several national monuments are represented, including El Malpais, Bandelier, and Kasha-Katuwe Tent Rocks, along with a couple of historical parks, including Chaco and Pecos. Cultural attractions delight visitors in the Rio Grande Valley.

Hubs: Albuquerque and Santa Fe, New Mexico

Albuquerque (population 450,000) is by far the largest community in the high-desert region. Highlights include its Old Town historic district, the Indian Pueblo Cultural Center, and the skyscraping Sandia ("watermelon") Mountains, the crest of which can be reached by car or aerial tram as well as on foot. Hot air balloons are a common sight here.

Glamorous **Santa Fe** ranks among America's most beautiful cities. It owes its charm to its unique amalgamation of Pueblo, Hispanic, and Anglo cultures. An ordinance issued decades ago stipulated that new buildings be faced with adobe or a look-alike material, and as a result Santa Fe exhibits a remarkable unity of style. The state capital is known for its opera and symphony orchestra, art galleries and museums, and historic central plaza.

AROUND ALBUQUERQUE

Several Native American communities, both old and new, are but a short drive from Albuquerque. Stroll through a restored kiva in a state park, visit well-preserved churches in an area where the Spanish conquered the region's indigenous peoples, see petroglyphs reflecting centuries of habitation by the Anasazi, and tour a politically independent modern-day Pueblo community.

1. Coronado Historic Site

Very easy stroll, with negligible distance; allow 30 minutes
Map: USGS: Bernalillo

GETTING THERE: From Albuquerque, take Interstate 25 north 15 miles to exit 242, Bernalillo. Drive 2 miles west on US Route 550, then turn right on Kuaua Road.

ON THE TRAIL: Located on the west bank of the Rio Grande, on the site of the ancient community of Kuaua ("evergreen" in the Tiwa language), this state monument offers imposing views of the Sandia Mountains. It has extensive low-walled ruins and a museum filled with objects from the colonial period, which began with Spanish explorer Francisco Vázquez de Coronado's failed 1540 expedition to find the Seven Cities of Cibola. But the restored kiva, in which archaeologists uncovered colorful murals dating from the 14th to 16th centuries, steals the show. Exact reproductions line its interior.

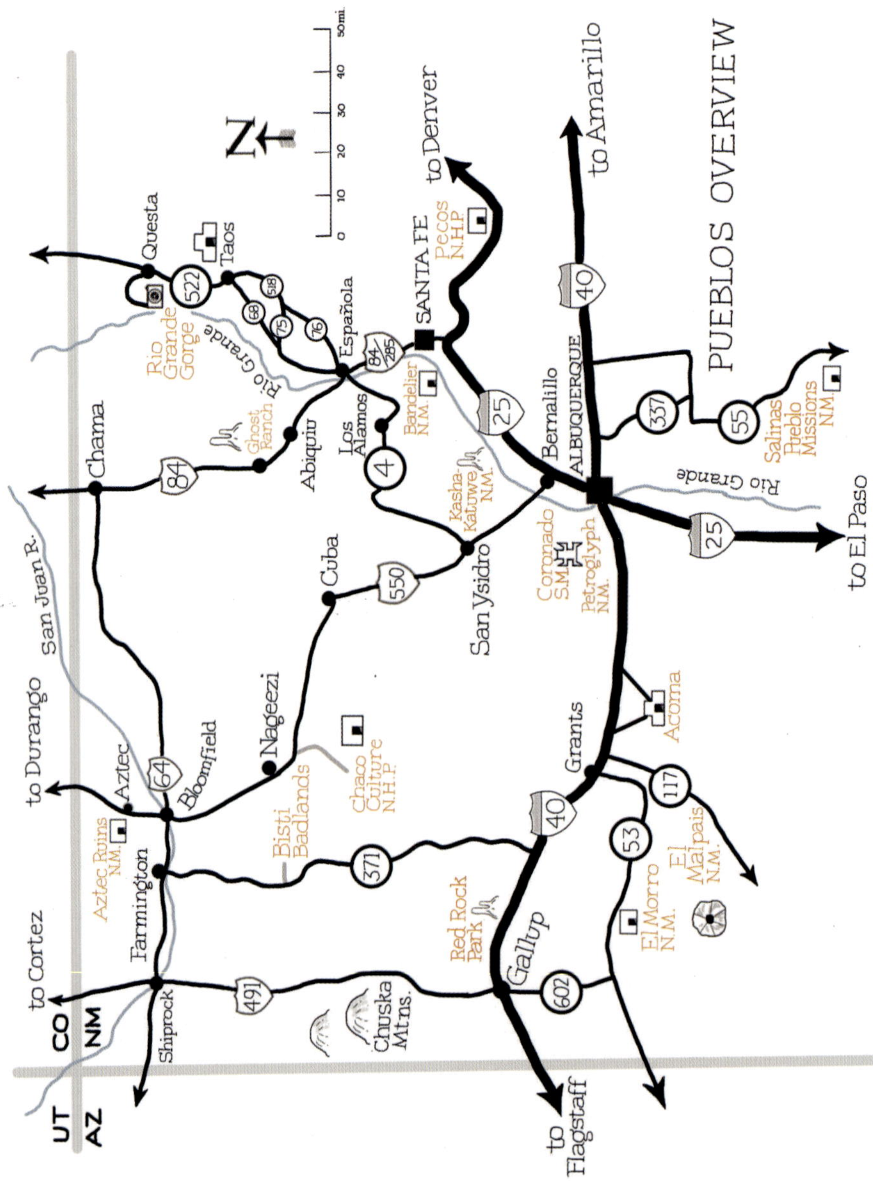

2. Salinas Pueblo Missions National Monument

Very easy strolls, with negligible distance; allow 30 minutes per site
Maps: USGS: Punta de Agua, Abó, and Gran Quivira

GETTING THERE: From Albuquerque, go east 17 miles on Interstate 40 to Tijeras. Pick up NM 337, which heads south to intersect NM 55. One of three units of the monument, Quarai, is off this road about 47 miles south of I-40. Continue on NM 55 to Mountainair to reach the others. Gran Quivira is 25 miles south of town on NM 55; Abó is 9 miles west of town on US Route 60.

ON THE TRAIL: The monument commemorates sites at which the Spanish conquered and attempted to convert New Mexico's indigenous peoples. **Quarai** has a large, well-preserved church with red masonry walls. Prior to the invasion, this pueblo served as an important center of trade between peoples of the Rio Grande and the Plains Indians. The visitor center is at **Abó**, which features another church and a large, unexcavated pueblo. Abó was abandoned after a raid by Apaches in 1672. **Gran Quivira** boasts two churches in addition to excavated ruins. At all three locations, the Spanish forced the Indians to mine salt, which was used to process silver in colonized Mexico.

3. Petroglyph National Monument

All trails easy; distance and time variable
Maps: USGS: Los Griegos and The Volcanoes

GETTING THERE: Drive west from downtown Albuquerque on Interstate 40 to exit 154. Go north on Unser Road and follow signs to the visitor center. Literature available there will direct you to various units of the park.

ON THE TRAIL: Petroglyph National Monument offers opportunities to see images abraded, carved, and pecked into the basalt boulders of a 17-mile escarpment. Geometric forms, birds, reptiles, hands, and crosses reflect centuries of occupation by indigenous peoples and early Spanish settlers. Though urban encroachment threatens the monument, private lands continue to be acquired.

Rinconada Canyon offers a 2.25-mile loop away from the sights and sounds of the city. **Boca Negra Canyon** features several short trails. Along one of these is a petroglyph of Kokopelli, a hunchbacked flute player—or possibly an itinerant peddler—thought to symbolize hunting, rainfall, and fertility. Most recently added to the monument is **Piedras Marcadas Canyon**, where a 1.5-mile loop accesses some four hundred petroglyphs, the best of which are concentrated around post #5. By some reports, the Anasazi regarded this canyon as a portal between worlds.

Farther west on I-40, the **Volcanoes Day Use Area** north of exit 149 contains no rock art, but a pleasant 3.25-mile trail executes a figure eight around twin cinder cones while offering a panorama of the metropolitan area and its mountainous backdrop.

4. Acoma

Very easy stroll, with negligible distance; allow 1 hour for guided tour
Permit required for photography; restrictions apply
Map: USGS: Acoma Pueblo

GETTING THERE: From Albuquerque, head west on Interstate 40 for 52 miles to exit 108. Turn south onto NM 23 and proceed 12 miles to the visitor center. A bus transports guests to the mesa top.

ON THE TRAIL: Known as the Sky City, Acoma is one of nineteen politically independent communities in New Mexico inhabited by descendants of the Anasazi, who apparently joined existing settlements after prolonged drought farther west led them to migrate to the region. Concentrated in the Rio Grande Valley, these communities are home to more than forty thousand people. They welcome visitors, charging modest entrance fees in most cases. Several times a year, they sponsor sacred dances and hold feasts on saints' days. Spanish colonial efforts to convert these Native Americans succeeded only superficially, with the Indians fusing Catholic beliefs and their more traditional ones. Persecution led the residents of many villages to rise up in the Pueblo Revolt of 1680, which temporarily drove out the conquerors.

Celebrated for its pottery, Acoma in many ways seems representative of contemporary Pueblo life. Poor by US standards but picturesque, the village is positioned 350 feet above the surrounding countryside on a forlorn, sheer-sided mesa. Only a few people inhabit the mesa year-round; most reside in the valley, where modern conveniences are available. The tour includes a visit to a 17th-century mission church. According to folklore, some tribal members starved to death on nearby **Enchanted Mesa** when a rockslide prevented them from descending the cliffs.

EL MALPAIS NATIONAL MONUMENT AND VICINITY

The lava fields of western New Mexico failed to impress Spanish explorers, who dismissed the region as El Malpais ("the badlands"). But visitors will delight in its caves and bridges, cinder cones and sandstone bluffs. The monument's east and west perimeters are not connected by road. Drive 72 miles west of Albuquerque on Interstate 40 to exit 89, turning south on NM 117 to access the east side, or continue 8 miles farther on I-40 to Grants, turning south on NM 53 to access the west side. Although an information station along NM 53 is staffed seasonally, the main visitor center is east of Grants at exit 85.

5. Lava Falls

Moderate 1.25-mile lollipop loop; allow 45 minutes
Sturdy boots recommended
Map: USGS: North Pasture

GETTING THERE: Drive 72 miles west of Albuquerque on Interstate 40 to exit 89. From I-40, drive south on NM 117 for about 36 miles. The trailhead is near the southern boundary of El Malpais National Monument.

ON THE TRAIL: This cairned route, which traverses the region's youngest lava flow, is rated moderate because of its ankle-twisting potential.

NEARBY: On the drive back to I-40, pause to visit lovely **La Ventana Arch** (a 0.25-mile out-and-back), at the head of **The Narrows** section, where a lava flow extends to the cliffs. Unfortunately, sky is not visible through the span from the viewing area.

6. El Calderón Trail

Easy 3-mile lollipop loop; allow 1.5 hours
Map: USGS: Ice Caves

GETTING THERE: From Grants on Interstate 40, take NM 53 south for about 21 miles to the parking area.

ON THE TRAIL: Straddling the Continental Divide at 7500 feet in elevation, this diverse loop satisfies the requirements for Vulcanism 101. From the parking area, proceed clockwise. The first attraction, off a short spur, is **Junction Cave**, an extensive lava tube that can be explored by experienced spelunkers (permit required). Back on the main trail, pass dual sinkholes and then, at 0.75 mile, another lava tube, home to various species of bat. The trail climbs gently toward a junction at the halfway point. Continue straight ahead, reaching the reddish **El Calderón Cinder Cone** in short order. The dormant volcano's eruption 115,000 years ago shaped the surrounding landscape. From inside the caldera, an optional trail climbs 100 feet to circle its lip. Backtrack to the junction for the quickest return to your car.

NEARBY: **Ice Cave and Bandera Volcano**, a private concession just west of El Malpais on NM 53, offers two easy out-and-back hikes: a 0.5-mile round-trip to a spectacular ice cave formed by a collapsed lava tube and a 1 mile round-trip to the caldera of a volcano that last erupted ten thousand years ago.

7. El Morro National Monument

Easy to moderate 2-mile lollipop loop; allow 1 hour
Map: USGS: El Morro

GETTING THERE: From Albuquerque, take Interstate 40 west 72 miles to exit 81 for Grants. Turn left (south) onto NM 53. Continue 41 miles, then turn left onto the signed spur for El Morro. Park at the visitor center at the end of the spur.

ON THE TRAIL: El Morro ("the bluff") houses prehistoric ruins and inscriptions that hikers can enjoy at close range. Its two trails can be combined into an educational loop.

Start at the visitor center. When the trail forks, go right on the very easy **Inscription Trail** leading to **Inscription Rock**, a sandstone cliff face on which aborigines, Spaniards, and later arrivals engraved symbols, names, and messages. A perennial pool accounts for the area's magnetic pull.

At mile 0.25, turn left onto the moderate **Headland Trail**, which ascends 250 feet to **Atsinna Ruin** ("place of writings on rock"), a partially excavated pueblo with 875 rooms. When done enjoying Atsinna, continue counterclockwise to descend the bluffs and complete the loop.

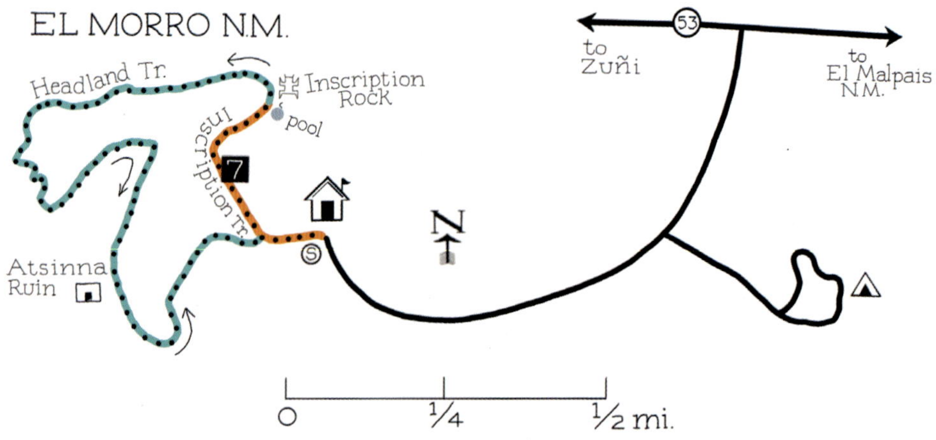

AROUND GALLUP

The area featured here lies within easy reach of the hubs of Cortez, Colorado (Chapter 4), and Flagstaff, Arizona (Chapter 6).

8. Red Rock Park

Moderate 5-mile loop, including spur, with exposure; allow 2.5 hours
Map: USGS: Church Rock

GETTING THERE: From Albuquerque, drive west on Interstate 40 almost to Gallup near the border of Arizona. Take exit 31 onto County Road 566, following signs for Red Rock Park. The interface between roads and trails here can be confusing. Before lacing up your boots, take a minute to scout out both trailheads by car, as you must walk between them later to complete the loop. To do so, where CR 566 forks near the park entrance, first take the road on the left, which will lead past a rodeo arena to the kiosk for the **Pyramid Rock trailhead.** Then backtrack to the fork and take a left, passing an unkempt campground. The **Church Rock trailhead**, where the hike begins, is at the end of this fork. Park here, adjacent to the local post office.

ON THE TRAIL: Once a state park, Red Rock currently is administered by the county. Don't be deterred by the fact that its facilities have fallen into off-putting disrepair.

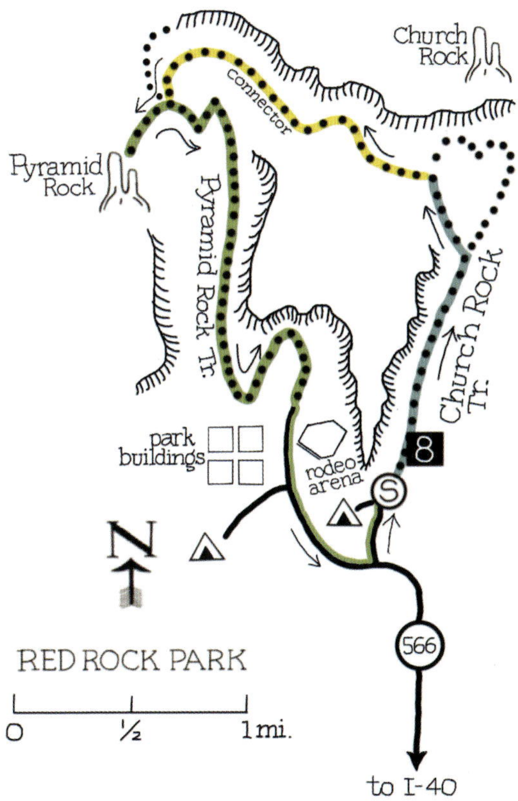

Pyramid Rock towers over the landscape near Gallup.

From the Church Rock end, the trail begins inauspiciously, crossing a denuded field before ascending along the right side of a wash to dodge a pour-off. Above the pour-off, continue climbing with the aid of near-vertical pecked-in steps, following what may well be the world's most elaborate cairns. The latter seem ubiquitous—except in the few places where you most need them.

At mile 1, arrive at a major junction. The path to the right, leading to the base of **Church Rock**, is surprisingly easy to lose, so turn left instead. The signage here, although typically overzealous, can be confusing; it indicates that you are following the Church Rock Trail, when in fact this is a connector to Pyramid Rock.

At mile 2.5, pass through a hikers' maze and soon reach an unsigned but important fork. Ignore cairns pointing toward a trail to the right, which swings back the way you came. Instead, continue straight ahead for several yards toward a set of metal poles at a second unsigned junction.

To the right, stair-steps climb to **Pyramid Rock** (elevation 7500 feet), a worthwhile 0.5-mile out-and-back if the spirit moves you. Otherwise, bear left to begin the 2-mile traverse toward the Pyramid Rock trailhead, paralleling the red cliffs and passing numerous hoodoos. Inexplicably, the trail markers fade in and out for the duration of the hike. Past a knife-edged ridge, you can spot rodeo buildings below. When the trail drops to a lower terrace, watch carefully for cairns. You need to double back sharply left here, facing Church Rock, for the final descent. Road-walk from the trailhead kiosk to your car on the route you scouted previously.

9. Bisti Badlands

Easy off-trail hiking; allow 3–4 hours
Map: USGS: Alamo Mesa West

GETTING THERE: From Albuquerque, take Interstate 40 west to exit 53 and turn north on NM 371. At milepost 70, go right onto a gravel road signed for **Bisti/De-Na-Zin Wilderness** (ignoring an earlier sign, which corresponds to a different trailhead). After 2 miles, the road ends at a T. Turn left and proceed 1 mile to the parking lot on the right.

Bisti Badlands, like a scene out of a Salvador Dali painting

ON THE TRAIL: Of the strange badlands that define northwestern New Mexico, most lie on the Navajo Reservation, in areas where visitors may not be welcome. Bisti (Navajo for "shale hills") is an exception. This pocket wilderness protects a surreal landscape of hoodoos, spires, and petrified wood in the Lewis Shale stratum. Wander at will or follow suggestions presented below.

Examine both sides of the orientation sign at the kiosk. Walk through the gate and follow footprints due east up shallow Alamo Wash toward two low hills stained red from the oxidation of coal. Pass to the left of the hills and continue east, paralleling a fence in the distance to your left. When the fence bends north, you have two options. One is to follow it to its end, then proceed straight ahead toward a formation shaped like a sphinx. Turn east to investigate an area replete with winged buttes.

The more traveled option from the bend in the fence is to bear east-northeast up the wash, proceeding straight ahead toward a pair of dark brown buttes resembling bears' ears. Go left of them and then swing to the right of a lower, lone butte, staying on the south side of the wash. Soon you arrive at the **Cracked Eggs**, which may remind you of cow pies. Round two bays to the east to access an area replete with major hoodoos and logs of petrified wood in 0.25 mile. From here, if you cross the shallow wash and walk a short distance to the north, you arrive at **Flattop Arch**. It's easy to connect directly to this point from the wing area mentioned above. Or, you can continue on an eastward trajectory about 0.5 mile from the petrified logs to visit **Dragon Arch**.

If time is short, an alternate plan is to veer to the right of the two red hills from the parking lot, crossing shallow De-Na-Zin Wash. Head toward another pair of red hills positioned ahead to the right (at about two o'clock). Beyond this point is a fancifully eroded area that one author calls a "Grand Canyon mock-up." Ascend somewhat for the best views.

CHACO CULTURE NATIONAL HISTORICAL PARK

From Albuquerque, take Interstate 25 north to Bernalillo. Turn left onto US Route 550 and continue about 130 miles. Colorful breaks give way to distant mesas and buttes and finally to the mountainous highlands of central New Mexico. Between mileposts 112 and 113, go left on County Road 7900, and travel 8 miles to the junction of CR 7950, which is unpaved. Turn left here and continue on CR 7950 for 15 miles. A high-clearance vehicle is recommended. If you want to camp in the park, reserve a site online.

The Rome of Ancestral Puebloan civilization, Chaco features twelve major sites built between 850 and 1150 CE. The Anasazi built confidently in the middle of this low, wide canyon instead of embracing the cliffs as at Mesa Verde, which was settled later. Chaco's masonry is by universal acclaim the finest in all the Southwest.

Residents of the canyon—which may have supported a population as large as two thousand in its heyday—established more than one hundred outlying pueblos throughout the San Juan Basin, whether to ease population pressure or as insurance against drought. Roads connected these outliers to the metropole. Water control systems, including irrigation, enabled the Chacoans to wrest a living from a harsh environment.

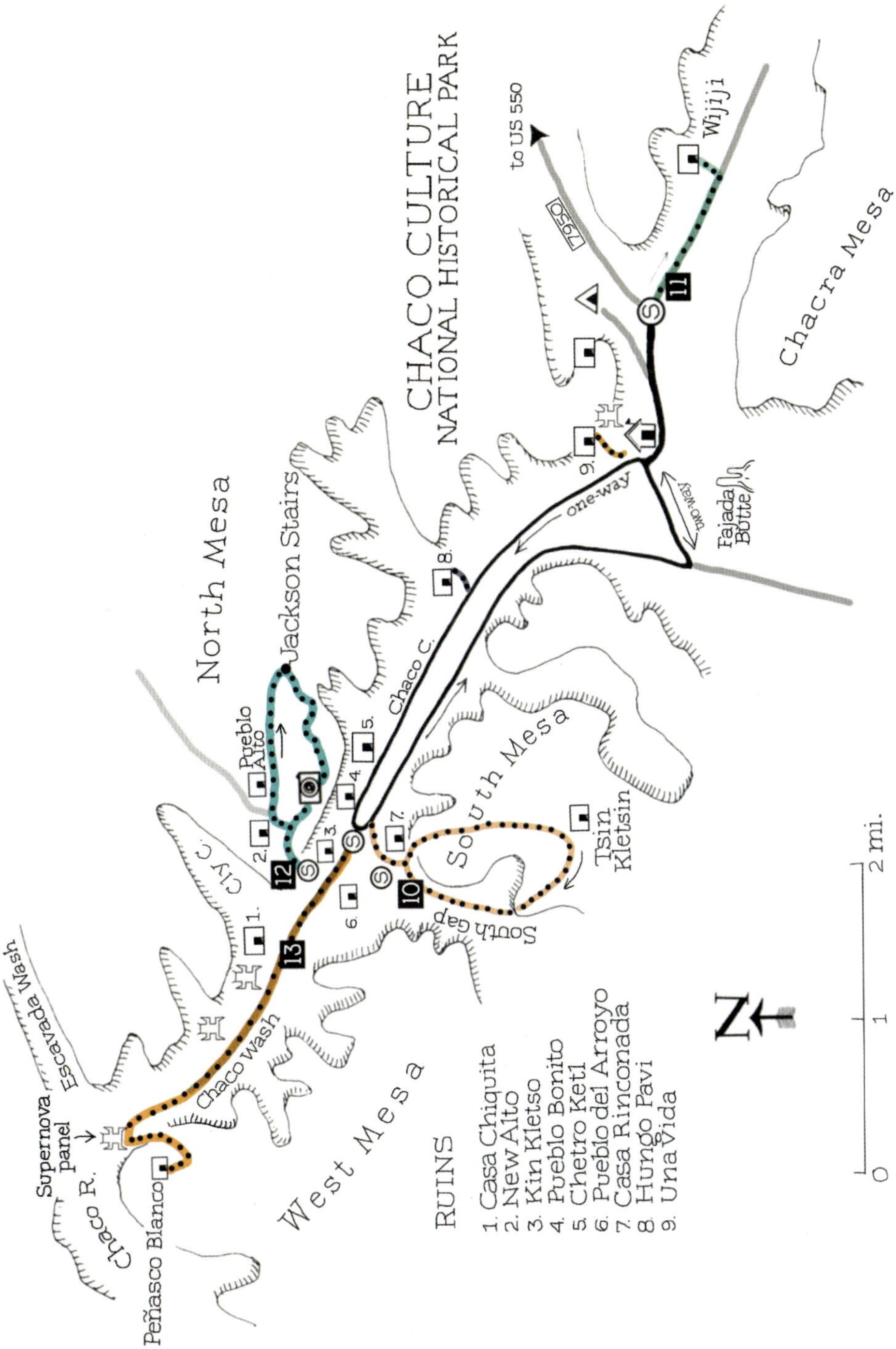
CHACO CULTURE
NATIONAL HISTORICAL PARK
to US 550
Wijiji
Chacra Mesa
Fajada Butte
one-way
one-way
North Mesa
Jackson Stairs
Pueblo Alto
Chaco C.
South Mesa
Tsin Kletsin
South Gap
Cly C.
Chaco Wash
Escavada Wash
Supernova panel
Chaco R.
Peñasco Blanco
West Mesa
RUINS
1. Casa Chiquita
2. New Alto
3. Kin Kletso
4. Pueblo Bonito
5. Chetro Ketl
6. Pueblo del Arroyo
7. Casa Rinconada
8. Hungo Pavi
9. Una Vida
N
0
1
2 mi.

All this construction required an elaborate social structure, complete with a bureaucracy to collect information, make decisions, and respond to contingencies. One of the "great houses" here—Pueblo Bonito—may have evolved into an administrative and religious center, with Pueblo Alto above it serving as a commercial entrepôt. The nature of the relationship between center and periphery is controversial, but it seems that when Chaco was depopulated in the 12th century, linkages among outlying communities collapsed, yielding increased autonomy coupled with decreased security.

In season, rangers conduct daily tours, but most visitors opt for self-guided walks. Pueblo Bonito, Chetro Ketl, and Casa Rinconada, which each have easy 0.5-mile trails winding through or around them, should not be missed. Allow approximately an hour at each site. D-shaped **Pueblo Bonito** ("beautiful town") is the largest site, with up to 800 rooms and 33 kivas. **Chetro Ketl** ("rain town"), a 500-room structure adjacent to Pueblo Bonito, is noteworthy for its uplifted platform plaza. In ancient times, the two sites were connected to the mesa top by foot- and handholds. **Casa Rinconada** ("box canyon house"), erected around 1100 CE, is located among a number of small villages on the south side of Chaco Wash. Here the main attraction is an impressive great kiva. The size and location of this ceremonial chamber suggest that it served the community as a whole rather than belonging to a particular clan.

Pueblo del Arroyo ("gully house"), across the canyon from Pueblo Bonito, contains a large plaza. A short trail leads to **Hungo Pavi** ("reed spring village"). Finally, **Una Vida** ("one life"), behind the visitor center, is an older, partially excavated dwelling. The remains of a hogan and corral indicate subsequent Navajo occupation. From marker #5 on the 0.25-mile loop trail, a rudimentary path ascends to a remarkable petroglyph panel.

For the backcountry trails described below, obtain permits at the visitor center. All lack shade and water, so plan to hike early or late in the day during summer.

10. South Mesa

Moderate 4-mile loop; allow 2 hours
Permit required
Map: USGS: Pueblo Bonito

GETTING THERE: From the park's visitor center, drive west on the park road to Casa Rinconada. Reach the trailhead from marker #10 of the Casa Rinconada loop.

ON THE TRAIL: **Tsin Kletsin** ("charcoal place") commanded a panoramic view of six other major buildings from the second story of one of its kivas and thus may have served as a communications center or relay station.

After ascending on switchbacks to a point just below the rim, the trail climbs a short chimney, swings widely left, and levels out. It bends right before heading to the ruin, visible from afar. On the windswept mesa, 450 feet above the valley, Pueblo Bonito, Chetro Ketl, Casa Rinconada, and Pueblo del Arroyo all are clearly discernible; this may be the best view in the park. From the ruin, the trail turns west and descends into South Gap on its way back to the parking area.

11. Wijiji

Very easy 3-mile out-and-back; allow 1.5 hours
Permit required
Map: USGS: Pueblo Bonito

GETTING THERE: From the park's visitor center, drive east for about a mile to the trailhead.

ON THE TRAIL: Of the backcountry sites open to the public, Wijiji ("greasewood") is the best preserved and most easily reached.

The route follows a service road. Wijiji, against the left canyon wall, contained one hundred rooms and rose three stories. Built early in the 12th century, it was one of the last of Chaco's great houses. Look for a petroglyph panel on the bluffs.

On the return, you face **Fajada Butte**, where an astronomical marker known as a "sun dagger" was discovered in the 1970s. In conjunction with three carefully positioned rock slabs, this petroglyph enabled Chacoans to determine the dates of solstices and equinoxes—information invaluable for both agricultural and religious reasons. The fragility of the marker led the Park Service to close the butte to tourists, but a film shown at the visitor center analyzes its role in indigenous culture. Other sites with solar calendars include Kin Kletso and Casa Rinconada.

12. North Mesa

Moderate 5.5-mile loop; allow 3 hours
Permit required
Map: USGS: Pueblo Bonito

GETTING THERE: From the park's visitor center, drive west on the park road to Kin Kletso.

Chaco Canyon, the metropolis of the Anasazi world, contained great houses like Casa Rinconada.

Ancestral Puebloans often aligned their dwellings' doors and windows.

ON THE TRAIL: This wonderful hike allows you to visit two major ruins and to attain excellent vantage points on several others. The trail ascends improbably through a couloir in the Cliff House Sandstone. At the top, it veers to the right, hugging the rim. About 0.75 mile of walking over slickrock brings you to **Pueblo Bonito Overlook**.

Here the trail forks. Turn left, climbing steadily for 0.5 mile to reach **Pueblo Alto** ("high town") and **New Alto** atop North Mesa, 350 feet above the valley floor. Of the two structures, the latter is better preserved, though the partially excavated Pueblo Alto is considerably larger, with 135 rooms.

The trail continues in front of Pueblo Alto. It heads up a side-canyon, revealing the **Jackson Stairs**, a set of pecked-in "Moki" steps by which inhabitants of the mesa top accessed Chetro Ketl. No worries—the trail doesn't use these steps; rather, it continues on the slickrock bench, eventually descending through a crack that returns you to the overlook at mile 4.25 to close the loop.

13. Peñasco Blanco

Easy 6.5-mile out-and-back; allow 4 hours
Permit required
Map: USGS: Pueblo Bonito

GETTING THERE: From the park's visitor center, take the park road west to Pueblo del Arroyo.

ON THE TRAIL: Handsome Peñasco Blanco ("white rock") perches atop West Mesa. The trail winds through a section of Chaco Wash that abounds in rock art, most notably a pictograph believed to represent a supernova that lit up the sky in 1054 CE, creating the Crab Nebula.

Shortly after setting forth, you pass **Kin Kletso** ("yellow house") and **Casa Chiquita** ("small house") on your right. Look for petroglyphs along the cliffs, especially at the mouth of the first significant side-canyon on the right beyond Casa Chiquita. Opposite the second side-canyon, the trail veers left, leading in a few hundred yards to the Supernova panel, along the base of the cliff.

Next the trail ascends about 150 feet to **Peñasco Blanco**. Overlooking the confluence of the Chaco River and Escavada Wash, this imposing structure originally had three stories. Return the way you came.

SAN JUAN BASIN

The featured hikes are accessed from US Route 550, north of the turnoff for Chaco. Because the local economy revolves around fossil fuel extraction, the basin is scenically a bit of a sacrifice zone.

14. Ah-Shi-Sle-Pah Badlands

Easy freelance exploration, with routefinding; allow 2–3 hours
Colorful route marker recommended (see below)
Map: USGS: Pueblo Bonito NW

GETTING THERE: Take US Route 550 north to Nageezi, about 3 miles past the turnoff for Chaco. Go left onto County Road 7800, which begins as paved but soon turns to packed dirt. Intersect CR 57 at mile 12.25. Turn left and continue another 3 miles to the Ah-Shi-Sle-Pah Wilderness Study Area on the right.

ON THE TRAIL: From the parking lot, walk 0.5 mile down the dirt road to the rim. Turn left and proceed about 100 yards to find a reasonably safe route to the floor of otherworldly "Purple Hat Gulch." Explore upstream (right) a short distance to its end, then turn around and continue to intersect very shallow **Ah-Shi-Sle-Pah Wash**. To guarantee you will recognize this junction on your return, mark it with a colorful object, such as a construction flag. Don't count on finding cairn-making material in these barren wastes. Remember to take your marker with you when you return.

From here, explore the bay to the left, then head across the shallow wash toward "Hoodoo Central." Proceed clockwise from the hoodoos around the upper amphitheater of the wash to circle back around to the gulch where you exit.

15. Aztec Ruins National Monument

Very easy 0.25-mile out-and-back; allow 45 minutes
Map: USGS: Aztec

GETTING THERE: From Albuquerque, take Interstate 25 north to Bernalillo. Turn left onto US Route 550 and continue to the town of Aztec, near the Colorado border. Go left onto NM 516. Immediately past the Animas River bridge, take a right onto Ruins Road and continue to its end.

ON THE TRAIL: The name Aztec derives from Anglo settlers' mistaken belief that the ruins were Mesoamerican in origin. In the 12th and 13th centuries, this was one of the major Anasazi (Ancestral Puebloan) communities of the Southwest, housing up to seven hundred people. The paved trail acquaints you with this 450-room complex. Archaeologists think that the pueblo may have been built and abandoned by Chacoan Anasazi and then later reoccupied by people influenced culturally by Mesa Verde. Of special interest is an enormous, lovingly reconstructed kiva into which native music is piped. The kiva occupies a portion of the plaza once used for communal activities.

NEARBY: To tour **Salmon Ruins**, take US 550 south from Aztec to Bloomfield. Turn right on US 64 and follow signs to the site.

16. Anasazi Arch

Difficult 0.5-mile out-and-back, with routefinding and scrambling; allow 45 minutes
Map: USGS: Cedar Hill

GETTING THERE: From Albuquerque, take Interstate 25 north to Bernalillo. Turn left onto US Route 550 and continue to the town of Aztec, near the Colorado border. From Aztec, go northeast on US 550 for 11 miles. Turn left onto County Road 2300, a good unpaved road, and reset your trip odometer. Reaching a fork at mile 1.25, go right on CR 2310 and proceed 2.75 miles. Immediately past a compressor station, turn right onto a short spur. You should be able to spot the arch on the skyline to your left. About

Free-standing Anasazi Arch boasts an impressively large opening.

50 yards before the track ends, park near a fire ring in a clearing to the right of an amphitheater.

ON THE TRAIL: Don't let pumpjacks, industrial noise, and heavy truck traffic deter you from visiting this sublime freestanding arch with a 125-foot rise. From the parking area, follow an unofficial trail north into the amphitheater, just to the left of a tall monolith. Soon you arrive at the first of three obstacles, all of which involve ascending short, steep sandstone chutes with the aid of rock piles and pecked-in foot- and handholds. At the top, Anasazi Arch (a.k.a. Cox Canyon Arch), a true original, comes into view. Swing around to the right to tackle the second obstacle. Your final hurdle occurs immediately below the arch; it can be bypassed to the left. Circle around the arch to attain different vantage points.

NEARBY: The San Juan Basin contains an estimated three hundred natural windows, arches, and bridges. Consult locally available literature if you'd like to sample more.

KASHA-KATUWE TENT ROCKS NATIONAL MONUMENT

A natural playground of sorts, Kasha-Katuwe is nothing short of hallucinogenic. Its conical formations, which stand up to 90 feet high, are the residue of ancient volcanic eruptions. The Canyon and Cave Loop Trails can be combined into an unforgettable loop.

17. Tent Rocks

Moderate 3.25-mile lollipop loop, with exposure; allow 2 hours
Trekking poles recommended
Map: USGS: Cañada

New Mexican tent rocks recall similar formations in Turkey's Cappadocia.

GETTING THERE: From Albuquerque, drive north on Interstate 25 to exit 259. Pick up NM 22. Follow signs to Kasha-Katuwe Tent Rocks National Monument. Turn left on Forest Road 266. A kiosk marks the trailhead.

From Santa Fe, drive south 5.5 miles on US Route 84/285 to I-25 and proceed to exit 264. There, take NM 16 past the dam that contains Cochiti Lake and turn left onto NM 22. Follow signs to the monument, located along FR 266. A kiosk marks the trailhead.

ON THE TRAIL: Begin on the **Canyon Trail**, passing two junctions with the Cave Loop Trail on the left (which you will take on the way back) as you stroll up the sandy wash. The walls of **Tent Rock Canyon** soon pinch in. The shade-filled canyon features two short sets of narrows. A shallow alcove on the left harbors a squiggly petroglyph.

Where the canyon appears to dead-end at about mile 1, a sign directs you to turn right, entering a passageway to a higher level. From here the trail climbs in earnest over rocky terrain, offering excellent views of the rhyolite formations, many of which are capped with balanced rocks. Once it tops out, 625 feet above the valley floor, you can visit two overlooks. Exposure at the second may prove frightening to some.

Now retrace your steps to the nearer of two junctions with the **Cave Loop Trail**. Go right, ascending slightly. Once you pass the eponymous cave, the trail drops down for a close encounter with more tent rocks before returning to your car.

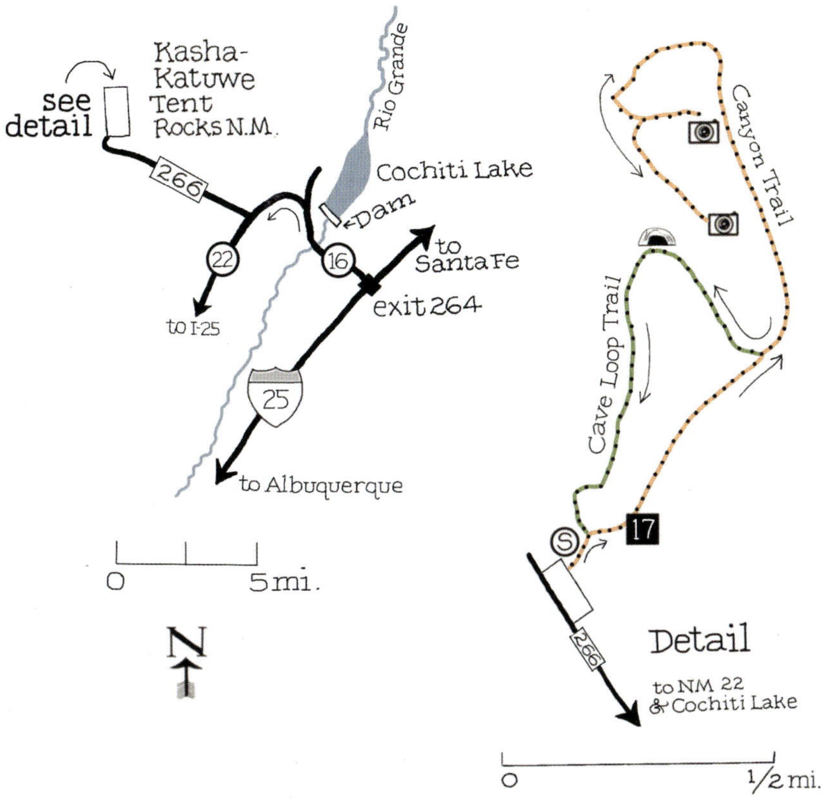

PECOS NATIONAL HISTORICAL PARK

Pecos is the site of a 600-room community constructed around a central courtyard. With the coming of Spanish conquistadors and Franciscan missionaries, centuries of intercultural conflict ensued. Visitors will see ruins from the era of conquest as well as Pueblo Indian structures.

From Santa Fe, head south on US Route 84/285 for 5.5 miles to Interstate 25, then travel east on I-25 for about 17 miles to Glorieta. Exit here, taking NM 50 east 8 miles to the park.

18. Ruins Trail

Very easy 1.25-mile lollipop loop; allow 1 hour
Map: USGS: Pecos

GETTING THERE: The trail starts at the visitor center. Watch an interpretive video before setting out.

ON THE TRAIL: The Ruins Trail allows you to inspect the mission church, a reconstructed kiva, and the remains of many other ancient buildings while soaking up the mountain scenery. Guided tours, some of which focus on the Civil War Battle of Glorieta Pass, are available year-round.

Franciscan Friars commandeered Native American labor to build a thick-walled mission church at Pecos.

BANDELIER NATIONAL MONUMENT

Named in honor of a prominent anthropologist/explorer, Bandelier National Monument occupies the forested Pajarito ("little bird") Plateau. It is geographically diverse, ranging from 5300 feet elevation near the Rio Grande to more than 10,000 feet in the Jemez Mountains. The crucial geologic event in regional natural history was the eruption of **Jemez Volcano** more than one million years ago, which blanketed the area with white volcanic ash, or tuff. Streams cut deep canyons through this soft material, exposing underlying basalt. Eventually, the volcano's center collapsed, producing massive **Valle Grande** caldera. Pyramidal formations called tent rocks, composed of tuff that hardened when hot gases escaped from the volcano, are a local specialty.

Another legacy of vulcanism was enhanced soil fertility. In consequence, Bandelier contains the greatest aggregation of prehistoric dwellings in our national park system. Members of the large Anasazi (Ancestral Pueblo) farming community that flourished until about 1550 CE built multistory apartments, sometimes enlarging preexisting caves in the soft tuff.

From Santa Fe, take US Route 84/285 north 15 miles to Pojoaque. Here turn left onto NM 502. Continue on NM 502 to its junction with NM 4, a left turn. About 5 miles past the town of White Rock you arrive at the spur road to Bandelier on the left, which descends to the park visitor center. The Juniper Campground is to the left of NM 4 just past this junction. Note that during the May to October high season, you can only enter Bandelier by means of a vehicle shuttle system starting at both Juniper Campground and the nearby town of White Rock.

19. Tyuonyi Overlook

Moderate 2-mile point-to-point; allow 1 hour
Vehicle shuttle or equivalent required
Map: Trails Illustrated 206: Bandelier National Monument

GETTING THERE: With two vehicles, leave one at the park visitor center. Drive the second back to NM 4. Turn left and proceed a short distance to Juniper Campground. Start the hike here, near the amphitheater.

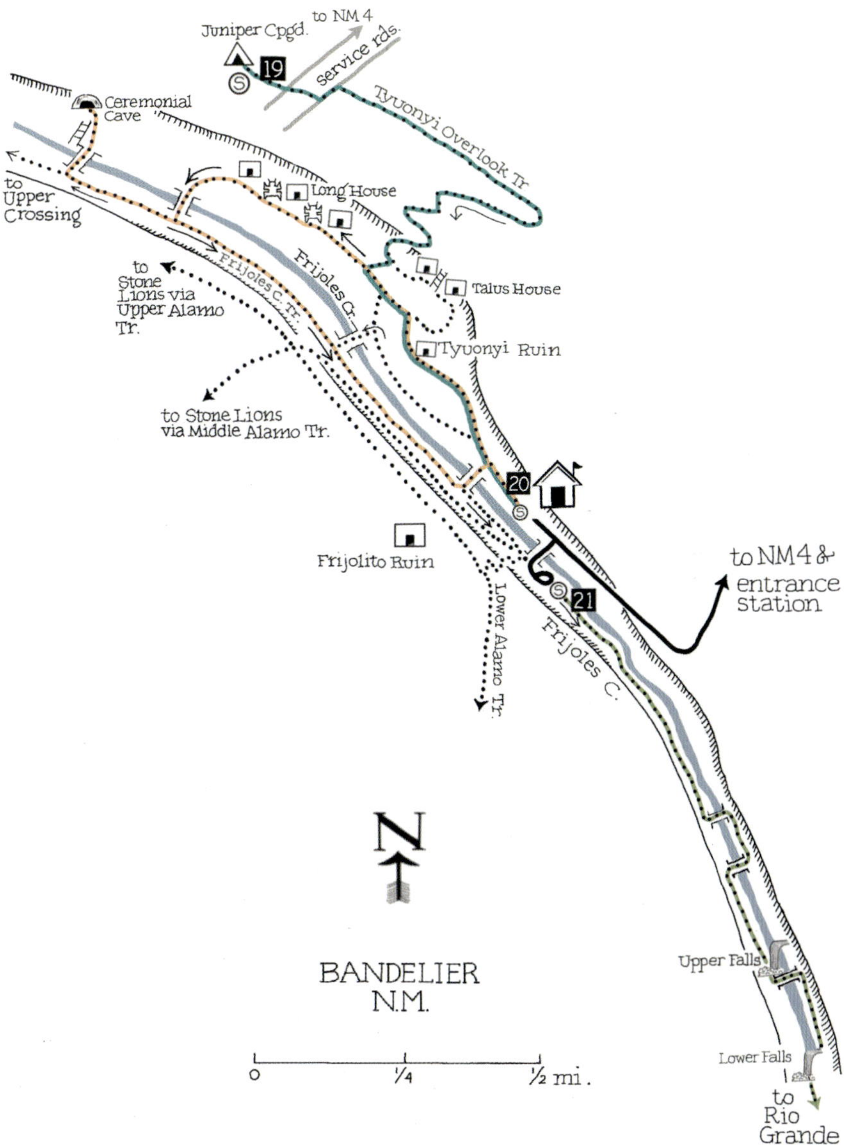

ON THE TRAIL: Formerly known as the Frey Trail, this well-constructed path was once the sole route into Frijoles Canyon. It soon crosses two service roads. At the second road, turn left and walk about 50 feet. Turn right to rejoin the trail proper.

As you reach the canyon rim, sweeping views greet you. The trail contours right and abruptly switchbacks 400 feet to the canyon floor, passing tent rocks along its way. **Tyuonyi** ("place of treaty"), a large, circular apartment house, is visible en route. At the base of the cliff, the trail intersects with the Frijoles Canyon loop near **Talus House**, a restored cliff dwelling. Turn left here and continue to the visitor center. If you didn't leave a car here, plan to catch a shuttle back to Juniper Campground.

20. Frijoles Canyon

Easy 2-mile loop; allow 1.5 hours

Map: Trails Illustrated 206: Bandelier National Monument

GETTING THERE: Park at the visitor center.

ON THE TRAIL: This walk is a must for all visitors to Bandelier, for it loops around the cave, cliff, and surface dwellings of lovely **Frijoles Canyon**, inhabited between the 11th and 16th centuries.

Begin on the **Nature Trail** along the right (east) side of the creek. Bear right at the first two trail junctions nearby, passing Tyuonyi Ruin (see Hike 19). Just beyond Tyuonyi, continue hiking straight upcanyon, paralleling the right bank of the creek and

Prehistoric Indians remodeled caves in Frijoles Canyon for shelter.

ignoring side trails on the left and right. You soon come to a second set of foundations and cave dwellings, collectively known as **Long House**. There is rock art here, as well as a cave housing an estimated fifteen thousand bats during the summertime.

Next, cross the bridge across Frijoles Creek and turn right. At mile 1, recross the creek and ascend to Alcove House in **Ceremonial Cave**, 150 feet above the canyon floor. Reached by ladders, the ruin sports a reconstructed kiva. Backtrack to the west side of the creek and turn left onto the Frijoles Canyon Trail, which returns you to your waiting car.

21. Falls Trail

Easy to moderate 5-mile out-and-back; allow 2.5 hours
Map: Trails Illustrated 206: Bandelier National Monument

GETTING THERE: Begin downstream from the visitor center, near the picnic ground.

ON THE TRAIL: This popular trail crosses Frijoles Creek on wooden bridges, descending gradually. It stays somewhat above the stream on its way to an overlook of 75-foot-high **Upper Falls** at mile 1.25.

Now the trail gets rougher. Descending on switchbacks, it recrosses the creek on a bridge before swinging down to a viewpoint for somewhat less impressive **Lower Falls**, 50 feet high. Crossing the stream three more times on stones and logs, the trail enters open, scrubby country, where it meets the **Rio Grande** at mile 2.5, a 700-foot drop from the visitor center. This is your turnaround point.

22. Capulin Canyon Backpack

Moderate 22.5-mile loop, with optional 5-mile out-and-back; allow 3 days
Permit required; trekking poles and water filter recommended
Map: Trails Illustrated 206: Bandelier National Monument

GETTING THERE: Park at the monument visitor center.

ON THE TRAIL: This trip gives you a good feel for Bandelier's backcountry, taking you from sweeping views on mesa tops to the floor of three canyons. In addition to designated campsites in the valleys, at-large camping is allowed on the mesa tops. Fire ravaged the area in 2011, and in times of drought some trails may be closed.

Start out by hiking west on the Frijoles Canyon Trail (see Hike 20). The gentle ascent through a wooded area involves several stream crossings on logs or rocks. About 0.5 mile past Ceremonial Cave, the canyon narrows considerably and you walk between 100-foot-high cliffs of tuff. Reaching **Upper Crossing** at mile 5.5, turn left onto the **Upper Alamo Trail**, climbing to a windy mesa top. The perch delivers 360-degree views of the surrounding peaks. At about mile 6.75, intersect first the trail along the Frijoles Canyon rim and then the trail to **Alamo Canyon**. Go right at each of these junctions, heading south and dropping 400 feet into Alamo Canyon at mile 7.75.

Follow the canyon downstream for a short distance before gradually climbing out past tent rocks to another plateau at mile 8.75. At the intersection here, turn right toward the lip of **Capulin Canyon** ("Capulin" translates as "chokecherry") and begin a precipitous 600-foot descent to the floor. Reaching the bottom at mile 9.75, turn left

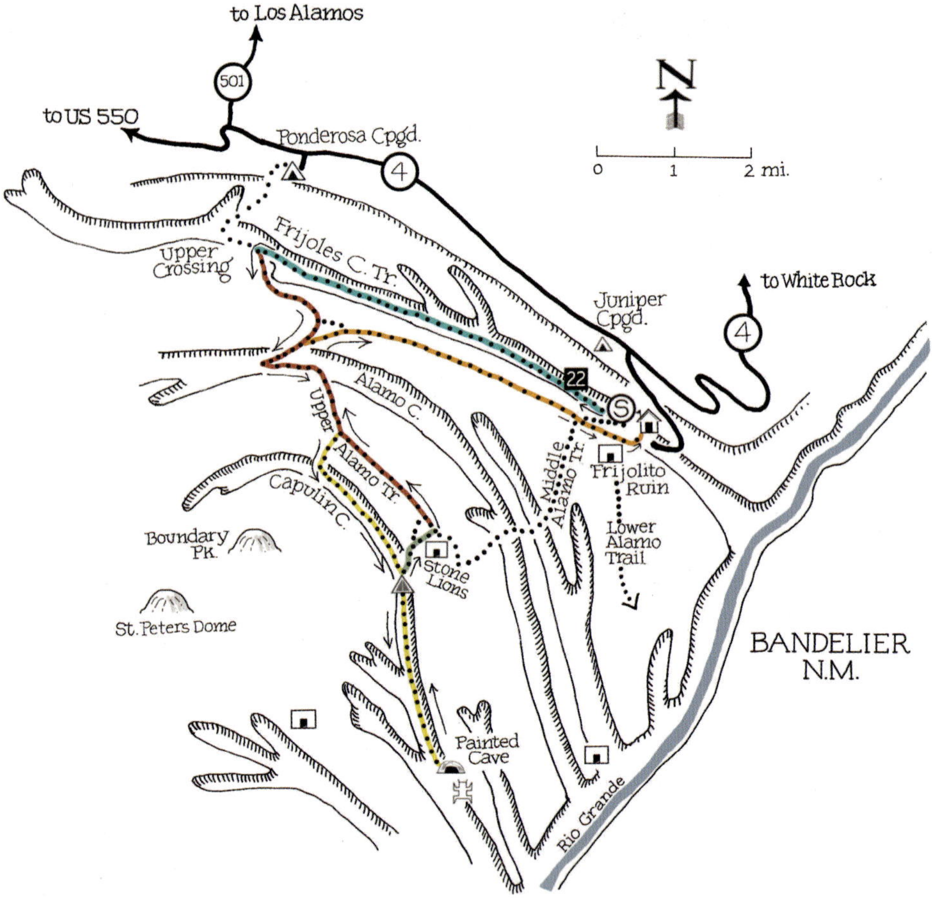

and head down the canyon through heavy timber to the backcountry ranger's cabin and designated camping zone at mile 11.75.

Those with time to spare will find it worthwhile to hike downcanyon to **Painted Cave** (5 miles round trip), with its reddish pictographs. Sacred to the Pueblo people, the shallow cave is perched 50 feet above the floor, but the drawings are visible from below. Pack binoculars if you opt for this side trip.

Back in the camping zone, locate the junction with the **Middle Alamo Trail**. Go north on that trail, climbing out of Capulin Canyon. At mile 13.25 you reach a pair of Y trail junctions. Turn right at the first junction; immediately to the right of the second, pay your respects at the severely eroded shrine of the **Stone Lions**, a pair of crouching mountain lions carved from volcanic rock. Hikers are implored not to disturb this ancient archaeological site in any way.

From here, turn left (northwest) onto the Upper Alamo Trail and climb back to the mesa top between Capulin and Alamo Canyons. Come to another intersection at mile 15.25. Stay right, continuing on the Upper Alamo Trail; you may remember this section of trail, which you hiked previously. Drop into Alamo Canyon at mile 16.75.

Then climb to the mesa on the other side. At mile 17.75 you leave the Upper Alamo Trail, picking up a trail on the right, which heads southeast.

The next stretch is relaxing and beautiful, paralleling the lip of **Frijoles Canyon**. You come to a fork at mile 20.75. The path on the left drops directly down to Frijoles Creek, while the one on the right returns to Alamo Canyon. Continue straight ahead along the rim to **Frijolito Ruin** at mile 21.75. Finish with a 500-foot descent into Frijoles Canyon, enjoying bird's-eye views of ruin sites below.

23. Tsankawi Ruins

Easy 1.5-mile lollipop loop; allow 2 hours

Map: Trails Illustrated 206: Bandelier National Monument

GETTING THERE: From the monument's visitor center, return to NM 4. Turn right and drive 11 miles to the unobtrusive parking area, directly opposite the start of NM 502.

ON THE TRAIL: The ostensible attraction of this detached unit of Bandelier is an unexcavated 350-room pueblo, built in the 15th century, that looks like rubble to the untrained eye. Nevertheless, Tsankawi ("village between two canyons at the clump of sharp, round cacti") deserves a visit for its panoramic views and points of interest.

The trail begins two levels below the mesa occupied by the dwelling. After you climb a short ladder, the path soon forks. Go left toward the base of the upper cliff, stopping to inspect petroglyphs at marker #6. Then proceed to the top using another ladder and cross the mesa to **Tsankawi Ruins**, a masonry surface structure that once boasted two or three stories.

From the ruin, drop back to the lower level on a third ladder. Petroglyphs and cave dwellings abound; scout for rock art, especially around marker #18. The trail follows a well-used path worn nearly a foot deep into the volcanic tuff to close the loop. Turn left to get back to the parking lot.

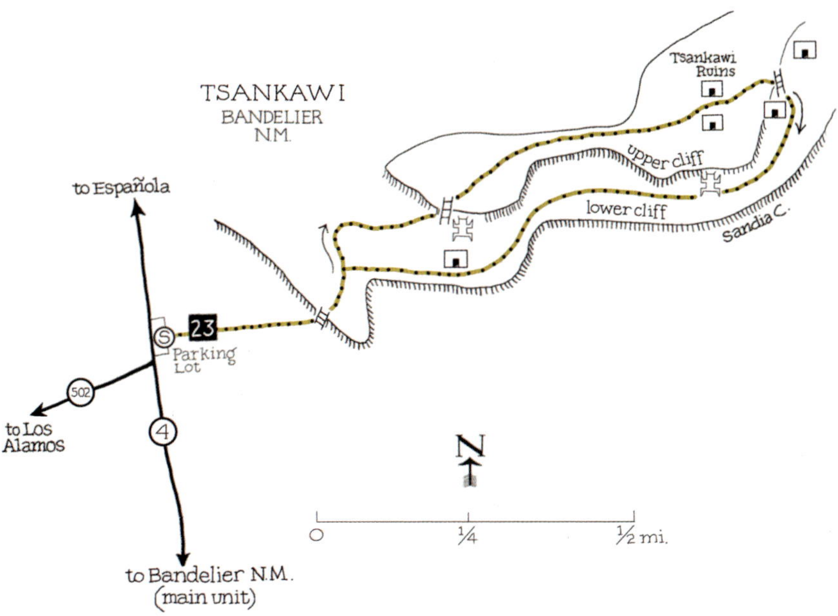

Technicolor cliffs around Echo Amphitheater, a favorite subject of painter Georgia O'Keeffe

NEARBY: Take a one- or two-hour guided tour at **Puye Cliff Dwellings** on the Santa Clara Indian Reservation. From Santa Fe, drive north to Española on US Route 84/285. At a fork on the north end of the commercial strip, go left, following signs to Los Alamos. Cross the Rio Grande and turn left onto NM 30 toward Santa Clara. Entering the reservation, continue several miles to a traffic light. Turn right onto Road 601, signed for Puye. In about 6.5 miles, go right again and proceed to the visitor center/gift shop to book your tour. Tours leave on the hour. A van conveys you to surface ruins on the mesa top. Later you descend by ladder and on a well-worn path of volcanic tuff to the cliff sites. Here the ancient Indians inhabited hollowed-out caves. Scan the high walls for petroglyphs. Binoculars prove useful here.

GHOST RANCH AND VICINITY

Once the residence of legendary artist Georgia O'Keeffe, Ghost Ranch is now a privately operated facility north of the diminutive settlement of Abiquiu. More than one hundred movies have been filmed on the property. All trails are open to the public.

From Santa Fe, drive north on US Route 84/285. Where the roads split, take US 84 northwest for about 35 miles. Turn right at milepost 224 into **Ghost Ranch Education and Retreat Center.** At a fork in the road, go left and proceed to the Welcome Center, where you can register and obtain a site map. Modest fees apply, and since the property is privately owned, federal land passes are not valid here.

For an interesting nearby destination related to O'Keeffe's work, head a few miles north of Ghost Ranch. Where the highway bends sharply right between mileposts 228 and 229, turn left at a marked road for **Echo Amphitheater**, the subject of many of O'Keeffe's masterpieces. A very easy, paved trail (0.25-mile out-and-back) leads to the alcove's mouth.

24. Chimney Rock

Moderate 2.5-mile out-and-back; allow 1.5 hours

Trekking poles recommended

Map: USGS: Ghost Ranch

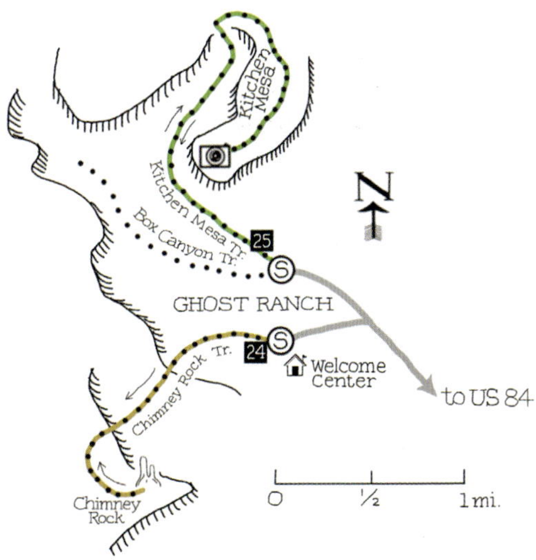

GETTING THERE: Start at the visitors' parking area near the Welcome Center.

ON THE TRAIL: The trail ascends for about 0.25 mile. After leveling out on a plateau, it climbs more steeply to a ridgeline significantly higher than **Chimney Rock**. At the top, the trail turns left and proceeds downhill to the overlook. The rock is a muscular pinnacle of Entrada Sandstone. You also enjoy commanding views of the **Rio Chama** (a tributary of the Rio Grande) and its environs. The colorful landscape is captivating—a little slice of Utah transported to New Mexico. Return as you came, taking care to locate the start of the descent at trail marker 18.

25. Kitchen Mesa

Difficult 5-mile out-and-back, with exposure, routefinding, and scrambling; allow 3 hours
Trekking poles recommended
Map: USGS: Ghost Ranch

GETTING THERE: From the Welcome Center, drive back toward US Route 84 until you reach a major fork in the road. Turn left, following signs, and proceed to the road's end. Park here.

ON THE TRAIL: Begin by hopping across the stream to your right. At mile 0.25, arrive at a hill with trailside exhibits pertaining to Coelophysis dinosaurs, which once roamed the area. From here the trail deteriorates markedly. Round the base of Kitchen Mesa to enter "Kitchen Canyon." A bruising 600-foot climb, partly on a dirt surface, commences at mile 1. Expect considerable exposure on the slippery, narrow path. About halfway into the climb, the route starts to favor rock. The last part of this leg requires a 15-foot scramble up a stable, boulder-lined chute, utilizing good handholds and footholds. It is easier than it appears.

Attaining the top, bear right to meet a wash at mile 1.5. Cairns may peter out here. Follow the wash for a few hundred feet, then cross it and make for the top of Kitchen Mesa. Once on top, you enjoy smooth sailing as you follow a clear trail to an overlook of Ghost Ranch and Abiquiu Lake.

NEARBY: From the same parking lot, you can hike to the head of watery **Box Canyon**. The moderate 3.75-mile out-and-back involves a gradual 500-foot climb, with numerous stream crossings at its upper end.

26. Plaza Blanca

Easy 1.5-mile lollipop loop, with routefinding; allow 1.5 hours
Map: USGS: Ghost Ranch

GETTING THERE: *This hike is on property belonging to the Dar Al Islam Mosque. Register online in advance to obtain the access code.* Drive south from Abiquiu on US 84 and turn left onto NM 554. In about 0.5 mile, turn left onto County Road 155. Reach the mosque's locked gate at 3.25 miles. Enter the access code and follow the dirt track about 0.5 mile, going right at a fork near its end. Park here.

ON THE TRAIL: Among Georgia O'Keeffe's best-known paintings of badlands are those of what she called the "Black Place" (near Nageezi, southeast of Farmington) and the "White Place," an isolated, pinnacle-studded ridge. To access the latter, go through the hiker maze to the right of the parking lot and proceed about 15 yards down the road to a social trail on the left. Follow it east to **Plaza Blanca Valley** at mile 0.25.

Upon reaching this point, you can either invent your own route or follow the plan outlined here. If you opt for the latter, turn right at the valley, paralleling the fluted

Taos Pueblo suggests how abandoned Anasazi great houses may have looked and functioned.

massif a short distance until you come to a reddish hogback. Circle behind the hogback, picking up a faint path. After several ups and downs the path intersects a major wash on the back side of the massif. Turn right and amble up the wash, which soon constricts to form a narrow slot. Near its end, you can scramble up the alabaster ledges of a side-canyon on the left to the top of the basin.

Now reverse course and head back down the wash, going past the path behind the massif that you took earlier. Jog somewhat to the south here around the prow of a major ridge. Doing so will take you into the upper end of the wash that you crossed initially. Find two small arches in the ridge to your left on your way to rejoin the social trail to the parking lot.

TAOS AND VICINITY

No trip to northern New Mexico would be complete without a visit to historic Taos. Although NM 68 is the quick way to get there from Española, a more colorful option is to take the route referred to as the **High Road**. Winding through the pine and aspen uplands of Carson National Forest, this 52-mile drive on NM 76, NM 75, and NM 518 links a series of Hispanic villages celebrated for fine weaving, fiery chiles, and religious fervor. The Spanish Rio Grande region, with exquisite mission churches such as the ones at **Chimayó**, **Las Trampas**, and **Ranchos de Taos**, remains the center of the Penitente sect, whose members practice rites of self-mortification during the Lenten season.

The town of Taos has served as a haven for writers and artists dating back to the era of D. H. Lawrence and Georgia O'Keeffe. Excellent local museums highlight Indian culture, but pride of place goes to **Taos Pueblo** ("town of the red willows"). Tucked between the Rio Grande and the Sangre de Cristo Mountains, the pueblo is one of the oldest continuously occupied communities in the United States. Its interconnected adobe dwellings today house 1800 residents.

Farther north, you can hike into the Rio Grande Gorge.

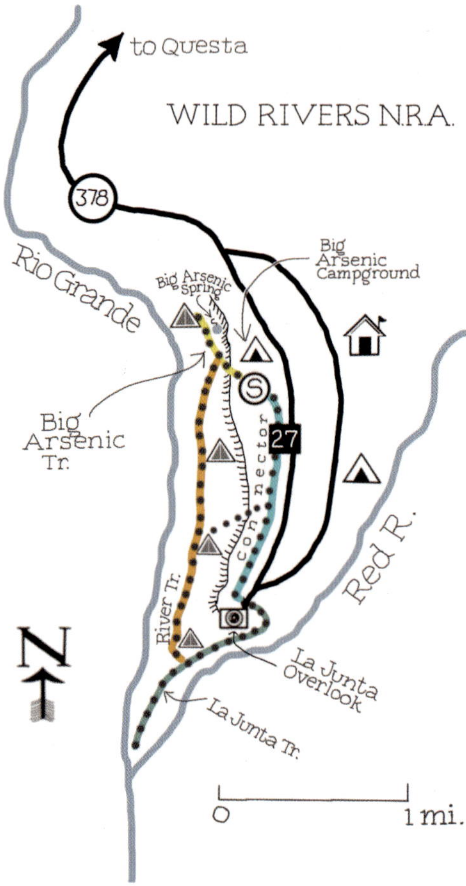

27. Rio Grande Gorge

Moderate 2-mile out-and-back; allow 1.5 hours

Map: USGS: Guadalupe Mountain

GETTING THERE: In Taos, pick up NM 522. About 2.5 miles north of Questa, turn left onto NM 378, traversing Rio Grande del Norte National Monument to enter **Wild Rivers National Recreation Area** at about mile 10. After stopping for information, continue along the paved loop road to Big Arsenic Campground to start the trail.

ON THE TRAIL: A marvel of masonry and engineering, the **Big Arsenic Trail** switchbacks 675 feet down black volcanic cliffs to a fork at the canyon floor. Turn right, heading upstream to **Big Arsenic Springs** at mile 1. Shortly past this point, campsites complete with lean-tos line the banks. Scout for petroglyphs to your left near the fourth of these structures. Return as you came.

You can make this a 7-mile loop by proceeding downstream to the confluence of the Rio Grande and Red River at mile 4. To return, follow the **La Junta Trail** 800 feet to the rim and road-walk north to your car. Back on top, **La Junta Overlook** affords the best views around.

CHAPTER 6
PAINTED DESERT

With hubs in Flagstaff and Page, this chapter concentrates on the national parks and monuments and prehistoric dwellings of northeastern Arizona. From easy day hikes amid the red buttes of Sedona to rugged backpacking trips into the Grand Canyon, from the austere Petrified Forest to the poetic Rainbow Bridge, attractions galore enchant the visitor. An auto tour of the Hopi Reservation rounds out the chapter.

Hubs: Flagstaff and Page, Arizona

Flagstaff (population 66,000), one of the largest communities in the high-desert region, sits in the shadow of the San Francisco Peaks, the eroded remnants of an ancient volcano. The city's 7000-foot altitude makes it comfortable even during the summer, and its **Museum of Northern Arizona**, dedicated to the perpetuation and promotion of local Native American cultures, should not be missed. At nearby Lowell Observatory, the former planet Pluto was discovered in 1930.

Page (population 7600) was founded in 1957 to facilitate the construction of Glen Canyon Dam on the Colorado River. The dam flooded the riparian paradise of Glen Canyon to create 186-mile-long Lake Powell, thereby spawning a lucrative tourist industry. In town, the fascinating **Powell Museum** documents the career and voyages of John Wesley Powell, the legendary explorer of the Green and Colorado Rivers who went on to head the US Geological Survey.

FLAGSTAFF EAST

On the outskirts of Flagstaff, you can tour Sinaguan ruins and hike to craters and natural bridges that inspire wonder.

1. Walnut Canyon National Monument

Easy trails totaling 1.25 miles; allow 1 hour
Map: Trails Illustrated 856: Flagstaff, Sedona

GETTING THERE: Take Interstate 40 east from Flagstaff for 7.5 miles to exit 211. Follow signs to Walnut Canyon National Monument.

ON THE TRAIL: The monument protects four hundred structures once inhabited by people of the Sinaguan culture. Stop at the visitor center to see natural history exhibits and rock art reproductions. The easy **Rim Trail** (a 0.5-mile round-trip) leads to scenic overlooks and reconstructed surface sites.

A steep descent from the visitor center takes you to the easy 0.75-mile **Island Trail**, which loops around a small, isolated mesa in the center of the canyon. Numerous small cave ruins are tucked beneath the Kaibab Limestone cliffs, with more sites coming

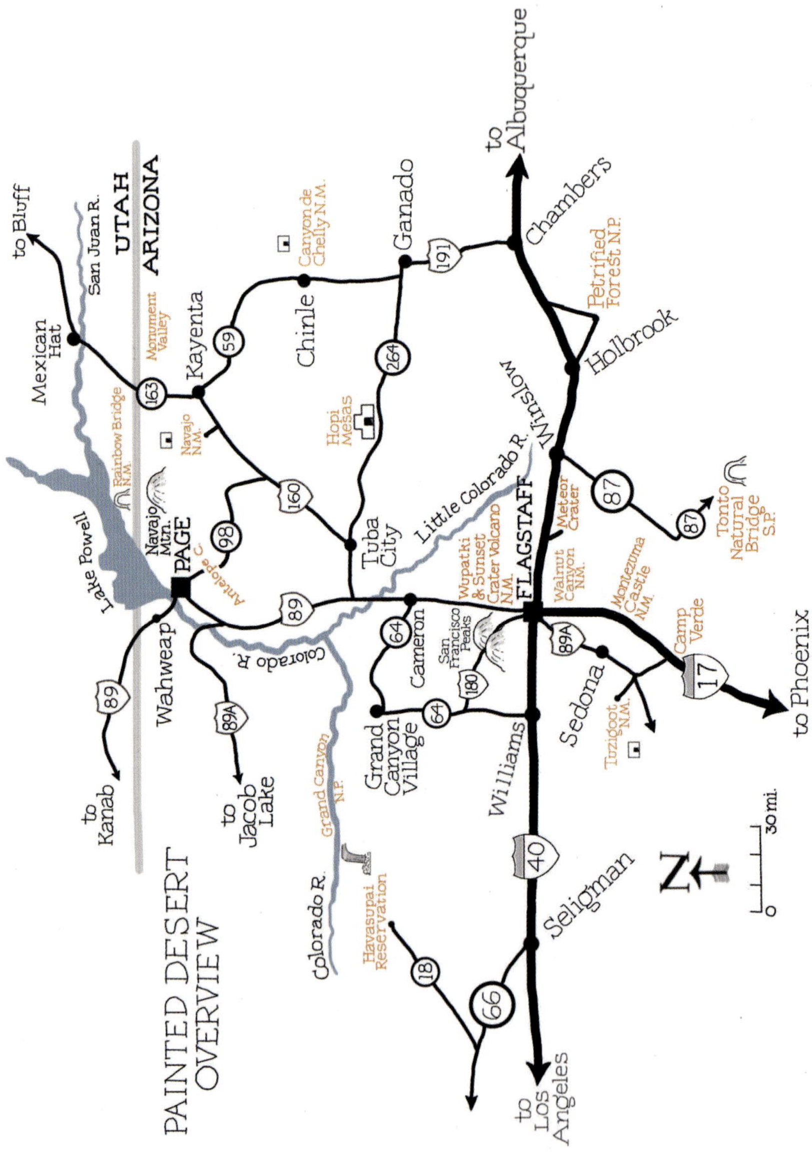

into view on either side of the 400-foot-deep canyon. The Sinaguas inhabited Walnut Canyon for some 150 years before leaving it for parts unknown around 1250 CE. They may have joined kin already established in the Verde Valley south of here.

2. Meteor Crater

Easy 3.5-mile loop; allow 2 hours
Map: USGS: Meteor Crater

GETTING THERE: Drive east on I-40 about 35 miles past Flagstaff to exit 233 and follow signs 5 miles to Barringer Meteor Crater. Fees apply.

ON THE TRAIL: The starkly beautiful Meteor Crater, a privately run "national landmark," is one of the world's largest impact sites, at 550 feet deep and almost a mile across. Films and exhibits at the museum detail how and why the collision occurred nearly fifty thousand years ago, while the Astronaut Hall of Fame demonstrates the crater's use as a mock moon surface for Apollo mission training. A **Rim Trail** encircles the crater, but entry into the depression is forbidden. Hour-long guided tours run regularly.

3. Tonto Natural Bridge State Park

Moderate cumulative 1.25-mile out-and-back; allow 1.5 hours
Trekking poles and river shoes recommended
Map: USGS: Pine

GETTING THERE: From Flagstaff, take Interstate 40 east to Winslow and turn south on AZ 87. In about 65 miles the highway joins AZ 260 to zigzag down the **Mogollon Rim** on the southern edge of the Colorado Plateau, which defines the boundary between the Upper and Lower Sonoran life zones. About 3 miles past the delightfully kitschy town of Pine, near milepost 263, turn right onto Forest Road 583 and proceed to the state park.

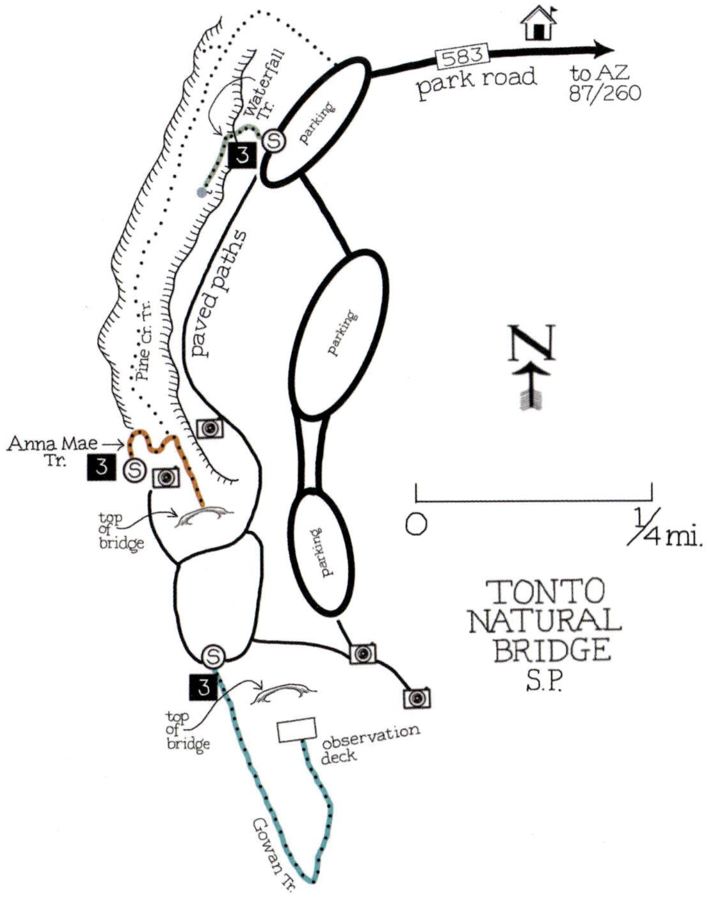

Top: A collared lizard poses on a chunk of jasper; *bottom*: Onyx Bridge spanned a shallow wash before its 2021 collapse

ON THE TRAIL: What a find! Allegedly the world's biggest travertine span at 180 feet high by 150 feet wide, Tonto Natural Bridge is visible from overlooks at the end of the park drive, but can be appreciated in its full magnificence only by descending into Pine Creek Canyon. Do so twice to access both sides of the tunnel-like formation.

Start out on the **Gowan Trail** (0.5 mile out-and-back), which drops 300 feet to an observation deck under a ribbon of water falling off the lip. Even when dry, the colorful boulders at the bottom are slippery as glass, making it difficult and dangerous to walk beneath the bridge.

Returning to the rim, locate the **Anna Mae Trail** (0.5 mile out-and-back) and descend to the rock-choked streambed. Cross the creek and pick your way toward the massive span, pausing to admire a window on the left. Once again, the topography deters exploration of the bridge's underside, though the rocks here do not pose as much of a hazard. The lacy travertine gives off a rococo vibe.

Unless you relish the prospect of boulder-hopping, skip the **Pine Creek Trail** in favor of the **Waterfall Trail** (0.25 mile out-and-back), which leads to a seep spring adorned with maidenhair ferns.

PETRIFIED FOREST NATIONAL PARK

With its distinctive Chinle Formation badlands, Petrified Forest National Park protects one of the world's highest concentrations of petrified logs, formed when trees were buried under mud, ash, or sediment. In each case, an oxygen-free environment prevented rotting. Over time, although the logs' original shapes and forms remained intact, cryptocrystalline structures replaced their cellular membranes. Wood thereby turned to stone, often brilliantly hued agate or jasper. The colors present in the fossilized logs reflect the types of minerals (e.g., manganese, iron, cobalt, copper, or chromium) involved in those exchanges. Please refrain from collecting souvenirs; an estimated ten tons of petrified rock are pilfered annually from the park.

In recent years the park has doubled in size and added several backcountry routes. Informative leaflets are available at either the Painted Desert Visitor Center or the Rainbow Forest Museum, located respectively at the north and south ends of the 26-mile-long scenic drive. Short, paved pathways allow people to visit attractions like the **Giant Logs** and 110-foot-long **Agate Bridge**. The featured hikes are presented in the order of north to south.

From Flagstaff drive east on Interstate 40 for 92 miles to Holbrook. Take US Route 180 for 20 miles to the southern part of Petrified Forest National Park, or continue 26 miles farther east on I-40 to access its northern section.

4. Painted Desert

Moderate 4-mile out-and-back, with routefinding and scrambling; allow 2 hours
Trekking poles recommended
Map: USGS: Kachina Point
GPS coordinates: 35.06310°N, 109.47321°W

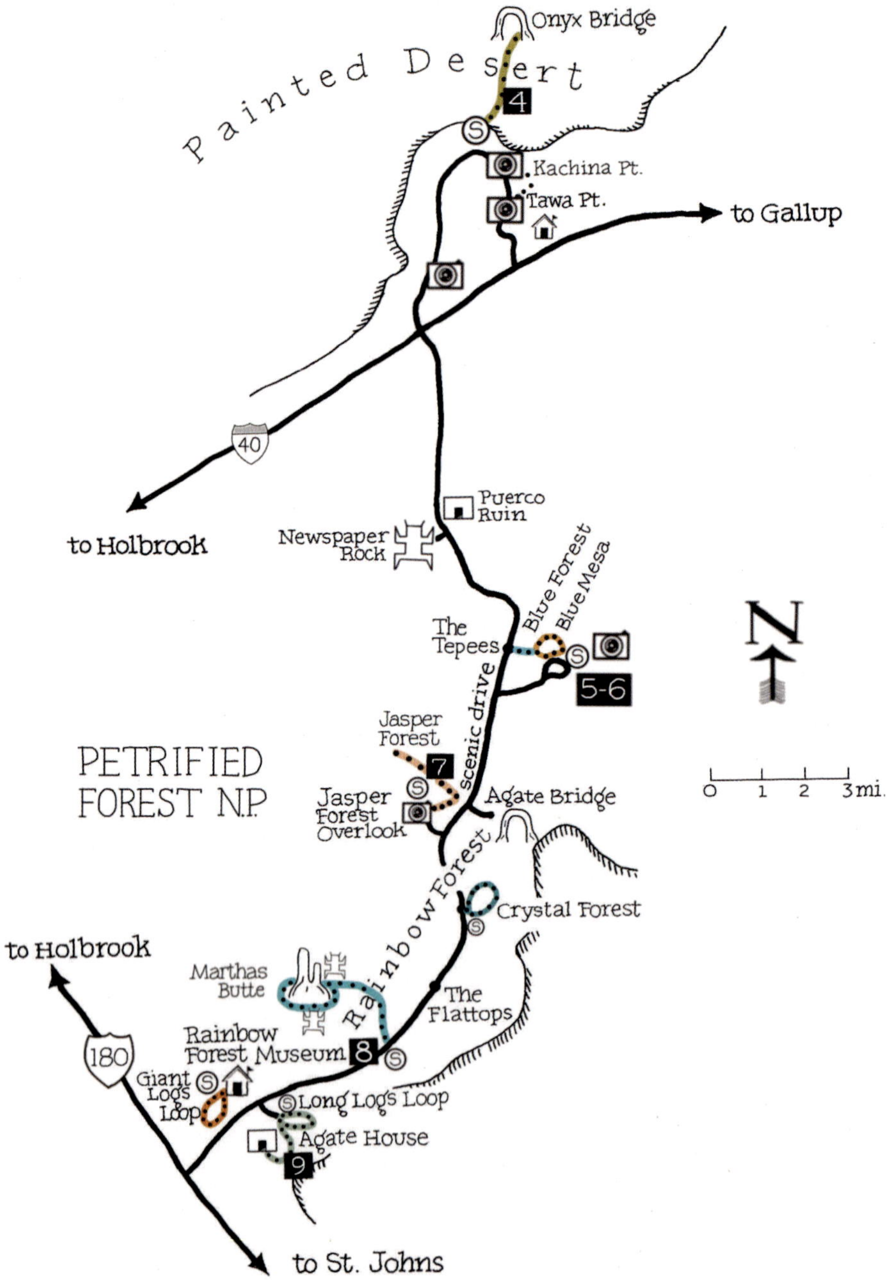

GETTING THERE: From the park's north entrance station, continue a short distance to the Painted Desert Inn and park in its lot.

ON THE TRAIL: Onyx Bridge, which collapsed in 2021, was a 30-foot-long petrified log span from the Triassic period. The surrounding terrain is still well worth exploring.

Locate the trailhead immediately to the left of the historic inn. Before starting out, look directly to the north toward shallow, braided Lithodendron ("tree rock") Wash. Orient yourself by taking note of what appears to be the largest bush in the middle of the dry streambed, about 2 miles distant. It sits between a low mesa on the left and a taller, two-tiered hill on the right. The bush, in close proximity to Onyx Bridge, will be your point of reference.

The constructed trail descends about 250 feet on switchbacks to the base of the cliff, paralleling a blindingly white ridge. At the bottom, pick up a hiker-made trail that passes between a set of ruddy hills. The trail swings to the west, gently descending a small ravine. On your left, though more apparent on the return trip, an old masonry structure occupies the bottom of one of the ravine's branches. Just beyond, at about mile 1, your route veers north to hit a broad wash. Cross this wash, but do not follow it. Instead, continue north across a lightly vegetated bench, effectively cutting a meander of **Lithodendron Wash**. Find an obvious break in the intermittent arroyo walls and drop down into the drainage.

Around a bend in the center of the wash sits the orientation bush that you spotted from the trailhead—the largest of several tamarisks in this vicinity. Enter the channel to the left of the bush and continue for about 150 yards until you arrive at a shallow, 5-foot-wide side-canyon to the west. Follow this side-canyon about 100 yards to a point where it divides, marked by a large chunk of petrified wood. Go right here and then take an almost immediate left into yet another small ravine. Clamber a short distance up this rocky chute. At the top, turn right to locate what's left of Onyx Bridge. Some unusual formations can be found to the west of the ancient conifer log.

From the bridge, you can spot the inn on the skyline. Use it as your beacon on the way back.

5. Blue Mesa

Moderate 1-mile lollipop loop; allow 45 minutes
Map: USGS: Adamana

GETTING THERE: From either entrance, take the main park road to the 3.5-mile spur loop for Blue Mesa and park near the kiosk.

ON THE TRAIL: This, the premier trail in the park, winds through orderly Chinle badlands. Descending steeply about 100 feet from the overlook along an asphalt path, you quickly reach a signpost at the start of the loop. Bear right to explore the purple-and-white banded formations, stopping at exhibits en route. The color that sets the mood here reflects the presence of carbon, cobalt, or copper in the soil. Close the loop and return to the mesa top.

6. Blue Forest

Moderate 1.5-mile point-to-point, with exposure, routefinding, and scrambling; allow 2 hours
Vehicle shuttle or equivalent required; trekking poles recommended
Map: USGS: Adamana

Top: The Blue Mesa Trail winds through brooding badlands; *bottom*: Neatly sliced petrified logs on Crystal Forest Loop

GETTING THERE: Using two vehicles, drive down the main park road from either entrance station. Leave one vehicle at The Tepees pullout, about halfway between the Newspaper Rock and Blue Mesa spurs. Drive the second vehicle to the spur for Blue Mesa and park at the designated trailhead.

ON THE TRAIL: Although the Blue Forest Route has a huge wow factor, it poses special challenges. People who fear heights should avoid this hike. Hazards include a knife-edged ridge and two short, steep ascents/descents on slippery scree. Before setting forth, obtain a copy of the trail brochure at the visitor center, which includes a helpful map and blow-by-blow photographs depicting the route.

Drop down from the Blue Mesa overlook (see Hike 5) and follow the loop counterclockwise a short distance to the "Whispers from the Past" exhibit. Look to the right to inspect your proximate goal, a low ridge sporting a few trees. Leave the paved trail here, following footprints up a shallow wash. Round a hill on its right and continue up the ravine on narrow switchbacks. Loose rocks make them safer to ascend than descend. Top out near the trees.

An indistinct path continues west toward the exposed ridge mentioned above. Take special care here. Past this point, the route continues to favor ridgetops. When the path plunges down a rocky draw at about mile 1, slow your pace lest you stumble on the slick ball-bearing slope. Some people might feel more comfortable turning around at this point. You won't miss much if you do.

For hikers who continue, the route now descends slowly toward The Tepees. When it bottoms out, join a deteriorated roadbed built by the Civilian Conservation Corps during the Great Depression, which continues to the scenic drive.

7. Jasper Forest

Easy 2.5-mile out-and-back, with routefinding; allow 1.25 hours
Map: USGS: Agate House

GETTING THERE: From either park entrance, take the scenic drive to the spur marked for the Jasper Forest, just south of Agate Bridge, and park in the lot.

ON THE TRAIL: The shards of petrified wood littering the ground in the Jasper Forest owe their deeply saturated colors to high concentrations of manganese and iron oxides. Most people experience the area only from the overlook. This hike offers an opportunity to get up close and personal.

The route begins to the right of the parking lot. Descend on a social trail that heads east back toward the park road. About 30 yards shy of that road, near the start of a big bend, turn left into the Jasper Forest drainage and pick up a badly eroded conglomerate roadbed. In all likelihood you will lose this track several times in the next mile, but you can't go too far wrong if you stick close to the cliffs on the right. Consult your topo for enlightenment. The hike ends where the canyon forks; the leaflet describing this route shows an image of a hoodoo that enhanced the area before its 1941 collapse.

NEARBY: About 2 miles farther south along the scenic drive is the very easy 0.75-mile **Crystal Forest Loop**. A paved path leads to logs inlaid with deposits of amethyst and quartz.

Ancient builders used unconventional materials at Agate House.

8. Marthas Butte

Easy 2-mile out-and-back, with routefinding; allow 1 hour
Map: USGS: Agate House

GETTING THERE: From either entrance, take the scenic drive to the bridge over Dry Wash, just south of milepost 22. Park along the east side of the road.

ON THE TRAIL: Petroglyph panels and an unusually positioned petrified log are highlights of this off-trail hike. Two stubby "ears" of Wingate Sandstone top the Chinle Formation butte.

From the parking lot, cross the road and drop into the wash on a social trail that, though obscure at times, continues all the way to your destination. Just a few minutes into the trip, the wash bends sharply east. Exit the wash to the left here and ascend slightly. From here on out, Marthas Butte to the northwest will be in view the entire time. Adjacent to it is a white hill sporting a petrified trunk known as **Walkers Stump**. Large Wingate Sandstone boulders that splayed off the butte line its base. Petroglyphs have been etched into the black desert varnish on some of these boulders.

Circumambulating the butte in a clockwise direction with its far (northwest) side equating to twelve o'clock, you will find a small set of concentric circles at nine o'clock. These circles comprise a solar marker, which is pierced by a shaft of sunlight at dawn on the summer solstice. Most of the other rock art may strike visitors as crude, with the exception of a significant collection at five o'clock.

9. Agate House

Easy 2.5-mile lollipop loop; allow 1 hour
Map: USGS: Agate House

GETTING THERE: Begin at a parking area across from the Rainbow Forest Museum at the south end of the park.

ON THE TRAIL: This popular walk delivers a one-two punch, winding past an extensive stand of petrified logs and visiting a reconstructed Sinaguan dwelling. The first 0.25 mile is paved. Turn right at the fork here, proceeding to the unique archaeological site, the walls of its seven rooms composed entirely of petrified wood. Back to the fork, wander the **Long Logs Loop** before returning to your car.

NEARBY: Behind the Rainbow Forest Museum, take a stroll on the very easy 0.5-mile **Giant Logs Loop**, which allows you to inspect some of the park's largest specimens.

CANYON DE CHELLY NATIONAL MONUMENT

Beautiful Canyon de Chelly (de-SHAY), home to more than sixty Anasazi sites, lies on the windward side of the Lukachukai and Chuska Mountains. The monument's name is a corruption of the term *tsegi*, meaning "rock canyon" in Navajo. Scenic drives hug both rims of the canyon, and all overlooks here are worth your time. Along South Rim Drive, stop at the 800-foot needle called **Spider Rock**, legendary

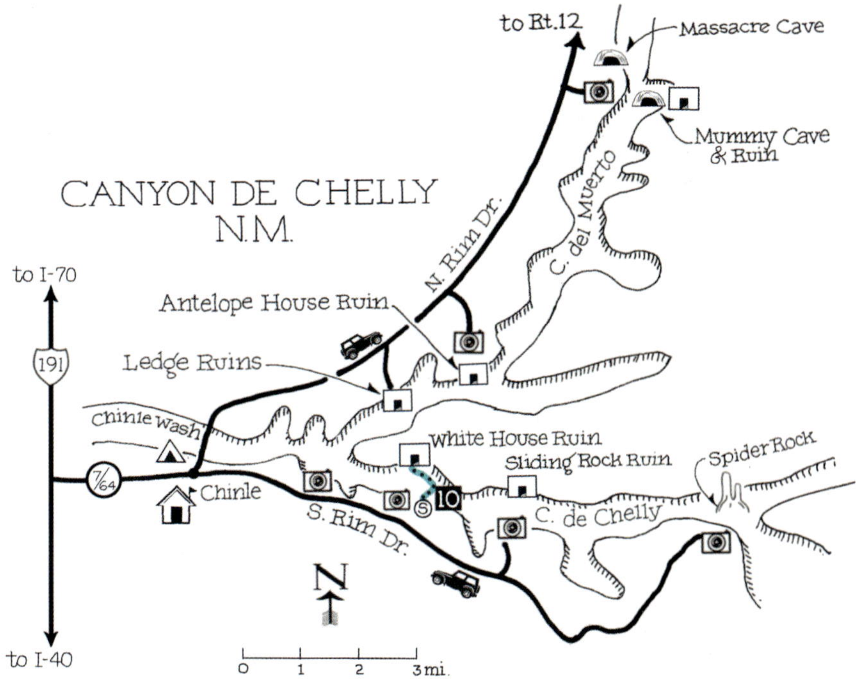

home of Spider Woman, said to have taught Navajos the art of weaving. On North Rim Drive, stop at the overlooks for Massacre and Mummy Caves. In 1805, Spanish soldiers seeking to punish and deter raids on their settlements slaughtered 115 Navajos who had been hiding in what came to be called **Massacre Cave**. At **Mummy Cave**, prehistoric burial remains were found in a 50-room ruin. The 1849 expedition that explored this site named the tributary in which it is located Canyon del Muerto ("canyon of the dead"). Below the rim, visitors are restricted to a single trail unless they opt to hire a local guide.

From Flagstaff, take Interstate 40 east to exit 333 for Chambers. Turn north onto US Route 191. Follow this highway 87 miles to Chinle. Turn right onto Route 7/64 and proceed to the visitor center.

10. White House Ruin

Moderate 2.5-mile out-and-back; allow 2 hours
Map: USGS: Canyon del Muerto

GETTING THERE: The trailhead is 6 miles from the monument's visitor center along South Rim Drive.

ON THE TRAIL: The trail fishtails 600 feet to the canyon floor. Near the bottom, it passes through two tunnels. Upon reaching the sandy wash, turn left to proceed to the site, crossing a small bridge. The ruin lies straight ahead on the right. Once home to nearly one hundred people, it has two tiers. The canyon walls are streaked with desert varnish, dark mineral traces that rains have leached from the sandstone.

NEARBY: South of Ganado along US 191, stop at the **Hubbell National Historic Site**. The Park Service runs tours of the beautifully appointed home of John Lorenzo Hubbell, who established a trading post in 1878 that continues to operate.

AROUND SEDONA

From Flagstaff, travel south on US Route 89A for 29 miles to Sedona. This knockout drive through the Coconino National Forest follows the main fork of **Oak Creek**, which cuts a sandstone gorge up to 2500 feet deep. Several campgrounds line the road; in season, reserve sites in advance.

By universal agreement, fashionable Sedona (named for Sedona Schnebly, the wife of the town's first postmaster) boasts scenery approaching that of southern Utah in grandeur, though it differs both ecologically and geologically. The uplands of this exclusive resort town lie within the oak-pine ecosystem, rather than in the pinyon-juniper or sagebrush plant communities. Massive ponderosas creep up the landscape's ramparts and monoliths. The area is a frequent film location as well as a mecca for New Agers with a passion for crystals and so-called "vortex" sites, or places replete with spiritual energy.

Although Sedona is surrounded by sedimentary formations, you also see evidence of vulcanism. A cross section of rock layers in some ways resembles that of the Grand Canyon farther north. The deepest exposed layer is Redwall Limestone, which forms vertical cliffs in the Grand Canyon. But the 1000-foot-thick Schnebly Hill Formation that dominates Sedona's landscape does not occur at all in the Grand Canyon—or anywhere else. A member of the Supai Group, it forms most of the prominent buttes around town. Color variations arise from differences in mineral content and oxidation.

For purposes of orientation, familiarize yourself with local traffic patterns. Coming from the north, you enter a zone of trendy restaurants and shops. Just past here you reach the so-called Y, where US 89A and AZ 179 diverge. By local custom, directions are given from this junction. Parking for Sedona's dense network of trails is regulated by the **Red Rock Pass** system. You must purchase a pass in town and display it on your dashboard at trailheads to avoid a ticket, holders of federal Senior or Access passes excepted. Red Rock Passes are widely available at local stores and hotels as well as picnic areas and certain trailheads.

11. West Fork Oak Creek

Easy 5-mile out-and-back; allow 2.5 hours
Map: Trails Illustrated 856: Flagstaff, Sedona

GETTING THERE: The hike begins off US Route 89A at the confluence of Oak Creek and West Fork, 10.5 miles north of the Y in Sedona. Parking fees apply. Be prepared for rock-hopping, and don't attempt the trip during spring runoff or when flooding threatens.

ON THE TRAIL: The trail begins by crossing **Oak Creek** on a small footbridge and then crosses the **West Fork** near a shallow pool. Here you enter the heavily forested russet-and-white gorge.

Anticipate frequent stream crossings but little elevation gain. At about mile 2.5, a ledge overhangs the right bank. Though the trail continues for another mile until the walls close in, this makes a good turnaround point. Fall colors in West Fork are over the top.

NEARBY: About 1.5 miles past West Fork on US 89A is popular **Slide Rock State Park**, where erosion-sculpted chutes create kid-pleasing waterslides.

12. Soldier Pass and Brins Mesa

Moderate 7-mile loop; allow 4 hours
Map: Trails Illustrated 856: Flagstaff, Sedona

GETTING THERE: From the Y in central Sedona, drive southwest on US Route 89A and turn right on Soldier Pass Road. Continue about 1.25 miles to Rim Shadows Drive. Bear right onto this suburban street. Turn left on Canyon Shadows Drive, then turn left on Forest Road 9904 and locate the Soldier Pass Trailhead at the back end of the lot.

ON THE TRAIL: The loop detailed here combines segments of four different trails to offer what is arguably the finest walk in the region. It contains everything a hiker might desire: arches and pools, varied plant communities, and superlative views of some of Sedona's renowned buttes.

Begin on the **Soldier Pass Trail**. In short order you reach a T intersection, to which you will return at the end of the hike. Go left here, stopping to inspect **Devils Kitchen** sinkhole. The trail briefly follows a jeep road before branching off to the right. You soon come to an unmarked drainage containing the so-called **Seven Sacred Pools**.

Take the spur trail on the right to check them out. Although unimpressive-looking, these pools serve as a year-round water source for wildlife.

Back on the main trail, turn right to continue up the canyon. The Soldier Pass Trail again meets the jeep road, which ends at a fence at mile 1.25. Go through the fence, entering **Red Rocks–Secret Mountain Wilderness**.

Near a signboard, an unmarked path heads toward the arches. To visit them, detour onto this path, scrambling uphill toward a redrock cliff. You soon reach a fork. The right branch accesses two of the arches, while the left traverses a sandstone terrace to the third. All are cliff-wall spans, formed when joints in the sandstone parallel to the sheer face widened and deepened, breaking through to the alcoves beneath.

Returning to the main trail, begin a brisk climb. At the top, the Soldier Pass Trail ends at a T intersection with the **Brins Mesa Trail**. (Opting for a bypass trail short

Classic Sedona: soaring crimson buttes graced by a century plant

of the intersection shaves about a mile off the hike.) Bear right on this lofty tableland to witness a breathtaking tableau. The deep, narrow chasm across the way is Mormon Wash. Just before the Brins Mesa Trail begins its descent, you arrive at a natural R&R spot. From that clearing, you can amble along a social trail to appreciate the **Earth Angel** spire close-up.

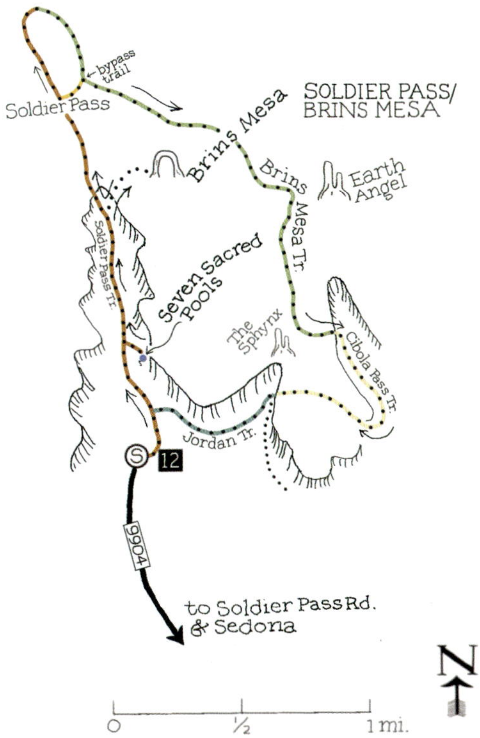

Back at the clearing, switchback down the trail, contouring around the formations to your right. Within 1 mile you reach a large parking lot. Go through it and walk down the road to join the **Cibola Pass Trail**. Follow this trail up a low ridge to a barbed-wire fence. On the other side you receive stellar views of several monumental rock formations, including **The Sphynx**, above you on the right. Descend to join the **Jordan Trail**. Go right and continue to the familiar intersection with the Soldier Pass Trail, near the sinkhole. Turn left and proceed to your car.

13. Coffee Pot

Easy 2.75-mile out-and-back, with scrambling; allow 1.5 hours
Map: Trails Illustrated 856: Flagstaff, Sedona

GETTING THERE: From the Y in central Sedona, go southwest onto US Route 89A for 2 miles to Coffee Pot Drive. Turn right and continue to a T intersection with Sanborn Drive. Turn left, then quickly take a right onto Little Elf Drive, which ends where it intersects Buena Vista Drive. Go right and locate the parking lot to your left. This is the designated lot for the Sugarloaf Trail, but other paths also originate here.

ON THE TRAIL: Start by walking north on the **Tea Pot Trail**, heading for the redrock cliffs. Reaching a three-trail junction, take the path on the extreme right, following cairns toward the powerlines. At the powerlines (mile 0.5), turn right to remain on the Tea Pot Trail. Pass a spur that loops around **Sugarloaf Hill**. Almost immediately, reach an unsigned junction with the **Coffee Pot Trail**. Turn left here, following a two-track. The track swings left to head a draw, or gully, then goes right, paralleling the cliffs. Ignore branching side-trails.

At mile 1, arrive at a slickrock flat. Here the trail goes left, but you turn right onto a slickrock path that soon follows a ledge. When the route seems to end, scramble to

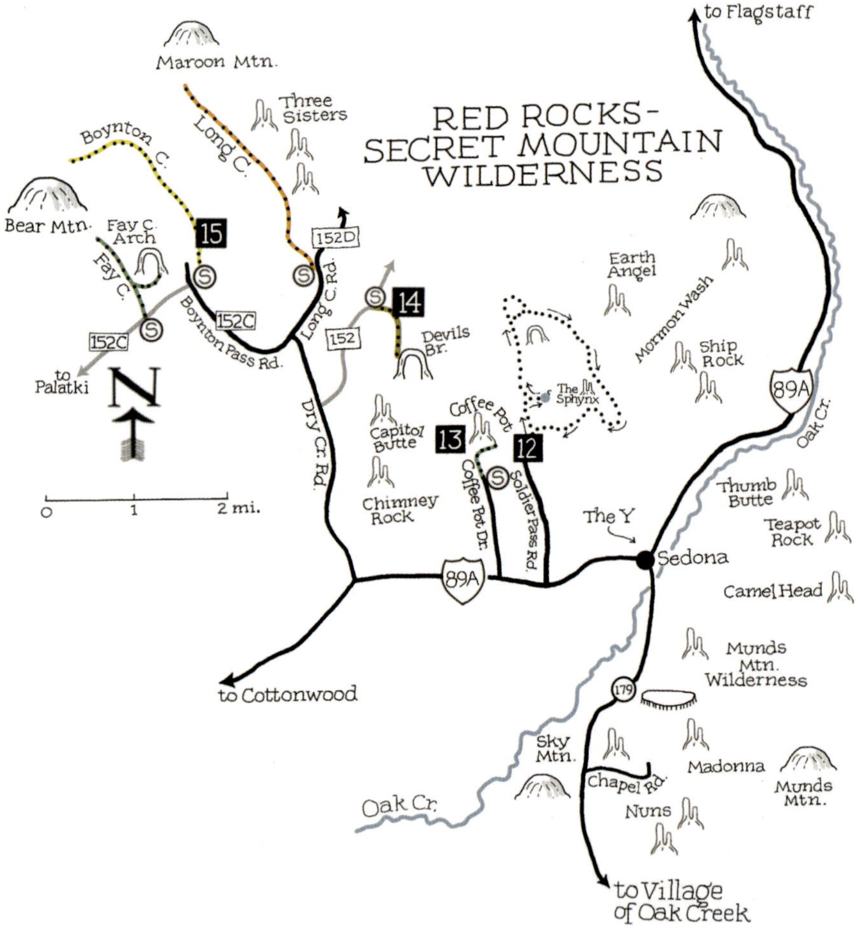

the next ledge, 10 feet above. Continue for about 100 yards until the "spout" of the Coffee Pot appears overhead and you can proceed safely no farther.

14. Devils Bridge

Moderate 3.75-mile out-and-back, with scrambling; allow 2 hours
Trekking poles recommended
Map: Trails Illustrated 856: Flagstaff, Sedona

GETTING THERE: From the Y in central Sedona, go southwest on US Route 89A for 3.25 miles. At the traffic light, turn right onto Dry Creek Road and drive about 2 miles. Turn right here onto Forest Road 152. Continue 1.5 miles, parking in a large lot.

ON THE TRAIL: This trail in Red Rocks–Secret Mountain Wilderness ascends to the Verde Valley's largest span, about 50 feet across. To say that the area receives heavy use would be an understatement. On weekends, especially, it becomes Party Central.

Start out by walking northeast on FR 152, a rocky "road" suitable only for drivers who are callously indifferent to the fate of their vehicles. After 1 mile, reach a signboard that marks the path to the arch. Turn right onto a onetime jeep track, which you follow for 0.5 mile to its end. From here a trail branches off to the right, clambering up perilously steep steps. Devils Bridge rewards breathless hikers where the trail tops out. Thrill-seekers wait their turn to be photographed crossing the span.

15. Boynton Canyon

Moderate 6-mile out-and-back; allow 3 hours
Map: Trails Illustrated 856: Flagstaff, Sedona

GETTING THERE: From the Y in downtown Sedona, go southwest on US Route 89A for 3.25 miles to a traffic light. Turn right onto Dry Creek Road. In about 3 miles, you reach the intersection of two forest roads, FR 152C and FR 152D. Go left on FR 152C, Boyston Pass Rd., and continue for 1.5 miles to a junction. Take a right and proceed 0.25 mile to the trailhead, just outside the Enchantment Resort.

ON THE TRAIL: This much-loved trail ascends gorgeous Boynton Canyon. It skirts the resort on the right, passing twin spires that mystics revere as a vortex spot. After the first mile the trail dips to the canyon floor, where the going becomes much easier. Turn around where the canyon narrows and the trail is obscured by brush.

NEARBY: Backtrack to the T intersection of FR 152C and 152 D. Go straight here, following FR 152D, Long Canyon Rd. In about 0.5 mile you will reach the trailhead for **Long Canyon**. The moderate 6-mile out-and-back offers views of the spindly **Three Sisters** and the still-higher eminence of **Maroon Mountain**. At the canyon's upper end, a freestanding double arch adorns the horizon.

Paralleling Boynton Canyon to its west is popular **Fay Canyon**. Reach it by backtracking 0.25 mile from the Boynton Canyon trailhead and bearing right onto a mostly unpaved road. The parking area is 0.5 mile down this road on the right. Stroll up the trail about a mile before doubling back to your vehicle. If you wish, scramble up a steep, rocky path on the right at mile 0.5 to view one of Sedona's most beautiful arches.

16. Cathedral Rock

Difficult 1.5-mile out-and-back, with scrambling; allow 1.5 hours
Trekking poles recommended
Map: Trails Illustrated 856: Flagstaff, Sedona

GETTING THERE: From the Y in central Sedona, drive south 3 miles on AZ 179 to a roundabout. Turn right onto Back o' Beyond Road. Continue about 0.5 mile to a large parking area on the left.

ON THE TRAIL: Cathedral Rock, a celebrated vortex or meditation spot for New Agers, dominates the landscape south of Sedona. A congested trail climbs 600 feet up slickrock slopes to a breezy notch between its twin buttes. Those nervous about heights may prefer either to sit this one out or to stop short of the top. The climb involves class 3 scrambling, but no significant exposure.

After crossing a wash, the cairned route ascends about 150 feet to a flat slickrock expanse appropriately called **The Vista**, where it intersects the **Templeton Trail** (see Hike 17). Just past this intersection the climb begins in earnest, marked by stripes of white paint as well as Sedona's signature cairns, composed of rocks encased in wire mesh baskets. Where the going gets rough, look for helpful foot- and handholds pecked into the rock. The most challenging segment, which covers about 125 vertical feet, comes at a false summit one level below the saddle. Beyond this point, the pitch moderates. After congratulating yourself at the summit, enjoy a restful intermezzo, complete with views of **Courthouse Butte**, the **Madonna and Nuns**, and **Munds Mountain.** Loose gravel recommends caution on the return.

NEARBY: The most arresting views in town are enjoyed from the local airport, another alleged vortex site. From the Y in central Sedona, take US Route 89A southwest for 1 mile. Turn left on Airport Road and proceed 0.5 mile to a tiny parking area atop the mesa. An easy 3.5-mile trail, the **Airport Loop**, circles this lofty perch.

17. Templeton and Easy Breezy Loop

Easy 5-mile lollipop loop; allow 2.5 hours
Map: Trails Illustrated 856: Flagstaff, Sedona

GETTING THERE: From the Y in central Sedona, drive south 3 miles on AZ 179 to a roundabout. Turn right onto Back o' Beyond Road. Continue about 0.5 mile to a large parking area on the left.

ON THE TRAIL: The Templeton Trail, extending from Bell Rock to Oak Creek, is part of a dense network around Cathedral Rock. With two vehicles, the hike can be completed as a point-to-point, but the loop described here makes for an ideal alternative.

From the parking lot, cross a shallow wash and ascend to the junction of the **Templeton Trail**, a few hundred yards distant. Turn right and lateral along the slickrock below the butte. At about mile 0.5, the trail begins its descent about 150 feet to relaxing creekside beaches, reached at mile 1.

Backtrack to the junction with the Cathedral Rock Trail and continue straight ahead along the same contour line. This section of trail, much less traveled than its eastern counterpart, stays on slickrock benches for much of its length. Nearing AZ 179 at about mile 4, turn left onto the less clearly defined **Easy Breezy Trail**. Suffer traffic noise until the path veers away from the road. All the way back to the parking lot, the Easy Breezy flirts with the same shallow wash you crossed at the outset. While deficient in big views, it offers a serene stroll through the woods.

18. Baldwin Trail

Easy 2.5-mile loop; allow 1.5 hours
Map: Trails Illustrated 856: Flagstaff, Sedona

GETTING THERE: From the Y in downtown Sedona, drive south on AZ 179 for 7.5 miles. Turn right on the Verde Valley School Road, which is paved for the first 3.75 miles. Continue on to an ample parking area on the left at mile 5.

ON THE TRAIL: The Baldwin Trail, frequented by hikers, bikers, and equestrians alike, offers reach-out-and-touch-it views of Cathedral Rock, Sedona's most photographed landmark. From the parking lot, cross the road and turn right onto the trail, which encircles a nameless butte. Cross a low saddle at the halfway point, then descend to a junction with the **Templeton Trail** (see Hike 17). Detour right for a short distance

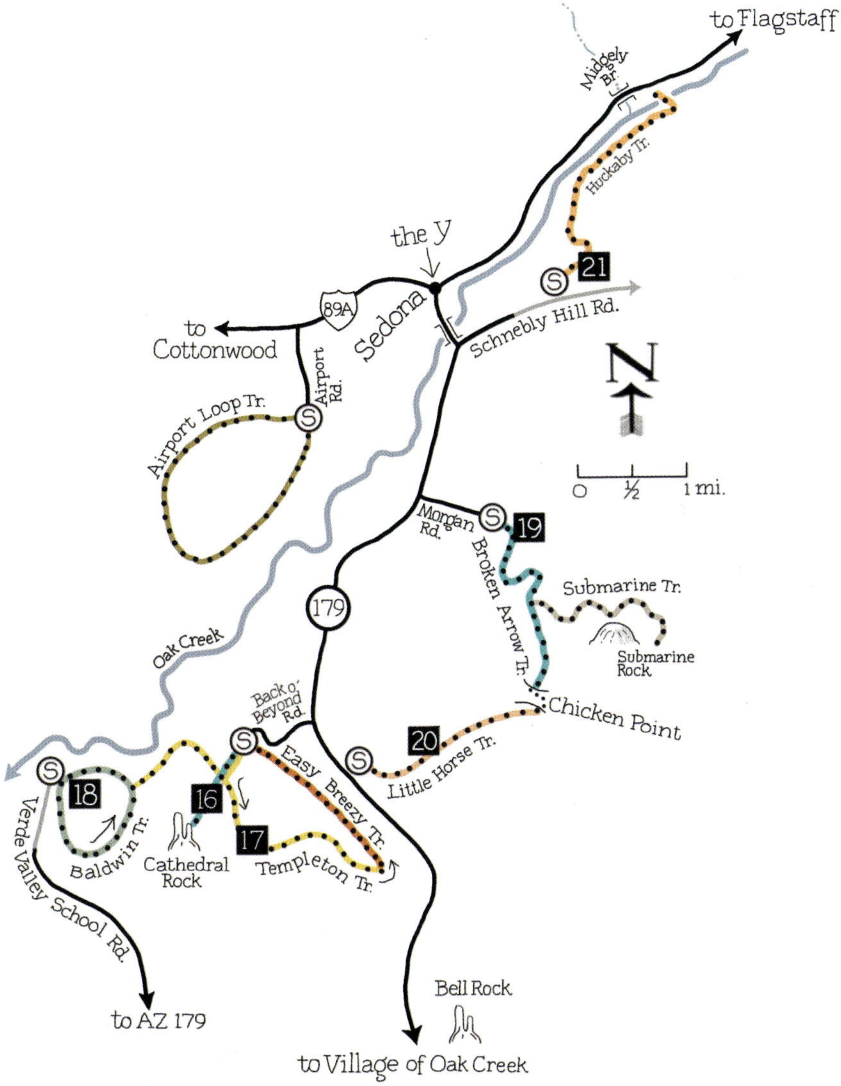

to chill out at sandy beaches along Oak Creek. Back at the junction, go left to return to your car.

19. Broken Arrow Trail

Moderate 5-mile out-and-back, including spur; allow 2.5 hours
Map: Trails Illustrated 856: Flagstaff, Sedona

GETTING THERE: From the Y in central Sedona, drive south on AZ 179 for 1.5 miles. Turn left onto Morgan Road, which leads 0.75 mile through the Broken Arrow subdivision to the parking lot.

ON THE TRAIL: The name "Broken Arrow" derives from a Western filmed here in the 1940s. The trail, across slickrock and packed sand, heads south toward Battlement Mesa, paralleling a jeep road that receives heavy traffic. At 0.5 mile, stop to see the **Devils Dining Room**, a fenced-off sinkhole. A worthwhile spur (1 mile round trip) to **Submarine Rock** branches left at mile 0.75. Crossing the jeep road, the spur descends into a wash before contouring around the back of the rock to the north face, where it is easiest to climb. Flat on top, the large bald provides an ideal place to drink in the scenery.

Return to the main trail, which climbs gradually along the base of **Twin Buttes**. You cross several slickrock flats, the last of which overlooks iconic **Bell Rock**, before topping out near **Chicken Point**. Retrace your steps back to the parking lot.

20. Little Horse Trail

Moderate 4.5-mile out-and-back; allow 2 hours
Map: Trails Illustrated 856: Flagstaff, Sedona

GETTING THERE: From the Y in central Sedona, drive south on AZ 179 for 3.5 miles to a parking area on the left. Find the trailhead at the south end of the lot.

ON THE TRAIL: This popular trail ascends 400 feet to a saddle that overlooks many of Sedona's landmarks. Jeep tours also frequent the pass, reaching it from the other side (see Hike 19).

After 0.25 mile, bear left at the junction with the Bell Rock Trail. The Little Horse follows a wash to a platform from which you can admire the modernist Chapel of the Holy Cross at the base of the Twin Buttes. A short spur on the left leads to the chapel. The main trail swings to the right past the buttes and takes advantage of a slickrock ramp to attain **Chicken Point**. Views here are superb.

NEARBY: With two cars, you can combine the trails for Little Horse and Broken Arrow (see Hike 19) into a moderate 3.75-mile point-to-point.

21. Huckaby Trail

Moderate 2.75-mile point-to-point; allow 1.5 hours
Vehicle shuttle or equivalent required
Map: Trails Illustrated 856: Flagstaff, Sedona

GETTING THERE: At one end of this trail is Midgely Bridge, which sits astride a tributary of Oak Creek. Drive two vehicles 5.5 miles north of Sedona on US Route 89A. Leave one car here. Demand for parking spaces at the picturesque bridge often exceeds supply, so plan accordingly. To reach the other end, return to Sedona in your second vehicle. From the Y at the center of town, drive south on AZ 179 for 0.25 mile. Just beyond the Tlaquepaque shopping mall, turn left onto Schnebly Hill Road and continue about a mile to a parking area.

ON THE TRAIL: This varied hike, which incorporates a shady creekside stroll, links **Schnebly Hill** and Midgely Bridge. Both point-to-point and out-and-back hikers should start at Schnebly Hill.

Find the trail on the north end of the lot. Go left at a junction at mile 0.25. Dipping down to Bear Wallow Wash at mile 0.5, the trail next ascends to a ridge at mile 1, which

In the spring, blooming ocotillo cacti abound along Sedona trails.

treats hikers to views of the Steamboat, Wilson Mesa, and Mitten Rock. Follow the ridgeline a short distance before descending steeply to **Oak Creek** at mile 1.5. Walk along its shady east bank, rock-hopping across the shallow stream at mile 2.5, where **Midgely Bridge** looms straight above. The trail continues a bit past the bridge before reversing course and switchbacking 200 feet up to the parking area in the final 0.25 mile.

22. Palatki Ruin

Easy 1-mile out-and-back; allow 2 hours
Reservations recommended (call 928-282-3854)
Map: Trails Illustrated 856: Flagstaff, Sedona

GETTING THERE: From the Y in central Sedona, drive southwest on US Route 89A. At mile 3.25, turn right on Dry Creek Road. Turn left at the stop sign at mile 6 and continue 1.75 miles to a fork. Take a left onto Forest Road 152C and follow this good unpaved road to its end at a T intersection. Go right onto FR 795, which dead-ends in 6 miles at Palatki ("red house"). (See map on page 160.)

ON THE TRAIL: A homestead serves as headquarters for the Palatki Heritage Site, a Sinagua complex in the Coconino National Forest. At the time scheduled for your tour, you will be instructed to walk to two cliff dwellings, both in south-facing alcoves. You also will have ample opportunity to view rock art along the cliff face.

NEARBY: To visit **Honanki Ruins**, backtrack to the start of FR 795 to its fork and hang a sharp right onto FR 525, a rough dirt road through private land. The parking lot is 4.5 miles from the junction. An easy 0.5-mile out-and-back trail gives access to Honanki ("badger house"), which dates to the 12th and 13th centuries.

SINAGUA COUNTRY

The Sinaguas once-farmed areas around contemporary Flagstaff, including both the bucolic Verde Valley and the high plateau beneath the **San Francisco Peaks**. The most recent eruption in that chain occurred in 1085 CE at Sunset Crater north of town, now a national monument. Mineralized ash deposited during that seismic event fertilized the soil, enabling generations of aboriginals to farm these benchlands successfully.

23. Sunset Crater Volcano National Monument

Easy 1-mile loop; allow 30 minutes
Map: Trails Illustrated 856: Flagstaff, Sedona

GETTING THERE: From Flagstaff, take US Route 89 north for 12 miles. Turn right onto the scenic byway connecting Sunset Crater Volcano and Wupatki National Monuments (Forest Road 545) and drive about 4 miles. Trailhead parking is on the right.

ON THE TRAIL: Scaling the red cinder cone of **Sunset Crater** is verboten, but you can walk near its base on the **Lava Flow Trail**, which includes a stop at a lava tube. Branching off a 0.25-mile paved loop, the trail descends slightly and proceeds counterclockwise, paralleling a fenceline around a flow of basaltic a'a lava. Of the three basic forms of lava, a'a—composed of sharp, rough clinkers—is the hardest to cross. Fortunately,

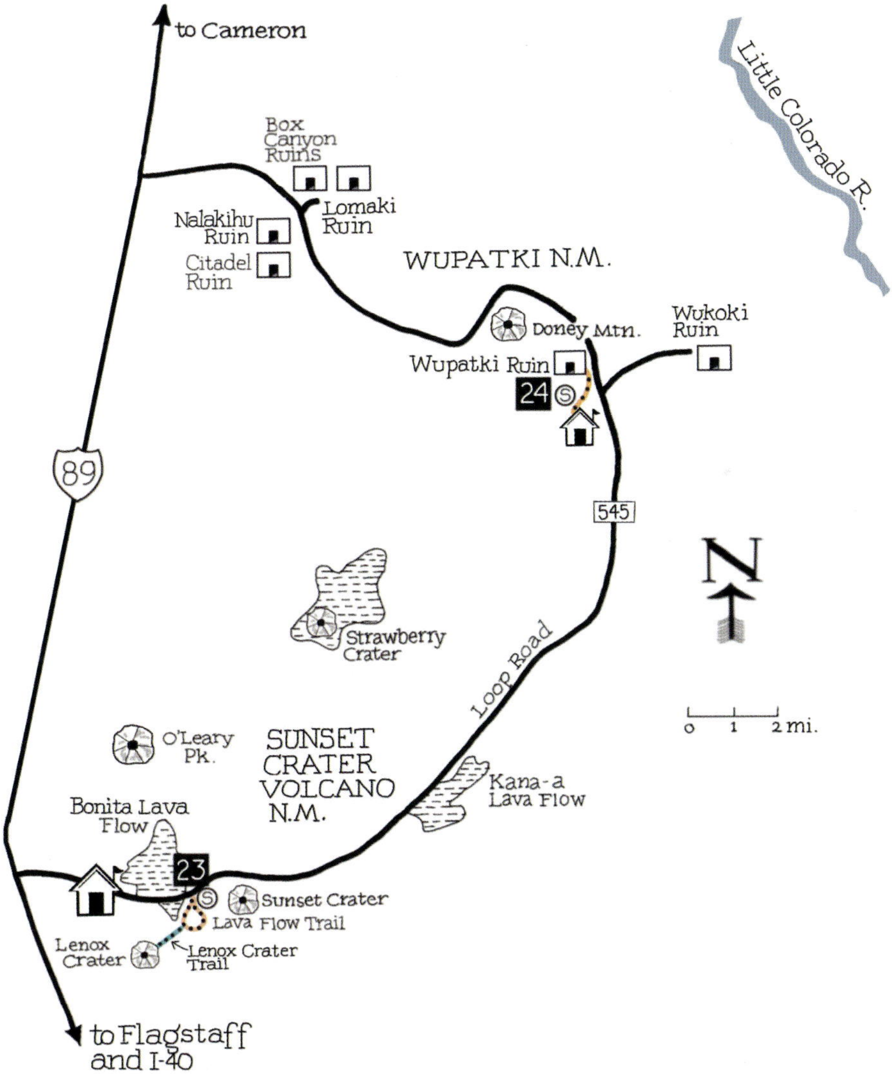

the trail surface is composed of packed dirt and ash. At its end, the trail links back to the paved pathway.

NEARBY: At the other end of the parking lot begins the **Lenox Crater Trail**, a moderate 1.5-mile out-and-back that climbs 300 feet to a cinder cone for a bird's-eye view of Bonita Lava Flow.

24. Wupatki National Monument

Very easy cumulative 1-mile out-and-back; allow 1 hour
Map: Trails Illustrated 856: Flagstaff, Sedona

GETTING THERE: From Flagstaff, take US Route 89 north for 26 miles and turn right onto Forest Road 545 (Loop Road), the northern end of the loop road connecting Wupatki and Sunset Crater Volcano National Monuments. Short trails lead to accessible sites off this road.

ON THE TRAIL: Together, Wupatki and Sunset Crater protect close to 2700 Neolithic ruins, a mere fraction of which are open to the public. Because of the fragility of these sites and their historical and scientific value, the backcountry is off-limits, with the exception of occasional ranger-led overnight trips.

The pueblos were erected in the early 13th century. About 5 miles from the highway, the first attraction is **Lomaki** ("beautiful house" in Hopi), a multistory apartment building at the end of a 0.5-mile spur. **Box Canyon Ruins** are nearby. A short distance farther down the loop, on the right, visit unexcavated **Citadel Ruin**. Positioned on a knoll composed of volcanic rock, it grants fine views of the towering San Francisco Peaks and surrounding countryside. Adjacent to Citadel Ruin is the **Nalakihu** site ("house standing alone").

At the visitor center, find the most extensive cluster, **Wupatki** ("tall house"), which contains a large outdoor amphitheater and a smaller, elliptical structure believed to have been a ball court. Ball courts were widely used by Mesoamerican indigenous peoples such as the Mayans and Toltecs; the presence of such a structure here attests to the extent of their cultural influence. Just beyond the visitor center, a 3-mile spur road leads to the **Wukoki** ("wide house") trailhead.

25. V-Bar-V Ranch

Easy 0.75-mile out-and-back; allow 1 hour
Map: USGS: Casner Butte

GETTING THERE: From Flagstaff, take Interstate 17 south to exit 298. Here pick up Forest Road 618. The pavement ends at a bridge over Beaver Creek in about 2.5 miles. Shortly thereafter, where three roads intersect, turn right toward the visitor center.

ON THE TRAIL: The Hopis claim this cliffside Sinaguan site in the Verde Valley as an ancestral legacy. The most striking inscription on the enormous slab is a sun dagger that functioned as an astronomical calendar.

26. Tuzigoot National Monument

Very easy 0.25-mile out-and-back; allow 30 minutes
Map: USGS: Clarkdale

GETTING THERE: From Flagstaff, drive south on US Route 89A for about 50 miles to Cottonwood. At a traffic light on the west side of town, pick up AZ 260 (a.k.a. Historic 89A, or Main Street, which becomes Broadway). Continue a few miles to the junction with Tuzigoot Rd. Turn right here and proceed to the monument.

ON THE TRAIL: The name Tuzigoot derives from the Apache for "crooked water." The structures protected here were built around 1000 CE. In pre-Columbian times, members of the Sinaguan and Hohokam tribes coexisted peacefully in the fertile Verde Valley, with the Sinaguans sharing their masonry skills and the Hohokams teaching their neighbors how to irrigate crops. Take a short, self-guided tour of this impressive structure, which housed more than two hundred people, and check out the outstanding exhibits inside the visitor center.

27. Montezuma Castle National Monument

Very easy 0.25-mile loop; allow 30 minutes
Map: USGS: Camp Verde

GETTING THERE: From Flagstaff, take Interstate 17 south to exit 289, and follow signs for Montezuma Castle. For Montezuma Well, take exit 293 for McGuireville and continue east 5 miles.

ON THE TRAIL: Early settlers mistakenly imagined that this well-preserved dwelling along Beaver Creek was erected by Aztecs from Mexico. One of the Southwest's most jaw-dropping archaeological treasures, **Montezuma Castle** was fashioned of limestone blocks and river stones in the 12th century. Fifty people inhabited this five-story structure, which is set like a jewel in the cliff. Too fragile to enter, it can be admired from a viewpoint behind the visitor center. The trail stops at another ruin before returning to the parking lot.

NEARBY: **Montezuma Well**, a detached unit of the monument, can be accessed by an easy, 0.5-mile loop. Fed by perennial springs, the pool formed when the roof of a limestone cavern collapsed. Local tribes utilized this reliable water source in their irrigation systems. Remnants of their ancient dwellings ring the sinkhole.

The impregnable fortress of Montezuma Castle commands a placid, verdant canyon.

GRAND CANYON NATIONAL PARK: SOUTH RIM

Carved by the Colorado River over millennia while surrounding benches uplifted, the gorge—278 miles long, up to 18 miles wide, and a mile deep—inspires awe and wonder like no other place. Nothing can prepare you for how it feels to contemplate the majestic side-canyons, the colorful buttes flanking the river, and the play of light and shadow on layered cliffs. As explorer Major John Wesley Powell put it, the Grand Canyon is "a land of music" that "cannot be adequately represented by speech."

"Discovered" by the Spanish in the mid-16th century, the canyon remained largely uncharted by white men until the Powell expeditions journeyed down the Green and Colorado Rivers in 1869 and 1872. But Native American artifacts, including split-twig figurines of mule deer and bighorn sheep dating back as far as 3000 BCE, have been found at some of its thousands of archaeological sites, and the Havasupai Indians—whose ancestors constructed a number of rim-to-river trails—continue to farm in their small reservation west of the main corridor (see Hike 33). Throughout the park, you will find overlooks galore, rewarding nature trails, and the chance to descend thousands of feet, reading geological history as you go.

From Flagstaff, take US Route 180 northwest to AZ 64. Follow this road to Grand Canyon Village. From Page, go south on US 89 for 59 miles to Cameron and turn right on AZ 64, which follows the Little Colorado River. The latter is the more dramatic approach route. Along the way, be sure to stop at the **Little Colorado River Navajo Tribal Park** near milepost 286 which overlooks the tributary. Fees apply.

Entering the park, enjoy your first peek into the Grand Canyon at Desert View, where you can visit the **Tusayan Ruins and Museum**. Between here and Grand Canyon Village, 24 miles farther west, Lipan, Moran, Grandview, Yaki, and Yavapai Points all merit inspection. From the village, Hermit Road continues west 8 miles to Hermits Rest. Free shuttle buses connect numerous locations along the rim. The Hermit Road remains closed to private vehicles from March through November.

Because the park receives up to six million visitors per year, 90 percent of whom opt for the South Rim, it is imperative to reserve well in advance for lodging along the rim as well as overnight hiking below. Xanterra Parks & Resorts holds the lodging concession. For backcountry permits, contact the Backcountry Information Center (BIC). To improve your chances, apply online at the earliest possible time: the first day of the month, four months before your desired starting date. Walk-in permits may be available at the BIC, adjacent to Maswik Lodge in the Village.

Backcountry trails in the park vary tremendously in length and difficulty. Only three are maintained. From the South Rim, hike either the Bright Angel or South Kaibab before attempting any of the unmaintained routes. Rangers question permit-seekers about prior experience and check for essential gear.

By far the most important imperative of Grand Canyon hiking is to carry sufficient water. Bear in mind that the ascent normally takes at least twice as long as the descent, and requires at least twice as much water. A minimum of one gallon per person per day is essential, and it is often advisable to exceed this requirement, even to double it in summer when hiking dry trails.

Before you descend, stroll along the rim to familiarize yourself with the canyon's major rock strata. In this vicinity those layers, from top to bottom, are as follows: Kaibab Limestone (gray); the Toroweap Formation (very narrow, gray); Coconino Sandstone (white and sheer); the Hermit Shale and Supai Group (red and sloping); Redwall Limestone (red or light gray, thick and sheer); Temple Butte Limestone (thin, purplish); Muav Limestone (mottled gray); Bright Angel Shale (greenish gray, narrow and sloping); Tapeats Sandstone (brown and vertical, below the Tonto Rim); and the Vishnu Group (the dark, jumbled basement rocks of the Inner Gorge). The oldest layers here date back 1.7 billion years.

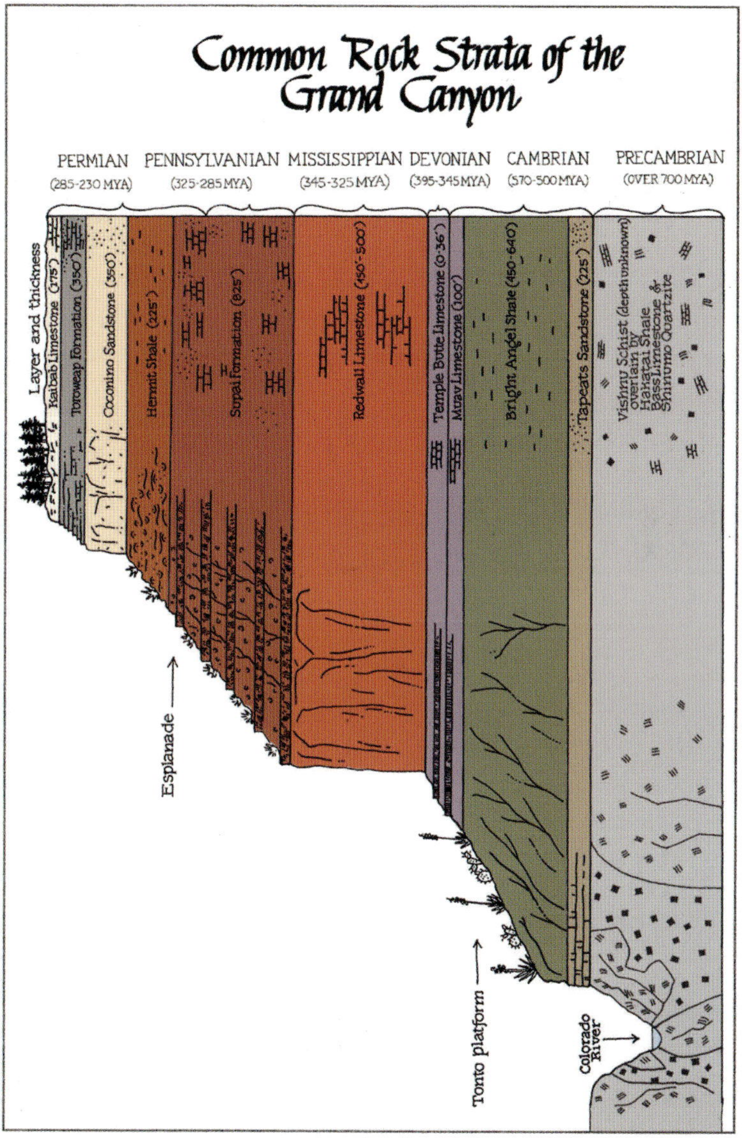

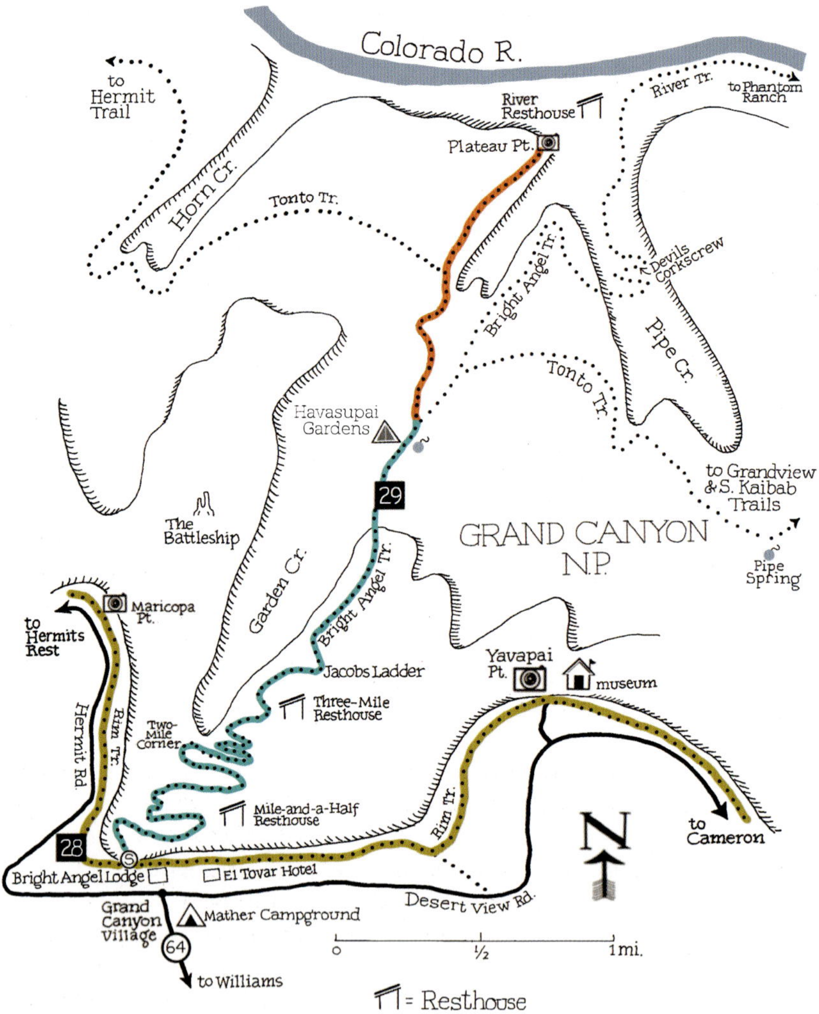

A trip into the Grand Canyon is a journey through geologic time. It is also a journey toward the equator, ecologically speaking, since every 1000 feet down equals 300 miles of southward travel. This change is especially evident in respect to the North Rim descents, which traverse the Canadian, Transition, Upper Sonoran, and Lower Sonoran life zones—meaning that the hiker here effectively travels from Canada to Mexico in a mere 14 miles!

28. Rim Trail

Very easy (where paved) to easy (where unpaved) point-to-point, up to 9 miles, using shuttle bus to return; allow up to 4 hours

Maps: Trails Illustrated 207: Grand Canyon National Park, or USGS: Bright Angel

GETTING THERE: Start at any of several locations along the South Rim.

ON THE TRAIL: The Rim Trail extends all the way from Pipe Creek to Hermits Rest. The most scenic sections are from Yavapai Point to the El Tovar Hotel (1.5 miles, paved), Bright Angel Lodge to Maricopa Point (1.5 miles, paved), and the Abyss to either Pima Point (2 miles, unpaved) or Hermits Rest (3.5 miles, unpaved). In all of these sections, the road is relatively far from the rim. The trail becomes braided and indistinct as it approaches Hermits Rest.

29. Bright Angel Backpack

Difficult 12-mile out-and-back to Plateau Point; allow 2 days, and consider a layover

Permit required for camping; trekking poles and headlamps recommended

Map: Trails Illustrated 207: Grand Canyon National Park

GETTING THERE: Begin at Bright Angel Lodge in Grand Canyon Village.

ON THE TRAIL: The Bright Angel Trail, which extends from the South Rim to Havasupai Gardens Campground and beyond, is the park's "easiest" and most popular inner canyon trek. This superhighway of sorts receives heavy use not only from hikers but also from mule parties traveling to and from Phantom Ranch, on the north side of the river. Expect your senses to be assaulted by equine droppings along the way, and when you encounter mule trains, quietly step aside (standing above the trail) to let them pass. From May through September, water is available at two trailside shelters. Camping along the trail is only allowed at Havasupai Gardens, which has water year-round.

The **Bright Angel Trail** follows the east side of the **Garden Creek** drainage for most of its length. Prominent formations visible along the way include the **Battleship**, Cheops Pyramid, Brahma Temple, and Tower of Ra. Near the start of its descent, the trail goes through tunnels in the Kaibab and Toroweap strata. Hunt for rock art just below the second of these tunnels. Tight switchbacks speed your passage through the Coconino Sandstone. Just beyond is **Mile-and-a-Half Resthouse** in the Hermit Shale, where water (in season), shelter, and toilet facilities are available. In the Supai Formation, more pictographs adorn light-colored rocks above the trail at Two-Mile Corner.

Continue downward to **Three-Mile Resthouse**. At mile 3.5, the Jacobs Ladder switchbacks plunge 500 feet to the base of the sheer Redwall Limestone cliffs. The gradient abates from here to the creekside oasis of **Havasupai Gardens** at mile 4.5, where aborigines once farmed. Beyond this idyllic campground, continue to **Plateau Point** at mile 6, on the edge of the Inner Gorge, which offers excellent views of the river 1200 feet below. The **Tonto Trail** comes in halfway between the campground and the overlook.

Finish with an ascent of the Bright Angel Trail. In hot weather, start the climb well before dawn, using headlamps. Although higher means cooler in the Grand Canyon, the sun's increased strength as the day wears on more than offsets any advantage gained from elevation. Keep your pack as light as possible for the climb, which takes about three hours for hikers in good condition. Refreshments await at Bright Angel Lodge, where the journey ends.

30. South Kaibab Backpack

Very difficult 16.25-mile semi-loop with exposure, plus side trips; allow 3–4 days
Permit required; water filter, trekking poles, and headlamps recommended
Maps: Trails Illustrated 207: Grand Canyon National Park, or USGS: Bright Angel

GETTING THERE: Catch a shuttle bus to the Yaki Point trailhead (elevation 7200 feet), just east of Grand Canyon Village.

ON THE TRAIL: Among Grand Canyon trails, the **South Kaibab Trail** is the most direct from rim to river, but with a 4500-foot vertical drop it is a serious knee-buster and, unlike the Bright Angel Trail to its west, it has no water stations. Especially in the summer heat, hikers who plan to combine the two in a loop should descend on the former and return on the latter.

Also in contrast to the Bright Angel Trail, which takes advantage of a geologic fault, the South Kaibab Trail favors ridgetops, offering expansive vistas but little if any shade. The trail begins by switchbacking to aptly named **Ooh Aah Point**, 600 feet below the rim at mile 1. At mile 1.5, 1150 feet down, you reach **Cedar Ridge** in the Coconino, a popular destination for day hikers. Enjoy unrivaled views of Cheops Pyramid, Sumner Butte, and other North Rim temples from this broad platform.

In the next 0.5 mile, descend to a saddle east of O'Neill Butte and enter the Supai Formation. The trail levels out somewhat as it heads for Skeleton Point (at mile 3), seeking a break in the Redwall's sheer limestone cliffs. From here it plunges remorselessly 500 feet to the Tonto Rim at mile 4.5, intersecting the **Tonto Trail**, which links numerous South Rim pathways into an efficient network.

Shortly thereafter you attain **The Tipoff**, on the lip of the Granite Gorge, with its ancient, primarily metamorphic rock. Here begins the no-nonsense 1500-foot drop to

Gnarled and weathered juniper skeleton perched on Cedar Ridge

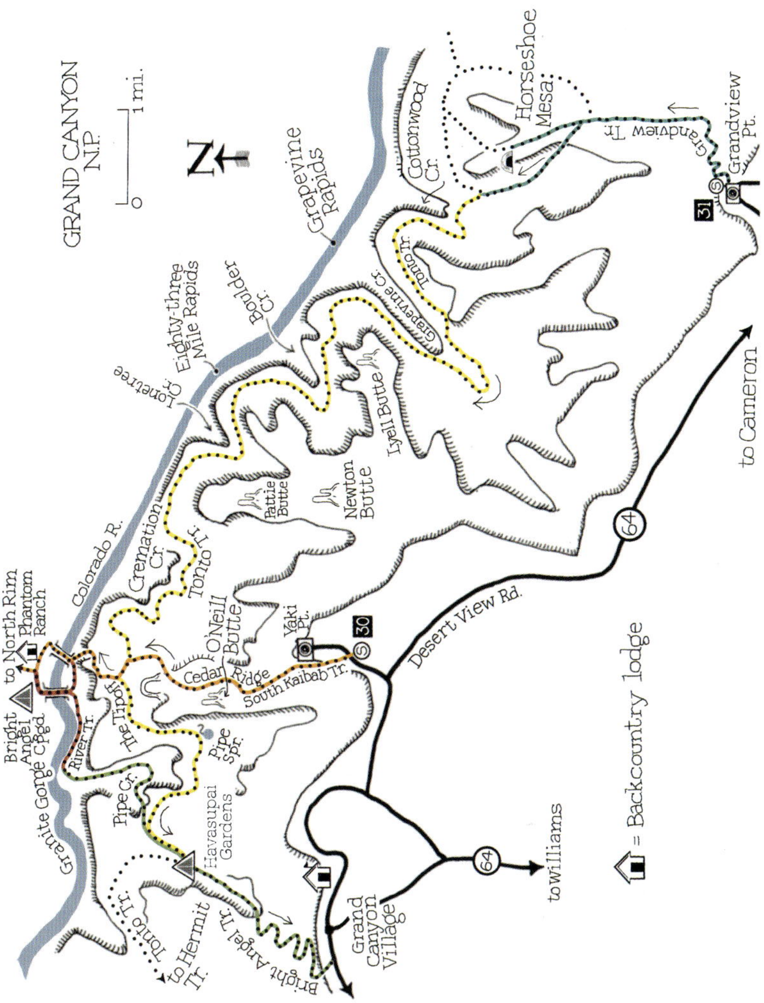

the canyon floor. The Colorado River and the dual suspension bridges spanning it pop into view. Turn right at the trail junction just above the river. Here hikers enter a tunnel transporting them to Kaibab Bridge at mile 6.25. Crossing it, you pass the River Ranger Station on the way to the **Bright Angel Campground** at mile 7. Rodent-proof food containers and pack hooks are provided. At rustic **Phantom Ranch**, about 0.5 mile farther on, cold beer and soft drinks are available for purchase, as are meals, if arranged in advance. Rooms can be reserved up to thirteen months ahead; on shorter notice, try for a cancellation.

It is wise to schedule a layover day in the canyon bottom to allow your joints and muscles to recover before the 9.25-mile return trip to the South Rim on the Bright Angel Trail. If you like, you can use that time to hike to glorious **Phantom Overlook** (a moderate 3.25-mile out-and-back, with 1000 feet of elevation gain) along the **Clear Creek Trail**, which branches off the North Kaibab just past Phantom Ranch.

Leaving the campground, follow the **River Trail** west to Silver Bridge at mile 0.75. Continue along the south bank to the waterless **River Resthouse** at mile 1.5, intersecting the **Bright Angel Trail**. After a relatively flat stretch, ascend 1200 feet up Pipe Canyon on the **Devils Corkscrew** switchbacks to Garden Creek. Expect some exposure here. At mile 3, the trail attains the Tonto Rim. It levels out again, making a beeline for bucolic **Havasupai Gardens** (mile 4.75). Plan to spend a night here, arising before dawn to execute the 4.5-mile, 3250-foot ascent to Grand Canyon Village on the Bright Angel Trail.

In hot weather, start the climb well before dawn, using headlamps. Three-Mile Resthouse and Mile-and-a-Half Resthouse have toilets and seasonally available water. The ascent to Bright Angel Lodge along the rim normally takes three hours for hikers in good condition.

Variant. A difficult 13-mile alternative route does not enter the Inner Gorge, but rather uses the **Tonto Trail** to connect the South Kaibab with the Bright Angel Trail. Although gonzo hikers sometimes complete this loop in a long day, most people find it more enjoyable to reserve a night at Havasupai Gardens. Connect with the Tonto at mile 4.5 and head west for 4 miles to the campground, stopping to refill water bottles in **Pipe Spring** at the halfway mark.

31. Grandview Backpack

Very difficult 33-mile semi-loop; allow 5 days
Permit required; water filter, trekking poles, and headlamps recommended
Map: Trails Illustrated 207: Grand Canyon National Park

GETTING THERE: Hop the shuttle to the trailhead at Grandview Point, 9 miles east of Grand Canyon Village.

ON THE TRAIL: Journeying down the Grandview and up the Bright Angel Trail is not for everyone. Only serious hikers in excellent condition with prior Grand Canyon experience should attempt the trip, which involves a 16-mile waterless stretch on the rolling Tonto Platform. During summer, hikers need to carry at least two gallons of water apiece and restrict travel to the early morning and late evening hours. But the rewards outweigh the hardship. Solitude is virtually guaranteed, and by universal agreement this is one of the most impressive parts of the canyon.

Built by a miner in the late 19th century, the unmaintained **Grandview Trail** is in decent shape and not hard to follow. Though steep, it offers some shade, particularly toward the top. At a saddle in the Coconino Sandstone at mile 1, enjoy views into Hance Canyon to the east. **Horseshoe Mesa**, 2600 feet below the rim at mile 3, is a day hiking destination in its own right. Three trails descend the Redwall from here. Yours is the trail on the left. Before leaving the mesa, continue straight ahead on the Grandview to explore a limestone cave complete with stalactites.

Next, pick your way down the westernmost trail to **Cottonwood Creek**, at mile 4.5, where you intersect the Tonto Trail. Shade and seasonal water make this a good place to camp. With effort, you can scramble to the river both here and at **Grapevine Creek** (mile 9), the next drainage to the west. Having perennial water in its upper end, this canyon also makes for desirable camping.

Boulder and Lonetree Creeks, at miles 14.25 and 17 respectively on the Tonto Trail, occasionally contain water, but expect to find none until **Pipe Spring** unless otherwise informed by the backcountry office. Therefore, you should plan to make a dry camp along the Tonto Trail. Fortunately, hiking is fast on the scrubby platform, which delivers peerless views of temples across the river. Occasionally you can peer into the Inner Gorge, watching hawks ride the thermals and specklike rafts negotiate fierce rapids.

At mile 22.25 comes **Cremation Canyon**, which received its name from charred human remains left by the Havasupai tribe. Beyond the west arm of Cremation Canyon at large camping is not permitted. After heading the canyon's three substantial lobes, you meet the **South Kaibab Trail** at mile 24.5. From there it is about 2 miles to Pipe Spring, where you can replenish your water, and 4 miles to **Havasupai Gardens**. Take the **Bright Angel Trail** to burn some fat while returning to the South Rim.

In hot weather, start the ascent (3250 feet over 4.5 miles) well before dawn, using headlamps. Three-Mile Resthouse and Mile-and-a-Half Resthouse have toilets and seasonally available water. Your pack should be as light as possible for the climb to Bright Angel Lodge on the rim, which normally takes three hours for a hiker in good condition.

32. Hermit Backpack

Very difficult 26.5-mile semi-loop, with exposure; allow 4 days
Permit required; water filter, trekking poles, and headlamps recommended
Maps: Trails Illustrated 207: Grand Canyon National Park, or USGS: Bright Angel

GETTING THERE: Catch a shuttle bus to the trailhead at Hermits Rest, stopping briefly at Pima Point to study your route from above.

ON THE TRAIL: The Hermit Trail, built for tourists by the Santa Fe Railroad Company, is the most celebrated of the non-maintained routes from rim to river, and arguably the most beautiful. Camping is confined to designated sites. The Hermit Creek, Monument Creek, Salt Creek, and Horn Creek sites have pit toilets. Inquire with the backcountry ranges about water availability.

From **Hermits Rest**, take a service road to the trailhead. At the rim, switchback through rocky terrain, bearing right at the intersections with the **Waldron Trail** and right again where the trail to the bird-lover's paradise of **Dripping Springs** at mile 1.75 splits off. The latter connects with a very difficult route down to the river via Boucher Creek. French Canadian prospector Louis Boucher was the hermit for whom the trail was named. Next descend to **Santa Maria Spring**, which has water and a small shelter. The trail skirts the eastern edge of Hermit Creek gorge. By now you have entered the Supai Group. Fourmile Spring, noted on some topo maps, ran dry years ago.

The trail zigzags to **Lookout Point**, which offers splendid views of the temples and canyons across the river. Around a bend is a long, gently sloping section of trail. You may encounter rock slides in this vicinity, prior to the big Redwall descent at mile 5. The steep switchbacks on the west side of Cope Butte are called the **Cathedral Stairs**. At the base of yet another set of switchbacks you attain the Tonto Rim at mile 6. Bear left onto the **Tonto Trail**. Walk for 1.25 miles until you drop into the creekbed, arriving at **Hermit Camp**, a comfortable facility with water and a toilet.

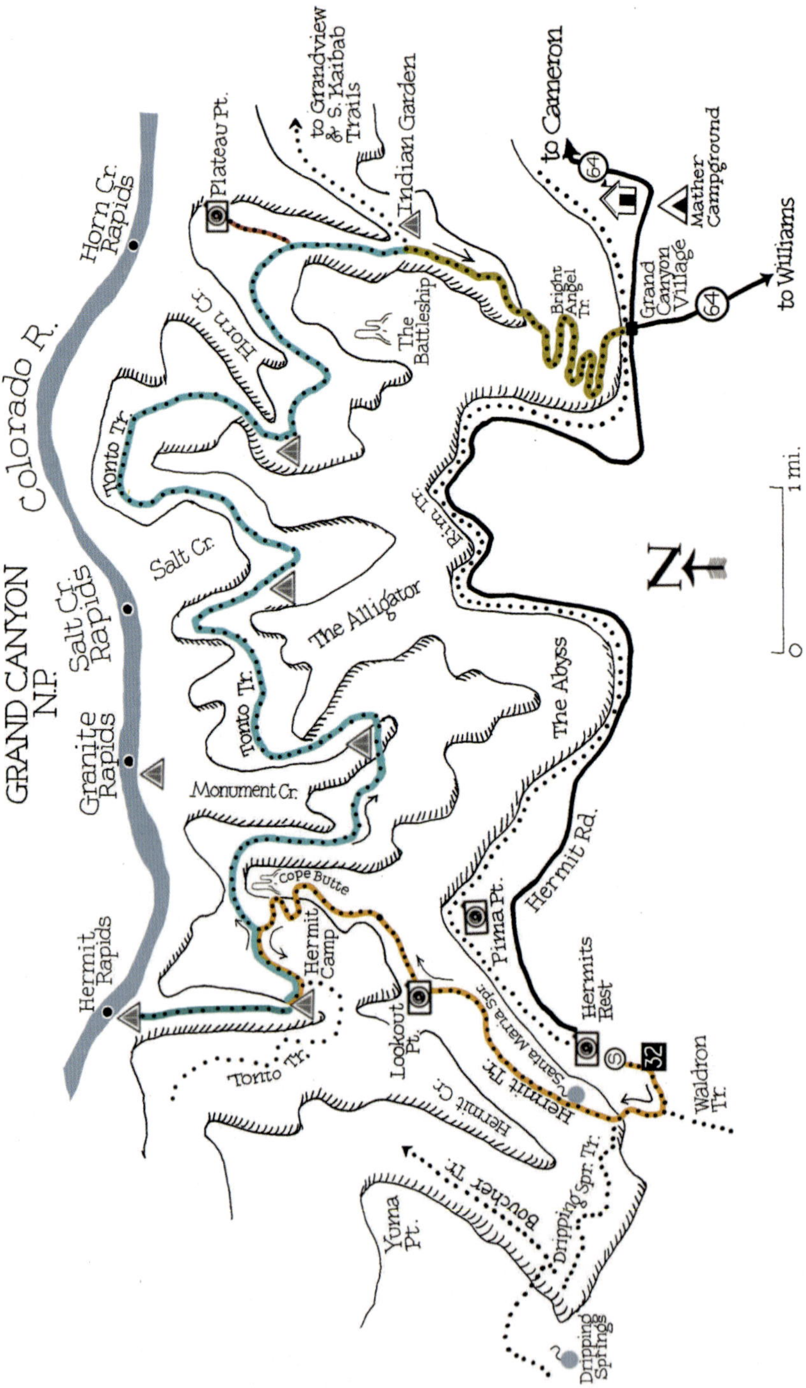
GRAND CANYON N.P.
Colorado R.
Horn Cr. Rapids
Salt Cr. Rapids
Granite Rapids
Hermit Rapids
Plateau Pt.
to Grandview & S. Kaibab Trails
Indian Garden
to Cameron
64
Mather Campground
to Williams
64
Grand Canyon Village
Bright Angel Tr.
The Battleship
Horn Cr.
Tonto Tr.
Salt Cr.
The Alligator
Tonto Tr.
Rim Tr.
The Abyss
Monument Cr.
Cope Butte
Hermit Camp
Lookout Pt.
Pima Pt.
Hermit Rd.
Hermits Rest
32
Waldron Tr.
Santa Maria Spr.
Hermit Tr.
Hermit Cr.
Tonto Tr.
Boucher Tr.
Dripping Spr. Tr.
Yuma Pt.
Dripping Springs
N
0
1 mi.

The 1.5-mile side trip down Hermit Creek to the river is delightful and unchallenging. Unless the year has been particularly dry, you may find pools along the way. The beach here is extremely rocky, but it's fun to watch rafts negotiate turbulent **Hermit Rapids**, formed by a boulder fan at the confluence. Swimming is not recommended.

From Hermit Camp, backtrack to the junction with the Tonto and turn left, heading rather precipitously up Cope Butte. The Tonto Trail follows the lip of **Monument Canyon** for some distance before dropping into the drainage about 3.5 miles past Hermit Camp, some 10.75 miles from the start. The scenic beauty of this part of the trip is unexcelled, with haunting views of the Inner Gorge. Monument Canyon receives its name from a spire that dominates its upper reaches. Water found in the official camping zone past the spire is potable when filtered. You can reach the river with relative ease to watch boats shoot Granite Rapids.

The Tonto Trail goes past a sphinx-like butte and out the east arm of Monument Creek. Back on the Tonto Rim, it swings around a formation called the **Alligator**. Above is **The Abyss**, a beautiful red amphitheater. The trail is frightfully exposed here. **Salt Creek**, the next major drainage, 3.5 miles past Monument Creek, takes a while to circumambulate. There is a campsite at mile 14.25.

At mile 18.25 comes the similar Horn Creek system. Check with rangers about water availability in Salt Creek, and do not filter water found near Horn Creek, which is radioactively contaminated from old uranium mines. About 1.5 miles past Horn Creek, the trail forks. Drop your pack and hike down the trail to the left 0.75 mile to appreciate the outstanding vistas from **Plateau Point**.

Back at the fork, keep following the Tonto Trail. Within 0.75 mile you will reach **Havasupai Gardens Campground**, where you'll find cottonwoods, fireplaces, toilets, and a cast of thousands. Most hikers reserve a campsite here in anticipation of the arduous ascent to the rim on the **Bright Angel Trail**. In hot weather, start the climb well before dawn, using headlamps for illumination. The climb normally takes three hours for a hiker in good condition. Three-Mile Resthouse and Mile-and-a-Half Resthouse have toilets and seasonally available water.

33. Havasu Backpack

Moderate 22.5-mile out-and-back; allow 2–3 days

Check with the park before attempting this. A 2024 flash flood closed this trail indefinitely.

Maps: USGS: Supai and Havasu Falls

GETTING THERE: From Flagstaff, take Interstate 40 west to exit 123 for Seligman, a 1950s time-warp town on legendary Route 66. Turn west on Route 66 toward Peach Springs. Route 18 branches off to the right just past milepost 110. Follow this road more than 60 miles to its end at an enormous parking lot on **Hualapai Hilltop**.

ON THE TRAIL: This trail on the Havasupai ("people of the blue-green water") Reservation rewards visitors with two transcendently beautiful waterfalls. Expect to pay a hefty fee for the privilege of hiking and camping here. The busy trail is frequented by mule trains bearing supplies to the village of Supai, as well as by friendly dogs in search of handouts or companionship. Since mules have the right-of-way, step aside to let them pass.

Travertine lacework at Mooney Falls

More than half of the 2000-foot elevation loss comes in the first mile, as the trail corkscrews down a Coconino Sandstone ridge. Views of Mount Sinyalla dominate the descent to the floor of **Hualapai Canyon**, in the Supai Formation. Although the canyon walls are low, they are close enough together to provide shade. Large boulders line the trail around mile 4.5. Within another mile, water gurgles close enough to the surface to support cottonwoods and redbuds.

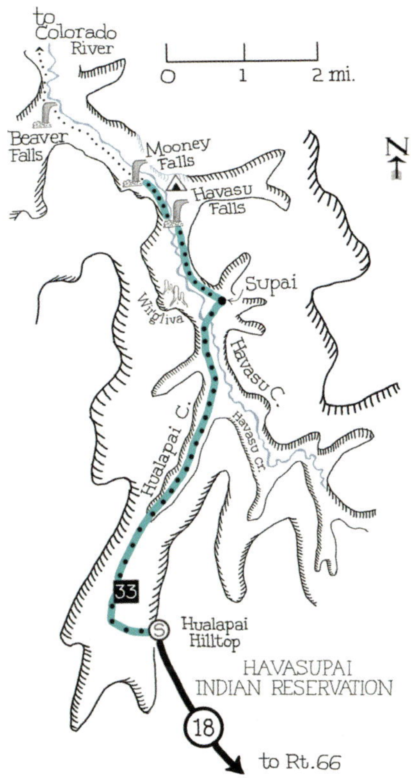

The junction with luxuriant **Havasu Canyon** comes at mile 6.5. Turn left, following signs. The trail parallels an irrigation ditch on its way to **Supai** (population 200) at mile 8. A pair of sandstone buttes, the Wii'igliva, preside over the town, which is encircled by fractured cliffs. Stop at the Tourist Office to complete your required paperwork. Supai, the last place in the country where mail continues to be delivered on muleback, offers unexpected amenities, including a café, grocery, lodge, museum, and (yes) a post office.

Follow a sandy road toward the campground. Along the way, pause to visit **Upper and Lower Navajo Falls**. The original waterfall in that location was washed out in 2008 but has since made a comeback. The magic begins at mile 9.5, when you spy the luminous turquoise waters of 100-foot-high **Havasu Falls**, which spills into a travertine bowl. This verdant paradise, with its lush hanging gardens, attracts birds and butterflies, and its idyllic beach proves irresistible. Dissolved limestone gives the water a milky appearance. You can refresh your tired feet in the bracingly cold pools or even swim if you're feeling brave. Just 0.5 mile beyond the waterfall is the shade-filled campground, strung out between miles 10 and 11 along the creek at the top of the Redwall.

From the campground, the trail switchbacks toward breathtaking **Mooney Falls** at mile 11.25 aided by a system of ladders, stairs, and chains that will strike terror in many hearts. It passes through two tunnels blasted out of the travertine before plunging to the base of the 190-foot cascade. Spray from the waterfall compounds the hazard. But even those who chicken out near the end are rewarded with outrageous views. Ambitious hikers undeterred by stream crossings and bushwhacking can press on, accessing 30-foot-high **Beaver Falls** 2 miles downstream before reaching the river at mile 16.5. Allow at least an extra day if you want to pursue that option.

PAGE SOUTH

As mentioned previously, Page was established by the federal government for the purpose of constructing Glen Canyon Dam. Today it serves as a basecamp for exploring once-remote venues, either on foot or by boat. For hiking opportunities northwest of town, across the border in Utah, consult Chapter 7.

34. Antelope Canyon

Upper canyon: Easy 0.25-mile out-and-back; allow 2 hours for guided tour, including group shuttle to the canyon, from Page; lower canyon: Moderate 0.5-mile loop; allow 1 hour for guided tour from parking area

Map: USGS: Page

GETTING THERE: The signed turnoffs are 2.5 miles south of Page on opposite sides of AZ 98, near milepost 299.

ON THE TRAIL: Visit Antelope Canyon, a much-photographed slot on the Navajo Reservation, in summer when the sun is high. Both the upper canyon, to the east of the road, and the lower, to the west, merit attention. Don't enter the canyon if rain threatens; flash floods have caused fatalities.

The upper canyon, known as **The Corkscrew**, draws more crowds. It is popular because of the light beams that appear around noon when sand is tossed near an illuminated surface. Guided tours of the lower canyon, a.k.a. **The Crack**, are longer and less strictly regimented. Ladders assist on the descent and ascent, with a stroll along the rim closing the loop.

Tickets for Antelope Canyon are also valid for same-day entry to **Waterholes Canyon**, about 6.5 miles south of Page on US Route 89 near milepost 542. From the bridge, visitors can explore the canyon independently upstream (east) for 1.5 miles. Downstream travel through deeper narrows, is technical, requiring specialized gear and expertise.

35. Horseshoe Bend

Easy 1.5-mile out-and back; allow 1 hour

Map: USGS Dagger Peak, AZ

GETTING THERE: From Page, drive south on US Route 89 for 4.25 miles. Near milepost 545, turn right into a gigantic parking lot signed for Horseshoe Bend. To beat the crowds, plan this hike for early morning. Fees apply.

ON THE TRAIL: South of the dam, the Colorado River snakes through what's left of lower **Glen Canyon**. Raft companies offer float trips down this 15-mile stretch of flat water between Page and Lees Ferry. The highlight is a meander that loops lazily around a Navajo Sandstone promontory. From the parking lot, follow the heavily trafficked cairned route as it descends a few hundred feet to a platform overlooking the bend. Turn right at the rim and walk a short distance for the best vantage point.

Mesmerizing interplay of light, color, and undulating walls in Lower Antelope Canyon

Soft, pink dawn greets Horseshoe Bend.

SCENIC DRIVE: HOPI MESAS

The Hopi population of about ten thousand is concentrated on three fingers of **Black Mesa** southeast of Page, Arizona. A deeply traditional tribe, the Hopis do not normally permit photography or sketching in any of their twelve villages. Some villages allow people who register at the local office to visit, provided they behave respectfully, but at present, most sacred tribal dances are closed to the general public. Archaeologists believe some drought-stricken Anasazi settled here because of the presence of reliable springs at the mesa bottoms.

A must for all visitors is ancient **Oraibi** on Third Mesa. Dating from the 10th century CE, Oraibi is the oldest continuously inhabited community in the United States. Second Mesa's **Hopi Cultural Center and Museum** acquaints guests with tribal history and crafts for a small admission fee. Farthest east is **First Mesa**, the reservation's pottery-making capital. Sign up at the village information center for a guided one-hour stroll through **Walpi,** a settlement perched on a ridge so narrow that it accommodates just two rows of buildings. The natural wonders of the reservation include **Coalmine Canyon**'s ethereal badlands; tour companies operate out of Tuba City on the Navajo Reservation.

To reach the reservation, from Page, drive south on US Route 89 to the junction of US 160. Turn left, heading east to Tuba City. There, pick up AZ 264, the major road through Hopiland.

NAVAJO NATIONAL MONUMENT

If you want to visit cliff dwellings but the crowds at Mesa Verde leave you cold, Navajo National Monument may be your cup of tea. In addition to countless smaller sites, it protects Keet Seel (the largest in Arizona) and Betatakin. The Navajos are culturally and linguistically unrelated to the Anasazi; the monument's name refers only to the surrounding reservation. Campsites, available on a first-come, first-served basis, are free.

From Page, take AZ 98 south for 66 miles to the junction of US Route 160. Turn left (east) here and continue to AZ 564. Turn left onto AZ 564, which climbs 9.5 miles through a slickrock wilderness to the visitor center.

36. Betatakin

Moderate 3- or 5-mile out-and-back; allow up to 4 hours
Map: USGS: Betatakin Ruin

GETTING THERE: Park either at the monument's visitor center or at the designated Betatakin parking lot, depending upon which of two tours you select.

ON THE TRAIL: Betatakin (Navajo for "alcove dwelling") can only be visited on ranger-led tours. During summer, these leave twice daily. The 8:15 AM tour (5 miles round trip) takes the trail from Tsegi Point to the floor of forested Tsegi Canyon, while the 10:00 AM tour (3 miles round trip) accesses the ruin from the **Aspen Trail**. The 135-room apartment building occupies a vaulting amphitheater. Erected in the late 13th century, this multilevel dwelling was "discovered" by John Wetherill's party in 1909. Admire rock art to the right of the ruin. Because of a rockfall hazard, visitors are no longer allowed to enter Betatakin.

NEARBY: The very easy **Sandal Trail**, a 1.25-mile out-and-back from the visitor center, leads to a Betatakin overlook.

37. Keet Seel Backpack

Moderate 17-mile out-and-back; allow 2 days
Permit required; river shoes recommended
Maps: USGS: Keet Seel Ruin and Tall Mountain

GETTING THERE: Park along the spur road to the lot for Betatakin, north of the monument's visitor center.

ON THE TRAIL: Keet Seel is open during the summer. Visitation is limited to 20 people per day. Call for reservations (928-672-2700) up to two months in advance and attend a required orientation the afternoon before setting forth.

The trip begins with a 1000-foot descent into **Tsegi Canyon** over rock and deep sand. Reaching the floor, you follow a stream course most of the way, passing four small waterfalls as well as some intriguing rock formations and climbing about 400 feet in the last 5.5 miles. The stream has cut a deep arroyo whose sides restrict your views, and you may encounter pockets of quicksand in the wash. Since grazing livestock have polluted the groundwater, wait to replenish your supply at a pristine spring near the ruin.

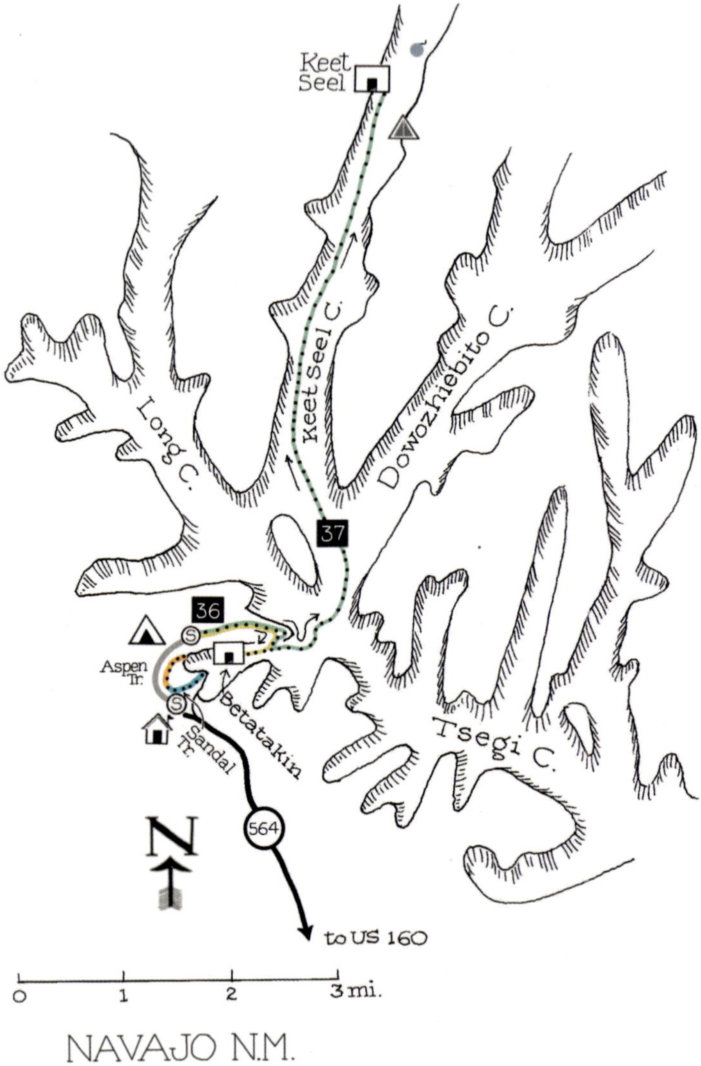

Drop your gear at the campground and approach the on-site ranger's cabin to tour **Keet Seel**, situated under a cavernous Navajo Sandstone overhang where the canyon opens up. This unforgettable pueblo, with its 155 rooms, was "discovered" by Richard Wetherill in 1895; its name is Navajo for "empty dwellings." To prevent damage to the fragile ruin, the hour-long tours are limited to five people.

RAINBOW BRIDGE NATIONAL MONUMENT

Surrounded by the Navajo Reservation, this postage stamp–sized entity protects spectacular **Rainbow Bridge**, the largest of its kind in the world, measuring 275 feet across and 290 feet high. Most visitors arrive by boat from **Wahweap Marina**, just west of

Page off US Route 89, a 100-mile, six-hour journey. The adventurous few set forth on foot by means of the North and/or South Rainbow Trails. Together, these trails nearly encircle 10,400-foot-high **Navajo Mountain**, considered sacred by traditionalists, who refer to it as the "head of the earth." At the base of this isolated peak lies some of the most rugged and spectacular wilderness in the Southwest. Hiking permits must be secured in advance from Navajo Nation Parks and Recreation (see Contact Information at the end of the book).

There are several ways to complete this hike, all of which pose logistical challenges. For those with sufficient time, the recommended option is to start on the South Rainbow Trail and finish on the North, which necessitates a shuttle or some equivalent. Inquire locally to hire a driver if you lack two vehicles. The North Rainbow is slightly longer but arguably more scenic. Some people prefer an out-and-back, while others arrange to hike to the bridge and return by boat. The following write-up details the full circuit.

Whichever option you choose, be aware that trailhead theft can be a problem, so leave nothing of value in your car.

38. Rainbow Bridge Backpack

Difficult 27.5-mile semi-loop; allow 4 days

Permit and vehicle shuttle required; high-clearance or four-wheel-drive vehicle, water filter, and trekking poles recommended

Map: Trails Illustrated 213: Glen Canyon National Recreation Area

GETTING THERE: From Page, take AZ 98 for about 40 miles. Turn left onto unpaved Navajo Mountain Road (Route 16), the condition of which can vary annually or even daily, and continue about 35 miles to a fork.

For the **South Rainbow Trail**, turn left at the fork. Drive about 5 miles, passing a barn to the left and a house on the right. Turn right just before a large sandstone dome. Because the road gets extremely rough, it might be advisable to walk the last 2.5 miles to the trailhead.

For the **North Rainbow Trail**, turn right at the fork. Proceed to the now defunct Navajo Mountain Trading Post, 6 miles away. About 4 miles past the former trading post is a four-way intersection with another dirt road near Navajo Begay butte. Several buildings occupy this junction. Continue straight ahead for about 3 miles to a Y. Bear left here and continue 2 miles to Cha Canyon parking area. Near the end, where the road descends a slope, it deteriorates badly.

ON THE TRAIL: The **South Rainbow Trail** begins amid dilapidated stone buildings called **Rainbow Lodge**, once a thriving dude ranch operation. A large cairn indicates the trailhead, and red mileposts mark the route. In the first 5 miles, anticipate tiring ups and downs as you cross the arms of **First** and **Horse Canyons**. Be careful not to lose the trail as you approach Sunset Pass at mile 5, which offers astounding views into **Cliff Canyon**, 1600 feet below. Although the 2-mile descent is steep and rocky, the canyon's winsome lower reaches make up for it. First Water Campsite, at mile 8, has flowing springs and sometimes even small pools. The more scenic campsites lie a mile farther on, where deep alcoves provide shelter.

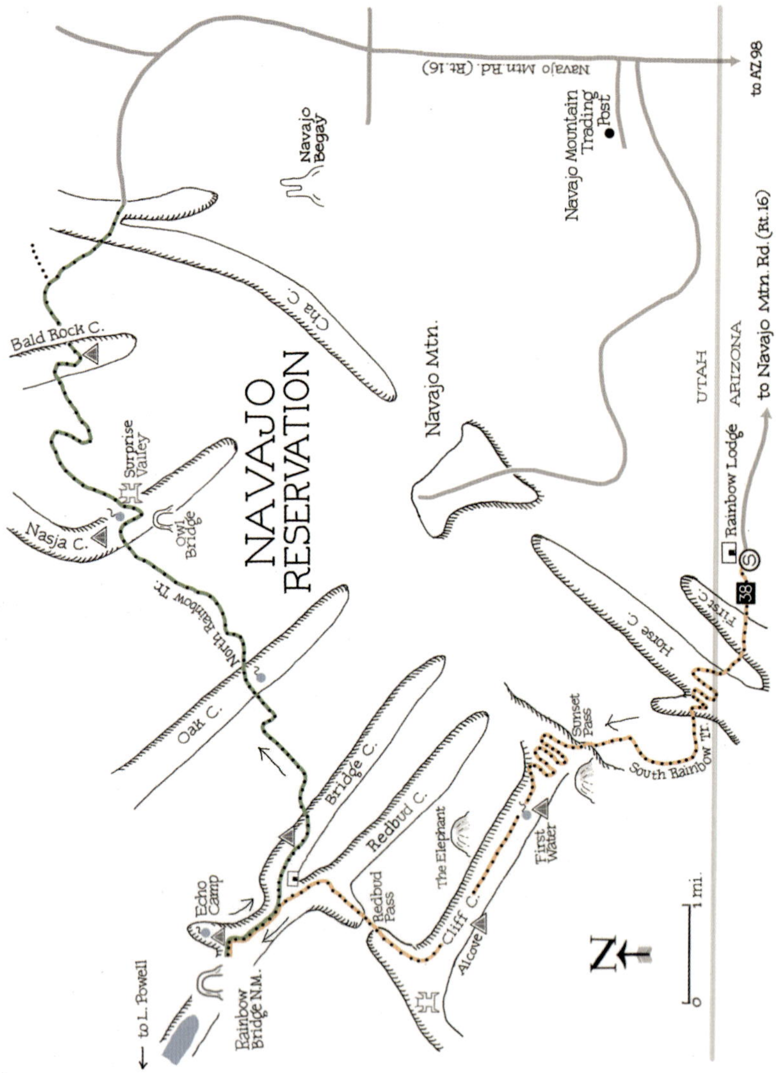

You can't miss the junction at 9 miles with the first sizable side-canyon to the right, opposite a massive alcove and not far past **The Elephant**, a sizable slickrock dome. Hunt for rock art 50 yards to the left of the junction. Turn right up the side-canyon, which gets progressively narrower as it climbs toward **Redbud Pass**, at 9.5 miles. The pass was blasted out in 1922 by John Wetherill, a member of the first party of Anglos to visit Rainbow Bridge. The trail goes through a narrow cleft to extraordinary **Redbud Canyon** at 10 miles. A recent rockfall may make this area cumbersome to traverse. Turn left and walk downstream.

Near a small ruin at 11 miles, Redbud meets **Bridge Canyon**. The South Rainbow Trail forks left here, heading downstream. After a while, Bridge Canyon dives deeply into the earth. The trail ascends slightly up to the right bank of the arroyo and remains on a shoulder the rest of the way. In about 0.25 mile you can spot the bridge. A spur on the right goes to **Echo Camp** at mile 13—a spring-fed grotto marred by decades-old junk left by horse parties.

From here, it's a flat, easy walk to **Rainbow Bridge**. At high water levels (not seen in decades), Lake Powell can back up under the Navajo Sandstone span. Out of respect for Native American spiritual traditions, stop short of the bridge rather than passing under it. Nearby plaques honor the Indian guides who led the Wetherill party. No camping is allowed in the national monument proper, but you can pitch your tent outside the perimeter.

To return via the **North Rainbow Trail**, backtrack up Bridge Canyon and take the left fork at the Redbud Canyon junction, 15.5 miles into the journey. Although the next 2 miles are steeper than the section near the bridge, good campsites exist in this area. Be careful not to lose the trail here. It goes up a side-canyon to the left and onto the slickrock rim. You may find a fair amount of water in upper Bridge Canyon as well as in some or all the systems to the east. Between these drainages you're usually walking on benches, savoring delicious views.

The trail to **Oak Canyon** is faint and often difficult to follow. This V-shaped canyon, at mile 19, offers cool mountain water to refresh thirsty hikers. About 3 miles farther is watery **Nasja Canyon**, the biggest and most beautiful along the entire route. There is a picnic table near **Owl Natural Bridge**. Climbing out of Nasja toward Surprise Valley, look for a Navajo petroglyph of a horse on the wall just above the trail.

Bald Rock Canyon, at mile 24.5, sports a cave and a small, unnamed arch. In the next 3 miles, cross two arms of **Cha Canyon**. Where the trail forks, about a mile before the end, go right. The second arm of Cha Canyon is shallow and, immediately beyond, a large cairn marks the parking lot.

Scalloped Navajo Sandstone juxtaposed against black volcanic rock in Snow Canyon State Park.

CHAPTER 7
CANYONS

This chapter's star attractions are Zion National Park and the North Rim of the Grand Canyon, located near the western edge of the Colorado Plateau. From hubs in St. George and Kanab, Utah, you enjoy ready access to several national monuments and state parks as well as to destinations across the border in Nevada and Arizona.

Hubs: St. George and Kanab, Utah

St. George (population 85,000) serves as a good jumping-off point. Located on the edge of the Mojave Desert in what is sometimes called Utah's "Dixie," this resort community offers numerous services. The early Mormon leader Brigham Young liked to spend his winters here.

The much smaller community of **Kanab** (population 4500) has developed a thriving tourist economy to supplement traditional mining and ranching. Local outfitters offer shuttle and guide services. North of town, Best Friends Animal Sanctuary, a no-kill shelter for injured and abandoned animals, welcomes the general public.

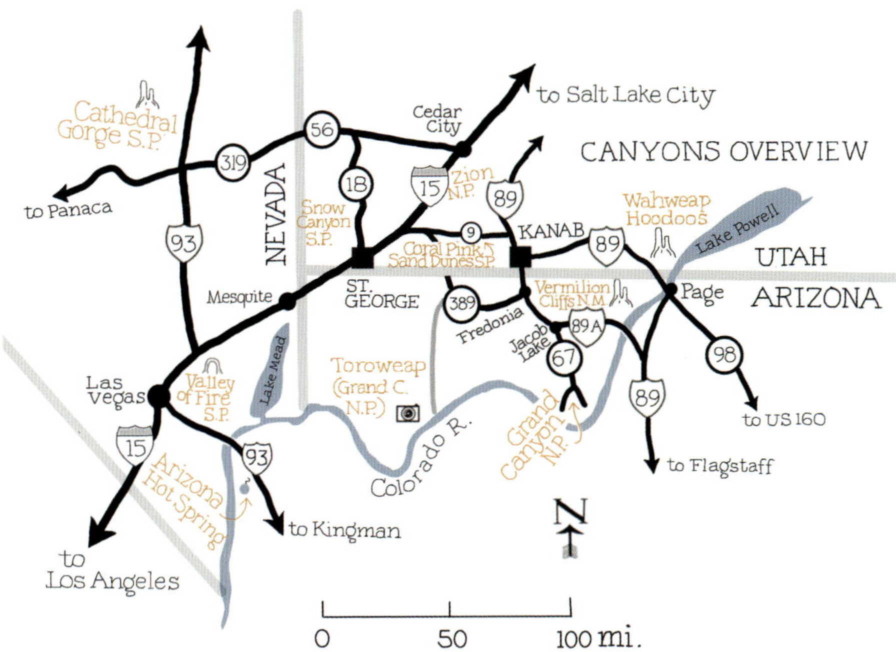

SNOW CANYON STATE PARK

Most visitors to southwestern Utah barrel toward Zion and Bryce, speeding past the hidden gem of **Snow Canyon** on the fringes of suburban Ivins. But the state park boasts scenery nearly as impressive as that found in its more renowned neighbors. Named after a pioneer family, this state park encloses 7000 acres of colorful canyons, slickrock domes, and ancient lava flows. Honeycombed with interconnected trails, it lies within the **Red Cliffs Desert Reserve**, designed to protect sensitive landscapes and save the desert tortoise from further decline.

To reach Snow Canyon, take Interstate 15 to exit 8, St. George Boulevard. Drive west to the T intersection with UT 18. Turn right and continue several miles to the second of two roundabouts. Go right, following signs to the south entrance.

1. Whiterocks Trail

Moderate 4-mile loop; allow 2 hours
Map: Trails Illustrated 715: Snow Canyon/Pine Valley

GETTING THERE: From the park's visitor center, drive north on the park road past milepost 11 to the turnout for Lava Flow Overlook.

ON THE TRAIL: This trip delivers a classic Snow Canyon experience. Start on the **Lava Flow Overlook Trail**. Within 0.75 mile, arrive at a junction with the **Whiterocks Trail**. Turn right and meander across lava flow benchlands affording exceptional views into West and Snow Canyons. The path swings northeast, crossing an outcrop of Navajo Sandstone. Ascend to another, higher bench near the park road. At a tall signpost, take the spur trail on the left to a sandstone dome harboring an amphitheater of surreal beauty. As you ascend the slope, your eyes take in only the elemental forms of deep blue sky and white cross-bedded slickrock—existence distilled to its simplest, purest components.

Scrambling into the amphitheater, pass a stock dam that creates a miniature marsh. Farther along, a tiny patch of living dunes contains pure white sand worthy of the Bahamas. Climbing higher still brings you to a pass overlooking a brush-choked defile.

Backtrack to the main trail and turn left at the signpost to reach UT 18. Turn right, following the busy highway for about 0.5 mile back to the north park entrance. Walk 0.5 mile down the scenic drive to return to your car.

2. Butterfly Trail

Easy 1.5-mile out-and-back; allow 1 hour
Map: Trails Illustrated 715: Snow Canyon/Pine Valley

GETTING THERE: From the park's visitor center, head north on the park road. The hike begins at the first turnout past mile marker 11.

ON THE TRAIL: The Butterfly and Petrified Dunes Trails share this trailhead. Go right at the initial fork, descending a sandstone slope and contouring past a petrified dune. In about 0.5 mile, the Butterfly Trail ends on a wide bench, where it joins the **Lava Flow Overlook Trail**. A right turn onto this trail leads to a lava tube, while a left turn

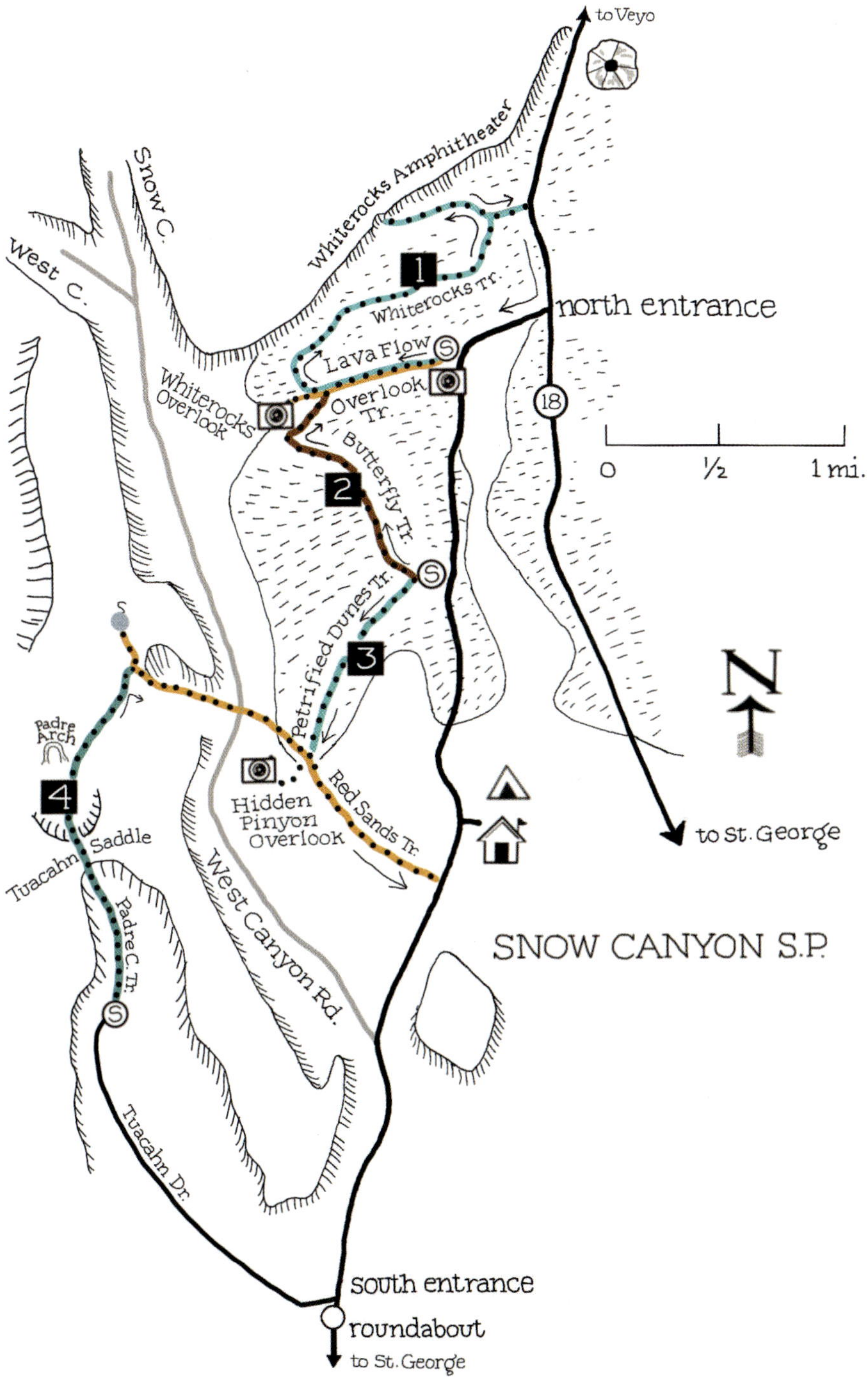
to Veyo
Whiterocks Amphitheater
Snow C.
West C.
1
Whiterocks Tr.
north entrance
Lava Flow
Whiterocks Overlook
Overlook Tr.
18
0
½
1 mi.
Butterfly Tr.
2
Petrified Dunes Tr.
3
Padre Arch
4
Hidden Pinyon Overlook
Red Sands Tr.
Saddle
Tuacahn
Padre C. Tr.
West Canyon Rd.
to St. George
SNOW CANYON S.P.
Tuacahn Dr.
south entrance
roundabout
to St. George

spirits you to **Whiterocks Overlook**. Coming back, look left to see the butterfly formation that gives the trail its name: two sizable sandstone slabs that lean against each other to create a V.

3. Petrified Dunes

Moderate 1.5-mile out-and-back; allow 1 hour
Map: Trails Illustrated 715: Snow Canyon/Pine Valley

GETTING THERE: From the visitor center, go north on the park road. The trailhead, which is shared with the Butterfly Trail, is located at the first pullout past mile marker 11.

ON THE TRAIL: This rugged trail offers unrivaled views of the Red Mountains to the west and ample opportunities for freelance exploration. Leaving the parking lot, take an immediate left at the junction with the Butterfly Trail (see Hike 2). From here ascend about 300 feet, following cairns and signposts, to traverse the Navajo Sandstone domes at the heart of the park.

The trail ends at a T junction; on the return, simply double back as you came or strike off on your own onto the cross-bedded ledges between the trail and the park road. In the vicinity, hunt for water-filled potholes, a tiny arch, and countless "Moki marbles," slippery round pebbles that have been freed from captivity in the surrounding rock. Few other places reward hikers with such surreal visions of frozen waves of sandstone against a typically cloudless azure sky.

4. Padre Canyon

Difficult 5-mile point-to-point, with routefinding and scrambling; allow 3.5 hours
Shuttling vehicles or equivalent required; trekking poles recommended
Map: Trails Illustrated 715: Snow Canyon/Pine Valley

GETTING THERE: Leave one vehicle at the parking area immediately south of the visitor center, where the hike concludes. To reach the trailhead, drive a second vehicle past the south entrance station toward a roundabout. Immediately before this roundabout turn right onto Tuacahn Drive. Continue 1.25 miles to the large lot at the end of the road. The trailhead is to the right of the Tuacahn Center for the Performing Arts.

ON THE TRAIL: This is a jungle gym of a hike, replete with fanciful forms. Depending on the time of year, wading seasonal pools may prove necessary.

After skirting private property, the path begins a rugged 600-foot climb up Padre Canyon to **Tuacahn Saddle** at about mile 1.5. Although initially gentle, the route steepens as the canyon narrows. Choose among several social trails that braid their way through talus. Toward the top, stay to the left of the ravine. When you attain the saddle, expansive views in both directions will help you ignore your aching calves.

The trail improves markedly on the descent. It drops down to cross two shallow washes, the second of which you follow for the next 0.5 mile. As you enter this second wash, detour left a short distance to a photogenic grotto. Returning to the main route, you soon attain the first of several ledges that require a downclimb. From here to the canyon's end, the route takes on a fun-house quality. Pause to admire **Padre Arch** before negotiating the second ledge. On the right, bypass a third ledge, which sports a pair of windows. Hikers may be tempted to drop through the bigger of these, but thankfully such a move proves unnecessary. Other minor obstacles in the vicinity include an oddly shaped slot that might be dubbed "the Birth Canal."

At mile 3, you intersect the **Red Sands Trail** (formerly Three Ponds Trail). Detour left here for 0.25 mile to visit the pellucid ponds. Then return to the junction, following a sandy wash for 1.5 miles to the park road.

AROUND ST. GEORGE

Beyond Snow Canyon State Park, the greater St. George area affords plentiful opportunities for hiking and exploration. A taste of its many splendors, from ancient rock art to slickrock dreamscapes, will whet the appetite for more.

5. Yant Flat

Moderate 4-mile out-and-back, with routefinding and scrambling; allow 3 hours
High-clearance vehicle recommended; road impassable when wet
Map: USGS: Harrisburg Junction

GETTING THERE: From St. George, take Interstate 15 north to exit 22 and turn left toward Leeds. Go through town and turn left onto Silver Reef Road. Zero out your trip odometer when the road passes under the highway. At mile 1.25, the road undergoes a name change to Oak Grove. Just past mile 1.5, bear left onto a gravel road (Forest Road 032) into **Dixie National Forest**, heading south. The road, with multiple wash crossings, hairpin turns, and sheer drops, offers big views but would be nerve-racking

Potholes dot the quilted floor of Yant Flat.

for acrophobes. At mile 10.65, notice FR 903 on the right. Park in a small lot across the road from this junction.

ON THE TRAIL: The secret's out! Reminiscent of the Wave and White Pocket formations in Vermilion Cliffs National Monument, Yant Flat (a.k.a. the Crazy Quilt) features stark expanses of cross-bedded sandstone that vary in color from bone white to cotton-candy pink. A photographer's paradise, it shows to best advantage in early morning.

On foot, follow a dirt track to the left through a pinyon and juniper forest. The old roadbed climbs gradually about 300 feet to the rim of your destination, which you reach at about mile 1.5. Here the trail abruptly ends at a slickrock dreamscape that is anything but flat. Go left, following the rim for about 200 feet until you reach a place where you can safely descend on ramps and ledges. The farther down you go, the more colorful the rocks become. It is relatively easy to scramble down to the first level and from there up to a viewpoint in the middle of the undulating sandstone, but any attempt to descend farther requires extreme caution.

Across the valley, though inaccessible from here, are the upper reaches of **Cottonwood Wash** (see Hike 6). Return as you came, using a diminutive arch on the horizon as your landmark.

6. Cottonwood Wash

Moderate 5.5-mile out-and-back, with routefinding and scrambling; allow 3 hours
Map: USGS: Harrisburg Junction

GETTING THERE: From St. George, drive north on Interstate 15. Take exit 18 for Hurricane and head east on UT 9/West State St. In about 1 mile, go left at a traffic light onto North 6300 West, which soon morphs into Old Highway 91. Proceed 2 miles to a warehouse on your left. Pull into the driveway and immediately go right onto an obscure unpaved road signed for **Red Cliffs Desert Reserve**. The road goes under I-15 to reach the trailhead parking lot.

ON THE TRAIL: The trail gives access to a psychedelic collection of hoodoos, beehives, and swirls in the area below Yant Flat (see Hike 5).

Begin by following a jeep road for 0.5 mile across a forlorn, fire-scarred landscape. Turn right at a signed intersection and descend to Cottonwood Canyon. At mile 1.5, arrive at the junction of Cottonwood Wash with a side-canyon on the left. The trail follows this side-canyon and crosses two humps before reaching a sandy slope. At the bottom of the slope, explore a prismatic slickrock depression replete with Moki marbles. Alternate routes are possible on the return, but because they are poorly marked, it is advisable to retrace your steps.

7. Tempi'po'op Petroglyphs

Easy 0.5-mile out-and-back; allow 1 hour
Map: USGS: Santa Clara

GETTING THERE: From St. George, take UT 18 north to UT 8. Turn left onto UT 8 to Santa Clara. Drive 1 mile west of town and turn left onto a road located immediately before a planned subdivision. In a few yards the pavement ends at a T intersection. Turn right here and continue to an informal parking circle.

ON THE TRAIL: Pecked onto boulders near the rim of **Santa Clara Canyon**, the Tempi'po'op ("rock writing" in Paiute) petroglyph panels feature carvings of animals, anthropomorphic figures, and geometric designs, some dating from the 1100s.

On foot, ascend the roadbed, turning right at a fork. At the top, go right again, following the canyon rim to a slickrock flat, which itself contains rock art. Locate a rudimentary path here that descends about 10 vertical feet. Continue along to the left at this level and also explore the one just beneath it to access multiple panels.

CATHEDRAL GORGE STATE PARK

Just across the border in Nevada is a landscape like no other. Buffy cliffs of compressed volcanic ash are cut through by short erosional channels narrow enough to make claustrophobes shiver. The smooth-walled slots typically end in rounded chambers, with just a hint of sky.

The twisty slots and fractal forms of Cathedral Gorge are Nevada's best-kept secret.

From St. George, take UT 18 north to its intersection with UT 56. Turn left here. At the state line, the route number changes to NV 319. Continue to Panaca. Turn right onto US Route 93 and proceed 2 miles to the main entrance.

8. The Caves

Easy freelance exploration with possible scrambling; distance negligible; allow 30 minutes

Map: USGS: Caliente

GETTING THERE: Follow the main park road north from the visitor center. Go right where the road forks and proceed to designated pullouts for The Caves.

ON THE TRAIL: The Caves has three adjacent units. In **Moon Cave**, both slots merit exploration. In **Canyon Cave**, the most extensive complex, don't miss the slot on the far right, which allows passage to the top of the formation. Look for a massive, seemingly bottomless pit here. A slot in **Cathedral Cave**, closest to the picnic area at the end of the road, has the feeling of a snail-type shower stall. The buildings in this vicinity were erected by the Civilian Conservation Corps during the 1930s.

9. Juniper Loop

Easy 5-mile loop, including spur; allow 2.5 hours

Map: USGS: Caliente

GETTING THERE: From the visitor center, follow the main park road. Where the road forks, go right and continue to its end at a ramada. The trail begins here, just north of The Caves.

ON THE TRAIL: Walk north up **Meadow Valley** on the Juniper Trail, paralleling the cliff face. At mile 0.5, take the spur on your right, which winds 0.5 mile up a canyon to a pavilion at **Miller Point Overlook**, climbing more than one hundred steps. The overlook also can be reached by car from a different park access road off US Route 93. You can extend the hike a mile if you continue to **Eagle View**.

Return down the steps and go back to the Juniper Trail. Turn right. The trail approaches the head of the valley before turning south, following a shallow wash past isolated spires and

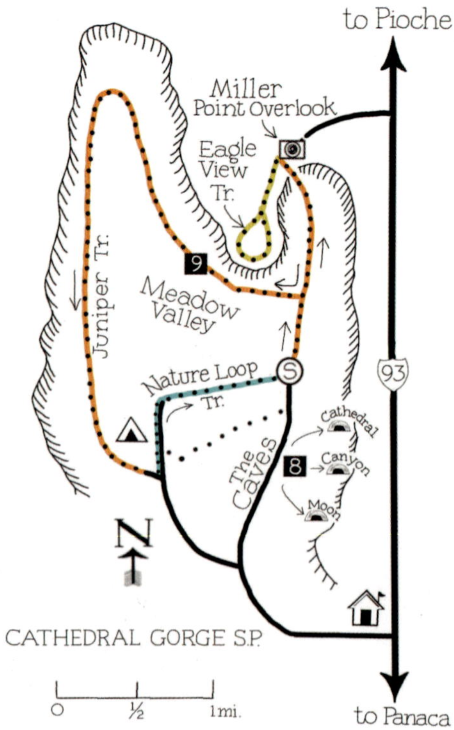

pinnacles to the well-appointed campground. Pick up the **Nature Loop Trail** and cross the valley to your car.

VALLEY OF FIRE STATE PARK

Geologically, southern Nevada belongs to the so-called **Basin and Range Province**. Its most obvious topographical features are long, parallel ranges that rise like waves across hundreds of miles of desert. But it lies close enough to the Colorado Plateau to share some of the latter's broken sandstone terrain, at least in certain isolated regions. One shining specimen is Valley of Fire State Park.

Adjacent to Lake Mead, Valley of Fire proves worthy of the fevered imagination of Dr. Seuss. This technicolor fantasyland in the Mojave Desert illustrates the ability of Aztec Sandstone (known elsewhere as Navajo or Nugget Sandstone) to mimic organic forms. Arches abound, and the aboriginal peoples who dwelled in the area left petroglyphs that offer a window into their way of life. The most distinctive panel, accessible from the campground loop road by a metal staircase, depicts an atlatl, the spear-throwing device used by Stone Age hunters. Well-marked trails take advantage of the park's whimsical topography. Be warned that low elevations can make hiking infernally hot during summer.

From St. George, take Interstate 15 south through a corner of Arizona, following the spectacular **Virgin River Gorge**. The abundance of Joshua trees here indicates

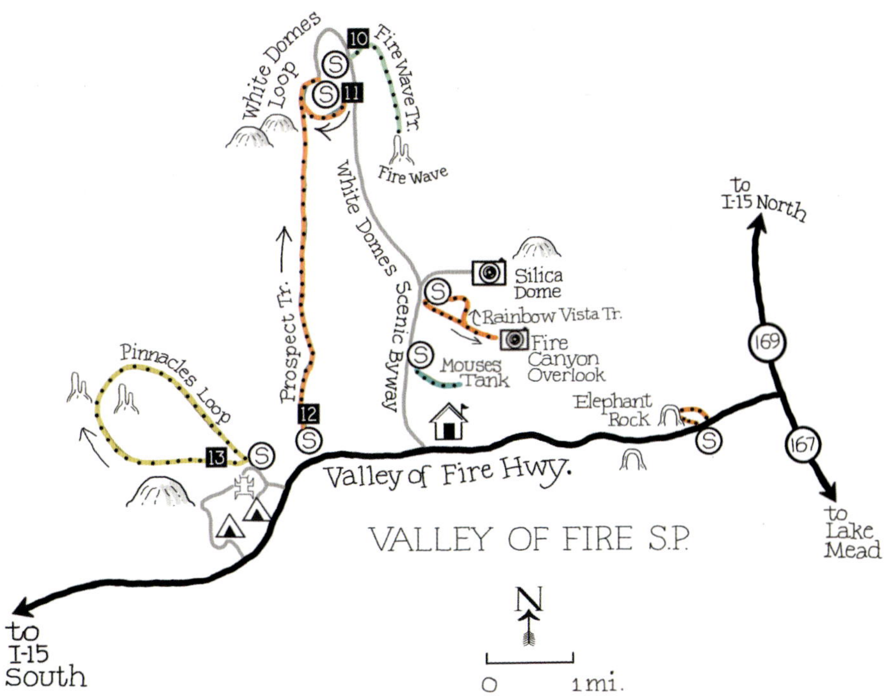

The Fire Wave, just steps off the scenic drive, was discovered and named by a German tourist.

that you are entering the Mojave Desert. Crossing into Nevada, take exit 93, signed for Logandale/Overton. Here pick up NV 169 and drive south about 25 miles. Just before the tollbooth for Lake Mead's Northshore Drive, turn right onto NV 169 enter the park.

Past the entrance station, a short loop leads to **Elephant Rock**, one of the park's signature attractions. Most other trails depart from either the **White Domes Scenic Byway**, which begins at the visitor center, or the campground. Easy out-and-backs lead to **Mouses Tank** (0.75 mile round trip), which enters a drainage past petroglyph panels to a rain-fed pool, and Fire Canyon Overlook along the **Rainbow Vista Trail** (1 mile round trip). The trails featured below tend to be longer and more challenging.

10. Fire Wave

Easy 1.25-mile out-and-back; allow 45 minutes
Map: Trails Illustrated 204: Lake Mead National Recreation Area

GETTING THERE: From the park's visitor center, head north on the scenic byway to parking lot #3, across the road from the trailhead.

ON THE TRAIL: The Fire Wave is a visually arresting outcrop of sandstone with beige and orange stripes. The clearly delineated route heads toward a canyon wall and then turns right, descending about 100 feet to the formation. Visitors are forbidden to walk on the Fire Wave, which has become a park icon since first receiving publicity a few years ago. Return as you came.

11. White Domes Loop

Moderate 1.25-mile loop; allow 45 minutes
Map: Trails Illustrated 204: Lake Mead National Recreation Area

GETTING THERE: From the park's visitor center, drive 5.5 miles along the White Domes Scenic Byway. The trailhead is located at the end of the road. Park here in a large lot.

ON THE TRAIL: Descend about 200 feet to the canyon floor, mostly on steps. Near the bottom, examine a former movie set. The trail then veers to the right. It negotiates a slot, passing two arches as it loops back to the rim. Back on top, turn right and walk along the road a short distance to your car.

12. Prospect Trail

Moderate 6-mile point-to-point, with some scrambling; allow 3 hours
Vehicle shuttle or equivalent required
Map: Trails Illustrated 204: Lake Mead National Recreation Area

GETTING THERE: To set up a shuttle, depart from the visitor center with two vehicles. Leave one car at the end of the scenic byway in the White Domes parking lot. In the other vehicle, return to the visitor center and drive west about 2 miles on NV 169 (a.k.a. Valley of Fire Hwy.), the main road through the park. The trailhead is to the right of the road, at the head of a sharp bend to the left.

ON THE TRAIL: This highly scenic route, marked by plastic ribbons, is the longest in Valley of Fire. It follows a dirt road for 2.25 miles to a low pass between mountains on the left and jagged cliffs on the right. Notice a small double arch just before you top out. As you cross the pass, yet another amazing arch comes into view. Descending, the trail negotiates a complex system of branching washes. Be prepared to circumvent some rocky pour-offs. This landscape is quintessential Valley of Fire, with flame-colored cliffs and candy-striped strata.

At about mile 3.5, whiter rocks start to appear. From a low saddle the trail drops into a steep arroyo to enter a narrow canyon. Bear right to join a wide, sandy wash at mile 4.75. In short order, you intersect the **White Domes Loop** (see Hike 11). Take either branch to ascend to the parking lot.

13. Pinnacles Loop

Moderate 5-mile loop; allow 2.5 hours
Map: Trails Illustrated 204: Lake Mead National Recreation Area

GETTING THERE: From the visitor center, drive west on the main park road (NV 169, a.k.a. Valley of Fire Hwy.) to the Atlatl Rock parking area, along the campground loop.
ON THE TRAIL: You are likely to enjoy seclusion as well as scenic grandeur on this recent addition to the park's trail system. From the parking lot, cross the road to a signboard. Turn left onto the marked route, which climbs almost imperceptibly, following a shallow wash. Pass a prominent mound of white rock at mile 0.5. At about mile 1.5, as you round a hogback, the pinnacles come into view.

When you reach them at mile 2, the trail veers to the right, taking advantage of a fissure through the blood-red cliffs. Objects of delight here include solution holes, balanced rocks, and knife-edged spires. A short scramble up a gully at mile 2.5 greets hikers with big views toward the north. From here the trail changes direction, cutting straight back to the parking lot across the open desert. Along the way, it traverses a zone that can only be described as barrel cactus heaven.

LAKE MEAD NATIONAL RECREATION AREA

Lake Mead on the Colorado River is an artifact of Hoover Dam, erected by the federal government during the Great Depression to generate electrical power. For many reasons, most notably the Southwest's ongoing drought, the reservoir currently is far below capacity. A white bathtub ring is clearly visible, and some beaches and marinas have been forced to close. However, such closures have not affected the area's intriguing trails.

To reach the national recreation area, from St. George, take Interstate 15 west in the direction of Las Vegas. The highway crosses the Utah border into the northwest corner of Arizona, following the spectacular gorge of the lower **Virgin River** into Nevada. Continue to exit 93, and then head south on NV 169, passing through the towns of Loganville and Overton. In about 25 miles, you arrive at the junction of NV 167. A right turn here takes you to Valley of Fire State Park, while a left onto NV 167 leads to Lake Mead National Recreation Area. Directions for the hikes described below start at this junction.

14. Redstone Loop

Easy 0.5-mile loop; allow 30 minutes
Map: Trails Illustrated 204: Lake Mead National Recreation Area

GETTING THERE: At the junction of NV 169 and NV 167, turn left (south) onto NV 167 into Lake Mead Recreation Area. Past the tollbooth, arrive almost immediately at a fork. Go right at the fork to stay on NV 167, Northshore Road. Continue to Redstone Picnic Area on the left at milepost 27.
ON THE TRAIL: The trail begins at a kiosk in the back of the parking lot. Follow it counterclockwise, climbing slightly to loop around a red dome. Freelancing to the south and west of the trail enables you to spot countless arches in the Aztec Sandstone.

NEARBY: The **Bowl of Fire** at milepost 18 along NV 167, Northshore Drive, lends itself to even more rugged off-trail exploration.

15. Liberty Bell Arch

Moderate 6-mile out-and-back; allow 3 hours

Trail closed May 15 through September 30 due to heat-related hazards; trekking poles recommended

Map: Trails Illustrated 204: Lake Mead National Recreation Area

GETTING THERE: At the intersection of NV 169 and NV 167, turn left (south) onto NV 167 to enter Lake Mead National Recreation Area, arriving almost immediately at a fork. Go right at the fork to stay on NV 167, Northshore Road. Follow Northshore Road—a knockout!—for 46 miles to the junction with NV 147. Turn left here. In 3 miles, turn left again onto NV 564, Lakeshore Scenic Drive. In 11 miles, turn left on US Route 93, a divided highway. The highway passes Hoover Dam and enters Arizona. At mile 4, turn left, taking a cut-across signed for the **White Rock Canyon trailhead**. Park here.

ON THE TRAIL: The trail leads not only to a memorable arch but also to gobsmacking overlooks of the Colorado River gorge.

From the kiosk, drop into the wash, walking under the US 93 bridge. At the first trail junction, bear right. Continue past a short narrows section to reach a second

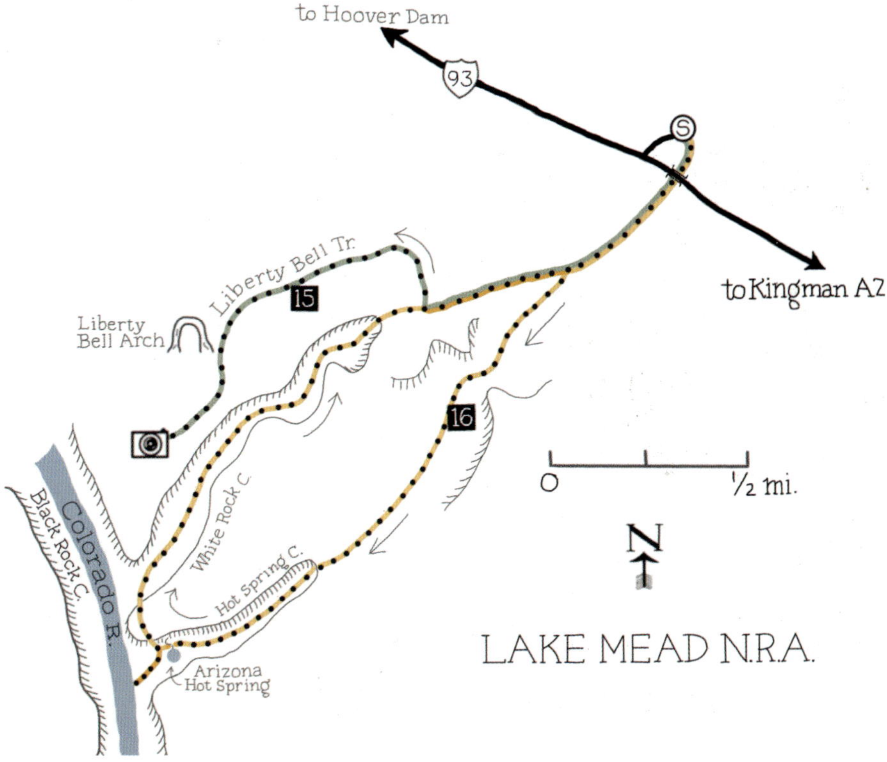

junction at mile 1. Turn right again, ascending a side wash. After leaving the wash, the trail climbs to a saddle, reaching an old magnesium mine with rusting equipment. Detour on a faint path to inspect the mine if you wish.

Back at the main trail, turn left and descend cautiously over scree to a major wash. Although Liberty Bell Arch is straight ahead of you, that fact is not immediately apparent because you are viewing the arch end-on. The trail climbs to an area on the left of the aptly named span. Huge conglomerate boulders close to its base add to the drama.

Beyond the arch, the trail ascends to overlooks of the free-flowing Colorado River, newly released from entrapment behind Hoover Dam. The bridge at the west end of Lake Mead is in view, and you may spot boaters lounging on the beaches of **Black Rock Canyon** far below. Retrace your steps to return to the parking lot.

16. Arizona Hot Spring

Moderate 6.5-mile loop, with routefinding and scrambling; allow 4 hours

Trail closed May 15 through September 30 due to heat-related hazards; river shoes and trekking poles recommended

Map: Trails Illustrated 204: Lake Mead National Recreation Area

Rugged Hot Spring Canyon has a funhouse quality.

GETTING THERE: At the intersection of NV 169 and NV 167, turn left (south) onto NV 167 to enter Lake Mead National Recreation Area, arriving almost immediately at a fork. Go right at the fork to stay on NV 167, Northshore Road. Follow Northshore Road for 46 miles to the junction with NV 147. Turn left here. In 3 miles, turn left again onto NV 564, Lakeshore Scenic Drive. In 11 miles, turn left on US Route 93, a divided highway. The highway passes Hoover Dam and enters Arizona. At mile 4, turn left, taking a cut-across signed for the **White Rock Canyon trailhead**. Park here.

ON THE TRAIL: Begin by descending to the wash and walking under the highway bridge. At mile 0.5, turn left onto a jeep road that you follow to a saddle with eye-popping views at mile 1. Descend over scree, reaching the floor of **Hot Spring Canyon** at mile 1.5. After the canyon slots up, minor, fun-filled obstructions become more frequent as you progress downstream. The spring, at mile 2.5, forms a series of small, thigh-deep pools in rapid succession. The water in the uppermost of these supposedly averages 111°Fahrenheit but feels far hotter, and you will want to hasten to the more comfortable lower pools. Signs warn visitors not to submerge their faces in the water, which contains microorganisms that can cause death if ingested.

Just below the last pool a 20-foot ladder eases your passage to the canyon's lower tier. Paraphernalia strung out by campers begins to appear. Many, if not most, visitors access the area from the **Colorado River**, where you can chill out on a rocky beach at mile 2.75. Since sheer cliffs make it impossible to follow the shoreline, you must backtrack about 5 minutes upcanyon to locate a rudimentary, exposed trail on the left. The path hops a saddle to the next drainage, **White Rock Canyon**, at mile 3.5. This part of the hike puts your navigational skills to the test, and poles come in handy.

The return up narrow White Rock Canyon, named for boulders washed down by flash floods, poses no major problems. If you have energy to spare, you can detour along the way to admire Liberty Bell Arch (see Hike 15), adding 2 miles to your trip.

ZION NATIONAL PARK

Zion, Utah's oldest national park, looks like Yosemite painted red, with Navajo Sandstone and the Kayenta Formation as the dominant strata. Its 6-mile scenic byway snakes through a magnificent canyon, carved out by the North Fork of the Virgin River, a Colorado tributary. More than 150 miles of trails branch off in every direction, leading to desert waterfalls, hanging gardens, and dazzling overlooks. Apart from the insanely large crowds that it attracts, Zion deserves its reputation as an earthly paradise. Visiting during the off-season is advisable, though bear in mind that some hikes—most notably the Virgin River Narrows—are not feasible at that time. Many of the best trips require a shuttle; companies based in Springdale offer that service. Zion's Kolob Canyons section, not connected by road to the rest of the park, is covered in Chapter 1.

From St. George, take Interstate 15 north to exit 16, picking up UT 9 to the south entrance station. Shuttle buses running from the gateway town of Springdale and the nearby visitor center transport people to points of interest in Zion Canyon.

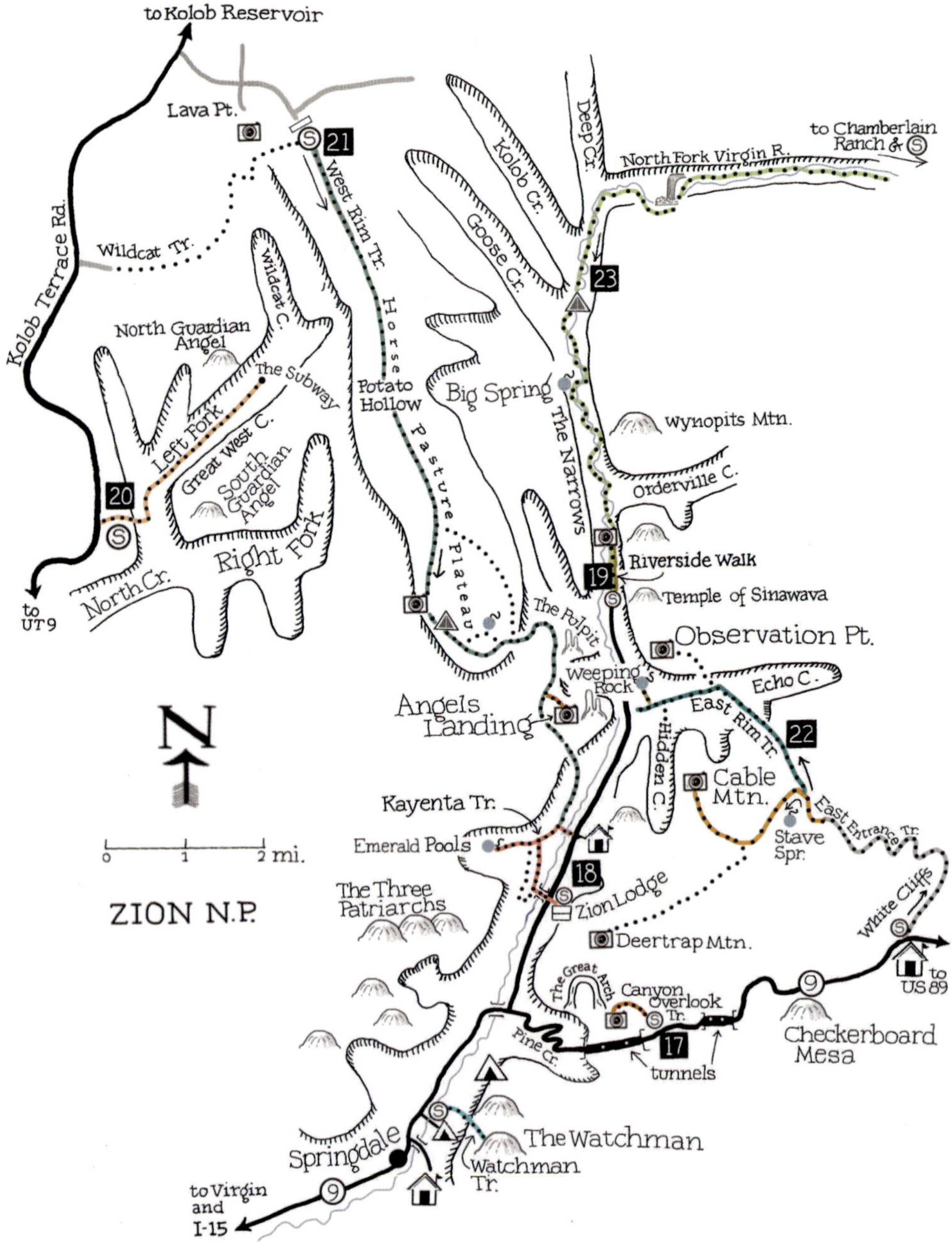
to Kolob Reservoir
Lava Pt.
21
West Rim Tr.
Kolob Terrace Rd.
Wildcat Tr.
Wildcat C.
North Guardian Angel
The Subway
Left Fork
Great West C.
South Guardian Angel
20
Right Fork
North Cr.
to UT9
Horse Pasture Plateau
Potato Hollow
Kolob Cr.
Goose Cr.
Deep Cr.
North Fork Virgin R.
to Chamberlain Ranch &
23
Big Spring
The Narrows
Wynopits Mtn.
Orderville C.
Riverside Walk
19
Temple of Sinawava
The Pulpit
Observation Pt.
Weeping Rock
Echo C.
East Rim Tr.
22
Angels Landing
Hidden C.
Cable Mtn.
Stave Spr.
East Entrance Tr.
Kayenta Tr.
Emerald Pools
18
Zion Lodge
The Three Patriarchs
Deertrap Mtn.
White Cliffs
to US 89
The Great Arch
Canyon Overlook Tr.
17
tunnels
Pine Cr.
Checkerboard Mesa
9
Springdale
The Watchman
Watchman Tr.
to Virgin and I-15
0 1 2 mi.
ZION N.P.

Private vehicles are prohibited on the scenic byway (though not on UT 9) between March and November. The popular Angels Landing requires a timed-access permit.

From Kanab, drive north on US Route 89 for 41 miles to Mount Carmel Junction. Turn left onto UT 9 and continue to the east entrance station. The spectacular highway winds among cross-bedded petrified dunes like **Checkerboard Mesa** and braves a dark, mile-long tunnel constructed during the 1920s. It then descends Pine Creek, passing the **Great Arch** (really an alcove) to intersect Zion Canyon.

17. Canyon Overlook

Easy 1-mile out-and-back, with exposure; allow 30 minutes
Map: Trails Illustrated 714: Zion National Park

GETTING THERE: Traveling west on UT 9, find the start of the trail at the west end of the first long tunnel you go through, about 5 miles from the park's east entrance station.
ON THE TRAIL: This nature trail, which is rather exposed despite protective guardrails, should top every visitor's list. It ends at a perch above the Great Arch, with inspiring views of Zion Canyon.

18. Emerald Pools

Easy 3-mile loop; allow 1.5 hours
Map: Trails Illustrated 714: Zion National Park

GETTING THERE: Start at Zion Lodge along the scenic byway, shuttle stop #5.
ON THE TRAIL: This short hike leads to several idyllic pools. Since wildlife depend on these water sources, refrain from swimming in them.

The **Lower Pool** is 0.5 mile from the lodge. Cross a footbridge over the river and turn right, following a very easy paved path. Here you pass under some gossamer waterfalls. The trail switchbacks 100 feet up to the **Middle Pools**.

The **Upper Pool**, reached by a picturesque but rocky 250-foot ascent, lies 0.5 mile farther on. Relax at the small beach, taking care on the uneven, slippery terrain. About 0.25 mile below the Upper Pool, turn left on the **Kayenta Trail**, which ends at Grotto Picnic Area. Here, pick up the **Grotto Trail** along the scenic byway to complete the loop.

19. Riverside Walk

Very easy 2-mile out-and-back; allow 1 hour
River shoes and trekking poles recommended beyond trail's end
Map: Trails Illustrated 714: Zion National Park

GETTING THERE: Start at the end of the scenic byway, shuttle stop #9.
ON THE TRAIL: Stroll along the Virgin River from the **Temple of Sinawava** on a placid, level trail. The lush gorge teems with life: dark green ferns, babbling springs, and miniature wildflower gardens. Most people turn back at a viewpoint beyond which the canyon is too constricted to accommodate a walkway. The intrepid continue upstream 2 miles farther to **Orderville Canyon**, wading through the rushing river over slippery cobbles before retracing their steps to the trailhead.

Zion's Emerald Pools Trail passes beneath a waterfall.

20. The Subway

Very difficult 9-mile out-and-back, with routefinding and scrambling; allow 8 hours

Permit required; trekking poles, river shoes, dry bag, and headlamp recommended

Map: Trails Illustrated 714: Zion National Park

GETTING THERE: From the visitor center, drive west on UT 9 about 15 miles to the town of Virgin. Turn right onto Kolob Terrace Road and proceed 8.25 miles to the lower Left Fork parking lot.

ON THE TRAIL: Truly a religious experience! The Subway is nature's answer to the Sistine Chapel, with pilgrims to match. Because demand for permits is heavy, apply well in advance of your visit.

The trip through the **Left Fork of North Creek** can be attempted from either the top or bottom. Because the former option, though undoubtedly more beautiful, requires technical equipment and involves swimming through cold pools, this book recommends the latter route. The Park Service allows 80 people in the canyon daily, selected by online lottery. Pick up your permit at the Wilderness Desk the day before your trip, and plan on an early start. Estimates of the hike's length vary widely, ranging from 6.5 to 9 miles. The higher figure feels more accurate, especially given the complexities of routefinding and the inevitability of mistakes. Plus, you will be wading much of the time, which slows upstream progress considerably, especially at higher water levels. Count on bushwhacking and plenty of boulder-hopping as well.

For the first 0.5 mile, the trail crosses a wooded mesa. Entering the Zion Wilderness, it drops down precipitously 400 feet in the next 0.25 mile, hugging the side of a basalt cliff. Scree slopes and exposure complicate your passage. Pause at the bottom to form a clear mental image of the route you have just traversed to prepare for the return trip. Although cairns and ribbons mark the junction, it is easily missed.

Initially wide and brushy, the canyon soon constricts, necessitating countless stream crossings. The **South Guardian Angel** looms above on the right. Side-canyons join from the left around mile 1.25. At about mile 2, the route becomes choked with boulders. Sometimes you can find paths leading up and around obstacles, but often you have no choice but to clamber over them. Around mile 3, just before a stream crossing, stop to appreciate about 70 birdlike **dinosaur tracks** that decorate vertical gray mudstone slabs on the left side of the canyon.

Past the tracks, negotiate another long and tricky obstacle course. Deliverance comes at mile 4, when you arrive at beautiful **Archangel Cascades**. Shallow water spills over ledges of crimson rock, enhanced by patches of green algae. Climb the ledges or detour to their right, alongside canyon walls festooned with spring-fed mosses and stained by minerals. At the top of the second cascade, the creek practically disappears into a deep, narrow crack.

Where the canyon bends sharply right, the Subway, situated below the **North Guardian Angel**, comes into view. Here the Navajo Sandstone cliffs pinch together above the ledgy Kayenta Formation, creating a keyhole effect. The architecture owes to deep, curved undercuts made by the stream. Circular potholes filled with

Tunnel-like walls rise above pellucid turquoise pools in the Subway.

turquoise water grace the slippery floor. Although the Subway can be dark as a cathedral inside, the effect is mystical rather than spooky. Not surprisingly, hikers from both the upper and lower trailheads congregate here. Other chambers beckon upstream, including the so-called Waterfall Room, but unless you are a human fly, don't attempt to access them from below.

21. West Rim Backpack

Moderate 15.25-mile point-to-point, including side-trip to Angels Landing; allow 2 days

Permit and shuttling vehicles or equivalent required; water filter and trekking poles recommended

Map: Trails Illustrated 714: Zion National Park

GETTING THERE: Leave one vehicle at the visitor center, to which you will return by shuttle bus from Grotto Picnic Area (stop #6). To reach the trailhead, drive a second vehicle west on UT 9 from the visitor center about 15 miles to Virgin. Turn right onto Kolob Terrace Road. Continue on this beyond-scenic road toward Kolob Reservoir, which climbs into heavy timber. At mile 21, turn right onto Lava Point Road, a dirt road that leads to primitive Lava Point Campground. Within a mile, you arrive at an intersection. Continue straight ahead to a Y. At the Y, go right for 1.25 miles onto a narrow, rutted track, descending a hill to reach the trailhead.

ON THE TRAIL: This varied trek leads to the rim and then to the floor of Zion Canyon. You can day-hike portions of the trail from the scenic byway, but substantial elevation gains make that option more daunting. Reserve permits online and, if necessary, arrange a shuttle to the trailhead in Springdale.

Crossing a vehicle barrier, follow the trail for several miles through the cool, semi-wooded uplands of **Horse Pasture Plateau**. This is fast, easy walking over level terrain, and before long the trail veers to the plateau's edge for a tantalizing glimpse of **Wildcat Canyon.** The trail next descends into **Potato Hollow** at mile 5, a humid, boggy valley teeming with aspens, flowers, and wildlife. (Did you remember your bug repellent?) Then it climbs several hundred feet, heading once again toward the plateau rim, which it hugs for the next few miles. Peering into the muscular pink-and-white domes of **Great West Canyon** is unforgettable, especially at dawn and dusk. Camp by reservation only in designated sites.

At the loop trail near the end of the forested plateau, bear right and continue along the rim. Where the trail begins its long descent to the floor of the main canyon, near mile 9.5, a sign points the way to a spring on the left. From the overlook to the Grotto Picnic Area, it is 4.75 miles, a 2500-foot descent offering little shade and no water. In hot weather try to complete this stretch before noon. The scenery leaves you gasping with delight, especially after you cross a low slickrock pass into Zion Canyon.

Only 2 miles from the conclusion of the trail, **Scout Lookout** at mile 11.25 supplies an outstanding vantage point. But nothing rivals the vista from **Angels Landing** (elevation 5785 feet). A rather hair-raising spur—1 mile round trip and very strenuous—climbs precipitously to the top of a tall fin jutting out into the canyon, nearly 1400 feet above the river. You can see the entire canyon at a glance. Although the spur has chain guardrails, its exposed, 500-foot climb can be frightening and is not recommended for children. Doff your pack, bringing only water and valuables as you join the inevitable conga line. (Most visitors approach Angels Landing from below, a 5.5-mile out-and-back that involves a 1500-foot elevation change and takes about 4 hours.)

Returning to the main trail, join the parade of hikers coming off the ridge. You drop down quickly on 21 no-nonsense switchbacks—nicknamed "Walters Wiggles," after the park's first superintendent—into shady **Refrigerator Canyon**. Attaining the canyon floor, you emerge into hotter, more open country and parallel the Virgin River the rest of the way. Eventually the trail crosses a bridge and ends opposite Grotto Picnic Area. Here, catch the shuttle to return to your car at the visitor center.

22. East Rim Backpack

Moderate 10-mile point-to-point, plus side trips; allow 2 days
Check with the park before attempting this. A 2019 cliff collapse closed this trail.
Map: Trails Illustrated 714: Zion National Park

GETTING THERE: Leave one vehicle at the visitor center, to which you later will return by shuttle bus from Weeping Rock (stop #7). To reach the trailhead, drive the second

Ribbon waterfall and spruce-clad domes along Zion's West Rim Trail

vehicle on UT 9 to the east entrance station and turn left to reach the East Entrance Trailhead. Otherwise, make arrangements with a commercial driver in Springdale.

ON THE TRAIL: This excellent adventure winds through forested country to the canyon rim before plunging 2150 feet to its floor. With an early start, it can be completed in a long day, though backpacking is preferable, especially if you throw in a side trip or two.

On foot, follow an abandoned roadbed up Clear Creek for 5 miles, passing massive peach-and-alabaster domes. The trail climbs through woodlands and turns into a narrow footpath. At mile 5.75, reach **Stave Spring** (the only water around, and often dry in summer; inquire about availability). Here, a side trip option presents itself. A level spur veers left; where it splits in about 0.5 mile, go right another 2.5 miles to **Cable Mountain Overlook**. If you chose this option, backtrack to Stave Spring to resume the featured itinerary.

At Stave Spring, pick up the **Echo Canyon Trail** heading northwest. From here it is 4.75 miles to the canyon bottom. Descend rapidly toward the rim alongside a neatly eroded wash. Views are panoramic, dominated by **Angels Landing** and **The Organ**, on the far side of a big bend in the river.

The trail now plummets to the floor of Zion Canyon. Along the way you meet three spur trails. The first detours to the right at mile 14.5, up 850 feet of switchbacks, to **Observation Point** (3.5 miles round-trip). At this junction, the Echo Canyon Trail merges with the **East Rim Trail**. About 1 mile farther down the trail, a second spur goes left to narrow **Hidden Canyon**, suspended almost 1000 feet above the valley. This exhilarating route, up to 3 miles round trip, clings to a cliff face initially and can be scary in spots, despite guardrails. The final spur, on the right, laterals to **Weeping Rock**, a spring festooned with hanging gardens. From the Weeping Rock junction, the main trail drops quickly to its terminus along the scenic drive.

23. Virgin River Narrows

Very difficult 16-mile point-to-point; allow 12 hours to 2 days
Permit and vehicle shuttle or equivalent required; water filter, trekking poles, river shoes, dry bag, and headlamp recommended
Map: Trails Illustrated 714: Zion National Park

GETTING THERE: Leave one vehicle at the visitor center, to which you later will return by shuttle bus from the Temple of Sinawava, shuttle stop #9. To reach the trailhead, drive the second vehicle east through the park on UT 9 about 2 miles past the east entrance, where an unpaved road branches off to the left. Take this road north for some 18 miles, crossing a wooden bridge over the river. Turn left and proceed 0.5 mile to the gate of Chamberlain Ranch. Continue 0.5 mile farther on the rough road to the parking lot. Allow at least an hour for the drive. Without two vehicles, hire a driver in Springdale.

ON THE TRAIL: In the minds of many, the Virgin River Narrows offers the ultimate in canyon-stream hiking. The settler who "discovered" the canyon in 1872 dubbed

Attempt the Zion Narrows when temperatures are high and water levels are low.

it "the most wonderful defile it has been my fortune to behold." Awe-inspiring red, black, and gold sandstone cliffs rise 2000 feet above the chasm, which is lined with cottonwoods and box elders much of the way.

Although the Virgin River Narrows is one of the most memorable of backcountry trips in all respects, do not underestimate it. Especially in high-water periods, the hike can be extremely fatiguing, since the river gets faster and deeper as it descends. Most of the way it tends to be shallow, but sometimes you encounter cold pools that can be up to 50 feet long. Because of minimal sun penetration, hikers can develop hypothermia even in midsummer. In fact, the canyon may be closed at times for that very reason, but also because of flash flooding, which has caused numerous fatalities. Aim for a June reservation, as that month tends to be both warm and dry.

The Park Service requires permits for all through-hikers, and limits the number of people who can be in the canyon on any given day. Hikers must satisfy age and height requirements. Reserve permits online for pickup at the Wilderness Desk in the visitor center.

Many hikers complete the trip in a very long day, which has certain advantages. It means that you can travel lightly and are unlikely to be caught unawares by adverse weather. But in all likelihood, it also means feeling rushed and exhausted.

For maximum enjoyment, plan to spend a night at one of a dozen designated campsites. If you lack dry bags, line each compartment of your pack with heavy-duty plastic garbage bags and put your sleeping bag, also wrapped in plastic, inside the main compartment. A pack lined in this manner will float, should it become necessary to swim. To protect water quality, the Park Service issues each camper a container for human waste.

At the trailhead, follow the dirt road across the river and continue for a few miles, crossing private property. The canyon here is wide and shallow, and the walking is easy. Pass a small cabin on the left at mile 1.5 as you travel through hilly country. Where the road starts to fade out, drop into the canyon and walk in the streambed. Although you will be descending from here on out, the 1300-foot elevation loss is barely perceptible.

For the first half of your hike, the river should be relatively shallow. The canyon walls grow progressively higher and closer together. At about mile 7, you reach a bankless section, where you probably cannot avoid wading, and also a pour-off, which you can skirt on the left. **Deep Creek**, entering at an angle from the right near mile 8, is a good landmark. It usually carries a large volume of water, making the river considerably colder, deeper, and swifter than previously. From here on, prepare to wade much of the time. Within the next 2 miles, two more tributaries—Kolob and Goose Creeks—also join the river on your right, but their mouths are relatively small, making them easy to miss. Designated campsites are concentrated between Deep Creek at mile 8 and **Big Spring** at mile 11, a luxuriant seep where you can refill your water bottles.

Below this point, the true narrows begin. The going gets rough, since you must cross the deepening stream countless times over slippery cobbles. Because the rocks aren't always visible below the turbulent surface, twisted ankles are a distinct possibility, and trekking poles to stabilize your gait prove indispensable.

Between Big Spring and **Orderville Canyon**, a large but often waterless tributary entering from the left at mile 13, chest-deep pools may require you to swim. In this vicinity you start to meet day-trippers coming up from the **Riverside Walk** (see Hike 19). At mile 15, exhale deeply upon reaching the 1-mile paved trail to the Temple of Sinawava.

AROUND KANAB

The area around Kanab, one of the hubs for this chapter, treats its guests to numerous hikes of national park quality. Recharge your batteries amid spectacular local arches, hoodoos, and dunes.

24. Coral Pink Sand Dunes State Park

Easy trail, with negligible distance; allow 30 minutes
Map: USGS: Cedar City

GETTING THERE: From Kanab, drive north on US Route 89 for 9 miles. Turn left onto Hancock Road and follow signs.

ON THE TRAIL: The park, a favorite of filmmakers, boasts sand of an uncommon hue. For obvious reasons, it receives heavy weekend use from all-terrain vehicle buffs. An interpretive trail extends into the dunes on a boardwalk.

25. Cobra Arch

Moderate 7.5-mile out-and-back, with routefinding and scrambling; allow 4–5 hours
High-clearance or four-wheel-drive vehicle required; trekking poles recommended
Map: Trails Illustrated 859: Paria Canyon/Kanab
GPS coordinates: 37.02088°N, 111.89581°W

GETTING THERE: Take US Route 89 east from Kanab for about 42 miles. Turn south on County Road 6020, Long Canyon Road, between mileposts 21 and 22 and reset your trip odometer. The unpaved road becomes rather hairy around mile 3, where it narrows and hugs a pointy ridge. Ignore side tracks branching off to the right. Bear left at the mile 5 junction. Around mile 6, patches of deep sand render the road unsuitable for passenger vehicles. Locate the parking lot on the right just past a fence at mile 7.75.

ON THE TRAIL: This remarkable 40-foot Navajo Sandstone span near the rim of **Buckskin Gulch** (see Hike 30) bulges out in the center while narrowing at either end. Cobra Arch is snakelike in both its appearance and its ability to mesmerize. GPS proves helpful in pinpointing its exact location. Keep in mind that the joy here resides more in the destination than the journey.

The register box is signed for the **Middle Trail**, which drops down into Buckskin Gulch in 1.5 miles. Begin on this trail, hugging the fence briefly to the edge of a cliff known as **The Dive**. Leave the Middle Trail here and turn left, continuing along the top of the formation. Straight ahead, notice a series of bays separated by rocky

Although tricky to locate, Cobra Arch amply rewards the persistent hiker.

headlands. Though hidden from view, the arch commands a shallow bowl under the second of these.

Round a few scallops, coming to an obvious break in the cliffs at mile 2.25. Cautiously descend to the lower level and follow cairns around its base. Cross a dune, then stay to the right of a large sand hill. From here the route continues mainly on rock, and although cairns may thin out, you want to proceed in a southeasterly direction toward a patch of red sandstone about 350 feet below the top of the cliff. The burnt-orange arch, at mile 3.75, faces south toward Buckskin Gulch. Its gorgeous setting atones for an otherwise humdrum trip.

NEARBY: **Edmaiers Secret** on West Clark Bench is a marvel of cauliflower (a.k.a. "brain") rocks, tepees, and delicate fins. A high-clearance or four-wheel-drive vehicle is required. To get there, take US 89 east from Kanab for about 42 miles. Turn south on CR 6020, Long Canyon Road, and proceed for 5 miles. At the junction, turn right and continue to the road's end at mile 6.75. Park and follow an abandoned track that trends west toward the Buckskin rim. From here, explore the area at will. Large potholes in the vicinity give this gem its alternate moniker, the **Water Pockets**.

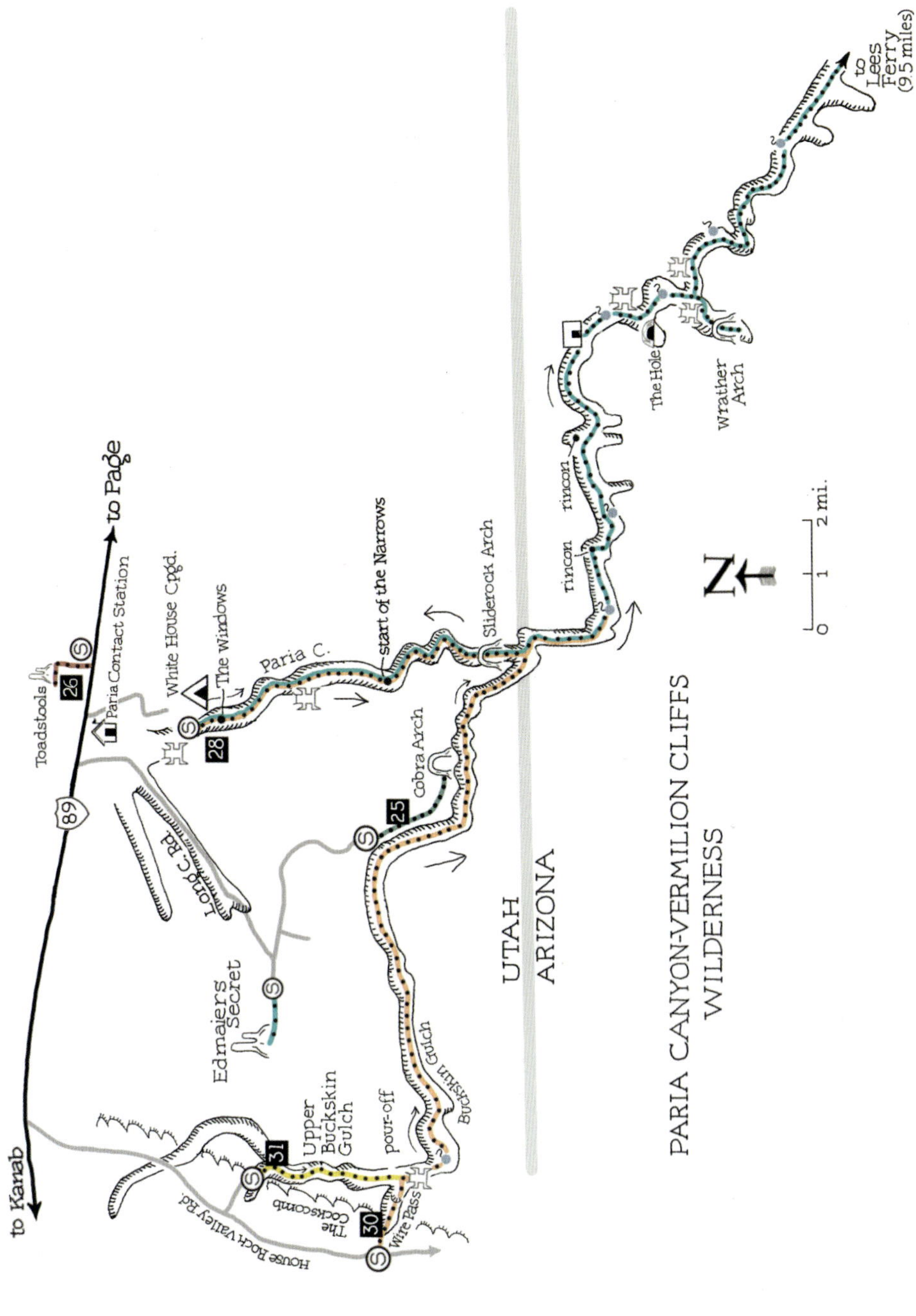
to Page
to Kanab
89
Toadstools
26
Paria Contact Station
White House Cpgd.
The Windows
28
Paria C.
start of the Narrows
Sliderock Arch
Long C. Rd.
Cobra Arch
25
Edmaiers Secret
Upper Buckskin Gulch
31
pour-off
Buckskin Gulch
The Cockscomb
30
Wire Pass
House Rock Valley Rd.
UTAH
ARIZONA
PARIA CANYON-VERMILION CLIFFS WILDERNESS
rincon
rincon
The Hole
Wrather Arch
to Lees Ferry (9.5 miles)
N
0 1 2 mi.

Whimsical, ultraphotogenic toadstools are a Grand Staircase-Escalante specialty.

26. Toadstools

Easy 1.5-mile out-and-back; allow 1.5 hours
Map: Trails Illustrated 859: Paria Canyon/Kanab

GETTING THERE: Drive east on US Route 89 from Kanab toward Page. Near milepost 19, about 1.5 miles past the **Paria Contact Station**, park in a marked lot on the left.

ON THE TRAIL: The Toadstools consist of a collection of pedestals whose Entrada Sandstone bases are protected from erosion by harder Dakota Formation caprocks. From the trailhead, pass through a hiker gate and walk directly up the wash. You will encounter two sets of hoodoos. The first set is predominantly reddish-brown. To reach the second set, which is white, turn left at the wash and walk a short distance. Explore to your heart's content, bearing in mind that the fragile structures are easily damaged.

NEARBY: To visit striated Chinle badlands featured in many Western flicks, turn north off US 89 at milepost 30.5 onto a dirt road (high-clearance vehicle required). Proceed 5 miles, following signs for **Old Pareah**. Arson unfortunately destroyed the movie set in 2006, but the banded, highly saturated hills more than merit a trip.

27. Wahweap Hoodoos

Easy 9-mile out-and-back; allow 6 hours
Map: Trails Illustrated 859: Paria Canyon/Kanab

GETTING THERE: From Kanab, drive east on US Route 89 toward Page. Near milepost 7, go north toward Big Water. Turn left here onto Ethan Allen Road. At a T junction, go left onto Fish Hatchery Road. About 3.25 miles from the highway, you reach Wahweap Creek. Park here.

ON THE TRAIL: Formations similar to the Toadstools abound near Lake Powell, though recent road closures make them harder to access. Of these the most renowned are the **Wahweap Hoodoos**, composed of ghostly pillars capped by chocolate brown conglomerate.

From the parking lot, pass through a fence and follow the main wash upstream. At mile 3.5, **Riverside Cove**, the first of three major collections of Entrada Sandstone hoodoos, materializes at the base of the cliff on the left. Within the next mile you arrive at **Hoodoo Central** and finally at the starkly white **Towers of Silence**, reminiscent of melted candlewax.

PARIA CANYON AND VICINITY

The wild and spectacular Paria (puh-REE-uh) River, which flows into the Colorado at Lees Ferry, Arizona, represents the ultimate in canyon hiking. Except in its lower reaches, the canyon, whose name means "muddy water" in Paiute, is relatively shady. The terrain is level or downhill all the way. Cliffs loom up to 1600 feet high. And the scenery is second to none: enormous sandstone alcoves streaked with desert varnish, hanging gardens of monkeyflowers, orchids and ferns, and two incomparable arches. The icing on the cake is the Paria's main tributary, Buckskin Gulch, which boasts the world's longest section of narrows.

Backpackers either can travel the length of the main canyon, from the White House Campground to Lees Ferry, Arizona, or execute a shorter semi-loop down Buckskin and back up Paria, from the Wire Pass trailhead to White House. Both options involve shuttles and require permits, for which you should apply well in advance. Because of potentially life-threatening flash flood hazards, check the weather report and stay clear if rain is predicted for the watershed. Conditions are most favorable in late spring, early summer, and early fall, though the canyon is very busy at these times, with competition for campsites near perennial springs. To minimize stream pollution, through-hikers are assigned "wag bags" for packing out human waste.

From Kanab, drive east on US Route 89 for 43 miles and turn right to reach the Paria Contact Station. If necessary, inquire locally about hiring a shuttle.

28. Paria Canyon Backpack

Moderate 37.25-mile point-to-point, plus side trips; allow 4 days
Permit and vehicle shuttle or equivalent; trekking poles and river shoes recommended
Map: Trails Illustrated 859: Paria Canyon/Kanab

GETTING THERE: Using two vehicles, drive east 30 miles on US 89 from the Paria Contact Station to Page, Arizona. Continue south on US 89 for 23 miles to the junction with US 89A. Turn right here and continue 19 miles to the bridge spanning Marble Canyon on the Colorado. Immediately past the bridge, turn right, entering **Glen Canyon National Recreation Area**, and drive 6 miles to **Lees Ferry**, the outpost below the Vermilion Cliffs where Grand Canyon float trips originate. Park in the long-term lot.

In the second vehicle, return to the Paria Contact Station. Drive 2 miles to the end of the dirt road to White House Campground.

ON THE TRAIL: From the trailhead, enter the canyon, which is shallow and dry at the start. You will remain in its bed for the next 28.25 miles. Normally the river starts flowing around mile 6.75 and you can count on splashing along in ankle-deep water for much of the way.

About 1.5 miles downstream you pass The Windows, a series of low holes gouged into the Navajo Sandstone cliffs. The walls quickly close in until you reach the **Narrows** about 4 miles from the trailhead. The deepest, darkest of these continue for 5 miles. Beautiful **Sliderock Arch** protrudes into the streambed at mile 6.25. Shortly thereafter, **Buckskin Gulch** comes in at mile 7; reserve time to explore this tributary.

A particularly beautiful part of the main canyon, capable of inducing a Zen-like mental state, begins 10 miles from the White House Campground. As the canyon slowly widens, you can camp on a sandbar on the left at 10.25 miles, opposite a fresh-water seep. Reliable springs also occur at miles 12.25, 20.5, 22, and 25.5. Noteworthy physical features in this section include an intimate grotto with a keyhole opening at mile 19 and **Wrather Arch**, 0.75 mile up a short side-canyon to the right at mile 20.5, a no-camping zone. Look carefully here, as the side-canyon's mouth is easily missed. It comes in shortly after a waterlogged straightaway stretch in the main canyon. The enormous arch ranks among the Southwest's ten largest, at approximately 200 feet

Backpackers stroll under Sliderock Arch, near the end of the Paria Narrows.

across. Be warned that the harrowing climb to the arch—especially the final steep scramble over talus and loose scree—may prove too much for some hikers.

The last spring is on the left canyon wall at mile 25.5. From here on, the trail touches base only occasionally with the river, which by now has cut through many layers of sandstone in rapid succession: the Navajo, Kayenta (starting below Wrather Canyon), Moenave, and Chinle strata. About 2.5 miles beyond the last spring, you face some tedious boulder-hopping in the streambed.

At mile 28, just before the river takes a 90-degree bend to the left, it is imperative, especially at high water levels, to locate a trail rising to the right of the stream. For the next 2 miles this trail stays high above the inner canyon, enabling you to bypass a nasty zone choked with brush and boulders. Only thrill-seekers should do otherwise.

After the trail returns to river level at mile 30, many good campsites are available. Filter river water if necessary. The canyon widens, and because shade is at a premium, avoid hiking this section in the midday summer heat. Immediately to the left of the trail at about mile 31.5, stop to admire some remarkable petroglyphs in a prominent field of boulders.

In the next few miles, pass the remains of old ranches and mining operations. At mile 36, cross into **Glen Canyon National Recreation Area**. Just before reaching Lees Ferry, explore John D. Lee's rustic homesite of **Lonely Dell**. A Mormon pioneer, Lee ran a ferry service here in the 19th century after participating in the 1857 Mountain Meadows Massacre, a notorious attack on a California-bound wagon train that claimed the lives of 120 migrants.

At the trail's end, turn left onto the road to Lees Ferry, retrieving your car from the long-term lot. Then, make the long drive back to White House Campground if you have another vehicle stationed there.

29. Cathedral Wash

Difficult 3-mile out-and-back, with routefinding; allow 2 hours
Map: Trails Illustrated 859: Paria Canyon/Kanab

GETTING THERE: From Lees Ferry, where the Paria Canyon hike ends, drive south toward US Route 89A. After marveling at an imposing collection of balanced rocks at mile 4, continue to mile 5. Park at the signed trailhead on the right.

ON THE TRAIL: This invigorating trek is best begun early in the day. Descend on stairs into the canyon on the west side of the road and pass through a culvert. Shallow at first, the wash sports lacelike walls formed when small rocks were released from imprisonment in the mudstone conglomerate. Expect minor hindrances, including pools and possible quicksand, in the first 0.75 mile.

Just below a powerline you encounter a deep pour-off that initially may look impossible to circumvent. Scout the route visually from the far-left edge of the chasm, paying attention to where people have stacked rocks to facilitate getting up and down. The descent begins about 25 yards to the right. First negotiate a 3.5-foot chute to the next level. Turn right and make for a wide ledge. You will need to "duck and cover" to avoid banging your head. Continue about 50 feet and descend to another ledge, aided again by a rock pile and numerous handholds.

From here the route to the canyon floor remains unproblematic. In the next 0.75 mile you encounter several moderately challenging obstacles, probably marked by cairns unless a flash flood has knocked them down. You pass through a short narrows section and then, just before reaching the river, a boulder zone. If you're lucky, you can watch rafts negotiating lower Glen Canyon's **Cathedral Rapid**.

NEARBY: At **Marble Canyon**, on US 89A adjacent to the spur to Lees Ferry, pause to walk across the old highway bridge, which has been pedestrianized. Look for condors roosting in the support beams; these magnificent raptors, with their enormous wingspans, were reintroduced to the Arizona Strip during the 1990s in a successful effort to save the species from extinction.

At the north end of Lees Ferry, the very easy River Walking Tour visits historic artifacts. About 0.25 mile from the trailhead, the difficult Spencer Trail (a 4-mile out-and-back with scrambling and exposure) climbs 1700 feet to the top of the Echo Cliffs. Drop 50 vertical feet from the designated endpoint to appreciate a Glen Canyon gooseneck.

30. Dive of Buckskin Backpack

Moderate 20-mile point-to-point; allow 2–3 days

Permit and vehicle shuttle or equivalent required; water filter, river shoes, and 30 feet of rope recommended

Map: Trails Illustrated 859: Paria Canyon/Kanab

GETTING THERE: To set up a shuttle for this hike, drive two cars east on US Route 89 from Kanab for 43 miles. Turn right to reach the Paria Contact Station. Here pick up the dirt road that extends 2 miles to White House Campground. Park one vehicle here. Returning to US 89 in your other vehicle, go west for 5 miles. Just after the highway cuts through the **Cockscomb** monocline, turn left onto House Rock Valley Road. With a bed of clay, this bumpy road's upper reaches are impassable when wet.

The Dive of Buckskin, a twilight world of echoes and twisting, constricted passages

Travel 8 miles to Wire Pass trailhead. If you lack two vehicles, inquire either in Kanab or at the Paria Contact Station about hiring a local outfitter. (See map on page 317.)

ON THE TRAIL: The so-called Dive is gothically spooky. In places, its 400-foot-high walls come so close together that you can touch both sides at once. That extreme narrowness prevents light from penetrating and creates a natural refrigerator effect. Repeated flash floods have sculpted the walls into gargoyles and left debris in their wake. As with all slots, every flood has the potential to change hiking conditions considerably. Obtain an update at the Contact Station.

From the parking area, cross the street to a wash, which soon slices through the Cockscomb at Wire Pass. To negotiate a dry-fall here, you may need to either scramble up to the right of the wash or lower your pack. At mile 1.75, you reach the intersection with Buckskin Gulch, gouged out of Navajo Sandstone. Turn right to proceed downstream. A few miles farther, bypass a rockfall high and on the right.

At about mile 8, at a bend in the canyon, is the hazardous **Middle Route** to the north rim. Here the canyon briefly widens just enough to permit camping. Sometimes there are stagnant "cesspools" just upstream from the start of this emergency escape route.

Unless flash flooding has blown it out, you may encounter a significant boulder jam at mile 11.5. If so, you will be thankful to have packed a rope. Scout carefully to weigh your options before proceeding. One alternative is to go up and over on the left, which requires a dodgy 20-foot downclimb. The other involves locating a chute in the middle of the rockpile through which you can lower yourself and your gear before squeezing through a ground-level passageway.

Flowing water usually begins less than a mile past this obstacle. Look for a popular campsite on the high, sandy bench to the left, at a big bend just short of the confluence. Turn left upon reaching the Paria River at mile 13, heading upstream toward White House Campground, 7 miles distant. For the next 3 miles you are strolling through the **Paria Narrows**, a no-camping zone because of flash flood danger. At mile 13.5, pass beneath lovely **Sliderock Arch**. Reaching the end of the narrows, continue to your next landmark, a collection of large stream-level erosion holes known as **The Windows**, at mile 18.5. The canyon widens considerably between this point and the trail's end at White House Campground, on the right.

31. Upper Buckskin Gulch

Easy 8-mile out-and-back; allow 4 hours

Map: Trails Illustrated 859: Paria Canyon/Kanab

GETTING THERE: From the Paria Contact Station, drive west 5 miles on US 89 to House Rock Valley Road, which is impassable when wet. Turn left and continue 4 miles to the Upper Buckskin spur on the left. Follow this spur to its end and park at the register box. (See map on page 317.)

ON THE TRAIL: Upper Buckskin is a neglected area, overshadowed by its better-known neighbors. But it makes for a delightful half-day stroll that enables you to explore the start of the canyon's narrows. Fees apply.

Enter the wash and follow it downstream. Within 0.5 mile, look for petroglyphs on the left wall. At mile 2, a side-canyon branches off to the left. Enter the narrows at mile 3 and intersect the Wire Pass route at mile 4. An alcove on the right contains rock art. Stop to admire a remarkable plaid tapestry wall on the canyon's left side. Then retrace your steps to return to your vehicle.

VERMILION CLIFFS NATIONAL MONUMENT

Vermilion Cliffs National Monument in northwest Arizona gives federal protection to a vast array of world-class locations, most notably Coyote Buttes and White Pocket. From Kanab, access these areas from the unpaved **House Rock Valley Road** (impassable when wet), 38 miles east of Kanab off US Route 89.

32. The Wave

Moderate 6-mile out-and-back, plus freelance exploring; allow 8 hours
Permit required
Map: Trails Illustrated 859: Paria Canyon/Kanab

GETTING THERE: From Kanab, drive east 38 miles on US 89. Turn south onto the unpaved, washboarded House Rock Valley Road (impassable when wet) and travel 8 miles. Park in the lot on the right.

ON THE TRAIL: Virtually unknown as recently as the 1990s, the cross-bedded pastel wonderland of The Wave—part of an administrative unit called **Coyote Buttes North**—has become one of the most sought-after tickets on the Colorado Plateau. Securing an audience with the Pope may be easier. Because only 20 individuals per day are allowed to enter the delicate area, the permit lottery is absurdly competitive. Ten permits are awarded through an online drawing, while the rest currently are selected at the BLM office in Kanab, Utah. Because hundreds of eager contestants may be vying for a handful of slots, meltdowns and temper tantrums are not uncommon. Successful applicants receive maps complete with detailed photos and directions.

Submit applications for the high-stakes internet lottery four months in advance. Choose the month you hope to visit and specify three dates within it, paying a small application fee. To enter the in-person drawing, show up at the Kanab BLM office by 8:30 AM on the day before you wish to hike. From mid-November to mid-March, competitions for Saturday, Sunday, and Monday slots are held the previous Friday. The odds of bagging a permit improve during the winter low season. People sometimes try to sneak into The Wave without official sanction. Be advised that the risk of getting lost (or worse; numerous fatalities have occurred) on the unmarked route is substantial, and that rangers patrol the area regularly. Fines for unauthorized entry are hefty, and violators face prosecution. For these reasons, precise directions will not be given below.

The route begins at the Wire Pass trailhead. To save time, hikers may want to spend the night prior to setting forth at **Stateline Campground**, 1.5 miles to the south, the northern terminus of the Arizona Trail. On foot, allow about 2 hours to reach The Wave. The area, composed of petrified Navajo Sandstone dunes stained by mineral oxides, stretches over an acre. It consists of an antechamber that opens out to other rooms. Just before reaching the antechamber, check out an amuse-bouche near the top of a sandhill to the left of the trail.

The technicolor swirls of The Wave enchant the lucky few who score permits.

If you ascend from the main body of The Wave and turn right, within a few hundred yards you come to a similar area sometimes identified as Wave Two. The colors of its stripes are softer and less saturated. Brain rock, hamburger, and oyster bed formations add to the area's trippy charm.

From Wave Two, locate a steep chimney ascending toward **Top Rock** at the apex of the formation. Not for the timid, this route provides access to numerous marvels, most notably **Melody Arch**, an incredible double span overlooking the desert to the north (GPS coordinates: 36.5928°N, 112.0020°W).

33. Coyote Buttes South

Moderately difficult freelance exploring with routefinding and scrambling; allow 4 hours for either unit
Permit and four-wheel-drive vehicle required
Map: Trails Illustrated 859: Paria Canyon/Kanab

GETTING THERE: Coyote Buttes South has two sections, Paw Hole and Cottonwood Cove. From Kanab, drive east 38 miles on US 89. Then turn south onto unpaved House Rock Valley Road, which is impassable when wet.

For Paw Hole: Take House Rock Valley Road 16 miles to the junction of a road to Lone Tree Reservoir. Turn left, arriving at an intersection in 1.25 miles. Go left again onto a very sketchy track and proceed 1.25 miles to the parking area.

For Cottonwood Cove: Drive south 19.75 miles on the House Rock Valley Road until you reach a corral opposite BLM 1017, Pine Tree Road. Turn left and continue 3 miles to a broken windmill. Just past the windmill, turn left onto BLM 1066. In about 6 miles, stay to the left of ramshackle Poverty Flat Ranch. Continue 2 more miles to the parking lot.

ON THE TRAIL: Happily, for those whose efforts to secure hiking permits for Coyote Buttes North have ended in frustration, mind-blowing Coyote Buttes South is less in demand. One reason for this discrepancy is that regular passenger cars cannot handle the rough, sandy access roads. If you are driving such a vehicle, your only recourse is to hire a local outfitter. Apply online for day-use permits, which are valid for each location.

As noted, Coyote Buttes South has two discrete sections. Although both venues are trackless, plentiful landmarks make navigation relatively straightforward. The main attraction of **Paw Hole** is its orange-and-white tepees, whereas **Cottonwood Cove** also features sandstone lace, brain rocks, and a memorable hoodoo, called the **Control Tower**. Both units have a high fun-factor and are well worth your time. The road to Paw Hole is much shorter but carries a greater risk of bogging down in deep sand. Ideally, travel in tandem with another vehicle.

34. White Pocket

Moderate freelance exploring, with routefinding and scrambling; allow 4 hours
Four-wheel-drive vehicle required
Map: Trails Illustrated 859: Paria Canyon/Kanab
GPS coordinates: 36.57328°N, 111.53734°W

GETTING THERE: From Kanab, drive east 38 miles on US 89. Drive south on House Rock Valley Road (impassable when wet) for about 20 miles to BLM 1017, Pine Tree Road. Zeroing out your trip odometer, turn left, and proceed 6.25 miles to a ranch. Shift now into four-wheel low gear. Travel north on BLM 1087, which undergoes a number change to 1086. Proceed to a Y at mile 10. Go left onto what appears to be the more obscure track and continue 5.5 miles, passing through a gate near the parking area.

ON THE TRAIL: The Southwest on steroids! This peerless destination is utterly surreal in its shapes, forms, and brilliant colors. Brown, red, and yellow swirls decorate its alabaster flanks. At this writing, permits are unnecessary. Visit White Pocket now, while you can still avoid jumping through bureaucratic hoops. That said, if you lack a four-wheel-drive vehicle, it would be folly to brave the area independently, since the approach roads contain treacherous sand traps. Better to hire a local outfitter in that case.

On foot, follow a sandy trail a short distance to the undulating slickrock mass with its polygonal cracks. The area is not large, but before setting forth, orient yourself so

The White Pocket resembles a petrified ice cream sundae.

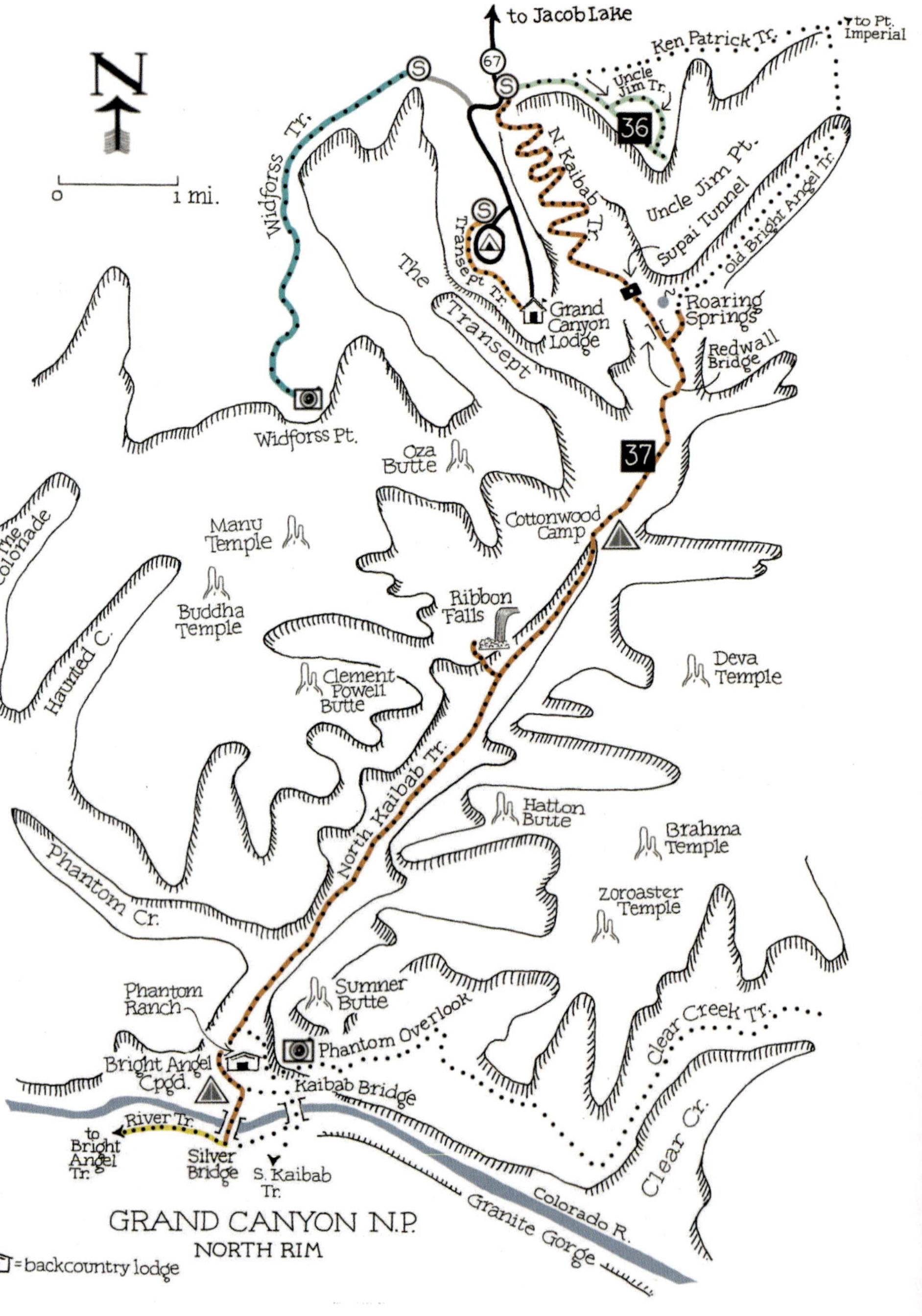
to Jacob Lake
67
Ken Patrick Tr.
to Pt. Imperial
Uncle Jim Tr.
36
N. Kaibab Tr.
Uncle Jim Pt.
Supai Tunnel
old Bright Angel Tr.
Widforss Tr.
0
1 mi.
Transept Tr.
The Transept
Grand Canyon Lodge
Roaring Springs
Redwall Bridge
Widforss Pt.
Oza Butte
37
Cottonwood Camp
The Colonade
Manu Temple
Buddha Temple
Haunted C.
Ribbon Falls
Deva Temple
Clement Powell Butte
North Kaibab Tr.
Hatton Butte
Brahma Temple
Phantom Cr.
Zoroaster Temple
Sumner Butte
Phantom Ranch
Phantom Overlook
Clear Creek Tr.
Bright Angel Cpgd.
Kaibab Bridge
River Tr.
to Bright Angel Tr.
Silver Bridge
S. Kaibab Tr.
Clear Cr.
Colorado R.
Granite Gorge
GRAND CANYON N.P.
NORTH RIM
=backcountry lodge

that you can locate your car at the end of the tour. **White Pocket Butte**, the formation that gives the area its name, serves as a landmark, as do many other features having unique personalities: natural tanks, folds, and striations, and rocks that seem to be melting under the desert sun.

GRAND CANYON NATIONAL PARK: NORTH RIM

Lieutenant Joseph Ives of the US Army, who beheld the Grand Canyon in 1857, famously derided the gorge as "altogether valueless," confidently predicting that his would be "the last party of whites to visit this profitless locality." But to Clarence Dutton, a member of the legendary Powell Expedition that explored the Green and Colorado Rivers just a dozen years later, the Grand Canyon was "by far the most sublime of all earthly spectacles." The six million pilgrims who flock to the national park every year give Dutton's perspective a ringing endorsement.

Though equally revealing of nature's artistry, the North Rim of the Grand Canyon differs in many ways from the South Rim (see Chapter 6). To begin with, the former ranges between 1000 feet and 1500 feet higher, and therefore tends to be cooler and wetter. For these reasons, it remains closed during the winter. The North Rim is also significantly farther from the river, so canyon views are not as intimate. Finally, because of its remoteness from population centers, it receives only a tenth as many visitors as its southern counterpart. People preferring a less frenetic experience therefore will find a lot to like in this unit. In addition to short trails leading to spectacular overlooks, backcountry opportunities beckon.

From Kanab, drive south on US Route 89A across the state line to Fredonia, Arizona. Turn left to stay on US 89A and proceed 32 miles to Jacob Lake. Here pick up AZ 67 south, which crosses the Kaibab Plateau, a region of ponderosa pines, quaking aspens, and lupine-covered meadows dotted with lakes. It is 30 miles to the entrance station and 14 additional miles to the visitor center. On arrival, stretch your legs on the easy **Transept Trail**, a spectacular 3-mile out-and-back along the rim between the visitor center and the campground.

35. Cape Royal

Very easy 0.75-mile out-and-back; allow 30 minutes
Map: Trails Illustrated 207: Grand Canyon National Park

GETTING THERE: From the visitor center, drive north 3.5 miles on AZ 67. Turn right onto Cape Royal Road and continue to the Y at mile 6. The left fork goes to **Point Imperial**, the park's highest overlook. For Cape Royal, turn right at the Y and continue about 14 miles to the parking area at the end of the Walhalla Plateau.

ON THE TRAIL: The Cadillac of North Rim overlooks, Cape Royal offers one of the Grand Canyon's supreme vantage points. The popular trail leads to **Angels Window**, a natural arch, and treats hikers to views of Wotans Throne, Vishnu Temple, and Freya Castle.

NEARBY: About 2.5 miles north of here, locate the inconspicuous trailhead for **Cape Final** on the right. The easy 4-mile out-and-back ascends gently through forested country to the east-facing perch, with Juno and Jupiter Temples in your sightline.

36. Uncle Jim Trail

Easy 4.5-mile lollipop loop; allow 2.5 hours
Map: Trails Illustrated 207: Grand Canyon National Park

GETTING THERE: From the visitor center, drive north on AZ 67 for about 2 miles and turn right into the North Kaibab parking lot. The trail begins immediately past the mule corral.

ON THE TRAIL: The highlight of this satisfying walk along a wooded plateau is the perspective it affords on the tight upper switchbacks of the North Kaibab Trail.

The hike begins on the **Ken Patrick Trail**, which extends 10 miles to Point Imperial. At about mile 0.75, where the paths diverge, turn right onto the Uncle Jim Trail and walk toward the canyon rim, from which the North Kaibab Trail comes into view as it snakes steeply down **Roaring Springs Canyon**. Continue along the rim to intersect a spur at mile 2 leading to prow-like **Uncle Jim Point**. Returning to the main trail, ascend gently through the forest to close the loop.

NEARBY: Across the main park road from the Uncle Jim trailhead, drive 1 mile down a dirt road to access the easy **Widforss Trail** (10 miles out-and-back), which winds through the forest to picturesque Widforss Point.

37. North Kaibab Backpack

Very difficult 28.5-mile out-and-back; allow 5 days, including layover
Permit required; water filter, trekking poles, and headlamps recommended
Maps: Trails Illustrated 207: Grand Canyon National Park, or USGS: Bright Angel

GETTING THERE: From the visitor center, take AZ 67 north for about 2 miles to the North Kaibab parking area on your right.

ON THE TRAIL: Shared by hikers and mule trains, the North Kaibab, considered the hardest of the three maintained trails descending into the inner canyon, passes through five life zones on its 5800-foot plunge to the Colorado River. The route is steep for the first 5 miles, following Roaring Springs Canyon to its junction with Bright Angel Creek below the Redwall. Water is available year-round at Bright Angel Campground and seasonally at Supai Tunnel, Roaring Springs, and Cottonwood Camp. You can also filter water drawn from the creek.

The ideal way to complete this hike involves spending the first and fourth nights at Cottonwood Camp (the halfway point) and the second and third at Bright Angel Campground near the river. But because Cottonwood Camp has few sites, securing reservations there is a crapshoot at best. Primitive camping along the trail is not allowed, and few hikers have sufficient strength and endurance to ascend the North Kaibab in a single day. One alternative is to cross over to the South Rim, ascending on the Bright Angel Trail (see Hike 29, Chapter 6). Long and expensive commercial shuttles run daily between the rims, which are 214 miles apart by road. All things considered, it may be best to wait until your stars align for two non-consecutive nights at Cottonwood.

Initially, the North Kaibab swings significantly west. Near the start of the Toroweap Formation, it traverses east and then drops down to **Coconino Overlook** at mile

Kaibab Bridge spans the Colorado River near Phantom Ranch.

0.75. This popular day hiking destination affords views of Bright Angel and Roaring Springs Canyons. From here the trail switchbacks boldly down through the Coconino Sandstone to the Hermit Shale stratum. Straightening out, it bears west before continuing its southward progress toward **Supai Tunnel**, 1425 feet below the rim at mile 1.75. Look for seep springs in the next 0.5 mile.

The trail meanders through pinyon and juniper vegetation to hit the top of the Redwall, at mile 2.75. **Redwall Bridge** spans the creek 3000 feet below the rim, and the trail remains suspended above the drainage as it continues its descent.

At mile 4.75, where the Muav Limestone and Bright Angel Shale layers meet, a 0.5-mile out-and-back heads east toward **Roaring Springs**. A rest station is here. Emerging from caves, these falls are the main water source for both rims.

Rejoining the main trail, pass the Pump House Ranger Station near the mouth of Manzanita Canyon. In this vicinity the trail finishes cutting through Tapeats Sandstone narrows. Within an hour or so, you reach **Cottonwood Camp** at mile 6.75, which has water, shade, and toilets. Terraces here once were farmed by ancient Indians, and evidence of their habitation can still be found. Take care not to disturb these artifacts.

Past Cottonwood Camp, the trail proceeds southwest toward the river, still some 1600 feet below. A cairned spur at mile 8 crosses a bridge over the creek and leads to **Ribbon Falls**, a 0.5-mile out-and-back. The cascade's environs are exceptional, featuring hanging gardens amid delicate travertine formations.

Back on the main trail, the canyon enters **The Box**, a zone of contraction, at mile 9. Here, cliffs composed of Vishnu Schist—among the canyon's oldest rocks—frame the streambed. The trail crosses the creek a few times on bridges through the spectacular narrows. Phantom Creek comes in at mile 12.5, and 0.5 mile later is the intersection with the **Clear Creek Trail**. Rustic **Phantom Ranch**, which accommodates a limited number of overnight guests (reservations essential), lies just above **Bright Angel Campground** at 14 miles. From here an easy stroll leads to the suspension bridges spanning the Inner Gorge.

With time to spare before returning to the North Rim, consider a side trip to **Phantom Overlook** along the Clear Creek Trail. Rated moderate, the 3.25 mile out-and-back climbs 1000 feet to this lofty perch, which offers exceptional views of the river and its Inner Gorge.

As noted previously, the return trip to the North Rim is long and exhausting if attempted in one day, not least because almost all the elevation gain comes in the last 7 miles. Hikers unable to secure a reservation for Cottonwood Camp on their ascent should plan on a layover day at Bright Angel Campground and a pre-dawn start, utilizing headlamps. One saving grace is that because water is abundant along the trail, your load will be lighter here than on other river-to-rim ascents.

38. Powell Plateau

Difficult 6.5-mile out-and-back; allow 4–5 hours
Permit and a high-clearance or four-wheel-drive vehicle required; trekking poles recommended
Map: Trails Illustrated 263: Grand Canyon West

GETTING THERE: From the visitor center, take AZ 67 to the North Rim entrance station. About 4 miles farther, turn left on Forest Road 422. Zero out your trip odometer here. At mile 2, turn left onto FR 270 and proceed to the junction with FR 223 at mile 4. Go right here. At mile 10, take a left onto FR 268. At mile 11, turn left onto FR 268B. At mile 11.75, turn right onto Swamp Point Road. Follow that track to its end at mile 19.5. Park at **Swamp Point**.

ON THE TRAIL: Pancake flat, the Powell Plateau juts out toward a big bend in the Colorado River near the "Camelot" formations (King Arthur and Guinevere Castles, Lancelot Point, Merlin Abyss, etc.). Begin by descending the **North Bass Trail** on overgrown switchbacks to **Muav Saddle**, 800 feet below the rim. Near a cabin dating to the 1920s, you arrive at a fork. Leaving the North Bass, hang a right here and climb, briskly at first, to Powell Plateau, with its blanket of ponderosa pines. Turn left at the top and follow the rim of **Muav Canyon**, enjoying big views to the east. The trail becomes increasingly obscure as you near Dutton Creek. Backtrack from here.

39. Thunder River and Deer Creek Backpack

Difficult 26.5-mile out-and-back; allow 4–5 days
Permit and high-clearance vehicle required; water filter, water cache, and trekking poles recommended
Maps: Trails Illustrated 263: Grand Canyon West, or USGS: Powell Plateau and Kanab Point

GETTING THERE: From the visitor center, allow 2 hours to drive to the trailhead. Take AZ 67 to the North Rim entrance station. About 4 miles farther, turn left on Forest Road 422. Continue 20 miles on FR 422 to FR 425 and turn left toward **Monument Point**, about 10 miles distant. When you pass Big Saddle Camp, take FR 292A, which deteriorates markedly in its last mile.

ON THE TRAIL: Thunder River—a frigid, beautiful waterfall emanating from a deep limestone cave—feeds into Tapeats Creek. Deer Creek, with a waterfall that plunges directly into the river from an exquisite set of narrows, is accessed from the same trail, making it feasible to combine them in one trip. The unmaintained routes are dry and dusty, with little shade and no water for most of the way. For that reason, planning to cache water around mile 4.5 for the return trip is highly recommended.

Start on the **Bill Hall Trail**, which plummets through the Kaibab Limestone before contouring around at the top of the Coconino Formation, a prominent band of white sandstone. Heading west, you come to a break in the Coconino, where the trail in effect has you doing a "controlled fall" down a talus slope dotted with pinyons and junipers. At mile 2, you intersect the gentler but longer **Thunder River Trail** on the so-called Esplanade, which has no equivalent on the South Rim. Mercifully, the trail levels out along this Supai Formation shelf. Walk on bare rock for a while, passing a boulder garden. At about mile 4.5, you arrive at a notch where the trail, taking

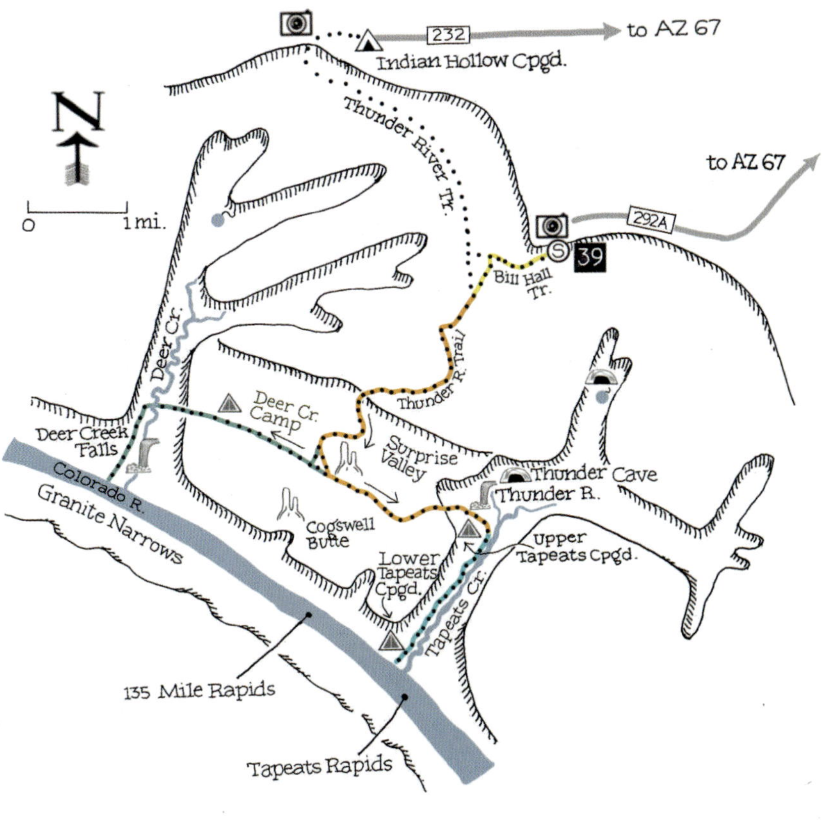

The Grand Canyon's forested North Rim towers above the temples of the inner canyon.

advantage of a rockslide, begins its 1000-foot descent of the Redwall. Establish a water cache near the top of the Redwall for the return trip, marking it with your name and the dates of your expedition.

At the base of the Redwall is **Surprise Valley**, which can be a furnace on summer afternoons. Here the trail veers to the right of a large butte, reaching an important fork at mile 6.5. The right fork enters the Deer Creek drainage. For now, turn left toward **Tapeats Creek**.

From the lip of Surprise Valley, the trail makes another 1000-foot descent on steep switchbacks to **Thunder River**, one of the world's shortest, at mile 9.5. Pause to enjoy an ice-cold drink (or shower!) gushing out of 3000-foot-deep **Thunder Cave**. Nearby cottonwoods offer shade. The trail parallels Thunder River on its way to the designated sites of **Upper Tapeats Campground** at mile 10.5.

Extend the hike if you wish with a 4.5-mile out-and-back to **Lower Tapeats Campground**, on the river. Under normal conditions, the trip is straightforward enough, though you may have to execute one or more fords, a dangerous practice at high water levels. If the creek is impassable, stay on the west bank the whole way. While it tends to be steeper and more hazardous than its eastern counterpart, you must be on that bank for the last plunge to the river. At the river is a sandy beach where you can watch rafts shoot **Tapeats Rapids**. Some people try to pick their way from here to Deer Creek, but that alternative, which involves hair-raising exposure on ledges above the **Granite Narrows**, is not recommended, especially for those carrying heavy packs.

When finished in the Tapeats drainage, return to the rim of Thunder River Canyon and continue on to the closer of two junctions with the **Deer Creek Trail** (mile 13).

Head west over a low pass to intersect the drainage. A short spur on the right at mile 14.5 goes to **Deer Spring**, a miniature Thunder River, which forms a 25-foot cascade as it gushes from a cave in the Muav Limestone stratum. Check out the manmade "thrones" behind the falls before pressing on to the main (north) fork of the creek.

Hike downstream to the top of the fluted narrows at mile 15.25 and ford the shallow creek. The trail hugs the west side of the drainage as it barrels down 0.5 mile to meet the Colorado. Idyllic **Deer Creek Falls**, with a 150-foot drop, creates a deep swimming hole at its base. Doubtless, you will have company from river parties, which monopolize camping rights in this dreamy spot.

From the river, it is a 10.75-mile return to Monument Point. Especially if your visit occurs during the summer, split the climb into two segments, eating an early dinner and hiking to your water cache on the Esplanade to camp. Finish the punishing ascent in the cool of morning.

THE ARIZONA STRIP

North and west of the Grand Canyon lies the remote area known as the Arizona Strip, which is largely disconnected from the rest of the state. Vermilion Cliffs National Monument, discussed previously, is on the Strip, as are Snake Gulch Primitive Area and the Toroweap (a.k.a. Tuweep) section of Grand Canyon National Park.

40. Snake Gulch

Easy 12-mile out-and-back; allow 5–6 hours
High-clearance vehicle and gaiters recommended
Map: USGS: Toothpick Ridge

GETTING THERE: From Kanab, take US Route 89A south 7 miles to Fredonia, Arizona and continue east on US 89A. In about 2 miles, turn right onto the paved Forest Road 22 (West Side Road) and reset your trip odometer. Soon the Kaibab Plateau looms ahead. At mile 16.5, enter Kaibab National Forest. Just short of mile 21, bear right to remain on FR 22. Shortly, the pavement ends. At mile 22.75 turn right at a sign for the **Kanab Creek Wilderness** onto a road that may contain deep ruts. At mile 24 turn right onto FR 642 and follow it to its end at mile 26.5.

ON THE TRAIL: Snake Gulch feeds into **Kanab Creek**, a tributary of the Colorado River. Because it served as a major byway in prehistoric times, the canyon system contains a wealth of polychromatic rock art, mainly depicting human heads and upper torsos. Reds predominate, but yellow and black pigments become increasingly common as you travel downcanyon. Although the length of the hike may seem intimidating, Snake Gulch is shallow, wide, and flat, with barely perceptible elevation change. Routefinding is a cinch, with social trails leading to all major sites. Be warned that the canyon can be an inferno in summer. Because the area saw heavy grazing in years gone by, prickly weeds like cheat grass thrive in the disturbed soil—hence the recommendation to don gaiters.

On foot, you soon arrive at the ruins of a cabin. Sign the trail register and follow the blocked-off two-track road down the canyon. Just past a fence near mile 2.25, the panels begin. Their beauty and sheer numbers make up for the blah scenery. You will find most of the pictographs on the north wall, with the greatest concentration occurring between mile 4 and Table Rock Canyon, a tributary on the left with a water tank at its mouth.

41. Toroweap Overlook and Saddle Horse Loop

Easy 1.5-mile loop; allow 1 hour
High-clearance or four-wheel-drive vehicle recommended
Map: Trails Illustrated 263: Grand Canyon West

GETTING THERE: From Kanab, go south 7 miles on US Route 89A to Fredonia. Turn right onto AZ 389 and drive about 8 miles. Between mileposts 24 and 25, look for the obscure turnoff onto County Road 109. Following signs for Tuweep, drive south on unpaved roads for 55 miles through open, lonely country to the Grand Canyon National Park boundary. Bear in mind that the washboarded roads sit atop a clay surface, making them impassable when wet. Without a four-wheel-drive vehicle you must park in a designated lot 2.75 miles shy of Toroweap Overlook.

ON THE TRAIL: The view from the overlook will blow your mind. In contrast to the main park corridor, the canyon here is a deep gash, with the Colorado visible 3000 vertiginous feet below. This is the one place where a common Grand Canyon moniker, the "Big Ditch," rings true.

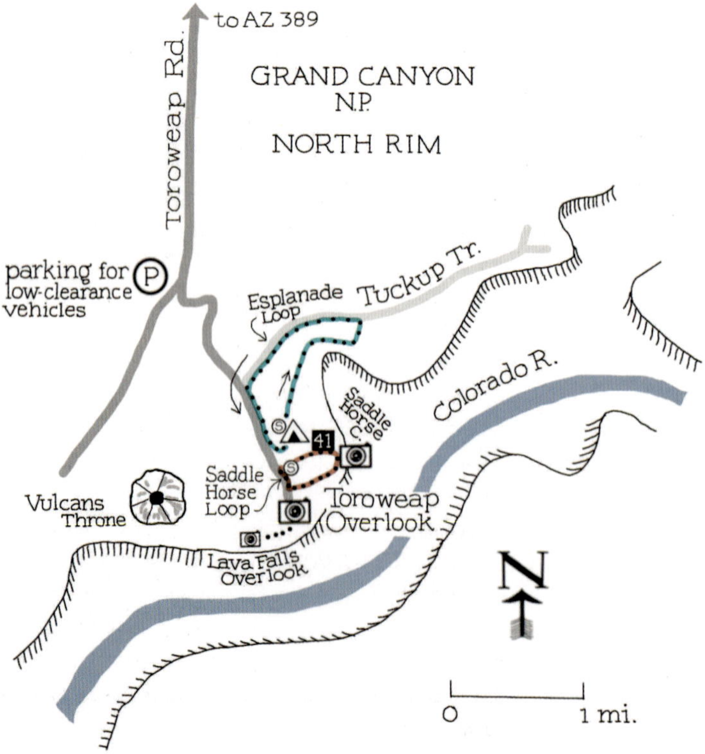

Slippery cinders along the very difficult 1000-foot ascent to Vulcans Throne pose a danger, while you are likely to lose the Tuckup Trail, notorious for fade-outs and false cairns, in short order. Opt instead for the **Saddle Horse Loop**, starting about a mile north of the overlook along the spur to the campground. Follow the spur a short distance until the trail branches off on the right. It visits two overlooks before returning to the road. Turn right and walk 0.25 mile along the road to your vehicle.

NEARBY: Although no longer indicated on the park brochure, the 3-mile **Esplanade Loop** gives a good feel for the backcountry. Start at site 10 in the campground and walk north on a jeep track near the rim of a side-canyon to meet the **Tuckup Trail** in about 1 mile. Turn left and proceed to the main road. Turn left and walk south along the road to your waiting car.

42. Whitmore Trail

Moderate 2-mile out-and-back; allow 1.5 hours
High-clearance or four-wheel-drive vehicle required
Map: USGS: Whitmore Rapids

GETTING THERE: From St. George, drive south on Interstate 15 to exit 4. Go east 1.75 miles and turn right, reaching the state line in 2 miles. Reset your trip odometer here. Proceed 62.25 miles down the unpaved Mount Trumbull Road (Route 257) to the Bar 10 Lodge. After this point the road deteriorates exponentially as it traverses exposed beds of sharp lava rock on its way to the overlook at mile 72.25. To avoid puncturing a tire, you may want to stop before the official start of the well-constructed trail.

You can also reach the trailhead from Toroweap (see Hike 41). Exit the park and travel 6.5 miles north. Turn left, following signs to Mount Trumbull. Total distance from the park boundary is 48.25 miles.

ON THE TRAIL: The Whitmore Trail is the shortest and easiest route to the bottom of the Grand Canyon. It takes advantage of a natural break near the bottom of the Tapeats Sandstone, passing to the right of a lava alcove sporting hexagonal columns of basalt at mile 0.5. At a small beach along the river, members of the polar bear club can enjoy a bracing dip while watching watercraft float by.

As J. R. R. Tolkien observed, “Not all those who wander are lost.”

ACKNOWLEDGMENTS

Many people have contributed to making this book a reality, starting with the savvy pros at Mountaineers Books, who have spoiled me forever with their painstaking attention to my manuscript. I am grateful to my sister-in-law, Hannah Hinchman, a prizewinning author/illustrator who lavished time and talent on the maps. Above all, I owe an unpayable debt to Lew Hinchman, my wonderful husband of more than four decades, who hiked with me every step of the way, proofread drafts for accuracy, and served as my technical consultant. The book simply would not exist without his companionship, encouragement, and generosity. Every author should be so blessed.

I dedicated the previous three editions of this work to Lew and to our son, Bryce. But this one is for the Glen Canyon Group of the Utah Sierra Club, in appreciation of their friendship, trail lore, and passion for wild nature. At a time when I was disinclined to take on a massive new project, even a labor of love such as this new edition, the fact that many club members egged me on made all the difference.

CONTACT INFORMATION

Acoma Pueblo, PO Box 309, Acoma Pueblo, NM 87034; (505) 552-6604; www.puebloofacoma.org

Arches National Park, PO Box 907, Moab, UT 84532; (435) 719-2299, or (435) 259-4351 for camping reservations; www.nps.gov/arch

Arizona Strip Field Office, Bureau of Land Management, 345 E. Riverside Dr., St. George, UT 84790; (435) 668-3200 www.blm.gov/office/arizona-strip-field-office

Aztec Ruins National Monument, 725 Ruins Rd, Aztec, NM 87410; (505) 334-6174; www.nps.gov/azru

Bandelier National Monument, 15 Entrance Rd., Los Alamos, NM 87544; (505) 672-3861; www.nps.gov/band

Bisti/De-Na-Zin Wilderness Area, Bureau of Land Management, Farmington Field Office, 6251 College Blvd., Suite A, Farmington, NM 87402; (505) 564-7600; www.blm.gov/visit/bisti-de-na-zin-wilderness

Black Canyon of the Gunnison National Park, 102 Elk Creek, Gunnison, CO 81230; (970) 641-2337; www.nps.gov/blca

Black Ridge Canyons Wilderness, Grand Junction Field Office, 2815 H Rd., Grand Junction, CO 81506; (970) 244-3000; www.blm.gov/visit/black-ridge-canyons-wilderness

Bryce Canyon National Park, PO Box 640201, Bryce, UT 84764; (435) 834-5322; www.nps.gov/brca

Canyon de Chelly National Monument, PO Box 588, Chinle, AZ 86503; (928) 674-5500; www.nps.gov/cach

Canyonlands National Park, 2282 Resource Blvd., Moab, UT 84532; (435) 719-2313; www.nps.gov/cany

Canyons of the Ancients Visitor Center and Museum, 27501 Hwy. 184, Dolores, CO 81323; (970) 882-5600; www.blm.gov/learn/interpretive-centers/CANM-visitor-center-museum

Capitol Reef National Park, HC 70, Box 15, Torrey, UT 84775; (435) 425-3791; www.nps.gov/care

Cathedral Gorge State Park, PO Box 176, Panaca, NV 89042; (775) 728-4460; parks.nv.gov/parks/cathedral-gorge

Cedar Breaks National Monument, 2390 W. Hwy. 56, Suite 11, Cedar City, UT 84720; (435) 586-9451; www.nps.gov/cebr

Chaco Culture National Historical Park, PO Box 220, Nageezi, NM 87037; (505) 786-7014; www.nps.gov/chcu

Coconino National Forest, PO Box 300, Sedona, AZ 86336; (928) 282-4119; for camping reservations: fs.usda.gov/activity/coconino/recreation/camping-cabins

Colorado National Monument, 1750 Rim Rock Dr., Fruita, CO 81521; (970) 858-3167; www.nps.gov/colm ; www.nmhistoricsites.org

Coral Pink Sand Dunes State Park, PO Box 95, Kanab, UT 84741; (435) 648-2800; stateparks.utah.gov/parks/coral-pink

Coronado Historic Site, 485 Kuaua Rd., Bernalillo, NM 87004; (505) 867-5351

Dead Horse Point State Park, PO Box 609, Moab, UT 84532; (435) 259-2614; stateparks.utah.gov/parks/dead-horse

Dinosaur National Monument, 4545 Hwy. 40, Dinosaur, CO 81610; (435) 781-7700; www.nps.gov/dino

Edge of the Cedars State Park, 660 W. 400 N., Blanding, UT 84511; (435) 678-2238 stateparks.utah.gov/parks/edge-of-the-cedars

El Malpais National Monument, 1900 E. Santa Fe Ave., Grants, NM 87020; (505) 876-2783; www.nps.gov/elma

El Morro National Monument, HC 61 Box 43, Ramah, NM 87321; (505) 783-4226; www.nps.gov/elmo

Escalante Petrified Forest State Park, 710 N. Reservoir Rd., Escalante, UT 84726; (435) 826-4466; stateparks.utah.gov/parks/escalante-petrified-forest

Farmington Resource Area, Bureau of Land Management, 6251 College Blvd., Suite A, Farmington, NM 87402; (505) 564-7600; www.blm.gov/office/farmington-field-office

Flagstaff Area National Monuments, 6400 US Hwy., Flagstaff, AZ 86004

Fremont Culture State Park, 1150 W. Clear Creek Canyon Rd., Sevier, UT 84766; (435) 322-3700 for camping reservations; www.desertusa.com/freut

Ghost Ranch Education and Retreat Center, 280 Private Dr. 1708, Abiquiu, NM 87510-2001; (505) 685-1000; www.ghostranch.org

Glen Canyon National Recreation Area, PO Box 1507, Page, AZ 86040; (928) 608-6200; www.nps.gov/glca

Goblin Valley State Park, PO Box 637, Green River, UT 84525; (435) 275-4584; www.stateparks.utah.gov/parks/goblin-valley

Grand Canyon National Park, PO Box 129, Grand Canyon, AZ 86023; (928) 638-7888; www.nps.gov/grca; www.grandcanyonlodges.com

Grand Canyon Trust, 2601 N. Fort Valley Rd., Flagstaff, AZ 86001; (928) 774-7488; www.grandcanyontrust.org

Grand Staircase-Escalante National Monument, Interagency Visitor Center, 755 W. Main St., Escalante, UT 84726; (435) 826-5499; www.blm.gov/visit/escalante-interagency-visitor-center

Havasupai/Havasu Falls Campground; www.havasupaireservations.com

Hopi Cultural Center, Route 264, Second Mesa, AZ 86043; www.hopiculturalcenter.com

Hovenweep National Monument, McElmo Route, Cortez, CO 81321; (970) 562-4282; www.nps.gov/hove

Kaibab National Forest, North Kaibab Ranger District, 430 S. Main St., Fredonia, AZ 86022; (928) 643-7395; www.fs.usda.gov/main/kaibab/home

Kanab Visitor Center, 745 E. Hwy. 89, Kanab, UT 84741; (435) 644-1300; www.blm.gov/visit/kanab-visitor-center

Kanarra Falls, www.kanarrafalls.com

Kasha-Katuwe Tent Rocks National Monument, County Rd. 22, Cochiti Pueblo, NM 87072; (505) 331-6259; www.blm.gov/visit/kktr

Kodachrome Basin State Park, PO Box 180069, Cannonville, UT 84718; (435) 679-8562; stateparks.utah.gov/parks/kodachrome-basin

Lake Mead National Recreation Area, 601 Nevada Way, Boulder City, NV 89005; (702) 293-8990; www.nps.gov/lake

Mesa Verde National Park, PO Box 8, Mesa Verde National Park, CO 81330; (970) 529-4465; www.nps.gov/meve

Moab Field Office, Bureau of Land Management, 82 E. Dogwood, Moab, UT 84532; (435) 259-2100; www.blm.gov/office/moab-field-office

Montezuma Castle National Monument, PO Box 219, Camp Verde, AZ 86322; (928) 567-3322; www.nps.gov/moca

Monument Valley Tribal Park, Box 360289, Monument Valley, UT 84536; (435) 727-5870; navajonationparks.org/tribal-parks/monument-valley

Natural Bridges National Monument, HC-60 Box 1, Lake Powell, UT 84533; (435) 692-1234; www.nps.gov/nabr

Navajo National Monument, PO Box 7717, Shonto, AZ 86045; (928) 672-2700; www.nps.gov/nava

Navajo Nation Parks and Recreation, PO Box 2520, Window Rock, AZ 86515; (928) 871-6647; navajonationparks.org

Paria Canyon–Vermilion Cliffs Wilderness, Arizona Strip Field Office, 345 E. Riverside Dr., St. George, UT 84790; (435) 688-3200; www.blm.gov/visit/paria-canyon-vermilion-cliffs-wilderness

Pecos National Historical Park, PO Box 418, Pecos, NM 87552; (505) 757-7241; www.nps.gov/peco

Petrified Forest National Park, 1 Park Rd. #2217, Petrified Forest, AZ 86028; (928) 524-6228; www.nps.gov/pefo

Petroglyph National Monument, 6001 Unser Blvd. NW, Albuquerque, NM 87120; (505) 899-0205; www.nps.gov/petr

Red Rocks–Secret Mountain Wilderness, Red Rock District, Coconino National Forest, PO Box 20429, Sedona, AZ 86341; (928) 203-7500; www.fs.usda.gov/recarea/coconino

Salinas Pueblo Missions National Monument, PO Box 517, Mountainair, NM 87036-0517; (505) 847-2585; www.nps.gov/sapu

San Juan Resource Area, Bureau of Land Management, 365 N. Main, PO Box 7, Monticello, UT 84535; (435) 587-1500; www.blm.gov/office/monticello-field-office

San Rafael Swell Recreation Area, Bureau of Land Management, 125 S. 600 West, Price, UT 84501; (435) 636-3600; www.blm.gov/visit/search-details/2187/2

Snow Canyon State Park, 1002 N. Snow Canyon Rd., Ivins, UT 84738; (435) 628-2255; stateparks.utah.gov/parks/snow-canyon

Sunset Crater Volcano National Monument, 6400 US 89, Flagstaff, AZ 86004; (928) 526-0502; www.nps.gov/sucr

Tuzigoot National Monument, PO Box 219, Camp Verde, AZ 86322; (928) 634-5564; www.nps.gov/tuzi

US Forest Service camping reservations; www.recreation.gov or www.fs.fed.us /recreation/reservations

Utah State Parks; (801) 538-7220; www.stateparks.utah.gov

Ute Mountain Ute Tribal Park, 480 Sunset Blvd., Towaoc, CO 81334; (970) 565-9653 ext. 330; www.utemountaintribalpark.info

Valley of Fire State Park, PO Box 515, Overton, NV 89040; (702) 397-2088; www.parks.nv.gov/parks/valley-of-fire

Walnut Canyon National Monument, 6400 US 89, Flagstaff, AZ 86004; (928) 526-3367; www.nps.gov/waca

Wupatki National Monument, 6400 US 89, Flagstaff, AZ 86004; (928) 679-2365; www.nps.gov/wupa

Zion National Park, 1 Zion Park Blvd., State Route 9, Springdale, UT 84767; (435) 772-3256; www.nps.gov/zion

FURTHER READING

Abbey, Edward. *Desert Solitaire: A Season in the Wilderness.* Touchstone: New York, 1990.

Adkison, Ron. *Best Easy Day Hikes Grand Staircase–Escalante and the Glen Canyon Region.* 2nd ed. Falcon: Helena, Mont., 2010.

Allen, Steve. *Canyoneering 3: Loop Hikes in Utah's Escalante.* University of Utah Press: Salt Lake City, 1997.

Bohan, William, and David Butler. *Great Sedona Hikes.* 5th ed. Self-published, 2018.

Butchart, Harvey. *Grand Canyon Treks.* Spotted Dog: Bishop, Calif., 1996.

Casey, Robert. *Journey to the High Southwest.* Globe Pequot: Chester, Conn., 2007.

Childs, Craig. *House of Rain: Tracking a Vanished Civilization across the American Southwest.* Little, Brown: Boston, 2007.

Copeland, Kathy, and Craig Copeland. *Hiking from Here to WOW: Utah Canyon Country.* Wilderness Press: Berkeley, 2008.

Day, David. *Utah's Incredible Backcountry Trails.* 2nd ed. Rincon: Orem, Utah, 2017.

DeCourten, Frank. *Dinosaurs of Utah.* 2nd ed. University of Utah Press: Salt Lake City, 2014.

Dodge, Natt. *Flowers of the Southwest Deserts.* Western National Parks Association: Tucson, 1985.

Fedarko, Kevin. *The Emerald Mile: The Epic Story of the Fastest Ride in History Through the Heart of the Grand Canyon.* Scribner: New York, 2013.

Fletcher, Colin. *The Man Who Walked Through Time.* Vintage: New York, 1989.

Gibson, Daniel. *Pueblos of the Rio Grande.* Rio Nuevo: Tucson, 2002.

Grubbs, Bruce. *Hiking Arizona.* Rowman & Littlefield: Lanham, Md., 2015.

Hansen, Eric. *On and Off the Beaten Path: Hiking Routes Near St. George, Utah.* Shop-Chicken, 2012.

Hoard, Dorothy. *A Guide to Bandelier National Monument.* Los Alamos Historical Society: Los Alamos, NM, 2009.

Hopkins, Ralph Lee. *Hiking the Southwest's Geology.* Mountaineers Books: Seattle, 2002.

Kelsey, Michael. *Non-Technical Canyon Hiking Guide to the Colorado Plateau.* 7th ed. Kelsey: Provo, Utah, 2018.

Kosik, Fran. *Native Roads: The Complete Motoring Guide to the Navajo and Hopi Nations.* Rio Nuevo: Tucson, 2013.

Laine, Barb, and Don Laine. *Best Short Hikes in Arizona.* Mountaineers Books: Seattle, 2005.

Lambrechtse, Rudi. *Hiking the Escalante.* University of Utah Press: Salt Lake City, 2016.

Martres, Laurent. *Photographing the Southwest: Volumes 1, 2, 3.* Photo Trip USA: Alta Loma, Calif., 2007–17.

Milligan, Tanya, and Bo Beck. *Favorite Hikes In & Around Zion National Park* 2nd ed. Sharp End: Boulder, Colo., 2013.

Molvar, Erik. *Best Easy Day Hikes: Zion and Bryce Canyon National Parks.* Falcon: Helena, Mont., 2014.

Noble, David. *Ancient Ruins and Rock Art of the Southwest.* Taylor Trade: Flagstaff, Ariz., 2015.

Parent, Laurence. *Hiking New Mexico.* Falcon: Helena, Mont., 2010.

Powell, John Wesley. *The Exploration of the Colorado River and Its Canyons.* Dover: New York, 1961.

Reisner, Marc. *Cadillac Desert: The American West and Its Disappearing Water.* Penguin: New York, 1993.

Roberts, David. *Sandstone Spine: Seeking the Anasazi on the First Traverse of the Comb Ridge.* Mountaineers Books: Seattle, 2006.

Schneider, Bill. *Hiking Canyonlands and Arches National Parks.* Falcon: Helena, Mont., 2017.

Stegner, Wallace. *Beyond the Hundredth Meridian.* Penguin: New York, 1992.

Stinchfield, Rick. *Capitol Reef National Park,* 2nd ed. Trails Books: Denver, 2019.

Stuart, David. *Anasazi America.* 2nd ed. University of New Mexico: Albuquerque, NM, 2014.

Tassoni, Peter. *A Hiking Guide to Cedar Mesa.* University of Utah Press: Salt Lake City, 2001.

Till, Tom. *In the Land of Moab.* Fable Valley: Moab, Utah, 2001.

Trevelyan, Julie. *100 Classic Hikes: Utah.* Mountaineers Books: Seattle, 2016.

Warren, Scott. *100 Classic Hikes: Arizona.* 4th ed. Mountaineers Books: Seattle, 2015.

Wilson, Dave. *Hiking Ruins Seldom Seen.* Falcon: Helena, Mont. 2011.

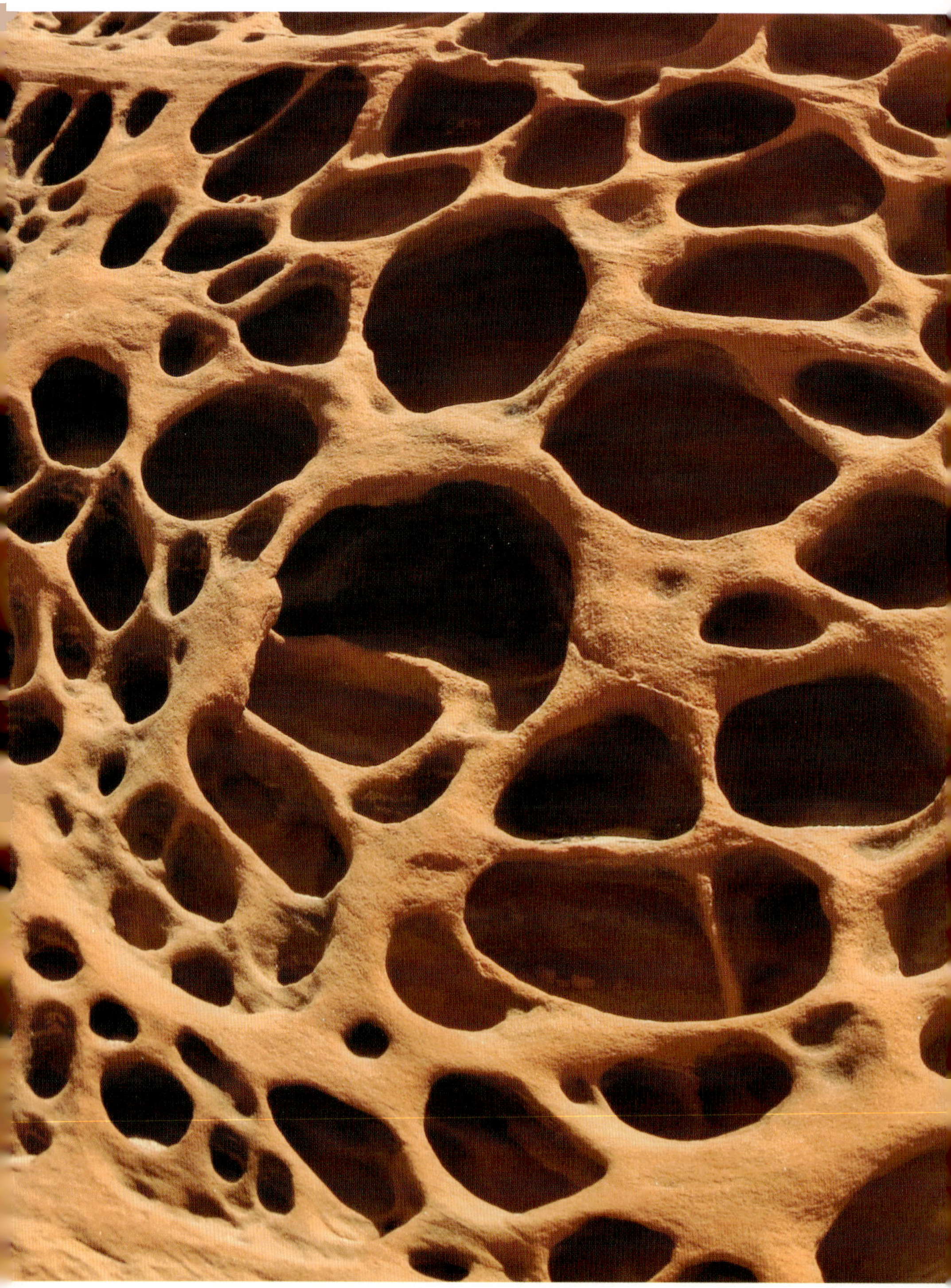

Sandstone cliffs sometimes assume a honeycombed appearance.

INDEX

M

N

O

P

Q

R

S

T

U

ABOUT THE AUTHOR

photo by Faye Serio

Sandra Hinchman was born, raised, and educated in upstate New York. In 1974, Sandy and her future husband, Lew, fell in love with the desert on a cross-country trip. Thirty-five years later, after retiring from their jobs as professors of political science at St. Lawrence and Clarkson Universities, respectively, the couple moved to Moab, Utah, in the heart of canyon country. Subsequently, they taught four times on the Semester at Sea Program, a floating college campus that circumnavigates the world. Wonderful as those experiences were, they helped the couple confirm that there is nowhere on the planet they'd rather be than the Colorado Plateau.

MOUNTAINEERS BOOKS

SKIPSTONE BRAIDED RIVER

recreation • lifestyle • conservation

MOUNTAINEERS BOOKS including its two imprints, Skipstone and Braided River, is a leading publisher of quality outdoor recreation, sustainability, and conservation titles. As a 501(c)(3) nonprofit, we are committed to supporting the environmental and educational goals of our organization by providing expert information on human-powered adventure, sustainable practices at home and on the trail, and preservation of wilderness.

Our publications are made possible through the generosity of donors, and through sales of more than 700 titles on outdoor recreation, sustainable lifestyle, and conservation. To donate, purchase books, or learn more, visit us online:

MOUNTAINEERS BOOKS

1001 SW Klickitat Way, Suite 201 • Seattle, WA 98134

800-553-4453 • mbooks@mountaineersbooks.org • www.mountaineersbooks.org

An independent nonprofit publisher since 1960

Mountaineers Books is proud to support the Leave No Trace Center for Outdoor Ethics, whose mission is to promote and inspire responsible outdoor recreation through education, research, and partnerships. The Leave No Trace program is focused specifically on human-powered (nonmotorized) recreation. For more information, visit www.lnt.org.

YOU MAY ALSO LIKE:

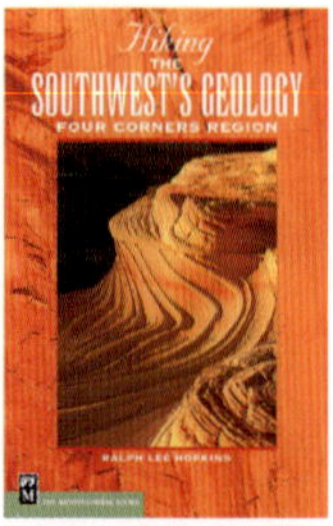